The Third Reich

THE THIRD REICH
CHARISMA AND COMMUNITY

MARTIN KITCHEN

PEARSON
Longman

Harlow, England • London • New York • Boston • San Francisco • Toronto • Sydney • Singapore • Hong Kong
Tokyo • Seoul • Taipei • New Delhi • Cape Town • Madrid • Mexico City • Amsterdam • Munich • Paris • Milan

PEARSON EDUCATION LIMITED

Edinburgh Gate
Harlow CM20 2JE
United Kingdom
Tel: +44 (0)1279 623623
Fax: +44 (0)1279 431059
Website: www.pearsoned.co.uk

First edition published in Great Britain in 2008

© Pearson Education Limited 2008

The right of Martin Kitchen to be identified as author
of this work has been asserted by him in accordance
with the Copyright, Designs and Patents Act 1988.

ISBN: 978-1-4058-0169-0

British Library Cataloguing in Publication Data
A CIP catalogue record for this book can be obtained from the British Library

Library of Congress Cataloging-in-Publication Data
Kitchen, Martin.
    The Third Reich : charisma and community / Martin Kitchen.—1st ed.
        p. cm.
    Includes bibliographical references and index.
    ISBN-13: 978-1-4058-0169-0 (pbk.)
    1. Germany—History—1933–1945. 2. National socialism—History. I. Title.
    DD256.5.K4756 2008
    943.086—dc22

                                                                2007035894

10 9 8 7 6 5 4 3 2 1
11 10 09 08 07

Set by 35 in 11/13.5pt Columbus
Printed and bound in Malaysia (CTP, KHL)

The Publisher's policy is to use paper manufactured from sustainable forests.

For Fiona, Steve and Ric

CONTENTS

ABBREVIATIONS

ADGB	General Association of German Trades Unions
AO	Foreign Political Organisation of the NSDAP
BDM	League of German Maidens
BNSDJ	Association of National Socialist German Jurists
BVP	Bavarian People's Party
DAF	German Labour Front
DAP	German Workers' Party
DDP	German Democratic Party
DFG	German Research Association
DFW	German Women's League
DNSAP	German National Socialist Workers' Party
DNVP	German National People's Party
DVP	German People's Party
EG	Einsatzgruppen (Murder Squads)
EK	Einsatzkommando (5 Commandos in a group)
ET	Special Troops (for the Einsatzgruppen)
FGA	Field Gendarmerie Division
Gestapa	Secret State Police Office
Gestapo	Secret State Police
GFP	Secret Field Police
Hiwi	Volunteer
HJ	Hitler Youth
HSSPF	Higher SS and Police Leaders
KdF	Strength Through Joy
KPD	Communist Party of Germany
Kripo	Criminal Police
KWG	Kaiser Wilhelm Society
LAH	Personal Standard Adolf Hitler
NS	National Socialist
NSBO	National Socialist Works Cell Organization

[x]

NSDAP	National Socialist German Workers' Party
NSF	National Socialist Women's Association
NSStB	National Socialist Students' Association
NSV	National Socialist People's Welfare
OC	Organisation Consul
OD	Order Service (Auxiliary Police in Occupied Russia)
OHL	Army High Command (First World War)
OKH	Army High Command
OKW	High Command of the Armed Forces
Orpo	Order Police
OSAF	Higher SA Leader
Osti	Eastern Industrial Company (SS)
OT	Organisation Todt (State Construction Company)
RAD	Reich Labour Service
RDI	Reich Association for German Industry
RKF	Reich Commissariat for the Strengthening of the German Race
RKFDV	Reich Commissar for the Strengthening of the German Race
RKK	Reich Chamber of Culture
RLB	Reich Land Association
RM	Reichsmark
RmfdbO	Reich Ministry for the Occupied Eastern Territories
RSHA	Reich Security Main Office
RuSHA	Main Race and Settlement Office
SA	Storm Section ('Brownshirts')
SD	Security Service
Sipo	Security Police
SOE	Special Operations Executive
SPD	German Social Democratic Party
SS	Protection Squad
SS-TV	SS Death's Head Squad
SS-VT	SS Auxiliary Troops (the origins of the Waffen-SS)
T4	Euthanasia Death Squad
UFA	Universal Film Company
USPD	Independent Social Democratic Party
UWZ	Central Migration Office
VBA	People's Association for the German Race Abroad
VDA	Association for Germans Abroad
Vomi	Ethnic German Coordination Office
WHW	Winter Help (NS Welfare Organization)
WVHA	Main Administrative Office for Business and Commerce (SS)
ZVfD	Zionist Association in Germany

AUTHOR'S ACKNOWLEDGEMENTS

I am most grateful to Heather McCallum who first suggested that I should write this book. It has proved to be a taxing, but rewarding experience, thanks to the help and encouragement of Laura Blake, Patrick Bonham, Mary-Clare Connellan, Alyssa McDonald and Christina Wipf Perry.

Evan Mawdsley and Jo Fox made a number of helpful and constructive criticisms.

All of the above have saved me from many slips and errors. Those that remain are entirely my own.

PUBLISHER'S ACKNOWLEDGEMENTS

We are grateful to the following for permission to reproduce copyright material:

Map 5 © 2007 by Jen Rosenberg (http://history1900s.about.com / library / holocaust / blmap.htm.) Used with permission of About, Inc. which can be found online at www.about.com. All rights reserved; Maps 6 and 7 after maps in Michael Burleigh (2001), *The Third Reich: A New History*, Pan Books: London by kind permission of Michael Burleigh.

Figures 2.1, 3.1, 3.2, 3.4, 4.1, 6.1 and 6.2 from Zentrum für Antisemitismusforschung; Figures 3.3, 4.3, 8.1, 10.1 and 10.2 from SV-Bilderdienst; Figure 5.1 with permission from Bundesarchiv/B145 Bild-F051620-0041; Figure 4.2, 'Reichsautobahnen', from Deutsches Historisches Museum, Berlin; Figure 7.1 from Münchner Stadtmuseum; Figure 9.1 from Felix-Nussbaum-Haus Osnabrück mit der Sammlung der Niedersächsischen Sparkassenstiftung © VG Bild-Kunst Bonn 2006

In some instances we have been unable to trace the owners of copyright material and we would appreciate any information that would enable us to do so.

LIST OF MAPS

Map 1   The Versailles Settlement

Map 2   The Gaue (1944)

1 Baden	15 Main-Franconia	29 Schleswig-Holstein
2 Bayreuth	16 Mark Brandenburg	30 Swabia
3 Berlin	17 Mecklenburg	31 Styria
4 Danzig-West Prussia	18 Moselland	32 Sudetenland
5 Düsseldorf	19 Munich-Upper Bavaria	33 South Hanover-Brunswick
6 Essen	20 Lower Danube	34 Thuringia
7 Franconia	21 Lower Silesia	35 Tirol-Vorarlberg
8 Halle-Merseburg	22 Upper Danube	36 Wartheland
9 Hamburg	23 Upper Silesia	37 Weser-Ems
10 Hesse-Nassau	24 East Hanover	38 North Westphalia
11 Carinthia	25 East Prussia	39 South Westphalia
12 Cologne-Aachen	26 Pomerania	40 Westmark
13 Electoral Hesse	27 Saxony	41 Vienna
14 Magdeburg-Anhalt	28 Salzburg	42 Württemberg-Hohenzollern

[xvi]

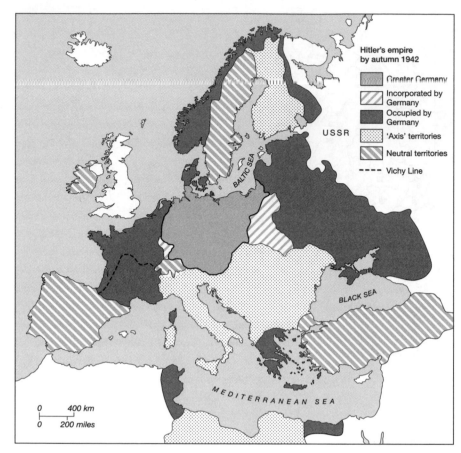

Map 3   Hitler's empire by autumn 1942

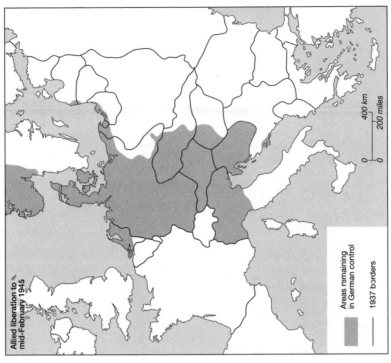

Hitler's Europe on the eve of
D-Day (6 June 1944)

Oslo

London

Leningrad

Berlin

Warsaw

Kiev

Paris

Prague

Vienna

Budapest

Belgrade

Bucharest

Odessa

Sofia

Rome

Athens

0   400 km

0   200 miles

Germany
and German-
occupied Europe

Allied fronts

1937 borders

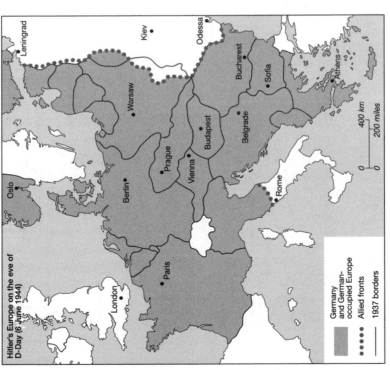

Allied liberation to
mid-February 1945

0   400 km

0   200 miles

Areas remaining
in German control

1937 borders

Map 4   The contraction of Hitler's Europe

Map 5   The death camps

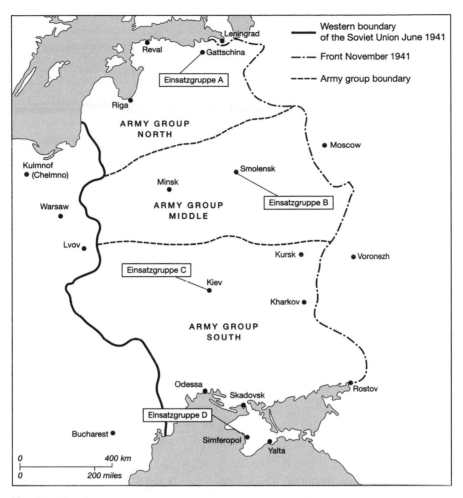

Map 6   Einsatzgruppen

Map 7   Invasion of the Soviet Union

CHAPTER 1

BACKGROUND

The intellectual debate

National Socialism was a uniquely German phenomenon and Germany alone is fully responsible for the appalling crimes committed in its name. But it was also in part a product of the times, conditioned by a profound malaise that festered within European society. This in no sense frees Germany from the heavy burden of accountability. The Third Reich was not an inevitable outcome of a world gone wrong, neither was it merely an aping of 'Asiatic' Stalinist terror, nor a desperate attempt to ward off the Communist threat. Other nations were affected by identical fears and influences, but no British prime minister bears responsibility for the murder of 6 million Jews and no French president blew his brains out in the basement of the Elysée after an unsuccessful attempt to conquer the world.

The Great War was an unmitigated horror that traumatized a generation and left the greatest minds perplexed. Walter Benjamin's 'Angel of History'[1] looked back in utter horror at the ruins of the past and was dragged screaming into the future. The British/German novelist Ford Madox Ford bewailed the fact that history once had seemed to hold all the answers, but was now devoid of any sense. The Austrian writer Egon Friedell announced that history did not exist, although that did not stop him writing numerous works on the subject, now long-forgotten. The Spanish philosopher Ortega y Gasset claimed that 'history is being turned upside down and a new reality is being created'. The publicist and historian Oswald Spengler trumpeted the slogan: 'optimism is cowardice'. All too many intellectuals plunged into a profound gloom and seemed hell-bent on the destruction of the intellect.

There was nothing new about such pessimism, but with the industrialized slaughter of millions in a war that seemed to make no sense it became singularly difficult to resist. The war appeared as a cruel vindication of the

[2] gloomy broodings of Schopenhauer and Nietzsche, of Burckhardt and Houston Stewart Chamberlain. In this world without meaning where, as Siegfried Kracauer argued, reality was a mere construction, there was a strong temptation to aestheticize violence, thereby discovering a sense of transcendence in a world without God, so that the mindless violence of warfare might be infused with some semblance of meaning. Ernst Jünger, Ernst von Salomon, Emilio Marinetti and Gabriele D'Annunzio saw in violence a transcendental quality that existed well beyond the realms of morality, history or rationality. This was a society dominated by paramilitary groups such as the Freikorps, Fascists and Nazis, by Bolshevik thugs, nihilists and anarchists. Europeans were fascinated by bandits and criminals, by outsiders and gratuitous acts of violence. Mass politics became militarized, whether it was in black-shirted Italy, brown-shirted Germany, the Austria of the Heimwehr, or the 'Comrade Mauser'[2] socialism of the Soviet Union. This sickness affected the vanquished powers and those that felt cheated by the peace settlement. The victorious powers were largely immune to this violence, but were left dangerously feeble in the face of strident calls for revision and revenge. The vast majority of the millions of French veterans were convinced pacifists. Britain mourned its dead and promised that such a tragedy should never again be allowed to happen. The United States withdrew from a Europe that had torn itself apart. The stage was empty upon which the dictators could strut.

The smug certainties of nineteenth-century bourgeois liberalism had begun to crumble long before the end of the century, as a fierce debate raged over the problems of modernity. Was it still possible to believe in progress after a war that proved so hard for memory to digest, or had society become so utterly decadent that it no longer welcomed the bracing effects of warfare? Did the war herald the beginning of a mass society in search of a sense of community and in need of unconditional obedience to unchallenged leadership? Wartime debates over civilization versus culture, the state and society, rights and obligations were hotly pursued and provided intoxicating material for radical ideologues. As the problems facing society became increasingly complex, the answers provided by the *terribles simplificateurs* seemed irresistibly attractive. Where reason was left perplexed or denied any legitimacy, faith could offer consolation. Faith – no matter in what, obedience – no matter to whom, self-sacrifice – regardless of the justice of one's cause, became a magic remedy, as Mussolini was one of the first to realize. The politics of the Big Lie and the scapegoat provided simple solutions to immensely complicated problems. The need for a comforting illusion was so strong that some of the greatest minds of the day

placed their extraordinary talents at the service of ignorance. As Gabriel [3]
Marcel argued, in a godless world without any other form of transcendence
it was all too easy to fall for the 'idolatry of class' or the 'idolatry of race',
and become an unquestioning devotee of a political religion.

The industrialized slaughter of the war gave new urgency to Nietzsche's
question as to whether mankind could make the 'solidified intelligence' of
technology serve rational ends, or whether it would be destroyed by the
power of its own invention. Such forebodings could easily be dismissed in
the light of Henry Ford and Frederick W. Taylor's vision of a brave new
world subject to the logic of technology that was enthusiastically emulated
not only in the capitalist West, but also in Lenin's Russia. Society could be
rationally planned and ordered, so as to be more efficient and to provide all
that was necessary for the good life. Architects and planners attempted to
design an environment that would be responsive to human needs. Eugenicists sought to improve the gene pool, by demanding the sterilization of all
those deemed to be carriers of genetically determined diseases or undesirable behaviour. In short, the application of rational intelligence could solve
all the problems, even those that beset a devastated Europe in a state of
turmoil. There were precious few who warned of the dangers to an open
society inherent in modernism. Prominent among them was the sociologist
Karl Mannheim, who wrote: 'the self-made sociological causes, which lead
to the cultural disintegration of liberal society, pave the way for dictatorial
forms. Unless a rational control of man, and of the self, keeps pace with
technological evolution, our present social order is bound to collapse.'

Then came the Great Depression, the technocrats' *Titanic*, and with it
the reverse side of the modern in the shape of mass unemployment, aliena-
tion and anomie, political crisis and revolt. There had always been a sense
of deep uneasiness at the heart of the modernist discourse. Walter Rathenau,
the most admirable of the Weimar republicans, expressed his deep unease
about the cold and rational technological world, which he as a leading
industrialist had done so much to shape. Schopenhauer's pessimism, transmitted via Kierkegaard's morbid meditations on mass society and Nietzsche's
intoxicating denial of the concept of objective truth, provided devastating
ammunition with which to attack the notion of progress. 'Progress' was no
longer viewed as improvement but rather as a process of self-destruction.
Human beings were reduced to anonymous cogs in a vast impersonal
machine as represented in films such as Fritz Lang's *Metropolis*, René Clair's
A nous la liberté and Charlie Chaplin's *Modern Times*. Spengler claimed
that civilization was destroying humanity. Gottfried Benn saw modern man
as an Icarus doomed by his own ingenuity. Civilization was reduced to

[4] T.S. Eliot's *Waste Land*. Some sought salvation in the dark and irrational forces of nature. Others struggled against existential ennui, and bitterly bemoaned their inconsolability as they searched for transcendence in a world without God, thus providing a model for Sartre, Camus and the post-war existentialists. The city was no longer the stimulating and exciting locus of the modern; it was now an 'asphalt jungle' and a 'Moloch', the brutal environment of Alfred Döblin's novel *Berlin Alexanderplatz*. For many 'America', once the land of freedom and opportunity, stood for all that was reprehensible about the modern world.

Ferdinand Tönnies had wrestled with these ideas and in 1887 had made the clear distinction between 'society' (*Gesellschaft*) and 'community' (*Gemeinschaft*). Society was the cold, artificial, bloodless world of the city and the market place, community the organic, traditional, emotional and harmonious life of village and countryside. In Tönnies' pessimistic vision society would eventually swallow up and destroy community, thus leaving people lost and helpless. The promise to a country that was torn apart to create a new sense of community was one of National Socialism's trump cards.

In his immensely influential book *The Revolt of the Masses* (1930), the Spanish philosopher Ortega y Gasset bemoaned the levelling down and standardization of thought, taste and material culture, of incomes, education, gender and sex that threatened the foundations of a civilization that was based on a clear distinction between an elite and the masses. For Ortega the masses were the intolerant and brutal advocates of direct action, as in Italian Fascism and Spanish anarcho-syndicalism. At the root of the problem was the blind belief that the staggering achievements of technology and the extraordinary improvements in living standards were somehow natural, preordained and self-evident. The technologists, the engineers and doctors were among the worst offenders. They were the '*sabio-ignorante*' (learned ignoramuses) who failed to realize that technology was turning people into barbarians. He rejected both the American and the Soviet models, and felt that Europe's only hope lay in a rejection of the dictators and of the nation state, to be replaced by a united Europe with firmly entrenched and genuinely liberal principals in which the individual was respected and rescued from the instincts of the herd. He thus arrived at a position very close to that of the amiable Austrian pan-Europeanist, Count Richard Coudenhouve-Kalergi, who, although a passionate opponent of totalitarianism, felt that democracy was little more than a poor substitute for a genuine aristocracy.

There was widespread agreement among intellectuals, of whatever political colouring, with Ortega's contention that civilization's progress

resulted in a cultural retreat, the atrophy of individualism and a loss of [5]
cultural vitality. Theodor Adorno, Max Horkheimer, Walter Benjamin,
Georges Sorel, Sigmund Freud, Paul Valéry and Hermann Hesse joined the
choir to sing a complex polyphonic lamentation over the ghastliness of
the modern world. Their works were peppered with words like 'anomie',
'transcendental homelessness', 'ambivalence' and 'rootlessness'. Max Weber
called for the 're-enchantment' of the world; Georg Simmel asked what
made society possible and insisted that the totality of human existence had to
be rescued from the pitiless reality of the world, thus providing deliverance
from the fragmentary with the restoration of integrality.

Karl Jaspers wrestled with these problems in 'The Intellectual Problems
of the Age' (*Die Geistige Probleme der Zeit*, 1931), which, with *The Revolt
of the Masses*, was among the most widely read and influential books in
the inter-war period. For Jaspers this was a period not only of political,
economic and social crisis, but first and foremost of a deep-rooted intellectual malaise. Mankind's knowledge and ability had become so vast and was
ever expanding, so that there were no longer any generally accepted and
binding transcendental values, leaving control in the hands of anonymous
experts and bureaucrats. Rationality was applied almost exclusively to
practical problems, leaving ample room for the irrational, as in the racial
hocus-pocus, the glorification of violence, and the restless vitality of
National Socialism. The crisis was generally accepted as a destiny from which
there was no escape, and mankind stood passive and helpless before the
antinomies of the individual and the collective, body and soul, being and
existence. This situation for Jaspers, far from being grounds for nihilism
and pessimism, offered a wide freedom of choice. There were no easy answers, but the individual struggle for elucidation could lead to the solution
of immediate problems. He sought thereby to preserve the philosophical
tradition of the ancients and Judaeo-Christian values against the assault of
the barbarians. His tragic-heroic stand against the forces of the irrational
found considerable resonance, particularly among students, and his short
book went through a number of editions.

Some, like the anarcho-syndicalist Georges Sorel and the Italian futurist
Marinetti, swallowed a heavy dose of Nietzsche and managed to convince
themselves that the war provided a purifying experience, an alternative to
the non-committal essence of the modern, and an opportunity to restore
order to the world. They turned their backs on the feeble and slavish
morality of the Judaeo-Christian tradition, and heralded the mystical experience of a tightly-knit community of supermen, whether of Ernst Jünger's
front-line soldiers, Sorel's striking workers, D'Annuzio's paramilitary thugs,

[6] the anti-Semitic, blood-and-soil regionalism of Maurice Barrès, or the close circle of precious young men around the poet Stefan George. The call was for 'action', 'revolution', 'struggle' or 'deeds'. Carl Schmitt, with his characteristic bluntness, announced that this was a state of emergency for which the only solution was the 'expulsion or destruction of the heterogeneous'. This cannot be dismissed as the vaguely ridiculous attitudinizing of an unworldly academic. It was symptomatic of a profound malaise that was to have truly frightful consequences.

Few thinkers reflected the problems and uncertainties of contemporary life more accurately and profoundly than Martin Heidegger who, in a remote hut in the Black Forest at Todtnauberg, pondered the gloomy predicament of modern man. In spite of its painfully convoluted and hermetic language, his major work of the period, *Being and Time* (1927), bears a remarkable resemblance to the novels of his contemporary, Franz Kafka, although Heidegger sadly lacked the latter's often overlooked and mordant sense of humour. Heidegger had served on the Western Front in a meteorological unit charged with making calculations for the use of gas during the 1918 offensive in the Champagne. Although it was a relatively safe posting, he was profoundly affected by the experience, which he claimed stripped everything away down to the basic core of the personality. That the individual was now forced to rely entirely on the self, without any of the material and spiritual comforts of civilization, he regarded as a valuable opportunity.

Heidegger set about stripping philosophy down to the basic problem of being, a process that he described as 'destruction'. He had been obliged to leave the Jesuit order because of health problems in 1909, and ceased to study for the priesthood in 1911. By 1919, after much heart-searching, he reluctantly came to agree with Nietzsche that God was indeed dead. Having 'destroyed' theology he set about the destruction of his mentor Husserl's phenomenology. Finally he set to work on the Western tradition of philosophy and metaphysics, which he felt had trapped thinkers since Plato in a second-hand and shopworn set of abstractions that had become autonomous, and which provided little more than 'useless' knowledge of the essence of things. He called for a fundamental rethinking of philosophy starting with the pre-Socratics, above all Heraclitus, the 'weeping philosopher' and the 'dark one', whose profound pessimism and extreme obscurity he found particularly appealing and worthy of emulation.

The German crisis of the spirit, with which thinkers as different as the historian Oswald Spengler and the theologian Karl Barth wrestled, was reflected in an extreme fashion in Heidegger's work. He agreed with 'conservative revolutionaries' like Ernst Jünger, Carl Schmitt, Moeller van den Bruck and Ernst Niekisch that Western civilization had degenerated into an 'exhausted pseudo-culture' that was hopelessly depraved, moribund and beyond redemption. Man as a 'rational animal' was condemned to 'wander through the desert of the earth's desolation'. Thinking had been reduced to mere intelligence, to Max Weber's dreary 'instrumental rationality'. Heidegger insisted that what Weber described as 'demystification' was in fact mystification – a blind faith in technology. Europe was helplessly trapped between the Soviet Union and the United States, both of which were godless mass societies which denied the individual all 'possibilities of being', which were driven by a blind faith in unbounded technology, recklessly heading towards an ecological disaster, and hostile to the heroic individual who dared to think, to create and to act. Heidegger's talk of the need for 'decisiveness' and 'authenticity' in a world from which the gods had fled and in which everyone is 'other' and where there is no self, accurately reflected the intellectual atmosphere of the age.

Whereas thinkers like Husserl and Weber insisted that the post-Socratic philosophical tradition offered the means of overcoming the present crisis, Heidegger violently disagreed. For Plato truth is something that is waiting for us to discover. Heidegger argued that it is not something that exists outside individual existence, and that each and everyone must discover truth on their own. But this was far from being a Promethean vision. Heidegger's individual existence was overshadowed by the certainty of death and by permanent anxiety. The call for courage in the face of nothingness offered precious little consolation. Heidegger's 'draft of being' left him dangerously susceptible to any promise of a new beginning, and hence to the lure of National Socialism. Here at last he saw an opportunity to make a critical decision and to play his part as 'an entire people [*Volk*] accepts the desolateness of modern man amid the process of being'. Heidegger was strongly influenced by Hölderlin, the first great modern German poet, who wrote of the need 'to assimilate to oneself all right and duties of the community, by law of nature and without any special individual liberties . . . to assimilate to oneself ineluctably and enduringly all friendships and enmities of the whole'. It was he who bemoaned the 'disunity' (*Zerrissenheit*) of Germany. For Heidegger, 'being in the world' (*Dasein*) also involved 'being with others' (*Mitsein*). If *Dasein* implied 'openness' (*Erschlossenheit*) this indeed was an opportunity 'to expose oneself to a new manner and means of acquiring being', the golden opportunity for the individual to be summoned out of 'lostness' into the 'they'. Germany had reached a new beginning and was at a moment of destiny in 'the encounter between global technology and modern man', a counter-movement to the

[8]   nihilism of the Western 'will to *techne*'[3]. A German was no longer condemned to an isolated life as an act of autonomy in a world without gods, but became an active participant in the life of the *Volk*. Plato's cave dwellers were now on the march, goose-stepping their way under Zarathustra's empty skies. This was an astonishingly naive leap of faith by a desk-bound intellectual, but it was one that Heidegger refused ever to regret. He never apologized for his shameful behaviour in Nazi Germany. On the contrary, he felt that Hitler had failed to live up to his expectations and owed him an apology.

    Heidegger's exact contemporary, the Catholic existentialist Gabriel Marcel, pointed out the seductive dangers of a godless world without any other form of transcendence. Ernst Jünger, whom Heidegger greatly admired, came to a similar conclusion when he wrote that socialism and nationalism were the two millstones by means of which progress pulverizes what is left of the old world. Jünger was a highly decorated and frequently wounded soldier whose brutally realistic account of his wartime experiences in 'Storm of Steel' (*In Stahlgewittern*, 1920), 'Copse 125' (*Das Wäldchen 125*, 1925), and 'Fire and Blood' (*Feuer und Blut*, 1925) provides an unequalled literary representation of war on the Western Front. In his further reflections on the war in 'The Personal Experience of Combat' (*Der Kampf als inneres Erlebnis*, 1922), 'Total Mobilization' (*Die Totale Mobilmachung*, 1930) and 'The Worker' (*Der Arbeiter*, 1932) Jünger turned his back on the liberal bourgeois idealism, which was one of the first casualties of the war. He now espoused a heroic nihilism in the face of the essential meaninglessness of the technological age. Arguing that it was irrelevant what one was fighting for, but that what mattered was how one fought, he concluded that mankind was physically, mentally and socially determined by the available technology. The soldier at the front and the worker in the factory stood in the same existential relationship to technological means, the soldier to his weapon, the worker to his machine. The modern soldier was thus the precursor of the modern worker. The heroic was no longer manifested in acts of outstanding individual bravery, but rather in the often meaningless and helpless fulfilment of one's duty as a 'representative individual', whether in the trenches or on the factory floor. In this age of the masses and machines, wars become wars of workers, not of knights, kings or citizens, with technology the consumer of mass-produced armies and with the state converted into a gigantic factory. The last war showed that 'civilization' is more profoundly attached to progress than 'culture', and the 'progressive' nations such as the United States and Britain turned out to be the winners, Italy and Russia the losers.

Jünger's nihilism and his vision of a superman were similar to Nietzsche's, but they came directly from his experience of total warfare, rather than from the death of God. This vision of a new soldier/worker state infused with a Nietzschean will to power was widely admired, particularly in Germany, and many, including Heidegger, imagined that it would be realized under National Socialism and provide a new sense of heroic community infused with a fearless dynamism. Although Jünger dedicated a copy of 'Fire and blood' to 'The National Leader Adolf Hitler', and although the Nazis made every effort to get him on board, he remained aloof. He was, as Walter Benjamin pointed out, far too much of an aesthete. He was a right-wing anarchist and something of a snob, who also had no sympathy for the Nazis' philistine aesthetics, crude racist ideas and knee-jerk anti-Semitism.

The constitutional and international lawyer Carl Schmitt was as much an opponent of the Weimar Republic as Jünger. He loathed the materialism of modernity and searched for transcendent values in a godless world. His basic assertion was that society and politics were based on natural enmity and conflicts of interest. Liberalism with its belief in compromise and moral universals was thus a denial of this basic reality, and parliamentary democracy with its perpetual debates amounted to a neutering of politics. Dictatorship, by which he meant the temporary Roman variety, was in his view far more democratic and better reflected the true interests of the people than rule by self-seeking elites and complex parliamentary procedures. He greatly admired Fascist Italy and drew up blueprints for a 'totalitarian state', but he still had serious reservations about the Nazis whom, like Jünger, he initially regarded as primitive rowdies.

Apart from his theoretical works, he played an active part in the destruction of the Weimar Republic. In 1932 he represented the state in Chancellor Papen's overthrow of the Prussian government[4]. Always an opportunist, he joined the Nazi Party in March 1933 and set to work on a 'racial renewal' of the law. He justified the murders during the Röhm Putsch of June 1934, called for a legal campaign against the 'Jewish spirit', and proclaimed that the will of the Führer was the highest law. In 1936 he fell foul of the SS and retired to the academic sidelines as professor in Berlin. The attack on Carl Schmitt from a National Socialist perspective was first launched by Hermann Koellreutter in *The German Führer State*, published in 1934, in which he condemned Schmitt for his 'non-racial legal formalism' and for his worship of the state as an abstract unit of power. For a National Socialist the state was made up of race and community, whereas Schmitt argued that the secondary issues of war and struggle were in fact central. National Socialists had similar reservations

[10] about Italian Fascism because of its emphasis on the central importance of the state.

Curiously enough this disreputable and discredited man was widely admired in left-wing circles in the late 1960s. They found his assertion that the liberal emphasis on human rights, individualism and the rule of law was based on an illusion, and that politics was all about power, leadership and decision-making, greatly to their taste. Furthermore, his prediction that there would be an increasing number of civil wars, wars of national liberation and supranational networks of guerrillas and terrorists appealed to their revolutionary romanticism.

Most intellectuals in this age of extraordinary ideological fanaticism rejected liberal democracy, which they saw as the source of all that was wrong with the modern world. It had spawned the tyranny of capital, of imperialism, of the Moloch of mass warfare, of bourgeois conformity and manners. In a more philosophical version, it was responsible for the subtler and even more terrible tyranny of metaphysics and language. Initially the majority of leading intellectuals stood resolutely on the extreme right and were, as Mussolini said of his compatriots, fascists, fascistophile, or afascist; but with the rise of Hitler the Soviet Union skilfully played the anti-fascist card, and was thus able to delude a large number of otherwise intelligent people into believing that theirs was an honourable, humane and progressive cause, part of a glorious tradition that went back to the French Revolution.

None of the previous strategies that had dominated the modernist discourse seemed adequate to solve the dichotomies between the intellect and the irrational, structure and mentality, technological progress and cultural pessimism. Liberal rationalism had brought no convincing solutions; conservatism seemed quaintly outmoded and sentimental. Bolshevism had resulted in terror, turmoil and an appearance of terrified, dreary, anonymous equality. Monarchy was absurdly snobbish, capitalism heartless and sordid, democracy delivered the mindless masses into the hands of the chattering classes. The modern, consisting of the masses, the market, materialism and Marxism, was widely rejected, but how could the forces of the irrational be intelligently instrumentalized to serve a new and essentially rational project? Most of the radical critics of the modern were far from being reactionaries in the sense of wanting to return to some idyllic pre-industrial world of proud artisans like Hans Sachs in Wagner's *Die Meistersinger*, or the sturdy yeomen of Merrie Olde England. Fascist ideologues like Giovanni Gentile or Alfred Rosenberg felt that the problem lay not in modern technology, but in a modern man who had become hopelessly degenerate. Ernst Jünger agreed, as did the cultural pessimist Oswald Spengler.

At the heart of the matter was the question of the masses. Jaspers argued that they were the product of the modern technological world. The masses were quite distinct from the old 'mob' or 'dangerous classes', who were deprived of civil rights and liberties, who were confined to a specific space within a rigidly hierarchical society based on estates or classes, and who could, in most instances, be controlled by a whiff of grapeshot. The masses had political rights, which were reinforced by an acceptance of theoretical equality. With universal suffrage they had political power, and through the majority vote they ensured, at least in the eyes of Nietzsche and his epigones, that quantity would triumph over quality, civilization over culture, and the animal over the noble.

The masses could be easily manipulated since the individual had been reduced to an automaton, prey to the instincts of the herd, deprived of all values and living only for the moment. Hatred of the masses was so intense that some entertained apocalyptic visions of mass murder. In 1908 D.H. Lawrence, whose mind Nietzsche had served to unhinge, thought that a gas chamber as big as Crystal Palace would help rid the world of some of this waste material. After the war he offered three cheers for the inventors of poison gas. G.B. Shaw, who Hitler and Goebbels greatly admired, agreed that the majority of Europeans did not deserve to live, but such were his charitable instincts that he felt that their deaths should be scientific and humane. An eminent divine, Dean Inge of St Paul's, pronounced the majority of mankind to be on a level with the apes. Vilfrido Pareto maintained that culture was impossible without hierarchy and exploitation. Josef Schumpeter, one of the many intellectuals who made the transition from socialism to fascism, agreed with Pareto on the need for a hero leader. Freud asserted that since the 'pleasure seeking and blindly destructive rabble' was unable to control its base instincts and was impervious to culture, it would have to be controlled by a 'superior class'. W.B. Yeats and T.S. Eliot enthusiastically agreed. Both felt that education should be the preserve of an elite, the remainder of the racial stock improved by systematic sterilization.

The liberal values of freedom, progress and reason were now no longer regarded as universally applicable, but were seen as the privilege of an elite. But of whom should this elite consist? Should it be an intellectual elite, as Freud and Ortega y Gasset would have it, or a power-political elite as in the writings of Pareto and Robert Michels? Would it be D.H. Lawrence's natural aristocracy, a group that combined intelligence with willpower as Mussolini suggested, or would it be Lenin's revolutionary vanguard? Whatever it was it would be based on leadership, demand obedience and have totalitarian aspirations.

[12]   Even democrats were often elitists. In 1926 a group of 64 German professors published a manifesto that claimed that a parliamentary republic was the best way of creating a sense of community and ensuring that 'living aristocratic values' were upheld. As the historian Friedrich Meinecke phrased it, an intellectual aristocracy was not incompatible with parliamentary democracy. A democracy that was not 'ennobled' by an intellectual elite was little more than the cacocracy of mob rule. By 1932 Meinecke had lost what little faith he had had in a parliamentary democracy that had declined into the capricious and arbitrary rule of the masses, but he denied that the answer lay in National Socialism. Even the left-wing British socialist, Harold Laski, later chairman of the Labour Party, argued that there was little more to democracy than majority rule.

Belief in an elite was but a small step away from Nietzsche's and Shaw's 'superman', Freud's 'super-father', or whatever variation of hierophant, dictator or charismatic leader. Jaspers, who was certainly no fascist, and who eventually came to the painful realization that he had been talking dangerous nonsense, argued that at this 'turning point in the order of existence', when Western civilization was faced with the alternatives of a 'new order of things or doom and destruction', there was need for a 'real leader' who would steer society away from this 'theoretical artificiality'. Heidegger was in broad agreement when he stated that modern science had brought society to the furthest possible distance from the philosophy of life (*Lebensphilosophie*) and managed to persuade himself that National Socialism resolved this 'encounter between planetary technology and modern man'. Jaspers, Ortega y Gasset, Michels and Mussolini all argued that the masses would blindly obey and follow their leaders and hence play the only role appropriate to them: to be instruments of history.

As early as the 1830s Gottfried Keller, a convinced democrat and republican, had warned of the demagogic and dictatorial potential inherent in democracy in his masterpiece 'Green Henry' (*Der grüne Heinrich*). Gustave LeBon, in his *Psychology of the Masses* (1895), had already shown how the masses could be manipulated, hypnotized and fall prey to mass suggestion. They were in need of transcendence, of belief whether it be religious, political or social. Sorel and Thomas Mann felt that the masses needed a myth or a mythical surrogate. Pareto called for an ideology, Michels for a 'fictive ethic'. The aim was to ensure a blind faith and obedience that would legitimize authoritarian rule, while at the same time unleashing and channelling the power that lay within them. By these means the aristocratic spirit of the elite would be transmitted to the inarticulate masses.

This elitist worldview was by no means confined to the right. Lenin [13] with his utter contempt for the masses was in full agreement. Adorno and Horkheimer argued that the ruling class had deliberately endowed the masses with a false consciousness by means of mass culture and the mass media. Truth was a monopoly of an estimable avant-garde, at the forefront of which was the Frankfurt School whose example the masses were to follow. They should eschew Benny Goodman and the great swing bands of the era, and listen attentively to the atonal serialism of Schoenberg, Webern and Theodor W. Adorno. Others, like Ernst Bloch, understandably felt that such forbidding fare would repel rather than illuminate the masses, and argued that the left should take a leaf from the right's more popular book, and stress the mythical, the irrational and the utopian, while at the same time ensuring that the elite pursued realistic, rational and realizable goals.

In the secure comfort of their studies, these effete intellectuals became apostles of violence, without which their modernist projects could not be realized. They applauded the Bolshevik struggle against 'enemies of the people', 'cosmopolitans' (another term for Jews), 'insects' and 'cancer'. Bloch managed to convince himself that violence was necessary in order for 'love' to prevail. Horkheimer put forward the absurd argument that violence was needed in order to get rid of violence. Lukács insisted that a brave new revolutionary world could not be made without violence. Brecht saw Stalinist terror as a necessary step on the way forward. The Webbs issued the stern admonishment that morality and reason could not be brought to the masses without violence. André Gide agreed, until he visited the Soviet Union, saw the future and realized that it did not work. Romain Rolland remained convinced that the Soviet Union, in spite of the appalling violence, was the only hope for humanity. Such pernicious nonsense continued to be perpetrated even after Stalin's death in 1953. Simone de Beauvoir spoke for her circle when she claimed in 1954 that the Gulag, through which some 10 million unfortunates passed, was the necessary price paid for progress.

This fatal fascination with violence was combined with a leadership cult with devotees on the left as well as the right. Hitler and particularly Mussolini had fan clubs that rivalled those of Lenin and Stalin. Some admired leadership for itself, regardless of its political content. G.B. Shaw held Lenin, Mussolini and Hitler in high regard and felt that Sir Oswald Mosley and his British fascist party offered the only solution to Britain's problems. Salvador Dali transferred his affection for Stalin to Franco. Dieu la Rochelle detested Communism, but admired Lenin and Stalin for their sterling leadership qualities.

[14]   Of all the dictators, Mussolini had the most distinguished list of admirers. Among them were the poets Ezra Pound, Rainer Maria Rilke and Gottfried Benn, politicians such as Winston Churchill and Konrad Adenauer, and an assortment of intellectuals from Sigmund Freud to Carl Schmitt and Oswald Spengler. None of these was able to transfer this admiration to Hitler, and indeed most of them found him utterly repulsive. Others had no such scruples. The psychoanalyst C.G. Jung managed to convince himself that Hitler was divinely inspired. Jean Cocteau described him as an artist of genius with an audacious vision for an exciting new Europe. The Norwegian Nobel Prize-winning novelist Knut Hamsun pronounced that Hitler spoke on behalf of all humanity. Another novelist, Louis-Ferdinand Céline, enthusiastically endorsed Hitler's anti-Semitism, and came to believe that he had restored faith in Europe's destiny.

The appeal of both Mussolini and Hitler was due to their charismatic leadership style that combined the heady mixture of nationalism and socialism. An irrational and emotionally charged attachment to the leader was reinforced by promises of the creation of a sense of national community that transcended class distinctions and which was reinforced by an extensive programme of social welfare. Mussolini had undergone a metamorphosis from socialist to rabid nationalist and Fascist. Oswald Mosley in Britain, and Josef Piłsudski in Poland, had experienced a similar mutation. 'Marxism', in whatever guise, never held the slightest attraction for Hitler, but his half-baked early radicalism was marked by venomous attacks on 'plutocrats', the 'thraldom of interest' and 'money-grubbing capitalism' that had a strong pseudo-socialist flavour. For Hitler 'socialism' meant concern for the collective good, the removal of all barriers of class and estate, the guarantee of a minimum standard of living, access to culture and equality of opportunity, except of course for non-Aryans and women. The important thing was to 'socialize people' and not worry about socializing banks and factories. Many of his most devoted followers were former Communists. Goebbels' first literary attempt was a play, written in 1920, entitled *The Working Class Struggle*. In 1923 he sympathized with the Communist Party's 'Schlageter Line' and with its denunciation of the bourgeoisie as 'idle, feeble and stupid', announcing that he was a 'German Communist'. He believed in 'state socialism' freed from internationalism and Jewish influences. He saw Locarno as a sell-out to Western capitalism and feared that Germany would probably get involved in a crusade against the Soviet Union. In 1931 he told Hitler that the party must become 'more Prussian, more active, and more socialist'. He described Hitler's economics guru, Gottfried Feder, as 'small and ugly', 'a puffed-up peacock', 'a conceited, vain, jealous fop' and was furious when he announced: 'We denounce all socialist tendencies.' Goebbels commented: 'Awful! I'm hopping mad with him!'[5]

Both Mussolini and Hitler believed that they practised a true form of Rousseauesque democracy. Mussolini's authoritarian democracy was based on the theoretical submission of a willing people to an elite leadership. Hitler's 'Führer democracy', a free-for-all claiming to be based on a clearly defined chain of command, was deemed to be a true articulation of the people's will, so that it was a dictatorship based on consent rather than coercion. Stalin adopted much the same stance, particularly during the war, when he gave himself the title of 'leader'. Similar rubbish was bandied about in Hungary under Gömbös and Horthy, in Piłsudski's Poland, Franco's Spain, Salazar's Portugal and Metaxas' Greece. The dictatorships were based on a Bermuda Triangle of charismatic leader, functional elite and the ignorant and irrational masses. One of the most indecorous sights of the age was the obeisance of distinguished intellectuals to the dictators, in the conviction that they devoted their energies to the common weal, and were the hope of the future. One by one the gods failed, and revealed themselves to be mean-spirited and vicious tyrants who, far from elevating their wretched peoples to a higher moral plane, had let loose their base and brutish instincts and thus caused untold misery. These heavily compromised intellectuals adopted all manner of ingenious strategies to extricate themselves from the burden of their guilt, at the basis of which was their indignation that the dictators had let them down.

Liberal individualism had suffered a severe setback during the war. The call now was for a united effort in defence of the nation in which the separate and single had to submit to the uniform and joint. Britain's National Union, France's Union Sacrée and Germany's Truce (*Burgfrieden*) were all expressions of the need for duty, sacrifice and submission for the common good. It was but a small step for this to turn into a sour chauvinism that asserted unique inborn national qualities and a clear delimitation from the other, whether in the form of ethnic or religious minorities, immigrants or neighbouring nations.

Germany, with its penchant for pretentious abstract concepts, eagerly adopted the notion of a 'popular community' (*Volksgemeinschaft*), which was an essential ingredient of popular discourse across a wide political spectrum from the Social Democrats to the radical right. It soon became a concept central to National Socialism, when the word '*Volk*' ceased to mean simply

[16] 'people' but took on a sinister racial connotation. The 'popular community' was transformed into a 'racial community', and an ideal of an exclusive folk that demanded submission and sacrifice replaced that of a general feeling of solidarity, designed to guarantee the security of the individual as well as that of the group. The National Socialist 'racial community' was thus driven by a collective selfishness. A distinction was made between Germans who were *Volksgenossen* and Jews who were *Rassengenossen*. Both can be translated into English as 'racial comrades', but the overtones of *Volk* give the first a wider meaning and, as Humpty-Dumpty said to Alice, the meaning of words is determined by power. The concept of a 'racial community' was at the very heart of National Socialism, even though it was obviously in blatant contrast to the social Darwinist free-for-all that was the other ideological bearing wall. The notion of 'community' had widespread appeal. Wilm Hosenfeld, the remarkable man who is remembered as the officer who saved the life of 'the pianist' (Wladyslaw Szpilman) in Roman Polanski's film, had been an enthusiastic member of the Wandervogel youth movement, relishing the thought of belonging to 'a racially German and pure-blooded association'. Later as a member of the SA he wrote: 'When one dons the SA uniform one is no longer one's own master. One is part of a greater community.' At the Nazi Party rally in 1936 he noted: 'Once again I am seized by the feeling of a great community.'[6] It took him many agonizing years to realize that National Socialism was riddled with contradictions and that the 'racial community' was a repulsive sham.

Fascist movements profited greatly from a widespread disillusionment with democracy. Nietzsche had proclaimed democracy to be a sign of decadence that amounted to rule by the second-rate. Nietzsche's friend, the great cultural historian Jacob Burckhardt, announced that democracy had destroyed Greek civilization. Sundry literati like Oswald Spengler, Othmar Spann and Moeller van den Bruck, saw democracy as a temporary phase soon to be replaced by dictatorship. Werner Sombart insisted that men must realize 'The Idea', that supra-individual something to which man must sacrifice himself, the concrete idea that appears within the group (*Verband*). He glorified war as a heroic response to 'the abject spirit of commerce'. Carl Schmitt, an ardent admirer of Fascist Italy, argued that since questions of value could not be quantified, parliamentary democracy was unworkable. Mass society had to be forged anew, the demystification of the world reversed, nihilism extirpated, by violent means if necessary. The 'true state', for Othmar Spann, was an organic state in which the individual lacks both importance and substance other than that which he borrows from the community in which he is incorporated. For both Fascists and Communists the word 'individual' implied utter contempt. The hero would replace the humanist, Christian humility give way to Germanic pride, discipline and sacrifice would supersede a wishy-washy idealism, and values would be transmogrified. Gottfried Benn and Ernst Jünger drank deep from this poisoned cup, as did a number of their colleagues across the Rhine.

The Italian corporate state was designed to guarantee the general good by a judicious admixture of the state and the private sectors. Class differences would be overcome by the realization that all were working together for the common good. Cooperation would take the place of the class struggle. It was a model that, in its many variations, had widespread support. The Papal encyclical 'Quadragesimo anno' of 1931 was critical of the role of the state within the Italian corporate state and stressed the importance of subsidiarity. It was a reaffirmation of Leo XIII's 'Rerum novarum' of 1891, but it also adopted many of the principal ideas behind the Fascist model. The encyclical served as a blueprint for Dollfuss and Schuschnigg's efforts to create a 'state based on the estates' (*Ständestaat*) in Austria.

State control over the economy had grown apace during the war as the nations braced themselves to mobilize their efforts. The result was what the German socialist economist Rudolf Hilferding called 'organized capitalism'. This model had considerable appeal across a broad political spectrum since it encouraged the hope that the vagaries of the market could be controlled, the masses integrated, and the private desire for profit made subordinate to the exigencies of the common good. Here left and right came close together, and the political discourse was peppered with such vague terms as 'national socialism', 'social nationalism', 'German socialism', 'national syndicalism' or 'organic syndicalism'. It thus came as no shock when Dieu la Rochelle spoke of the half-socialism of Hitler, the half-fascism of Stalin.

There was general agreement between the extremes of left and right that the political, social and moral crisis could not be overcome without the use of force. But how was this force to be organized? The Austrian experiment under Dollfuss, the 'millimetre Metternich', seemed to indicate that a dictator was necessary in order to bring the working class in line and integrate the masses. Then came the question of who that dictator should be. The problem in the Germany of 1932 was narrowed down to whether or not to accept Hitler. Was this ill-educated and unpredictable man a Parsifal or a Siegfried, or was he a dangerous rabble-rousing Jacobin? That so many distinguished minds faced such a dilemma was testament to the dangerous absurdity of a totalitarian project that most were to live to regret.

[18] Germany

Hitler was the creation of his times, the product of German history, who in turn made history in the course of 12 spectacular years between 1929 and 1941 and then, having failed spectacularly, directed a murderous orgy and a mass suicide on an unimaginable scale. He was a unique historical figure in that a nobody became an all-powerful dictator who altered the course of history, but who also left behind him nothing but a legacy of death and destruction. What was there in German history that made such an extraordinary phenomenon possible?

We have seen how the temper of the times was favourable to an authoritarian solution to the challenges of modernity, but this also serves to underline the uniqueness of National Socialism. Germany alone among the technically and culturally advanced states fell prey to a radical fascist movement that established an unchallenged dictatorship with breathtaking rapidity. Historians have spilt much ink on the question of whether this was due to the unique course (*Sonderweg*) of German history that made something like the Third Reich likely or, in an extreme form, inevitable. Obviously the fact that Germany since 1945 has developed into an admirable democracy, fully conscious of its obligations both towards its past victims as well as to the international community, shows that there were many positive features in the country's history. The *Sonderweg* thesis is further weakened when the course of Germany's development is compared with that of other comparable states. The social and economic structure, respect for the rule of law, the self-conscious bourgeois mentality, the educational and cultural norms, were comparable to those in France or Britain and were sufficient preconditions for a workable parliamentary democracy. Nevertheless National Socialism, although not the inevitable outcome of German history, was a uniquely German phenomenon, and it is therefore necessary to look at the peculiarities of Germany's development in order to find a clue to why such a highly civilized country should fall prey to such barbarity.

At the root of the problem is the phenomenon known variously as 'non-simultaneity' or 'unequal development'. Goethe had lamented the fact that for the Viennese Germany meant Austria, whereas for the Berliners it was Prussia. Schiller complained that 'the political begins where scholarship ends'. The united Germany of 1871 was a curious amalgam that many felt to be incomplete and which was still in search of an identity. It was a relatively loose association of states, dominated by an arch-conservative bureaucratic Prussia, in which the military caste played a dominant role, while parliamentary democracy and liberal institutions were far more developed in the

southern German states. The Prussian–German authoritarian state failed to
adjust to the new realities and challenges posed by an industrialized mass
society. Bismarck sought to frustrate bourgeois liberal emancipatory efforts
and bring the masses into line with programmes for social insurance and
plebiscitary appeals to nationalism, imperialism and even anti-Semitism.
Catholics and Social Democrats, comprising almost half the population, were
denounced as 'enemies of the Reich' and treated as pariahs.

Problems that generations in France and Britain had addressed had to
be solved immediately by the new German Empire. A nation state had to
be created and given a constitution. Rapid industrialization meant that a
solution had to be found to the social question, and this at a time when
Germany had overnight become the most powerful nation in Europe, yet
had still to find a role. An ingenious attempt was made to synchronize the
social and the political structures with an elaborate system of checks and
balances, but it did nothing to stop them being driven further apart. On the
one hand there was an authoritarian military state with its archaic warrior
caste, on the other a dynamic, modern industrial society with an organized
proletariat clamouring for a political voice. In such a situation the bulk of
the formerly liberal bourgeoisie moved steadily to the right, seeking the
protection of the authoritarian state and thus creating the phenomenon that
Thomas Mann called 'General Dr. von Staat'. Rather than seeking to defuse
inevitable social tensions by constitutional parliamentary means, Germany
decided to opt for a powerful state with a mission designed to court the
enthusiasm of the masses. Having bowed low to Bismarck's Realpolitik,
thus betraying their ideals, the bulk of the German bourgeoisie dressed
their humiliation as a victory for the 'German mission' and strengthened
their determination to resist the 'enemies of the Reich', both at home and
abroad.

Wilhelmine Germany was thus profoundly uneasy, riven with anxiety,
fearful of future contingencies. Could Germany as the 'empire in the
middle', encircled by the Ententes, survive as a great power? Would the
new Germany be destroyed in a war and left powerless? Would the enemies
within overthrow a political system that guaranteed the predominance of
the old conservative order? Liberalism had given way to nationalism. Concerns about an open society, liberties and tolerance were forgotten. Power
was now all that mattered as 'society' gave way to 'community'. Alien influences must be purged and Germans become more German. The soulless
influence of the enlightenment, democratic levelling, and the all-pervasive
and negative Jewish influence must be energetically countered. The German
people, free from these harmful outside influences, must then find 'living

[20] space' for their excess population by, in the words of Paul de Lagarde[7], advancing 'a few times fifty miles in the direction of Central Asia'. None of this would be possible, according to another leading cultural pessimist, Julius Langbehn, without a strong leader, the elimination of the Jews, whom he regarded as 'a temporary plague and cholera', along with their intellectual allies, the purification of the German race and a subsequent national rebirth. Wagner's frightful English son-in-law, Houston Stewart Chamberlain, argued that the idea of 'Man' was the pernicious product of the French Revolution. 'Mankind' does not exist, only 'men, various and different'. 'Mankind' was simply another term for 'racial chaos', and in his vision of a new tribalism 'race and the ideal together make up the personality of man'[8].

Such noxious ideas were initially entertained by a relatively small circle of cultural critics who had a horror of the masses, whom they saw as a major contributing factor to the curse of modernity, but they were on the agenda, to be eagerly vulgarized and radicalized by demagogues on the extreme right. A mass society developed with the remarkable rate of industrial growth, swelling the ranks of the Social Democratic Party (SPD) whose programme was alarmingly revolutionary, in contrast to its increasingly reformist practice. The authoritarian state felt threatened and demanded absolute loyalty and solidarity in the face of those it branded as 'enemies of the Reich'. This seemed to be achieved in the political truce of 1914, but within two years the old tensions resurfaced to become explosive in the moment of Germany's humiliating defeat.

On 29 September 1918 Hindenburg and Ludendorff told the Kaiser that the war was lost and that negotiations for an armistice based on President Wilson's Fourteen Points should begin at once. The High Command (OHL) set about placing the blame for a lost war squarely on the shoulders of the majority parties in the Reichstag, which on the previous day had agreed that Germany should become a constitutional monarchy. On 1 October Ludendorff gleefully told a group of senior officers: 'We shall now see these gentlemen enter various ministries. They can make the peace that has to be made. They can now eat the soup they have served up to us!' The changeover to a parliamentary regime was part of the 'revolution from above' masterminded by Admiral Paul von Hintze, a devious, blasé and ambitious opportunist who had been appointed secretary of state for foreign affairs in July. The 'stab in the back' legend, that was to play such a critical role in the downfall of the Weimar Republic, was thus carefully constructed in the late summer of 1918.

On 3 October Prince Max of Baden, the heir to the grand duchy and a man virtually without a political profile, was appointed chancellor.

Members of all the majority parties were given ministerial positions. Germany [21] was now a fully-fledged constitutional monarchy and there were raucous protests from the right. Heinrich Class, the president of the Pan-German League, called for an all-out offensive on the Jews, whom he held uniquely responsible for this disastrous turn of events. At a meeting of senior officials of the League in late October he quoted Kleist and said of the Jews: 'Kill the lot; you will not be asked the reason why at the last judgement.' The League's official newspaper, the *Deutsche Zeitung*, published an article by Baron von Gelbsattel which also blamed the Jews for this 'bloodless revolution', since democracy was 'of Jewish origin' and was an essential ingredient of Jewry's destructive potential.

On 23 October US Secretary of State Lansing called for Germany's unconditional surrender and demanded the Kaiser's abdication, terms that Ludendorff, who was simply looking for a breathing space, found totally unacceptable. Prince Max told the Kaiser that Ludendorff had to go or he would feel obliged to resign. Hindenburg and Ludendorff travelled to Berlin to confront the Kaiser, and in a stormy scene William accepted Ludendorff's resignation.

Meanwhile, the navy mutinied when ordered out to sea to confront the Royal Navy, while on 7 November a motley crew of socialists and anarchists under Kurt Eisner seized power in Munich. The king abdicated and a republican 'Free State of Bavaria' was proclaimed. On the following day, revolutionary sailors and workers took over control in Brunswick. By 8 November Düsseldorf, Stuttgart, Leipzig, Halle, Osnabrück and Cologne were in the hands of Workers' and Soldiers' Councils. The mayor of Cologne, Konrad Adenauer, calmly announced that he fully accepted the new circumstances.

By now it was clear that the Kaiser would have to go. The sailors in Kiel were the first publicly to demand his abdication. Then the prominent Social Democrat Philipp Scheidemann wrote to Prince Max at the end of October, saying that the Kaiser should abdicate in order that the armistice talks should proceed smoothly. The SPD leader, Friedrich Ebert who, unlike Scheidemann, was far from being a republican, suggested to the chancellor on 7 November that a regent should be appointed, arguing that unless William II were to go there would be a revolution. According to Prince Max he then added the famous words: 'I hate revolution like the plague.'

On the morning of 9 November Otto Wels, regional secretary of the SPD in Brandenburg, and a rough-hewn populist of exceptional courage and sound instincts, called for a general strike in protest against a decree by General von Linsingen, Commanding General in the Marches, which banned

[22] the Workers' and Soldiers' Councils. Ebert began negotiations with the Independent Social Democrats (USPD), the Revolutionary Shop Stewards and the Workers' and Soldiers' Councils (Arbeiter und Soldaten Räte) with a view to forming a government on the Bavarian model. Wels the pragmatist knew that Ebert's efforts to co-opt the extreme left were unlikely to succeed without military support. He therefore approached the Naumburg Light Infantry (*Naumburger Jäger*), a traditional regiment known for its loyalty to the Kaiser. Wels appealed to the other ranks to support the Social Democrats in their endeavour to create a new republican government. He met with a warm response. The news that the Naumburger had thrown their support behind the Social Democrats was a shattering blow to Prince Max and to the OHL. At Headquarters Groener, Ludendorff's replacement, had already come to the conclusion that the army would refuse to follow the Kaiser in an attempt to oust the Social Democrats and that he therefore had to abdicate. Hindenburg agreed, but refused to relay this unpleasant news to the All Highest. In the morning of 9 November Groener told the Kaiser: 'The Army no longer stands behind Your Majesty!' whereupon William II expressed his intention to abdicate. Prince Max then handed over the office of chancellor to Friedrich Ebert, the leader of the SPD.

In the early afternoon of 9 November Scheidemann addressed the crowds from a window in the Reichstag and announced the formation of a 'German Republic'. He did so largely to forestall the radical socialist Karl Liebknecht, who two hours later proclaimed a 'Free Socialist German Republic'. Ebert was furious with Scheidemann for thus jumping the gun, but was silenced by the Berliners' rapturous reception of his announcement.

The Weimar Republic was thus born of defeat, but Adolf Hitler, skilfully following the score written by Hintze and the OHL, was to insist that it was the cause of Germany's downfall. Had not a civilian signed an armistice when the German Army was still firmly entrenched on French soil? Had not Hindenburg and Ludendorff insisted that the army was undefeated? Had not the majority parties, in which Jews, Freemasons and Catholics played a disproportionate role, stabbed the fatherland in the back, only to crawl to Versailles and sign a humiliating peace? For Hitler this was 'Ebert's lemonade revolution', a scandalous act of national betrayal.

All the political parties in the Weimar Republic were in full agreement that the Treaty of Versailles, which every schoolchild knew was a *Diktat*, had to be revised. The National Socialists never tired of harping on this popular theme, using it to disguise their more radical aims and intentions. The attack on the Versailles settlement was part and parcel of the assault on the 'November criminals' who had founded the republic and who had signed the treaty. Admiral Hintze and his colleagues knew perfectly well that the peace would be extremely harsh, for all the idealistic nonsense in the Fourteen Points, and welcomed this fact, for it would further discredit the new republic and make it all the easier for the old elites to get back into the saddle. Furthermore, the Versailles settlement left Germany in a very strong position. Whereas in 1914 it had been contained by the Ententes between Russia, France and Britain, it was now bordered on the east by the weak secession states and the Franco-British *entente* was no longer *cordiale*. A bitterly resentful Germany still had the strongest economy in Europe, while the victorious powers began to have serious reservations about the treaty, so that the situation was highly favourable to a determined revisionist.

The 'revolution' of 1918/19 was incomplete. The Social Democrats, fearful of the threat from the left, and anxious above all to maintain law and order, had felt obliged to rely on the support of the army and the Freikorps. The price they paid was extremely high. The army, the judiciary and the civil service were left untouched. Their loyalty was to the old regime, not to the new constitution. The political parties also failed to adapt to the new system and clung to the old confrontational style appropriate to challenging a government without parliamentary responsibility. They were still devoted to furthering specific sectional interests rather than common concerns. Compromise, essential to the effective functioning of a multi-party democracy, was a dirty word for both left and right. Politics, as Carl Schmitt was loudly to proclaim, was a question of friend and foe. Enemies of the republic dominated the political discourse. The right hankered after the good old days before the war, while the left chanted: 'Democracy is not without blame, Socialism is our aim!' Anti-democratic ideas were no longer the privileged notions of irrational cranks and snooty critics of modern civilization, but were common currency in mass parties fired with a determination to destroy the republic by whatever means possible. Ernst von Salomon, one of Walther Rathenau's murderers, wrote:

> Where is Germany? In Weimar or in Berlin? It was once on the front, but the front collapsed. Then it was supposed to be at home, but home was a deception. It appeared in songs and speeches, but the tone was false. One spoke of fatherland and motherland, but niggers have that as well. Was it the people [*Volk*]? But they demanded bread and voted for fat bellies. Was it the state? But the state chattered about its form and found it in renunciation.

Millenarian visions of a 'Third Reich' and beguiling aspirations for a 'racial community' vied with versions of a workers' and peasants' utopia on

[24] the Soviet model. Liberalism was pronounced dead in 1932 by the philologist Jonas Lesser, who added: 'Young people know that intellectual compromises are at the root of all vices and lies.' The socialist satirist Kurt Tucholsky similarly mocked the pathetic notions of compromise and conciliation. Parliament was the despised locus of compromise, Oswald Spengler's 'alehouse table', and Edgar Jung denounced parliamentary government as 'rule by the inferior'. Dictatorship was the only answer, but in the age of the masses this had to be coupled with some democratic element. Moeller van den Bruck announced in his influential book *The Third Reich* of 1923 that liberalism would destroy the nation and that democracy and dictatorship were compatible. Democracy involved the people controlling their destiny, without being bound by constitutional restraints or procedural rigmarole, so that as long as the people were in agreement, a dictatorship could be democratic.

Moeller van den Bruck, Oswald Spengler, Edgar Jung and Ernst Jünger had little sympathy for a plebiscitary mass party such as the NSDAP, but they did it a great service in discrediting parliamentary democracy, undermining the republic, providing a cerebrally insolvent movement with some powerful intellectual weaponry and making the very idea of dictatorship acceptable in elite circles.

Hitler

Kurt Tucholsky[9] said of Hitler: 'The man does not exist. He is simply the noise that he makes.' That is the core of the problem of writing about Hitler, for no other great historical figure is as empty, shallow and barren. His background is obscure. We do not know who was his grandfather. His father was probably his mother-in-law's half-brother, and thus his wife's uncle. He was a school drop-out who twice tried to gain admission to art school but was unsuccessful due to his obvious lack of talent. He drifted into an aimless bohemian life in pre-war Vienna before volunteering in the Bavarian army in 1914, aged 25. During the war he displayed considerable bravery and devotion to duty, winning the Iron Cross second class in 1914, the Military Cross with crossed swords third class in September 1917, a regimental diploma for bravery and the wounded medal in May 1918, plus the Iron Cross first class and the service award third class in August 1918, but he showed no leadership qualities whatsoever, ending the war as a lance corporal. He was 30 years old in 1919, a total failure living in obscurity. He was a self-educated and absurdly arrogant know-all with an

acute case of arrested development; a man without friends and without [25]
any positive human attributes. His personal life remained pathetic throughout, and the great demagogue was absurdly gauche in a private setting.
On closer examination his tirades were rhetorically weak, totally lacking in
any intellectual substance, utterly humourless and ultimately boring. One
contemporary spoke of the man's 'sheer unpleasantness'. Friedrich Reck-
Malleczewan, himself an appalling old fraud and phoney aristocrat, described
him as a 'power-drunk schizophrenic' whose 'incantations of the great
Manitou' revealed his 'basic stupidity'[10]. He was one of the many *fleurs du
mal* that blossomed in the rich *völkisch* humus of post-war Munich. Until
1929 he was a spectacular failure who had gained a certain notoriety as a
twice convicted jailbird, a bank robber, blackmailer and accessory to murder,
the improbable leader of an absurd attempt to overthrow the government, the
crackpot drummer boy of Munich's beer halls, presiding over a court packed
with misfits and second-raters, rife with sordid sexual scandals and shameless
villainy. Once in power he lived in great splendour and amassed a huge
fortune while Goebbels' propaganda machine presented him as living an
austere life, devoting all his energies for the well-being of the German people.
He made huge sums from the compulsory sales of *Mein Kampf* and from the
advance on his 'Second Book' that was never published in his lifetime. He
was also paid royalties for his portraits on such things as postage stamps,
which brought in 50 million RM in 1937 alone. He never paid any taxes.

Hitler was the product of the masses and of Goebbels' propaganda. He
was nothing without an audience and he had an uncanny ability to read the
room and give his listeners exactly what they wanted to hear. He peppered
his speeches with foreign words such as 'Invasion', 'Terror', '*Defaitismus*'
and '*diffamieren*' to give them a certain intellectual edge and to impress his
semi-literate audiences. Any half-baked collection of clichés and prejudices
was dignified with the fashionably pretentious label of 'worldview'
(*Weltanschauung*). Propaganda was an integral part of Hitler's ideology. It
provided perlocutionary calls for action on wholly inadequate grounds and
worked as long as the regime was able to deliver at least some of the goods.
When propaganda became totally divorced from reality it could only
move the blindly faithful and left the average citizen in cynical disbelief.
Without accepting the once fashionable French linguistic determinism, Victor
Klemperer's argument in his insightful book *LTI: Lingua Tertii Imperii*
(The Language of the Third Reich) that the repetition of single words and
expressions to the extent that they entered everyday speech was the most
powerful of all propaganda weapons, is wholly convincing. Words such as
'fanatical', 'brutal', 'ruthless', 'merciless', 'uncompromising' and 'unbending'

[26]   took on a positive meaning. The new language provided, in Schiller's words, 'a language that writes and thinks for you'. This is particularly true of anti-Semitism. People were desensitized and the threshold of acceptance lowered, to the point that they became compliant with mass murder.

The hypnotic effect of his speeches on mass audiences was an immense boost to Hitler's self-confidence to the point that a certain poise grew first into a blissful egotism and then to megalomaniac proportions. He had a sleepwalker's unshakeable belief in his destiny that he was able to convey to others. At times this chthonian creature seems to be the fulfilment of the medieval Jewish prophecy that: 'At night time there shall come upon the earth a man of exceptional eloquence. All that is God's . . . must have its counterpart, its reverse in evil and negation. So it is with the word, the gift of speech.' His hypertrophic self-identification with the German people reached the point where he ordered a national suicide to accompany his own. 'The destiny of the Reich', he said, 'belongs to me alone', and a speaker at the 1936 party rally in Nuremberg announced in pseudo-religious terms: 'Now we are together, we are with him and he is within us and we are Germany.' Hitler declared his personal experience to be a genuine and authentic expression of the nation, claiming that he was Germany personified. In this romantic view the will of the leader replaced politics and law, with faith, conviction and passion taking the place of careful consideration and detailed planning. 'Thy will be done' was the first article of faith of all true believers. At the heart of what J.P. Stern called his 'solipsistic evil' was his conviction that his will was sanctioned by Providence, the will of John 5:30: 'I seek not mine own will, but the will of the Father which hath sent me[11].' His was the reverse of Immanuel Kant's concept of will, in that it failed to take into account the means whereby it could possibly be attained. Hence his childish tantrums when his will could not be done.

In 1930, admittedly after he had left the NSDAP, Otto Strasser wrote of Hitler:

> He is a sleepwalker, a real medium the like of which the craziest periods of human history tend to produce. He emerges from the shadows between night and day. How often have I been asked for the secret of Hitler's extraordinary oratorical talent. I can only explain it as an incredible intuition that enables him without fail to diagnose the discontents that plague his listeners. Whenever he tries to lend weight to his speeches with scholarly theories, extracted from other people's books that he had only half understood, he is unable to rise above a pathetic mediocrity. But when he casts aside these crutches, when he leaps forward and says whatever comes into his mind: then he is suddenly transformed into one of the greatest orators of the century.

He was the product of his times, who in turn altered the course of history. Like many Germans he failed to realize that the 'November revolution' of 1918 was not the cause of Germany's defeat, but its result. He was the unique product of this 'November crime' and throughout his career his successes were due to the failures of his opponents. He was indolent and indecisive until he made yet another reckless gamble, so that Goebbels gave him the nickname '*cunctator*'[12]. He had absolutely no organizational talent and brooked no argument or even discussion. He was fortunate to have in Gregor Strasser an organizational genius who built up the party, and in Ernst Röhm an activist that gave the party a revolutionary élan and uncompromising vitality. Both men fell foul of Hitler and were murdered in 1934. National Socialism was not a coherent ideology; it was served up in many different guises and remained essentially amorphous. Historians such as Michael Burleigh dismiss it as mere 'guff'[13], which it undoubtedly is in retrospect, but it would be unwise to dismiss it out of hand. Some impressive minds contributed to this devil's brew, countless otherwise intelligent people were intoxicated by it, millions were killed as it was put into practice. In a speech given in 1936 Hitler announced: 'National Socialism is not a doctrine of inertia, but a doctrine of conflict. It is not a doctrine of happiness and good fortune, but a doctrine of struggle and thus also a doctrine of sacrifice.' It should be noted that the German word for 'sacrifice' (*Opfer*) also means 'victim'. The call for 'sacrifice' was a deviously insidious form of emotional blackmail, an underhand means of wringing material benefits, as well as a form of quasi-religious confirmation. Such ambiguity is typical of so many of Hitler's remarks, serving to disguise their profound pettiness. As one intellectual remarked, this was 'politics fit for the kindergarten'.

It soon became apparent to the more intelligent Nazis such as Goebbels that Hitler was an indispensable figurehead, without whom the party would fall apart into a series of bickering factions. The Hitler myth was thus at the very core of National Socialism and without it the movement would fall prey to rivalries, factions, betrayals, infighting and intrigues and eventually self-destruct. Thus the Third Reich had no constitution; the 'will of the Führer' was the highest law. There was no politburo, and the cabinet soon ceased to meet. Hitler founded no dynasty and did not appoint a successor. His dictatorship could never have been reproduced. He left nothing behind him but a pile of rubble and a morally bankrupt nation.

The Weimar Republic collapsed in 1929 and overnight Hitler's NSDAP ceased being merely a fringe party and could no longer be ignored. Hitler had failed miserably in 1923 and with Stresemann's skilful revisionist policy, massive US credits and conservatives holding a monopoly of ministerial

[28] positions, there was no place for a party on the radical right. Everything changed with the depression, mass unemployment and three years of minority governments ruling by presidential decree. The catastrophic effects of the depression were compounded by an acute crisis of political identity. The leading figures to the right of centre, such as Hugenberg, Kaas and Schleicher, were sworn enemies of the republic who wanted an authoritarian presidential government. It was the right rather than the depression that destroyed the republic, with Papen locked in battle with Schleicher and Hitler biding his time, much to the displeasure of party activists, until he was called upon to step into the breach. The elites had no clear idea what Hitler stood for beyond a promise of a perpetuation of their authoritarian mode of personal and professional life, a 'non-political' society in which there would be no place for awkward democratic choices and compromises, and a reassuring vision of the restoration of a sense of community. A polymorphic Hitler with an eclectic ideology was to establish a polycratic state that was to satisfy the longings of the vast majority of an atomized *Volk*. Provided that one was not one of the targeted victims, such as Jews, Marxists or the handicapped, this allowed for a great deal of leeway for those within the 'racial community', membership in which became all the more desirable as those 'alien to the community' were ruthlessly exterminated.

Hitler's twin obsessions were with race and space. The two were intertwined. Hitler's worldview can be summed up in his phrase: 'Everything that has happened hitherto in the history of the world is an expression of the instinct for self-preservation of different races.' This may have sounded profound to some of the faithful, but it was never clear what he meant by race. Was he talking of the Germanic race, the Aryan race or the White race? How was racial identity to be established? Was it by measuring skulls to distinguish between Eastern (*ostisch*), Western (*westisch*), Northern (*nordisch*), Palatine (*fälisch*), East Baltic (*Ostbaltisch*) and Dinaric (*dinarisch*), or by some other arcane method? The Munich journalist and courageous opponent of National Socialism, Fritz Gerlich, took great delight in pointing out that according to the criteria established by Dr Hans E. Günther, whom Frick had appointed to a chair of racial research at the University of Jena, Hitler's nose betrayed him as being distinctly 'Mongolian'. His worldview was also 'Mongolian' according to Rosenberg's taxonomy. An added absurdity was that Himmler was a fervent admirer of Ghengis Khan and idealized the Mongols, in spite of their dubious racial characteristics, believing them to be the original inhabitants of Atlantis. Goebbels was impressed when the SS doctor Karl-Josef Gross pointed out to him that the criteria for racial selection were open to serious question, since most of the leadership would fail to pass the test. It was a popular joke that the ideal Aryan was blonde like Hitler, slim like Göring, tall like Goebbels and had a name like Rosenberg.

Hitler insisted that the Jews were a race but here too there was confusion about how they could be identified. Were they perhaps after all a religious community? Whatever they were they stood in the way of the Darwinian struggle between peoples and races for 'living space' (*Lebensraum*) and therefore had to be eradicated, not simply displaced. All of this was madness. Germany had absolutely no need whatsoever for living space and if the Jews really presented such a deadly menace as they did in Hitler's pathological vision it is curious that it proved relatively easy to murder 6 million of them in an alarmingly short space of time. The concept of *Lebensraum* came from Rudolf Hess who had picked up the notion from Karl Haushofer, professor of political geography at Munich University, with whom he first studied and then became his assistant and 'adoptive son'. It then became popularized in Hans Grimm's 'blood-and-soil' best-seller 'People Without Space' (*Volk ohne Raum*), published in 1926.

Hitler's spectacular successes enhanced his status as a charismatic leader and precious little stood in his way. The *folie à deux* between Hitler and the Germans began with a rapidity that took all by surprise. As Heinz Marr wrote in 1943 the permanent connection between the people and the Führer, a word that means 'leader', 'guide' and the person in the driver's seat, was proof against any form of intellectual doubt. Germans were led by a German who knew the essence of their kind. The Führer was the real essential 'me' to whom I must bend my will in order for me to be what I really am. At home the liberals, the Centre, the Social Democrats and the Communists were pitifully passive. Hitler put Germany back to work and restored a degree of social peace with a judicious combination of carrots and sticks. He used enough terror to force the doubters to toe the line, but not so much as to provoke resistance. In foreign affairs the British and French were unbelievably feeble, with only the French foreign minister Barthou prepared to confront the obvious menace. Hitler had a hyena's instinct for what was half dead and possibly his greatest achievement was the defeat of France. He was almost alone in realizing how weak and demoralized the country was and victory over Germany's hereditary enemy brought him to the pinnacle of his prestige and power.

He now had a megalomanic belief in his omniscience, and was able to convince others of his genius. He was the living embodiment of Gottfried Feder's insistence that a leader above all needs 'somnambulistic certainty',

[30] not knowledge as such, but will-power. This proved to be his undoing. The Soviet counter-attack in December 1941 made it obvious to a number of officials that the war could not possibly be won, and there is indication that Hitler knew in his heart of hearts that this was indeed the case. That month he told the Croat foreign minister Korkowit: 'I am absolutely ice-cold . . . If the German *Volk* should no longer be strong enough and ready to sacrifice its blood in order to preserve its very existence, it should disappear and be destroyed by another stronger power . . . I won't weep a single tear for the German *Volk*.' True to his word he ordered a national suicide, the ultimate sacrifice, on 19 March 1945, but the country was in such a state of terminal collapse that his maniac orders could no longer be carried out. Hitler's legacy was thus that of a murderer, of his opponents at home and abroad, of the Jews, of those outside the 'racial community' and finally of the Germans themselves. Pitifully few realized the dangers that lay ahead as they celebrated the 'national revival' in 1933.

CHAPTER 2

THE ORIGINS OF NATIONAL SOCIALISM

From Munich to Berlin

A minute party in Bohemia that represented the interests of the German speakers known as the 'Sudeten Germans' concocted a curious brew of nationalism and socialism, the two most powerful offshoots of the French Revolution, which was soon to prove potent and highly addictive. It was a mixture prescribed by the likes of Adolf Stoecker, Friedrich Naumann and Oswald Spengler that was to reach critical mass under National Socialism. The multinational Habsburg Empire was a hotbed of radical nationalism and anti-Semitism, and the traditionally internationalist socialist movement had become tinged with a nationalism that was to prove its undoing. The combination of these two powerful ideologies was potentially explosive. Nationalism could widen its appeal with a dose of socialist egalitarianism, and a socialism shorn of its internationalism was to prove considerably more attractive. The German Workers' Party (DAP), which was formed in Trautenau in 1904, combined extreme German nationalism with a befuddled sour-grapes socialism that was anti-capitalist and anti-bourgeois. It was an insignificant little group that would be of little interest had it not formed the basis of the Austrian Nazi Party. It was renamed the German National Socialist Workers' Party (DNSAP) after the war and soon established contact with Hitler's party in Munich. In 1926 Hitler was acknowledged as leader of what had become the Austrian branch of the NSDAP.

The syncretism of nationalism and socialism not only appealed to wild-eyed Sudeten German radicals or crackpot bohemians in Munich, it was a vision that attracted people as varied in both distinction and talent as Walther Rathenau, Ernst Jünger, Martin Heidegger, Ferdinand Tönnies, Werner Sombart, Oswald Spengler and Arthur Moeller van den Bruck. It was clearly an idea with a future, but few would have imagined this had they attended meetings of the DAP in the back room of a Munich alehouse in 1919.

[32]   The German party was founded on 5 January 1919 by Anton Drexler, a mechanic, and Karl Harrer, a journalist, in rooms provided by the *völkisch* Thule Society in Munich's most luxurious hotel, the Vier-Jahreszeiten (Four Seasons). It was quite separate from the Austrian DAP and was just another of the minute extremist groups that mushroomed in Munich in the post-war years, that listened to harangues from the likes of Gottfried Feder with his obsession with the 'thraldom of interest', or *völkisch* diatribes from the chronically alcoholic Dietrich Eckart. Drexler drew up a party programme that was a poorly written compilation of extreme anti-Semitic and racist slogans, along with perverted socialist notions spiced with a virulent nationalism. The German DAP aspired to be a mass party, appealing to all 'racial comrades who work with brain and brawn', but as a collection of hare-brained misfits it was unimaginable that this could ever happen. Small wonder then that Harrer had simply wanted a minute discussion group to meet occasionally and had initially opposed Drexler's idea of forming a party.

On 12 September 1919 Adolf Hitler, in his capacity as an army informant on fringe political groups in Munich, attended a meeting of the party at which 41 members were present. He was both fascinated and appalled by much of what he found. This witches' cauldron of distorted nationalism and parodic socialism was very much to his taste, but he was outraged that a party that professed to be anti-democratic should spend so much time in discussion and debate. He was determined to drag this handful of disgruntled misfits out from a shabby back room and into the open, in order to win a mass following. Hitler organized a meeting at the Hofbräukeller, a popular Munich watering hole, to be held on 16 October. The meeting was widely publicized, 111 people turned up, and Hitler made his first public address. It was a huge success. Hitler, at the age of 31, had at last found his vocation.

Hitler was in no sense an original thinker and *Mein Kampf* is a ragbag of shopworn notions and spiteful prejudice, an unreadable pyramid of piffle, but it would be a serious mistake to discount this all as mere balderdash that no one could possibly take seriously. Precious few people ever read the book and it has all too often been ignored or discounted by historians. It was not until March 1941 that Wilm Hosenfeld got round to reading it. He was amazed by what he found. He wrote to his son[1]:

> It is really surprising to discover the extent to which the Führer has already realised his demands, plans and thoughts and one has a very good idea of what will happen: for example a confrontation with the Russian system of government and among other things the final settling of the Jewish question in Europe. There won't be a single Jew left in Europe after Hitler.

This was an intoxicating ideology that inspired millions and was put into deadly effect. It appealed not only to an intellectual underclass of unhinged autodidacts and flat-earthers, along with rebellious bullyboys in search of some justification for deviant behaviour; it also appealed to people of discernment and intellectual distinction. We now know that this was all poisonous twaddle, although it still finds favour in certain quarters, but it is vitally important to understand why it had such an appeal to such a wide public.

The socialist elements of National Socialism have been emphasized of late, particularly by those desirous to discredit further the floundering socialist project. They should not be exaggerated, but neither should they be ignored. It is noticeable that National Socialism found many converts from the left who were attracted to its revolutionary rhetoric and its vision of a new and more equitable society. There was a widespread craving for community and a sense of belonging, which many felt had been partially fulfilled in the comradeship of the trenches and the 'fellowship of field-grey'. Community and belonging also involves discrimination and exclusion, as was made perfectly clear in the National Socialist concept of the 'racial community' (*Volksgemeinschaft*) in which race would override class, 'racial comrades' would unite in a struggle to the death against all rivals and enemies, and a new transcendent identity would be forged. National Socialism demanded certain fundamental reforms of the economy. It revived the ancient attack on usury in the form of a denunciation of the 'thraldom of interest'. It called for greater equality of opportunity, denounced the 'profiteers', 'plutocrats', 'materialists' and the complacent bourgeoisie with their selfish disregard for the common good, demanded that outmoded social divisions be removed, and issued vague promises of social justice for all members of the 'racial community'. Radical National Socialists, as we shall see, called for a revolutionary attack on capitalism and privilege, but this was diverted into an attack on 'Jewish capitalism' that led to the seizure of Jewish property and then to mass murder.

Hitler made a distinction between 'socialism', which he saw as a vital component of Nazism, and 'Marxism' or 'Bolshevism' under which rubrics he included both Communism and social democracy, and at times even those bourgeois parties that supported the idea of parliamentary democracy. Marxism, for which Alfred Rosenberg coined the phrase 'Jewish-Bolshevism', had to be rejected since it stood for internationalism rather than for the nation and the race, and was opposed to wars between nation states, thus failing to understand that endless struggle was the key to social existence. Socialism for Hitler meant an insistence on the paramount

[34] importance of collective well-being. This apparently came from an ancient Aryan tradition that upheld the rights of the individual (which could only be secured by being surrendered to the community), private property and the nation, all of which were denied by 'Jewish Marxists'. The justifiable needs of the working class could only be met within the framework of a nation state securely founded on racial solidarity. German socialism was based on the principle that the good of the community takes precedence over the good of the individual, and nationalism protects the community from outside threat. There could thus be no true socialism without nationalism, no nationalism without socialism. As Goebbels put it in 1930[2]: 'socialisation means placing the concept of the *Volk* above that of the individual'. Socialism for Hitler was not a matter of economics, it was a question of 'worldview' (*Weltanschauung*) – a hackneyed Nazi word that meant everything from philosophy to a gut feeling – of ethics and a return to fundamental religious values that had been perverted by the churches that were weighed down with Judaic ballast. It was the eclectic utopian vision of a muddle-headed autodidact, harmless enough when confined to cafés in Munich, but deadly dangerous when elevated to the state religion of Europe's most powerful nation.

The idea of the nation purged by a social-Darwinian struggle of alien elements to become ethnically homogeneous had been entertained by such organizations as the Pan-German League in the pre-war years, but it was still a fringe phenomenon on the far right. With Germany's shattering defeat and the humiliating Treaty of Versailles, the collapse of the monarchical order, the truncation of the Reich, a staggering reparations bill, hyperinflation, and a new state that was despised and discredited, all hope for the future was centred on the German people. National Socialists held no brief for the state as such, for this was for them an artificial construct. Goebbels, for all his admiration for Mussolini, condemned Italian Fascism out of hand because of its emphasis on the state. The economist, pollster and mass murderer Otto Ohlendorf, an idealistic and critical Nazi who had studied at the University of Padua and therefore had first-hand knowledge of Italian Fascism, shared Goebbels' dislike of a system that extolled the state above the race, as well as vigorously objecting to the way in which the state meddled with the economy. What counted were the people, the race and the nation. The German word '*Volk*' means both 'people' and 'race' so that as the radical right indulged in the cult of the Germanic and entertained all manner of anti-Semitic and racist fantasies the word took on an exclusively racist meaning. The national solidarity of 1914, along with the intoxicating vision of limitless war aims, fanned these atavistic hopes and desires, and was followed by a chronic post-war hangover. Germans now found themselves as despised minorities in the successor states in which they had enjoyed privileged positions. 'Racial comrades' in Poland, Czechoslovakia, Hungary and the Baltic States appealed for help from the fatherland, thus fuelling nationalist fervour. Germans abroad were particularly susceptible to the siren calls of National Socialism and were assiduously cultivated by the party.

Nationalism was a powerful integrative force that was irresistibly attractive to a defeated, divided and resentful Germany. It offered a vision for the future, transcended class divisions and thus had egalitarian and democratic aspects, while being based on essentially conservative values. It offered consensus amid disintegration, combined myth with mission, promised national rebirth within the tried and trusted framework of tradition, and offered a powerful antidote to revolutionary change while retaining a vigorous future-oriented dynamic.

Hitler had nothing but contempt for the revolution of 1918/19 in Germany. For him it was a 'pseudo-revolution', a treasonable revolt by a bunch of deserters egged on by Jewish agitators, a 'lemonade revolution'. These traitors had left capitalism untouched, left the state virtually intact, moral and ethical values unaffected. Whereas the French republicans in 1870 had fought in defence of the new order, thus preserving France's honour, the back-stabbers of 1918 had cravenly capitulated to a vindictive enemy. The only good thing they had done was to get rid of the monarchy, thus paving the way for a true republic. Hitler believed that revolutions existed essentially in the realm of ideas and that the widespread acceptance of a new ideology was the key to the successes of the French Revolution, Bolshevism and Italian Fascism. In Hitler's words: 'The victory of a party results in a change of government, the victory of a worldview is a revolution which fundamentally and essentially changes the condition of a people [*Volk*].' Like so much else, he fondly imagined that this was a profoundly original insight, when in fact it was a somewhat commonplace observation. As an electrifying speaker and a miserable writer he insisted that the victory of a worldview could be won only by oratory, not by the written word. In *Mein Kampf* he wrote that the French Revolution had been brought about by 'an army of rabble-rousers', and that the Bolsheviks had triumphed over illiterate hordes when 'thousands of agitators spun tales of a gleaming paradise'.

Both the French and Bolshevik revolutions were for Hitler the results of Jewish intrigues. Jews had spurred on the bourgeoisie to attack the aristocracy, propagated the destructive notion of the 'rights of man', and thus prepared the ground for the Jewish domination of Europe. Jews always

[36] supported the aspirations of the exploited and ignorant masses and, since they were far more intelligent, they could manipulate and use them for their own ends. This was the secret behind the Bolshevik revolution and the German so-called revolution of 1918/19. Hitler boasted that he always learnt from his enemies. From the Marxists he learnt the importance of parades, associations, party cells and propaganda aimed directly at the masses. He claimed to have a grudging admiration for Lenin and Trotsky, and to have learnt valuable lessons from Freemasons and from the 'Protocols of the Elders of Zion'. From all this he insisted on the need for a permanent revolution, with National Socialists as 'revolutionary reformers', constantly on the move, never losing their élan, refusing to relapse into bureaucratic routine and inertia.

Hitler was in no sense an original thinker, so that National Socialism was not identical with Hitlerism, but he did have an interpretative monopoly over its ideology and was the party's undisputed leader. Without Adolf Hitler there could never have been a National Socialism, and the movement would never have been successful without his commanding presence. Bismarck had been a powerful integrative force, in both a positive and a negative sense, in the unified Germany that he created. William II was a somewhat ridiculous figure who, try as he would, was never able to play this role to the full, and with the collapse of the empire in 1918 there was a wide-spread yearning for a figurehead, a new Bismarck or ersatz Kaiser. Some felt that the aged Field Marshal Hindenburg, who was elected president in 1925, fitted the bill. The victor of Tannenberg had about him the nimbus of past glories and the good old days, but, as a tired old man gradually descending into senility, he was hardly an electrifying figure who could reverse the humiliation of defeat in the Great War and restore Germany's fortunes. Hitler promised far more than the restoration of the frontiers of 1913. He offered a vision of a 'racial community' that would do away with outmoded social structures and class prejudice, creating a genuine merito-cracy in a 'national awakening' and a 'national revolution'. He promised to restore Germany's national honour and greatness, by territorial expansion and by the establishment of Germany's hegemonic position in Europe. He thus directly appealed to the chiliastic longings that slumbered in Germany and which his demagogic genius was to awaken and stimulate.

Hitler, who had enormous respect for the Catholic Church, its dogmatic rigidity, its intoxicating ritual, and even its insistence on celibacy, which meant that it could never fall into the hands of a self-perpetuating elite, saw National Socialism as a form of secular religion that in future would replace the churches. Goebbels constantly harped on this theme. On reading *Mein*

Kampf he asked himself whether Hitler was indeed the saviour. Later he confided in his diary: 'National Socialism is a religion' and agreed with Count Ernst zu Reventlow, co-founder with Jakob Hauer of the German Faith Movement (*Deutsche Glaubensbewegung*), a rival to the German Christians, that National Socialism must become 'the state religion of the Germans', adding: 'my party is my church'. During the war he announced: 'We do not need to know what the Führer wants to do – we believe in him.' On another occasion he said: 'This is the time for you to turn away from your false gods and bow down before him!' Göring said: 'All of us, from the humblest SA man to a prime minister, are from Adolf Hitler and through Adolf Hitler'. Such remarks prompted Goebbels, himself a master of overblown panegyrics to the Führer, to write in his diary: 'He literally crawls up Hitler's arse. If he wasn't so fat he would actually succeed in doing so.'

Hitler constantly talked in religious terms and endlessly repeated the word 'eternal'. The 'martyrs' of the Munich Putsch were 'my apostles'. The very concept of the 'Third Reich' was religious, as in 'Thy kingdom [*Reich*] come', a blasphemous reference to the Lord's Prayer. In 1935 Hitler proclaimed: 'You are resurrected in the Third Reich.' Two years later he told the party faithful: 'We are led by Providence and we act according to the will of the Almighty.' During the war he asserted: 'I humbly believe in providential grace.' Baldur von Schirach spoke of Hitler's birthplace in Braunau as 'a place of pilgrimage for German youth'. The Gauleiter of the Saar announced that Hitler was 'a greater and more powerful Jesus Christ'. Hanns Kerrl, the minister for church affairs, trumped this by proclaiming him to be 'the true Holy Spirit'. Carl Schmitt, not to be outdone, argued that Hitler had 'immediate or real presence'. The SS magazine *Das Schwarze Korps* waxed lyrical on the occasion of the Führer's 47th birthday on 20 April 1936 and wrote: 'You are love, you are power!' A Hitler Youth song claimed that the swastika and not the cross was the sign of earthly redemption. Students of ancient Germanic lore pointed out that the name 'Adolf' was made up of 'Ath' (divine act) and 'Uoffa' (creator), while from his exile in Holland the ex-Kaiser William, a student of eastern mysticism, took great delight in pointing out that the Nazis had got the swastika the wrong way round, their version symbolizing death and misfortune. Wartime death announcements often began with the words: 'He died with firm belief in his Führer'. Friedrich Stieves, in his highly regarded *History of the German People*, wrote that in 1933 Germany was the terminally sick man to whom Adolf Hitler said: 'Take up thy bed and walk!' The Swiss psychologist C.G. Jung proclaimed Nazi 'faith' to be a genuinely archetypical religious manifestation, a 'tragic experience' (*Erlebnis*). It was a religion in the sense of being

[38] the object of faith rather than of prudential thought, an absolute that demanded fanatical obedience, self-sacrifice, total submission to the Führer's oracular power, a freeing from the everyday and the humdrum, a search for transcendence. It was, however, a pseudo-religion, in that it was an example of what Pope Benedict XVI once called seeing man 'as no longer the gift of nature or the Creator: he is his own product', while mouthing the 'atheistic pieties' characteristic of National Socialism.

This new religion was a lethal mixture of familiar components, a magic spell that could not be broken. A radical, embittered and aggressive nationalism was combined with a total rejection of parliamentary democracy and the liberal concept of individual freedom. A virulent anti-Marxism was reinforced by a pseudo-socialism, the major component of which was a venomous anti-Semitism, a prejudice that one of the fathers of social democracy, August Bebel, once described as 'the socialism of fools'. Racism went hand in hand with exotic schemes for territorial expansion and a hubristic bid for hegemony.

At the root of all this was the cardinal importance of race. National identity was to be based not on a common culture, shared values and citizenship, but on race. Democracy and liberalism were diametrically opposed to this racial concept of nationhood, as was Marxism with its internationalism and its insistence that the class struggle was the key to the understanding of history. True socialism could only be realized in the 'racial community' in which all distinctions of class and status would be removed. Racism implied the radical removal of the alien other and all that threatened the health and vigour of this new Mendelian[3] order. The struggle between races, which was the driving force behind world history, necessarily involved a struggle between nations in which the purest and strongest would emerge triumphant.

A political movement with so many heady ingredients was bound to be fissiparous, was likely to be rent apart by factional rivalries, and would witness a cut-throat struggle for power among the leadership. It such a situation it was absolutely essential, as Joseph Goebbels was the first to realize, that there should be an uncontested leader, a mythical 'Führer', as the fount of all authority and the ultimate interpreter of the word. The future propaganda minister had many serious reservations about Hitler. He was infuriated by his dithering and his unwillingness to make awkward decisions. He was appalled by his indolence and bohemian ways. Above all he saw Hitler as the prisoner of a reactionary clique in Munich, bitterly remarking that Berlin, where he was the Gauleiter, was the head of the movement and Munich its arse. But Goebbels came to realize that the 'Hitler movement', as it was known ever since 1921, required that Hitler be

strengthened in his position as leader. Goebbels first referred to him as [39]
'Hitler', then as 'the boss' and by 1932 as the 'Führer'. As Hitler's power and
self-confidence grew apace Goebbels' reservations gave way to unreserved
admiration, idolatry and slavish submission. The Hitler myth held all these
destructive forces together until his suicide, and the key to an understanding of National Socialism lies in the reciprocal relationship between Hitler
and his followers, between the Führer and the *Volk*.

Charismatic leadership

Hitler cannot be explained away as a criminal maniac, an aberrant Austrian
who descended from the clouds on an otherwise healthy Germany, an evil
magician who bewitched an entire nation, or a historical accident that
defies historical analysis. There was also much more to National Socialism
than 'Hitlerism' with its fascinator raised to mythic heights by Goebbels'
brilliant propaganda and Albert Speer's cultic backdrops. But neither
was he the 'weak dictator', the structurally determined product of a specific
social configuration.

Max Weber's concept of charismatic rule remains the best interpretative
tool for an understanding of the reciprocal relationship between the Führer
(the word chosen by Weber) and his disciples and followers. This relationship is based on the 'affective surrender' to the leader and to his favours.
It is the secularized and modernized form of the leadership exercised by
the prophets and heroes of old. The leader is obeyed because of his unique
and exceptional qualities, not because of the office he holds. His charisma
is reinforced by success, but lasts only as long as his luck holds and these
qualities continue to be recognized. His closest associates are chosen not
because of their professional expertise, nor because of their social status or
family connections. Questions of competence or privilege are irrelevant; their
power resides purely in the trust placed in them by the leader. Charismatic
administration, for lack of a better word, is not hidebound by rules, regulations or precedent, but is essentially irrational. Decisions are taken on the
spur of the moment, either by the leader or by those in a position to interpret his will. The leader's will is the basis of all law, the means by which all
actions are legitimized. Charismatic leadership depends on faith in the leader
and in the recognition of his unique qualities; faith and recognition then
become a duty and obligation for the followers. Charismatic leadership can
only be preserved by due consideration for the welfare of the followers,
by a series of successes and by the affirmation of the leader as a man of

Figure 2.1   'Serve the Führer'

destiny, a man with a mission, one of the elect. For all his uniqueness the charismatic leader has to operate partly within a framework sanctioned by tradition, apparently within the bounds of the law, and relying to a degree on a predictable administration that in turn has to be loyal and subservient.

Charismatic leadership can only succeed in an atmosphere of crisis and uncertainty. The leader promises to overcome all the pressing problems and demands of his followers a leap of faith, absolute trust and fanatical belief. This is therefore not a conventional tyranny or dictatorship, since it is thereby given a form of plebiscitary legitimization and popular acclaim. The charismatic leader is further legitimized by his ability to overcome such crises with the result that when there is no further immediate crisis there is a dangerous temptation to create one in order to reinforce his charismatic power. It is truly astonishing that the faith of a large number of Germans in Hitler survived until the bitter end, and in some instances even after his suicide and a shattering defeat. At times it took on absurd dimensions as in the naive belief in the so-called retaliation ('V') weapons in the final stages of the war. Some even convinced themselves that Germany had developed a one-man plane that flew so fast that it had to fire backwards so as not to fly into its own bullets.

Crisis alone is not enough to launch the career of a charismatic leader. Society has to have a tradition of susceptibility to strong leadership and a devotion to the 'great men' of the past, in order to be able to put its faith in one individual. The leader must then satisfy such longings and aspirations. Once this reciprocal relationship has been established the leader can ignore established practice and act according to the biblical adage: 'It is written, but I tell thee . . .' The charismatic leader cannot be constrained by any legal, moral or traditional norms and is not required to give any rational justification for his actions. The further he distances himself from these norms, the stronger becomes the charismatic bond between leader and led. The self-confidence and sense of absolute certainty of the leader is then transmitted to his followers.

At the beginning of the nineteenth century many nationalists longed for a German Napoleon and it was widely felt that Bismarck, the 'white revolutionary' with his 'revolution from above', fulfilled this role. William II imagined that he could follow in the Iron Chancellor's footsteps, but his attempts at personal rule exposed him as a poseur and braggart. Hindenburg and Ludendorff, the victors of Tannenberg and the demi-gods of the High Command, basked in the adulation of the masses, but they suffered the ignominy of defeat. Hindenburg's attempt as president to act as an ersatz emperor and use his prestige to overcome the profound crisis that plagued the republic was a pathetic failure. Where was the new Bismarck who would unite the nation and restore Germany's prestige? Who could satisfy the widespread longing for a prophet? Who could lead the people out of their Babylonian captivity? Joseph Goebbels confided in his diary that Germany longed for a great man 'like the earth in summer for rain' and having toyed with socialism, which he rejected as being 'infected with Jewishness', felt that he might have found him in Adolf Hitler. On reading *Mein Kampf* in 1925 he asked himself: 'Who is this man? Half plebeian, half god? Really Christ or merely John the Baptist?' The Jesuit-educated Goebbels was one of the first to see the quasi-religious aspect of National Socialism.

Essential to charismatic leadership is a hardcore of fanatical believers who have undergone a form of conversion, a transmogrification of values, and who unquestioningly accept the interpretative monopoly of the leader. In order to strengthen the leader's hold over his followers subordinates are

[42] appointed not because of their expertise and competence, but for their unquestioning loyalty and devotion. Were this barony highly skilled and proficient they might be tempted to question the leader's superiority in all fields of endeavour, and thus dim his charismatic lustre. Their power resides in their immediate relationship to the leader, which in turn depends on absolute submission and fealty.

Once Hitler was in power his charismatic party organization with its special groups and offices had to coexist with the existing state apparatus with its professional bureaucracy bound by legal and administrative norms. The result was what Ernst Fraenkel was so judiciously to call a 'dual state'. Whereas civil servants called for fiscal probity and prudent house-keeping, Hitler blissfully disregarded economic feasibility and financed his gigantomanic plans by seizing Jewish property and by a system of state-sponsored mugging dressed up as voluntary contributions. The end result was a colossal debt that was to be paid off by a war of conquest and plunder. Such a system can only survive in a situation of permanent crisis and frantic activity without which it would become routine and humdrum, in which case the leader would rapidly lose his charisma. Hitler's quest for new crises to master and his staggering *va banque* tactics were eventually to take on grotesque proportions and end in a horrific suicidal *Götterdämmerung*.

The truly astonishing thing about Hitler is that a man of the utmost insignificance could attain such a position of absolute power and command such slavish loyalty. All other outstanding historical figures showed some early signs of talent, of leadership potential or vision. Hitler's background was that of an ill-educated, unemployed nobody in pre-war Vienna and Munich. He showed not the slightest signs of leadership during his army career and was not even selected for special training as an NCO. It was only when he discovered that he had exceptional gifts as a political agitator on the wilder shores of the extreme right in post-war Munich that his meteoric rise to power began, by which time he was over the age of 30. Even then, who could have thought that this bizarre character, ranting and raving to a selection of assorted crackpots in a Munich beer hall, would, within 12 years, be regarded as the national Messiah, the unchallenged dictator over a great nation? Even Hitler imagined that he would be only a rabble-rouser, winning mass support for some prominent figure on the extreme right. It was only after the failure of his putsch in 1923 and subsequent imprisonment that he began to think of himself as the all-powerful Führer, but this was still essentially wishful thinking. Hitler had no patience for administrative work and no organizational talent. Gregor Strasser was the organizational genius who rebuilt the party, but he and his brother

Otto had serious reservations about Hitler. Otto was on the far left of the party and was disgusted at the sight of Hitler hobnobbing with people he regarded as reactionaries. In an attempt to move the party sharply to the left he founded the Battle Group of Revolutionary National Socialists and openly challenged Hitler. Hitler beat off this challenge in 1930 and Otto Strasser prudently went into exile in 1933, first to Austria, then Czechoslovakia, Switzerland, Portugal and Canada, returning to Germany after the war and dying in Munich in 1974. Gregor shared many of his brother's left-wing views, calling for the nationalization of the banks and heavy industry, and disagreed with Hitler's tactics, arguing that the NSDAP should enter a coalition. Hitler soon began to have serious doubts about Gregor Strasser's heterodox views and accused him of idealizing the Jews, insisting that Jews were far more dangerous, base and diabolical than he could imagine. All this in spite of the fact that Gregor Strasser was a hair-raisingly virulent anti-Semite, with even Goebbels remarking about his 'Jewish mania'. He was soon to be charged with harbouring 'Jewish-liberal-democratic-Marxist-humanitarian' concepts such as his support for voting rights and corporate chambers.

Goebbels, who was appointed district party leader (*Gauleiter*) in Berlin in 1926, with his detestation of the bourgeoisie and his half-baked socialist notions, sympathized with the north-German group around the Strasser brothers. He first met Gregor in 1924, describing him as a 'sympathetic Bavarian apothecary', 'THE National Socialist' and 'a bear of a man'. In 1925 he became secretary to Strasser's Working Group Northwest that put revolution before evolution, socialism before the social, young before the old, and mounted a campaign against the 'bigwigs' in the Munich 'pigsty'. Goebbels approved of the fact that Strasser was 'a semi-Marxist' and vowed that he would fight for an 'idealistic socialism' that was rid of 'Jewish pollution'. By 1928 Goebbels was under Hitler's sway, enchanted by his 'wit, humour and sparkling intelligence', seeing in him a man 'with whom we can conquer the world'. He now saw Strasser as a '*Schweinehund*', a 'rotten capitalist', the 'Satan of the movement', who opposed Hitler. Goebbels had serious misgivings when in 1929 Hitler made a U-turn and made his peace with what he had days before called the 'bourgeois political gang' and supported the 'Steel Helmet referendum'[4]. He hoped that the NSDAP would out-trump the conservative German National People's Party (DNVP) in this unholy alliance, but he did not like the idea of Hitler hobnobbing with so many prominent reactionaries. But although he sympathized with aspects of what Hitler called the Strassers' 'drawing room socialism', he still sided with Hitler. He still complained that he was bone idle and wrote in his

[44]   diary in January 1930: 'Once again Hitler refuses to make a decision. He makes me vomit . . . He is no longer in control.' He complained that Hitler was an indolent ditherer, surrounded by a bunch of second-raters. Although he still clung to his inchoate socialist notions he realized the central importance of Hitler to the movement and decided that the 'Strasser nonsense' had to be destroyed 'root and branch'. He therefore gave his full support to Hitler in his struggles against his great rivals and challengers: Otto Strasser in 1930, Gregor Strasser in 1932 and finally Ernst Röhm in 1934. At the same time he continued to complain bitterly about the situation in Munich. When the SA protested against the 'Munich big shots' in 1930 he wrote in his diary: 'The SA kings are quite right to take up arms against the scandalous pigsty in Munich[5].'

The early years of the NSDAP

Germany was traumatized by a lost war and humiliated by the peace settlement, the currency was destroyed by hyperinflation, and the country was in danger of falling apart as regional antagonisms became inflamed, class antagonisms were exacerbated by chronic unemployment and the political system ground to a standstill. Between 1930 and 1932 only five bills passed in the Reichstag by majority vote, during which time there were 60 emergency decrees. In such a crisis situation latent longing for a strong leader was activated and Hitler's insistent promise of a 'racial community' was a beguilingly attractive answer to the problems of a society that appeared to be falling apart at the seams. He was violently anti-democratic, loathed the Weimar Republic, was passionately anti-Communist, and his anti-Semitism was a pathological obsession. But for most Germans democracy was discredited, the republic a miserable failure, National Socialism the only viable alternative to an abhorrent Communism, and Hitler was careful to moderate his anti-Semitism in his public addresses. Even when he relapsed into beer hall Jew-baiting he could count on a sympathetic hearing from traditionally anti-Semitic audiences.

A community is by definition exclusive and a racial community implied a concept of nationhood based on racial homogeneity. This was the core notion of the Germanophile 'blood-and-soil' apostles in Munich, who wallowed in a mythical Germanic past and who included Heinrich Himmler, Alfred Rosenberg, Baldur von Schirach and Walther Darré. It was championed by a number of small groups throughout the country and by Germans abroad. Nationalism was now combined with a virulent racism and was locked in battle with the internationalist Marxists, who were seen as responsible for Germany's defeat by a 'stab in the back' and who stood in the way of a glorious national reawakening. Munich provided rich compost on which such noxious ideas could thrive. Kurt Eisner, a somewhat woolly-headed journalist from Berlin and Independent Social Democrat, who had seized power in Bavaria in November 1918, was assassinated on 21 February 1919 by a young aristocrat who became an instant hero on the radical right. Munich then followed the example of Béla Kun's soviet Hungary when Ernst Niekisch proclaimed the end of the 'bourgeois capitalist age' and a soviet Bavaria. Had it not ended in a terrible bloodbath, the Bavarian Soviet Republic would have been regarded as pure operetta, the object of almost universal derision. It was run by a bizarre collection of doctrinaire Communists, dreamy pacifists, anarchic literati and outright crackpots. Lenin took a lively interest in their activities, and with his unerring inability to understand foreign countries, imagined that Catholic, rural, reactionary Bavaria had been transformed into the standard-bearer of the German proletariat. At the behest of the Social Democrat army minister, Gustav Noske, the White Terror made quick work of the republic, which had come under the dauntless control of the Communist Eugen Leviné. Soviet Munich quickly became the capital of the counter-revolution, a hotbed of sundry right-wing extremists who blamed recent events on the machinations of world Jewry, and agitators like Adolf Hitler found a ready audience for their hateful messages.

The DAP was just one of the many fringe groups in post-war, post-revolutionary Munich, which included the Thule Society, the Germanic Order, the Reich Hammer Association and the viciously anti-Semitic German Racial Defence League. This last soon had 200,000 members, mostly students, and was by far the largest and most influential of the groups on the radical right. Young students such as Rudolf Hess, Hans Frank and Alfred Rosenberg were enchanted by Dietrich Eckart's *völkisch* diatribes as they shopped around looking for an organization that best answered their needs and longings.

Such was the Munich in which Hitler, still in the army and attached to the 2nd Bavarian Infantry Regiment, was employed as an informant on radical movements. It was in this capacity that he attended a meeting of the German Workers' Party in September 1919. Anton Drexler, the party's founder, was much impressed by the newcomer, remarking, 'he's got the gift of the gab!' and Hitler felt instantly at home. He soon began to attend party meetings regularly. At the end of March Hitler left the army, determined to devote himself to politics. Captain Karl Mayr, under whom Hitler

[46] had recently served, was enormously impressed by Hitler's transformation
from simple soldier into a people's tribune and introduced him to Captain
Ernst Röhm, a swashbuckler who had served in General von Epp's Freikorps
and had played an enthusiastic part in the White Terror that put an end to
the Bavarian Soviet Republic. Röhm was responsible for supervising the disarmament of the Bavarian army and thus had a huge supply of weaponry
to pass on to paramilitary groups on the extreme right.

The NSDAP, as the party was renamed, thus had ready access to weapons
for its brown-shirted Storm Section (SA) led by an air ace from the
'Richthofen Circus', Hermann Göring. General von Epp generously provided
60,000 marks from army funds to enable the party to buy its newspaper, the
Völkischer Beobachter ('Racial observer'). Dietrich Eckart introduced Hitler
to extremist circles in Munich society, which included the piano-maker
Carl Bechstein, the publisher Hugo Bruckmann and the frivolously elegant
art historian 'Putzi' Hanfstaengl, an odious, self-serving character assassin and
amateur pianist. Initially Hitler made a rather gauche impression in Munich
salons, but he was already a local celebrity, an interestingly eccentric
curiosity for whom some society ladies had a certain motherly affection.

In May 1921 Hitler made his first big gamble, threatening to resign
from the party unless he was given full dictatorial powers as leader. At first
he saw himself as a drummer boy for General Ludendorff, whose head had
been stuffed with all manner of Germanic, racist and anti-Semitic claptrap
by his dreadful new wife Mathilde, and who was the unquestioned figurehead
on the lunatic fringe of the radical right. After Mussolini's March on Rome
in October 1922 Hitler began to think of himself as the German Mussolini.
His party now had 55,000 members and thanks to support from Ludendorff
and Röhm he stood at the head of a consortium of paramilitary groups that
included the SA, the German Fighting League (Deutsche Kampfbund), the
Oberland League, and the Reich War Standard (Reichskriegsflagge).

In the crisis year of 1923, with the occupation of the Ruhr and hyperinflation, Germany threatened to fall apart. The Nazi daily rag *Völkischer
Beobachter* denounced the 'Stresemann–Seeckt dictatorship' as another
Jewish conspiracy, pointing out that both men were married to Jewesses
and that the minister of finance Rudolf Hilferding was both a Marxist and a
Jew. Otto Gessler, the German Democratic Party (DDP) Reichswehr minister
since the Kapp Putsch, ordered the Bavarian minister-president von Kahr
and the local army commander, General von Lossow, to ban the paper.
Both men refused in an act of defiant insubordination, leaving Berlin in an
awkward quandary. Seeckt refused to take sides, just as he had done during
the Kapp Putsch. General von Lossow now began to talk of a march on

Berlin and the establishment of a national dictatorship, but it was Hitler [47]
who decided to act. His attempt to outfox Kahr and Lossow failed miserably, and the putsch attempt on 9 November ended in a hail of bullets
from Munich's police force. Sixteen of his followers were killed and became
the first martyrs of the 'National Revolution' to whom homage was rendered
every year on 9 November, and to whose memory Adolf Hitler dedicated
the first volume of *Mein Kampf*. The bloodstained swastika banner became
the movement's most sacred relic.

Hitler was given a derisory light sentence and spent a comfortable spell
in a minimum security prison in Landsberg where he dictated *Mein Kampf*
to his devoted secretary Rudolf Hess, the paper provided by Winifred
Wagner, a wilful Englishwoman, high-priestess of the Wagner cult and
prominent among Hitler's besotted female admirers. The NSDAP was banned
and Hitler, who was never interested in organization and administration,
let the party fall apart for fear that some rival might take over the reins
during his absence.

There was still a huge potential, at least in Bavaria, for a party on the
extreme right. The Racial Block (*Völkischer Bloc*), an alliance of the major
groups on the extreme right, won 20 per cent of the votes in the local
election in Bavaria, held in April 1924, one week after Hitler was sentenced.
In Munich they won an astonishing and alarming 35 per cent of the popular
vote. In the national elections of May 1924 the German Racial Freedom
Party (*Deutschvölkische Freiheitspartei*), a party founded in 1922 by former
conservatives on the extreme right wing of the DNVP, got 2 million votes
and returned 32 members to the Reichstag.

Hitler set about rebuilding the party as soon as he was released, insisting
that he was the unquestioned Führer and that 'Heil Hitler' should henceforth be the only acceptable form of greeting for 'party comrades'. The
situation was far from favourable. The currency had been reformed, the
economy was back on an even keel, Germany after Locarno once again
accepted by the community of nations with a seat in the League of Nations.
The party was badly split between the radical north and the reactionary
south, and Hitler was loath to confront this fundamental problem. The
NSDAP absorbed the German Racial Freedom Party in 1925, but by 1928
there were still a mere 100,000 members and the party won only 2.6 per
cent of the popular vote in the Reichstag elections that year, returning a
dozen deputies. With the radical right losing two-thirds of its votes within
four years it looked as if the party was on the way out. In addition, Hitler
was banned from public speaking in most of Germany until 1927, and in
Prussia until 1928.

[48]   The party now made a radical tactical change in a desperate attempt to keep afloat. Hitherto the National Socialists had aimed to win over the working class from the 'Marxist' parties and had failed miserably. Combined support for the Communists (KPD) and SPD remained virtually constant. Now the party concentrated on the urban petite bourgeoisie and the peasantry, on small businessmen, artisans and craftsmen, on white-collar workers and smallholders. In its new guise the NSDAP presented itself as a genuine people's party, open to all 'racial comrades' regardless of social background, with a flexible approach to the pressing issues of the day, an openness to innovative ideas, working for the 'national awakening' and set on building a 'racial community' that would overcome all antagonisms of class and estate, status and wealth.

Outwardly the most dramatic change took place in the summer of 1929 when Hitler joined forces with the media mogul Alfred Hugenberg and his DNVP in the referendum against the Young Plan to reschedule reparations. The bohemian revolutionary with his trench coat, boots and whip was suddenly transformed into a pinstriped conservative, sharing the platform with captains of industry, generals and aristocrats. The left wing of the party bitterly complained that Hitler had made a pact with the reactionaries, but the results of this new alliance were impressive. The party made substantial gains in local elections in 1930, rising from 1.7 per cent to 4.1 per cent in Mecklenburg-Schwerin, from 1.4 per cent to 7 per cent in Baden, and from 1.4 per cent to 11.3 per cent in Thuringia. As the economic and political crisis deepened there was a persistent craving among the masses for a saviour, a hero and a message. Hitler, for all his intellectual poverty, was somehow able to project an idealized view of a new society that struck an immediate chord with millions of alienated, frustrated and angry voters. This *terrible simplificateur* out of nowhere suddenly appeared on the national scene as a Parsifal or Siegfried, a holy simpleton who would bring salvation to a society going through a profound ontological crisis, by blissfully disregarding the complexities of modern life and by concentrating on the fundamentals: the nation, the race and the mortal dangers to the community posed by Jews and Marxists, whatever their stripe, along with the need for 'living space'. The conservatives imagined that they had tamed this unruly creature and that he would simply provide the electoral support that they needed to realize their plans for an authoritarian state. Very few realized the appalling dangers that loomed ahead. An exception was the liberal *Frankfurter Zeitung*, which in 1928 described Hitler as a man possessed by a demon, driven by a manic vision of atavistic origin, a dangerous fool left over from the days of the barbarian invasions.

The Reichstag elections of September 1930 were a dramatic demonstration of the mounting appeal of the puffed-up charlatanry, the hate-filled platitudes and racist banalities of National Socialism. Some 6.4 million voters, 18.3 per cent of the electorate, voted for the party and returned 107 deputies to Berlin. The NSDAP had twice the number of supporters as the conservative DNVP and was now the major party on the right. Hitler's charisma was further enhanced by this electoral triumph and his appeal was increasingly hard to resist. The party made impressive gains in local elections in 1930, winning 25.6 per cent of the popular vote in Bremen, 27.2 per cent in Braunschweig and 37.2 per cent in Oldenburg. The harder the depression bit, the deeper the political crisis, the greater the appeal of National Socialism to almost all sectors of the population. The Communists were able to win greater support from among the urban working class, but many from this milieu flocked to the National Socialists. Catholics in rural areas remained largely resistant to this blasphemous pseudo-religion. Hitler was careful not to indulge in crude anti-Semitic and racist rabble-rousing, which he left to his old crony Julius Streicher, the Gauleiter of Franconia, for this had precious little popular appeal and was widely regarded as tasteless, whatever one's personal views of the lesser breeds. *Mein Kampf,* with its primitive hate-filled diatribes, is a massive, crudely written and unreadable tome, which no one had sufficient stamina to read. Hitler seemed omnipresent, making 148 public appearances at huge rallies between April and November 1932, flying the length and breadth of the country in a truly astonishing effort at self-promotion. The sight of Hitler charging around the country in a supercharged Mercedes or in the open cockpit of an aeroplane enhanced the vision of a dynamic modern 'movement'. The constantly repeated themes in what amounted to a continuous electoral campaign from 1930 to 1932 were now 'community', 'national revival', the perfidy of the 'Weimar system' and the millenarian vision of a Third Reich. Hitler had no programme and proposed no concrete solutions. He simply promised that with will, determination and struggle all problems could be solved. It was precisely this lack of any tangible answers that made him particularly attractive and which separated him from the other leading politicians of the day. He had nothing to offer but blind faith and enthusiasm, which the crowds eagerly shared. The German people were not bewitched, bamboozled or baffled by Hitler. He provided the vision, the leadership, the determination and the sense of community for which they yearned.

The formula worked wonders. Hitler won an impressive 36.8 per cent of the popular vote in the presidential election in April 1932 against Hindenburg. The upward trend was clearly visible in a series of local

[50] elections. Then, in the Reichstag elections in July 1932, 13.8 million voters supported the NSDAP, which now was the largest faction in the Reichstag with 230 deputies. A substantial proportion of the increased support for the party came from those who had never before bothered to go to the polls, or those who had just been given the right to vote. Party membership rose from 400,000 in December 1930 to 1.4 million by the end of 1932. Hitler was now unquestionably the coming man on the right, courted by political brokers and lobbyists, businessmen and Protestant clergymen.

As the party went from strength to strength there was a growing sense of frustration and impatience among the rank and file. After two years of frantic effort the Nazis were still not in a position of power and had two-thirds of the electorate against them. Hitler refused to accept any offer other than that of the office of chancellor and many of his supporters thought such stubbornness mere folly. Money was beginning to run desperately short. The party was rent with dissention. Hitler's leadership was put in question. The Nazis suffered a major reverse in the Reichstag elections of November 1932, losing 2 million supporters and dropping from 37.4 per cent of the popular vote to 33.1 per cent, and with 196 seats returning 34 fewer deputies to parliament in Berlin. Many voters were concerned that the NSDAP was far too left wing, in spite of all Hitler's assurances to the contrary. The sight of the Nazis marching side by side with the Communists during the Berlin transport workers' strike was highly alarming, as was the mounting violence, reaching a peak in August when five Nazi thugs committed a brutal murder in the Silesian town of Potempa. They were condemned to death, but the sentences were commuted to life imprisonment, largely due to Hitler's impassioned intervention on behalf of these heroes. Local elections in Thuringia, where the NSDAP had previously done quite well, were even more disastrous with the party obtaining up to 35 per cent fewer votes in some areas. Yet just at this moment when the party seemed to be going rapidly downhill the lucky gambler won the jackpot when the power elite handed him the office of chancellor.

Much of the appeal of National Socialism came from the profound contradiction within it, which was never resolved. On the one hand was the grotesquely reactionary Wotan-worshipping *völkisch*-Germanic hogwash with its 'blood-and-soil' (*Blut und Boden* – soon to be shortened to '*Blubo*') ideology and romantic hankering after the pre-industrial world of Hans Sachs and the mastersingers of Nuremberg. On the other hand, like the Communists, this was a party of the young, determined to do away with all residues of a moth-eaten past and shopworn tradition, committed to a

dynamic and technologically advanced society run by a genuine meritocracy. Many of these young men were absorbed with what Götz Aly has
called a 'post-pubescent search for identity while puffed up with delusions
of omnipotence'[6]. Seventy per cent of party members were under the age of
40 in 1930, when Hitler was 41, Göring 37, Goebbels 33, Himmler 30,
Heydrich and Eichmann 26 and Josef Mengele only 21. National Socialism
was thus, as one wit put it, a fatal combination of Austrian madness and
Prussian efficiency, of atavistic fanaticism and sceptical pragmatism, of
romantic yearning and cynical careerism. The coarse brutality and criminal
activism of the SA with their pitched battles against the paramilitary forces
of the left, which left hundreds dead and brought Germany to the brink
of a civil war, was combined with resounding calls for law and order. The
contradiction was resolved by claiming that Nazi violence was self-defence
against Marxist terror. The Nazis thus appeared to many to be the only
conceivable guarantors of peace and quiet.

The NSDAP was a genuine people's party in that it had no class-specific
base. It was certainly not the tool of a sinister group of monopoly capitalists, nor was it merely the mouthpiece of a disgruntled petite bourgeoisie.
Its most striking characteristic was that it had a particular appeal to Protestants. From 1930 about half of its support came from rural areas and
Protestant towns with less than 5,000 inhabitants. Protestant to Catholic
supporters at the polls were in a ratio of two to one. German Protestants
had always tended to be nationalists, regarding Protestantism as the only
truly German religion, and the Hohenzollern monarchy in Prussia as closely
identified with the evangelical religion. Catholics were regarded as outsiders, unGerman, owing primary allegiance to Rome, and had been
persecuted in Bismarck's *Kulturkampf.* These rural and small-town Protestant
voters were at the core of the Nazis' electoral success, they were there in substantial numbers as early as 1928, and it was here that the largest percentage
of voters switched their allegiance from parties in the political centre to the
NSDAP by 1932. Another group that was particularly susceptible to the
siren calls of National Socialism was civil servants. Whereas white-collar
workers, who were less affected by unemployment than the industrial working class, tended to support the Social Democrats, civil servants complained
about Brüning's austerity measures and had never made their peace with
the republic. It was widely believed at the time that Hitler's success was
due in large part to a swarm of enthusiastic female supporters. This has
been shown to be pure myth. Only 7.8 per cent of those who joined the
party between 1925 and 1932 were women. That the party had propor-
tionally more female voters was due to the fact that more women than men

[52]   actually bothered to vote. White- and blue-collar workers were under-represented in the Nazi vote in 1930, civil servants and the self-employed over-represented. Nevertheless this was genuinely a people's party which had the advantage of not having much of a programme beyond a few vague promises of 'national revival' and the creation of the 'racial community'. A vote for the NSDAP was a vote against the republic, a protest against a political system that had ground to a standstill, remonstration against a drastic decline in the standard of living as politicians failed to deal with the acute problems of mass unemployment. Germany led the world in the beer-drinking stakes, so that the 43 per cent drop in beer consumption between 1929 and 1933 is indicative of the severe impact of the depression on every-day life. Since the Reichstag hardly ever met between 1930 and 1933 the political parties became increasingly irrelevant, giving rise to a widespread longing for a dynamic alternative.

Hitler had played a part in drawing up the party programme, which he made public in a speech at Munich's famous Hofbräuhaus on 24 February 1920. One of the first things he did when given dictatorial powers over the party in July 1921 was to insist that this programme should remain immutable. He repeated this in *Mein Kampf*, arguing that once one started tinkering with a party programme the door was open to debate for which there was no place in a party such as the NSDAP. He made a clear distinction between 'political parties' which stood for compromise and 'worldview parties' which had to proclaim their infallibility. The programme was a ragbag of conventional *völkisch* notions, anti-capitalism dressed up as socialism, and virulent anti-Marxism. When Hitler abandoned his anti-capitalist stance in 1928 and sought the support of industrialists and bankers, who were not surprisingly alarmed by talk of the 'thraldom of interest' and attacks on big business, he tried to placate the party's left wing by denunci-ation of a mysterious entity called 'Jewish capitalism'. Many of the party faithful, particularly in the SA, disapproved of the Führer hobnobbing with 'plutocrats' and continued to subscribe to a half-baked anti-capitalism and pseudo-socialism. In 1931 Werner Best, head of the party's Security Service (SD) in Munich, cooked up an emergency plan, known as the 'Boschheim documents', to overcome the economic crisis. It involved the abolition of money, compulsory labour service for all and the death penalty for those who dared disobey. The party's worldview was thus hopelessly inchoate and Hitler alone was its infallible interpreter. There were other prominent exegetes such as Alfred Rosenberg whose *Myth of the Twentieth Century* (1930) was hailed as second only to *Mein Kampf* as a canonical text of National Socialism, even though Hitler accurately described this unreadable piece of eclectic drivel as 'a plagiarised piece of scissors and paste rubbish', while readily admitting that he had never read the book. Then there was Heinrich Himmler, whose obsession with a mythical Germanic past, with quests for the holy grail and Atlantis and mystical speculations about the revival of an ancient religion, Hitler found utterly absurd. The party programme was certainly not a vote catcher and was largely ignored. The slogan was now 'Adolf Hitler is our programme'.

Hitler's 'programme' was not a blueprint for a new society, he did not set a rigid timetable, nor did he have an inflexible set of priorities. He was a master tactician, a breathtaking gambler, and a flexible opportunist who after lengthy hesitation would make split-second decisions. As Albert Speer said: 'Hitler would doze like a crocodile in the mud of the Nile before inflicting another drama on the world.' He was, however, limited and constrained by a set of *idées fixes* that makes it often appear as if he were following a set plan, the principal one of which was the notion of 'struggle' as in the title of his book *Mein Kampf.* He envisioned history as an endless social-Darwinian struggle to determine the strongest and the fittest. He declared war on the world as it existed and on the value system upon which it was based. Ultimately it would be war that would decide to whom this world would belong. As he wrote in *Mein Kampf:* 'Mankind grew to be great in endless struggle – it will be destroyed by endless peace.' In his 'Second Book' he wrote[7]:

> Politics is history in the making. History itself represents the progression of a people's struggle for survival. I use the phrase 'struggle for survival' intention- ally here, because in reality every struggle for daily bread, whether in war or peace, is a never-ending battle against thousands and thousands of obstacles, just as life is a never-ending battle against death.

Hitler believed that he had discovered the key to history in race, in much the same way in which Karl Marx believed he had found it in class. The German *Volk* as the quintessential representatives of the Aryan race was naturally superior to all other races, and it was thus imperative that it should be purified and strengthened by eliminating all elements that threatened its health and vigour. Dubious genetic material should be ruthlessly eliminated, miscegenation strictly forbidden. In 1938 Hitler told some leading officers that 'the world will and must belong' to 'this great racial core' of up to 110 million Germans. The German nation could only achieve its historic mission under an absolute leader who was blessed with the absolute certainty that he was guided by Providence. The Aryan masses were bound

[54]   together not only by blind devotion and absolute obedience to this superhuman Führer, but also by the ties of the 'racial community', which would
overcome all distinctions of class and estate and was thus the ultimate
expression of National Socialism. Such National Socialism was the absolute
opposite of Marxist socialism, which must therefore be ruthlessly exterminated. Democracy, liberalism and what Goebbels called the 'ideas of 1789'
also belonged on the rubbish dump of history.

There remained two absolutely imperative struggles. The first of these
was for the 'removal' (*Entfernung*) of the Jews, which Hitler saw as anti-
Semitism's ultimate goal. He believed that Jews were a racial rather than a
religious community that was bent, like the Aryans, on world domination.
Germans and Jews were locked in a life and death struggle. In these early
years it was never quite clear precisely what he meant by 'removal', but in
Mein Kampf he insisted that Jews had to be 'eliminated' (*ausradiert*). In 1925
he first suggested that they should be gassed. On 30 January 1939 he
announced that a future war would result in the 'annihilation of the Jewish
race in Europe'. His discourse was peppered with references to Jews as 'parasites', 'vermin', 'germs', 'maggots' and the like, suggesting that 'removal'
would involve something rather more than the suspension of certain rights
and the exclusion from civil society.

The second great struggle was for 'living space' (*Lebensraum*). In 1922
Hitler spoke of the 'destruction of Russia'. In *Mein Kampf* he wrote that
Germany would seize land in the Soviet Union and that 'this gigantic
empire in the east is on the brink of collapse' because of 'the Jewish parasites gnawing at its entrails' and because Bolshevism had rid Russia of its
German brainpower which was the basis of its former strength. He repeated
this need for *Lebensraum* in the east in his unpublished 'Second Book'
of 1928 and wrote that this 'eastern space' (*Ostraum*) would be Germany's
India.

A constantly repeated theme was that this was an issue of world power
or annihilation, a pernicious concept that had been common currency in
extremist circles during the war. For Germany to be a world power the
Jews would have to be destroyed and a vast empire carved out in the east.
None of this was in the party programme, nor did it feature in the election
campaigns. Hitler's mass appeal had nothing to do with this appalling
vision, although it was commonplace talk in the upper echelons of the
'old warriors'. Hitler's charismatic appeal lay elsewhere: in his promise to
give the nation back its dignity, to overthrow the unjust peace settlement, to solve the political and economic crisis, and to create the 'racial
community'.

Hitler's appointment as chancellor [55]

General Kurt von Schleicher, who was chancellor for 57 days immediately before Hitler, made a bizarre attempt to cobble together a coalition that would combine trades unionists and left-wing Nazis around Gregor Strasser, whom he offered the post of vice-chancellor. He was committed to an ambitious programme of public spending and the restoration of welfare programmes that Papen had abolished, but it was a disastrous failure. Strasser was at first inclined to accept; Hitler began to panic, fearing that he would lose control of the party, and made yet another dramatic threat to commit suicide. The party was beginning to share the feeling of resignation and helplessness that was widespread in German society. There were ominous signs that the party faithful were losing patience and that the party was falling apart. Steeled by Goebbels and Göring, Hitler soon recovered his composure and it was Strasser who lost the battle of nerves, throwing in the towel and resigning from all party offices. The trades unions did not trust Schleicher and refused to cooperate. The agrarians and most of the influential industrialists felt that Schleicher's programme smacked of socialism, and began to think of Hitler as a viable alternative. The chancellor's plans were in ruins and power now rested in the hands of the camarilla around the aged President Hindenburg, a group that represented the interests of big business, the agrarians and the military. Papen, smarting at his recent defeat, now saw a golden chance to get his revenge on Schleicher. He, like so many of his caste, imagined that he could manipulate Hitler, whose position seemed to be far from secure with the SA chomping at the bit, with the party rent apart by the Strasser affair and disheartened after the recent disappointing showing at the polls. A number of prominent editorialists proclaimed National Socialism to be a spent force, and several party functionaries reluctantly admitted that they were probably quite right.

On 4 January 1933 Papen met Hitler at the home of a mutual acquaintance, the Cologne banker Baron Kurt von Schröder, offering him the chancellorship in a joint cabinet. It all seemed quite absurd. Papen was in no position to make such an offer, he had virtually no support and his career hitherto had been a series of disasters. Hindenburg, the only man who could appoint a chancellor, was known to dislike Hitler intensely. In November 1932 Schröder had organized a petition, signed by a number of leading businessmen, asking the president to appoint Hitler chancellor, but it had been studiously ignored. Nevertheless, there were also powerful forces that were looking for an alternative to the crypto-socialist Schleicher. A number of generals, prominent among them Werner von Blomberg, the army

[56]   commander in East Prussia and a man well connected with the landowning
aristocracy, liked the idea of a Hitler/Papen government. Hitler promised
rearmament, a massive increase in the size of the army and an aggressively
revisionist foreign policy. Others of a more conservative cast of mind were
alarmed by the radicalism and anarchic violence of the SA. A scandal
involving financial aid for agriculture in eastern Germany, known as
Osthilfe, alienated the agrarians from Schleicher and made them much
more sympathetic to Hitler. The Nazis were also well represented in the
agrarians' powerful lobby, the Reich Land Association (RLB).

On 10 January Papen met Hitler again, this time at the Berlin villa of
Joachim von Ribbentrop, a sparkling-wine salesman who had married his
boss's daughter and had become a self-appointed expert in foreign affairs,
but all he had to say was that Hindenburg had refused point-blank to
appoint Hitler chancellor. The president repeated his adamantine opposition to a Hitler chancellorship on 18 January. Papen did not give up hope,
and continued to intrigue with renewed determination. On 22 January he
arranged a meeting between Hitler, Hermann Göring and Wilhelm Frick, with
Hindenburg's son Oskar and the president's chief of staff, Otto Meissner.
The president's son spent a considerable time alone with Hitler and was
much impressed by what he heard. He was in a very delicate position
because the investigation into the *Osthilfe* scandal revealed that the president had handed over his estate at Neudeck, which had been given to him
during the war by a grateful nation, to his son in an illegal attempt to avoid
paying death duties. Oskar felt that Schleicher had thus failed to protect
his father from the prying eyes of journalists who were out to destroy his
reputation. Papen continued to press the president, but he still refused to
consider appointing the 'Austrian lance corporal' either chancellor or army
minister. Hitler rejected the offer of the vice-chancellorship in a new Papen
administration and at another meeting at Ribbentrop's house on 27 January
Papen agreed to serve under Hitler. On the following day Hindenburg
refused to grant Schleicher emergency powers under Article 48, having
decided to appoint a government that had a parliamentary majority, in
other words a government that would include the NSDAP.

That evening Hindenburg appointed General von Blomberg army
minister. This was a serious breach of constitutional propriety in that only the
chancellor was in a position to appoint ministers, but Hindenburg felt that
he needed someone with direct authority over the army when he had been
deliberately misinformed that Schleicher was planning a *coup d'état*. Meanwhile, Papen and Hitler had drawn up their list of cabinet members. At the
last moment the DNVP leader Alfred Hugenberg accepted the offer of a

super-ministry that combined the portfolios of economics, agriculture and [57]
food. A number of Papen's aristocratic cronies were to be given ministries:
Konstantin von Neurath at the foreign office, Lutz Schwerin von Krosigk
at finance and Paul Eltz von Rübenach at the transport and post ministry.
The chairman of the right-wing veterans' organization Stahlhelm, Franz
Seldte, was suggested as labour minister. The ministry of justice was to be
given to Franz Gürtner from the DNVP. There were only two Nazis in the
proposed cabinet, Wilhelm Frick as minister of the interior and Hermann
Göring as minister without portfolio. Faced with a cabinet filled with reliable
conservatives and convinced that Hitler's bid for a one-party dictatorship
would fail for lack of parliamentary support, Hindenburg's objections
were finally overcome and in the afternoon of 30 January 1933 he appointed Hitler chancellor. Hindenburg's residual misgivings were evident
in that the handover took place in his private office rather than in a more
public ceremony.

Was there an alternative?

Hitler's appointment as chancellor was not inevitable and was dependent on a multitude of contingencies, but at that particular conjuncture it is
difficult to imagine another viable option. There could be no return to a
parliamentary democracy which had ceased to function for three years, for
which there was precious little enthusiasm in the Reichstag and which was
denounced by a powerful extra-parliamentary opposition. Some dreamt of
restoring the Hohenzollern monarchy, but this was a small minority with
no popular backing. Given the bitter hatreds between the KPD and SPD, with
the KPD denouncing the SPD as 'social fascists', even more contemptible
creatures than the National Socialists, there could be no united front on the
left, however desirable this might have seemed to a number of intellectuals.
The rigidly Stalinist KPD, slavishly following Moscow's dictates, making
tactical alliances with the NSDAP and with its apocalyptic vision of the
dictatorship of the proletariat, attracted millions of voters but had a strictly
limited mass appeal. There was some loose talk of a military dictatorship,
but the army, with its tradition of ruling by proxy and thus maintaining the
fiction of being apolitical, was strongly opposed to this. Many officers feared
that such a course of action would precipitate a civil war in which they
would be forced to take sides, something they had managed to avoid
during the Kapp Putsch. Some historians have argued that Hindenburg
should have disregarded constitutional proprieties and continued to support

[58] Schleicher, thus allowing the NSDAP to wither away. But Schleicher's quixotic attempt to build a left-of-centre alliance appalled Hindenburg, as had his handling of the *Osthilfe* scandal, which had sullied his name and alienated a powerful group of conservatives. Furthermore, government by emergency decree had been tried for three years and had failed miserably. There had been three shots at such a presidential government, under Brüning, Papen and Schleicher, but they had served only to worsen the crisis. Who but the wild-card Hitler offered any chance of success? Hitler could provide both a parliamentary majority and wide support from many diverse groups throughout the country. The bourgeois-conservative power elite was ready to ally with the German fascists in order to win mass support for an authoritarian regime. Hitler thus did not have to 'seize power', as Goebbels insisted he had done. Power was handed to him on a plate. Once he had done what was expected of him he could easily be shunted aside. He was a relative newcomer surrounded by experienced politicians who would keep him under close control. Above all there was Hitler himself: the charismatic leader, the power-hungry Führer who would settle for nothing short of the chancellorship, the people's tribune at the head of a genuine popular party, the visionary with a set of pat answers to the major problems of the day. There was no other figure with anything approaching the same popular appeal, or who could conjure up such enthusiasm. Disastrously, he appeared to be the right man at the right moment.

Hitler's dictatorship was not simply the product of the depression and the ensuing political crisis. It was a uniquely German affair. All democratic states suffered severely from the depression. In the United States the effects were even more catastrophic. It was only in Germany that the political culture and social structure were such that the exceedingly fragile consensus that held a pluralistic society together collapsed and the republic was left without legitimacy. Brüning's deflationary policies, designed to reduce demand as well as unit costs, thus stimulating exports, were seriously misguided at a time when world trade was chronically disrupted. Similarly, the 'hunger chancellor' continued to tighten the belt even when Germany went off the gold standard and when the Hoover Moratorium on reparations removed the restraints demanded in the Young Plan. Admittedly such a policy was conventional economic wisdom, and it was the Nazis who benefited from the pump-priming by the Papen and Schleicher governments. The republican party system fell apart, the historically weak liberal parties shrivelled, the Social Democrats lost much of their support and were locked in battle with the Communists, the unions were hopelessly weak during the depression, and the Centre Party moved steadily to the right when Monsignor

Kaas became head of the party in 1928. In the same year Hugenberg replaced Count Westarp as leader of the DNVP, resulting in a sharp rightward turn, the party calling for an end to 'the preponderance of Jewry in everyday life', and in 1930 the Democrats joined forces with the Young German Order, thus making a noticeable rightward shift. There was no conservative party with wide popular appeal capable of inoculating voters against the Nazi virus. In such a situation it was inevitable that the extremes on both wings would grow rapidly and for most Germans the threat from Communism was far greater than that from the extreme right. As the gap between the haves and the have-nots grew ever wider, the siren call of the 'racial community' became ever more seductive. The temptation to blame all present problems on Versailles, even after the peace settlement had been fundamentally modified, was so strong that a realistic approach to crisis management was virtually impossible. The elites were uncertain, confused and unable to stand together as they did in the United States and in Britain. Industrialists were torn between free traders and protectionists. Agrarians were given protective tariffs, generous subsidies and handsome tax relief, but were still unable to master a worldwide agricultural crisis. The highly privileged big landowners were deeply resented by the small farmers, so there was nothing like an 'agricultural estate' as promised by the NSDAP's farming guru Walther Darré. Industrialists and agrarians, along with the military, imagined that Hitler's brand of charismatic leadership and plebiscitary populism could be used to achieve their own immediate ends. They were so utterly blinded by their arrogant self-confidence and selfish concerns that they were unable to see the enormous risks they were taking, and most remained stubbornly blind to the horrendous damage they had done, both to Germany and to the world, as well as to their dire responsibility for that tragedy.

CHAPTER 3

HITLER AS CHANCELLOR

The foundation of the Nazi dictatorship

Many observers, particularly in the conservative camp, managed to convince themselves that the Hitler cabinet was in the direct line of succession to those of Brüning, Papen and Schleicher and that little had changed. Hitler had been remarkably moderate and restrained in the weeks before 30 January 1933, and there were only two National Socialists in the government: Wilhelm Frick as minister of the interior and Hermann Göring as minister without portfolio, but who also held a key post as minister of the interior in Prussia. In April Göring was appointed air minister, thus presaging major changes in Germany's foreign political stance, but for the moment all was comfortingly familiar. Hitler surrounded himself with conservative nationalists from Papen and Schleicher's governments along with Alfred Hugenberg, the newspaper magnate, film tsar and leader of the conservative party (DNVP) as the all-powerful 'economic dictator' who was both federal minister of economics and food, as well as Prussian minister for economics, agriculture and food. Franz von Papen as vice-chancellor showed his ability to get things wrong when he told a colleague that Hitler was 'now in our employ!' and added: 'In two months time we will have pushed Hitler so tightly into the corner that he will squeak!!' The Stahlhelm leader, Theodor Duesterberg, who refused a position in Hitler's cabinet, claimed that the new chancellor would soon be running in his underpants through the chancellery garden to avoid arrest. A perfect solution seemed to have been found with Hitler's charismatic appeal, his drive and dynamism providing popular support for an authoritarian solution to the crisis, while he was harnessed by experienced and responsible conservatives. The little drummer boy could soon be pushed aside once the necessary constitutional changes had been rammed through a compliant Reichstag.

Such illusions were by no means the prerogative of the right. On the left the Social Democrats fondly imagined that Hitler was not Mussolini, that Berlin was not Rome and that Germany would not fall prey to a fascist dictatorship. The SPD's official newspaper announced that Hitler was the prisoner of the reactionaries and that Berlin remained 'red'. The Communists were also blinded by an outmoded ideological approach, proclaiming that nothing had changed and that Hitler's government was no different from that of his immediate predecessors.

It came therefore as a rude awakening for the denizens of cloud-cuckoo-land to find themselves in the midst of a profound social and political upheaval that some distinguished scholars were later to label a revolution. This was certainly not a revolution like those in America or France, nor was it analogous to the industrial revolution. These three, for all their unfortunate side effects, were essentially progressive in that they gave rise to fresh creative and energizing impulses of incalculable consequences. National Socialism by contrast marked a barbarous regression, an unleashing of a crazed atavistic fever that, far from offering an avenue to the future, ended in total destruction and ruin.

The key to the dystopian National Socialist vision was the creation of the Aryan superman, secure within the 'racial community', made possible by the elimination of all those threatening elements such as the handicapped, people with genetically determined diseases, the congenitally asocial (defined as anyone unable to earn a living) and above all the Jews. The 'new Adam' was to conquer 'living space' in the east where the local population would be killed, driven away or become the helots of the master race. This amounted to the total negation of what Goebbels called 'the ideas of 1789', which included the rights of man, the ideals of freedom and democracy as enshrined in the American constitution, or the rugged individualism of the industrial revolution. This in turn was only possible because of Hitler's quasi-religious charismatic leadership, without which there could never have been the revolution within people's minds that enabled the regime to get so perilously close to achieving its aims.

Hitler moved with breathtaking speed, catching both opponents and sympathizers off balance, and within 18 months had established an invincible dictatorship. His first step was to persuade President Hindenburg to call fresh elections, for he hoped to gain the necessary two-thirds majority for constitutional changes that would spell the end of democracy in Germany. Much to the distress of his nationalist colleagues, he thus reverted to calling for a plebiscitary sanction and parliamentary approval for his radical anti-parliamentary course. The nationalists wanted nothing to do with the parliamentary rat race, but Hitler was well aware of the need for demonstrations of popular support, without which his charismatic appeal would wilt away. The 'ideas of 1789' were thus not entirely moribund, but he assured his nationalist colleagues that this would be the last election, and that there would be no return to parliamentary government.

Hitler had no intention of letting the whim of popular opinion determine the outcome of the election. On 31 January the KPD called for a general strike. It was an empty gesture given the high level of unemployment, but with the Reichstag dissolved on 1 February Hitler seized the opportunity to make use of Article 48 of the constitution and issued an emergency decree on 4 February 'For the Protection of German People'. This permitted severe restrictions on the freedoms of the press and of assembly in the event of any 'immediate danger to public safety' or in instances where 'the organs, organisations and offices of the state and its employees were insulted or mocked'. The KPD was unable to hold any meetings, and the Communist and Social Democrat press was effectively muzzled. On 17 February Göring, as minister of the interior in Prussia, ordered the police to shoot to kill at the slightest provocation, and five days later he enlisted 50,000 SA, SS and Stahlhelm men as auxiliary police. The frequent and flagrant abuses of the decree could be appealed to the High Court (Reichsgericht), but by the time any such cases were heard the election was long since over.

The brown-shirted SA were unleashed during the election campaign and systematically disrupted the meetings of the republican parties, beat up opposition politicians, and flung some 100,000 unfortunates into hastily improvised concentration camps. A former minister, Adam Stegerwald from the Catholic Centre Party, was viciously assaulted during a rally in Krefeld. The Social Democrat police chief of Berlin, Albert Grzesinski, was made to fear for his life and felt it prudent to resign. The offices of a number of republican newspapers were set alight and the SA murdered some 600 people in these early months. In June the Social Democrats fought back, shooting three SA men in the Berlin district of Köpenick. In the ensuing 'Bloody Week' the SA arrested 500 people, most of whom were brutally mishandled and 91 were killed, among whom was the Social Democrat provincial president of Mecklenburg. There was widespread revulsion against this wave of barbaric anarchism. General Ludendorff, Hitler's brother-in-arms in 1923 and a man who was firmly entrenched on the wilder shores of the *völkisch* movement, wrote to his old superior Hindenburg to express his disgust at these 'unbelievable events' and claimed that this was the 'blackest time in German history'.

Hitler conducted a brilliant election campaign, travelling tirelessly the length and breadth of the country in his private aeroplane, preaching his simple and persistent message of national redemption to vast and enthusiastic crowds. He denounced the 'November criminals' in apocalyptic terms as responsible for the last 14 years of economic deprivation, political wrangling and national degradation. He painted a vivid picture of a revivified and dynamic 'racial community' that would overcome all distinctions of class, estate and station. The economy would be invigorated by two four-year plans and 'national rebirth' ensured by the reassertion of family values and a return to the basic tenets of Christian morality. All this was left deliberately vague, and Hitler assiduously avoided making any concrete promises, but he spoke with such burning passion and utter conviction that he carried the crowds with him. There was no need for a carefully considered programme in such an emotionally charged atmosphere, and the opposition parties were left hopelessly demoralized, divided and cowed.

On 20 February Hitler addressed a group of prominent businessmen and assured them that there would be no further elections, and that whatever the outcome of the present polls he intended to create a powerful and unconstrained state. First he would achieve absolute power, then he would destroy all his opponents. The businessmen were delighted at what they heard, promptly got out their chequebooks and relieved the NSDAP of all financial worries.

At 9 o'clock in the evening of 27 February smoke was seen billowing though the roof of the Reichstag. Within minutes a dim-witted Dutch anarchist, Marinus van der Lubbe, was arrested in the Bismarck room and confessed to having set the building on fire. The National Socialists promptly announced that this was part of a Communist plot. Willy Münzenberg, the colourful Communist newspaper magnate, mounted a brilliant campaign claiming that the Nazis had planned the fire themselves in order to have an excuse for further emergency legislation. A *Brown Book* was published in Paris that purported that the Nazis were complicit in the fire, and which proved to be an extremely effective piece of anti-fascist propaganda. The claim that the Communists were behind the fire was soon shown to be false, and Münzenberg was later to confess that the material in the *Brown Book* was fabricated. Most historians now believe that van der Lubbe acted alone, but the suspicion that the Nazis were involved still lingers.

When Hitler was told of the fire he worked himself up into a towering rage and said that all Communist functionaries should be shot, and the KPD deputies in the Reichstag hanged. The Prussian ministry of the interior immediately set about drafting a new emergency decree, which was

[64]   promulgated on 28 February as the Decree for the Protection of the People and the State. It rendered the state of emergency permanent and suspended all the fundamental rights guaranteed in the constitution. A number of crimes, among them arson and treason, were made subject to the death penalty. Summary arrests were permitted and opponents of the regime could be flung into concentration camps under 'protective custody', a sinister euphemism typical of the Nazis' deformation of the language. Wilhelm Frick as minister of the interior could now disregard the sovereign rights of the states if he deemed that law and order were in jeopardy. This was an important step towards dismantling Germany's federal structure and creating a national police force. Although the decree was ostensibly designed to meet a Communist threat, and although van der Lubbe's trial in September showed that there was no evidence whatsoever that the KPD was involved, it remained in force until May 1945, so that the Weimar constitution was effectively suspended. Van der Lubbe was executed, even though arson had not been a capital offence at the time he committed the offence. Carl Schmitt scorned those who objected to such retroactive punishment and announced that the principle of 'no punishment without a law' had to be changed into 'no crime without a punishment'.

Prominent Communist functionaries were arrested on 28 February and the party's offices were closed, but the party was not banned so as to ensure that the left-wing vote remained split between the KPD and SPD. In all about 7,500 Communists were arrested, including the party boss Ernst 'Teddy' Thälmann, as were such prominent left-wing intellectuals as Egon Erwin Kisch, Erich Mühsam, Carl von Ossietzky and Ludwig Renn. The 'brown battalions' of the SA killed 69 of their more obstreperous opponents. The persecution of Communists continued apace with 18,243 of the remaining 60,000 party members being hauled up in front of the courts by 1935. The respectable German bourgeoisie heartily approved of these draconic measures and breathed a sigh of relief that the Communist menace had been so effectively crushed.

In spite of the violence, intimidation, mass arrests and muzzling of the opposition parties, the results of the election held on 5 March were disappointing for the Nazis. With 43.9 per cent of the vote they were left five seats short of a parliamentary majority, but with the support of Hugenberg's DNVP, who renamed themselves the 'Battle Front Black, White and Red' and allied with other smaller right-wing groups, the Nazis had a majority of 52.9 per cent. With an 88 per cent turnout a sizeable proportion of the electorate showed its determination to fight back, and the combined vote for SPD, KPD and Centre amounted to an impressive 41.8 per cent. The

Nazi vote had increased by 6.6 percentage points since their best showing in the elections of 1932, not a particularly impressive result under the circumstances, but they gained 20.7 per cent more votes in Lower Bavaria, 16.3 per cent more in Upper Bavaria and 13.8 per cent more in Württemberg, areas where the party previously had had little appeal. The majority of German voters had thus shown their approval of the emergency measures and their dissatisfaction with parliamentary democracy. People rushed to join the NSDAP and were contemptuously dubbed the 'March fallen' (a term that had been used to describe those who had died on the barricades in the revolution of 1848) by the 'Old Warriors'[1]. There were 1.5 million party members at the end of 1932, 3.1 million by 1 March 1933 and 4.5 million by the end of 1934. There was widespread concern that the 'March fallen' would make the party too big and unwieldy, thus lacking in revolutionary enthusiasm, but others thought that this was a highly desirable development that would keep the dangerous radicals in check. After June 1933 there were virtually no further admissions until 1 March 1937. This meant that the NSDAP with only one-third from the 'Old Warriors' was a party of opportunists and place-hunters. At its largest about 10 per cent of the total population were party members. A third of all teachers, civil servants and doctors were in the NSDAP, thus at more than three times the national average they were over-represented.

As soon as the ballots were counted the Nazis set about the systematic demolition of the republic's federal structure and the centralization of all power in Berlin, in a process known as 'coordination' (*Gleichschaltung*). It was a two-pronged offensive with SA thugs and party activists storming town halls and local government offices, chasing terrified officials away and hoisting the party's swastika flag. The authorities in Berlin claimed that such mayhem was proof of the state governments' inability to maintain law and order and Article 2 of the Reichstag Fire Decree was used to replace them with loyal Nazis. Police chiefs were also replaced by the party faithful.

The process was characteristically chaotic, and there was no carefully considered plan as to how the new state should be organized. Berlin issued ultimata and promulgated a Coordination Law on 21 March, but at the local level the SA took the law into its own hands and, determined to enjoy the fruits of victory, indulged in an orgy of mindless violence. In some states the Nazis met with considerable resistance. The Bavarian prime minister Heinrich Held bravely stood up to threats from the SA, but he got no support from local army units, which were given strict orders from Berlin not to meddle in domestic politics. Frick appointed a prominent Bavarian Nazi, Lieutenant-General Baron Franz von Epp, as head of the Bavarian

[66] government and Held had no alternative but to clear his desk. Heinrich Himmler began his remarkable career in law enforcement when he was made police chief in Munich and head of the Bavarian secret police, with Reinhard Heydrich as his brilliant and ruthless assistant.

On 21 March, the first day of spring, the regime celebrated its success in an impressive ceremony organized by Joseph Goebbels, who had just been appointed minister of propaganda. It was held at the Garrison Church in Potsdam where Frederick the Great lay buried. The humble other-ranker appeared before the field marshal in a morning coat and the 'people's chancellor' bowed before the soldier-president, who was moved to tears by this powerful symbolic representation of the continuity from the glorious Prussian tradition to the new Germany. Bishop Otto Dibelius, as General Superintendent of the Evangelical Church in Brandenburg, preached on the same text that was used by the court preacher Ernst Dryander at the outbreak of the Great War in August 1914: 'If God is with us, who can be against us?', thus appealing to the 'spirit of 1914' and giving the church's seal of approval to Hitler's efforts to build a new state. The day ended with a gala performance of *Die Meistersinger*, giving the chorus 'Awaken!' particular poignancy.

On the same day a decree was issued which made 'insidious attacks' on the government or the Nazi Party, even in the form of mild verbal criticism, a criminal offence that was to be tried in the recently constituted special courts, which were party rather than state institutions. On the following day Himmler as head of the SS opened the first official concentration camp at Dachau, near Munich, to provide accommodation for those who transgressed this new law. SS-Oberführer (Brigadier) Theodor Eicke was appointed commandant. There were already some forty-odd informal concentration camps built by the SA, the SS and the police where inmates were cross-examined, tortured, murdered or released at whim; but this was clearly an inadequate means of dealing with 100,000 political prisoners. On 20 June 1934 the SS was made solely responsible for the concentration camps, which were henceforth guarded by the SS Death's Head Units (SS Totenkopfverbände). Eicke was made inspector general of concentration camps and set up his Berlin office in the Gestapo headquarters at Prinz-Albrecht-Strasse 7.

The Reichstag met in the Kroll opera house on the afternoon of 21 March, immediately following the ceremony in Potsdam. The atmosphere was distinctly menacing. The building was draped with swastika flags and surrounded by the SA. Hitler changed his morning coat for party uniform. Göring as president of the Reichstag refused to allow the 81 Communist deputies to take their seats, and a number of SPD members had also been arrested or forced into exile. The result was that the new house was made up of 288 Nazi deputies and 278 others. There was only one item of business: a constitutional amendment known as the Enabling Act that was designed to put an end to the last vestiges of parliamentary rule and place legislative power exclusively in the hands of government. In order to win the necessary majority Hitler promised that he would make use of emergency powers only when absolutely essential, and that he would keep the state governments in place, and pointed out that the Act would remain in force only for four years. He kept none of these promises. Since the bill needed a two-thirds majority, all depended on the attitude of the Centre Party. The leadership under Monsignor Ludwig Kaas was not averse to an authoritarian solution to the crisis, and feared that opposition would result in restrictions on the freedom of the Catholic Church. Other weak spirits managed to convince themselves that the bill was aimed exclusively against the Communists, and took comfort from the fact that the bill was designed to last for only four years. The former chancellor, Heinrich Brüning, warned that the Nazis had no intention of keeping their word with regard to the Catholic Church, but only a handful of deputies heeded these perceptive words. Otto Wels from the SPD was the only deputy who had the courage to speak out against the bill. It was not an impressive performance, being conciliatory in tone, and it met with hoots of derision from the brown-shirted ranks. It was a sorry admission that the labour movement had missed the boat and had failed miserably to meet a deadly challenge. Hitler replied with a passionate speech that brought the house down. It was one of his most impressive performances in which on the spur of the moment he used every rhetorical trick to demolish the hapless Wels. When the votes were counted 444 were in favour and only 94 against. The bill had thus been forced through in a blatantly unconstitutional manner and was renewed twice, thus providing a pseudo-legal basis for 12 years of dictatorship. Göring as Reichstag president had refused to accept the duly elected Communist deputies, and the vote in the upper house was invalid because the state governments had been overthrown and were therefore without proper representation. Few were concerned about such niceties. There was virtually no one who was concerned about civil liberties and most Germans acquiesced in this shameful surrender. Across the Rhine Léon Blum spoke of a deplorable 'suicide, hara-kiri by a sovereign parliament sacrificed on a dictator's altar'.

On 31 March the government used its new powers to promulgate the Provisional Law for Coordination (*Gleichschaltung*) of the states (*Länder*) with

[68] the Reich. This merely sanctioned what had already happened throughout Germany. The Enabling Act now applied to the states, where governments no longer had to consult local parliaments and could rule by decree. A second bill made way for the appointment of state governors (*Reichsstatthalter*) who acted on instructions from Berlin. Hitler appointed himself governor in Prussia with Göring as prime minister, to whom the chancellor delegated his authority. This marked the end of the long and fruitful tradition of German federalism.

The situation was complicated by the fact that many of these state governors were also the local party bosses (*Gauleiter*), but state and party district boundaries did not coincide, resulting in permanent disputes over jurisdiction and precedence where state and party districts overlapped, and further confusion between state and party functions. The situation became even more confusing with the appointment of armaments commissars whose districts were again different from those of both the state governors and the Gauleiter. All three tended to ignore instructions from Berlin and established themselves as little Hitlers in their satrapies, considering themselves beholden to the Führer alone.

For all the talk about the unity of the National Socialist state there was from the outset a hopeless confusion between state and party, federal and state competence, the traditional ministries and the special plenipotentiaries. Hitler added to the confusion in that he was in many ways a 'hands-off' tyrant. He preferred to let his myrmidons struggle among themselves and let the strongest and fittest emerge triumphant. This corresponded to his view of life as an endless struggle, and it ensured that the Nazi movement never lost its activist dynamic by becoming bureaucratized. Indeed 'movement' (*Bewegung*) was at the very heart of National Socialism. Whence or whither was of little consequence as long as it was on the move. The end result of all this was that most of the leading figures in the Third Reich were a repulsive collection of brutish gangsters, crude and corrupt place-seekers and ruthless careerists who were made all the more dangerous because they had large numbers of highly intelligent and capable people who were willing to serve under them. As Karl Kraus, the Austrian wit, once said of National Socialism: Prussian efficiency was placed at the service of Austrian madness. There was a certain advantage in this system for it was possible to avoid unnecessary red tape and pointless paper shuffling, but far too much time and energy was lost on interdepartmental rivalries and the struggle for power and influence.

A senior civil servant wrote to Frick in June 1934[2]:

Legally the state governors are subordinate to you as minister of the interior.
Adolf Hitler is the state governor of Prussia. He has delegated his authority to
Göring. You are also Prussian minister of the interior. As Reich minister of the
interior Adolf Hitler and the Prussian prime minister are legally subordinate to
you. Since you are also the Prussian minister of the interior you are subordinate to the Prussian prime minister and to yourself as Reich minister of the
interior. I am not a legal scholar, but I am sure that such a situation has never
happened before.

It was Hitler who held this all together in a system known as the National
Socialist Führer State. With the passing of the Enabling Act he had formal
approval for his dictatorship. By courting Hindenburg he could claim to be
in the glorious tradition from Frederick the Great to Bismarck. But above
all his authority rested on the charismatic legitimization afforded to a people's
tribune able to galvanize the masses to a hitherto unknown degree. That
authority was further reinforced by a series of remarkable successes in both
domestic and foreign policy.

Hitler, the visionary with a mission, could not allow his power and
authority to be constrained or shared, either by parliament or by a cabinet.
He, not his ministers, made the decisions and he would brook neither argument nor discussion. Thus in July collegial debate in cabinet was banned.
Individual ministers henceforth worked on draft legislation that was then
forwarded via the head of the chancellery to the Führer for approval. An
edict of October 1934 required absolute obedience from ministers who were
henceforth not even allowed to resign, and who were forbidden to discuss
matters informally one with another. Cabinet had thus become a pointless
institution. It originally met every day, but only 19 times in 1934, 12 times in
1935, 4 times in 1936, 6 times in 1937 and for the last time in February
1938. Initially Göring, certain of support from Schacht, Darré, Seldte, Frick,
Kerrl, Rust, Frank, Neurath, Himmler and Lammers, used the Prussian
ministerial council to pass laws, since the Reich cabinet virtually never met.
Parliament merely served as a forum for Hitler's speeches and no longer had
any serious function. By the time war broke out in September 1939 the regime
saw fit to use the Reichstag to sanction legislation on only six occasions.

Gleichschaltung

Gleichschaltung resulted in all professional associations, societies and clubs
being brought under party control. Walther Darré, the party's agricultural

[70]   expert and author of such authoritative works as *On Blood and Soil* and *The New Aristocracy of Blood and Soil*, a long-term friend of Himmler's, took over control of Germany's farmers' associations and was given the title of Reich Farmers' Leader. At the end of June he was appointed minister of agriculture, and thus had complete control over all aspects of agriculture.

On 1 April the offices of the Reich Association for German Industry (RDI) were raided by the SA and a number of officials were dismissed, among them the vice-president Paul Silverberg who, although he was a Nazi sympathizer, was Jewish. The RDI was completely reorganized a couple of months later and its name was changed, although the initials remained the same to give the appearance of continuity. Gustav Krupp von Bohlen und Halbach was appointed president and, along with Hjalmar Schacht, the former president of the Reichsbank, organized the Adolf Hitler Fund, which collected money from industrialists for the NSDAP. In early May business was organized according to 'Reich Estates', amounting to the formation of compulsory cartels.

Gleichschaltung affected every walk of life. The professional organizations of doctors, lawyers and engineers were brought under party control, and henceforth there were only National Socialist beekeepers' associations and National Socialist cycling clubs. Even the village skittles team was closely watched by the party. As a result Germany's vigorous and varied club life withered, and people either stayed at home or visited the local pub where they learnt to keep an eye out for police informers.

Clearly there was no place in the new Germany for independent trades unions. At the beginning of April the head of the Trades Union Association (ADGB) Theodor Leipart, an obsequious toad-eater, offered the regime his organization's loyal support, even though on 4 April management had been given the right summarily to dismiss any worker who was under suspicion of 'activities inimical to the state'. He was rewarded when 1 May was made a legal holiday, thus fulfilling one of the labour movement's most fervent wishes. Once the jollifications of the Day of National Labour were over the SA stormed union buildings, all their property was seized, a number of trades union leaders were arrested and Leipart had no alternative but to dissolve the ADGB. The unions were replaced on 10 May by one single union, the German Labour Front (DAF) under Robert Ley, a vehement anti-Semite and notorious drunkard widely known as the 'Reich Piss Artist' (*Reichstrunkenbold*). His erratic behaviour was partly explained by the fact that part of the frontal lobe of his brain was missing, as a result of having been shot down during the war. He was both corrupt and an appalling womanizer, whose second wife was a drug addict and committed suicide.

He managed to crash his Mercedes when drunk, with the Duke and Duchess of Windsor on board, both of whom were undeterred in their admiration for Nazi Germany in spite of this unfortunate incident. All workers, blue or white collar, as well as the self-employed, were obliged to join the DAF, which had 25 million members by 1941 and supported a gigantic bureaucracy of 44,500 administrators and clerks. With the unions out of the way, there was no place for contract negotiations between labour and management over wages and working conditions. On 19 May 'labour executors' (*Treuhänder der Arbeit*) were appointed who were given full powers to set wages.

The regime now set about the systematic destruction of the political parties, which in any case had no role to play after the passing of the Enabling Act. By 10 June the party newspaper *Völkischer Beobachter* claimed without fear of contradiction that the 'party state' was dead. Most of the leading Communists had either been arrested or gone into exile after the Reichstag fire, but the party was not formally banned until the end of the month. Moscow appeared curiously indifferent to the destruction of the party and the martyrdom of its members. Hitler had not even bothered to issue an outright ban on the Social Democrat paramilitary organization Reichsbanner, which he regarded with total contempt as offering precious little resistance to his own bullyboys. It was gradually banned state by state. Meanwhile, the party was systematically harassed, meetings were banned, its newspapers censored, offices were raided and the rank and file became totally demoralized. Most of the party leadership moved to Prague, to oppose the regime from a safe distance. On 22 June Frick proclaimed the SPD to be 'an organisation hostile to the people and the state'. The remaining parties dissolved themselves in the weeks to come. The DNVP's leader, Hugenberg, caused a furore by demanding the return of the German colonies and eastward expansion in the course of an economic conference in London in June. This provided Hitler with an excellent excuse to oblige him to hand in his resignation. He was replaced by Kurt Schmitt, head of the Allianz insurance company, as minister of economics, while Walther Darré took over the agricultural portfolio. On 27 June a 'Friendly Agreement' was reached between the NSDAP and the DNVP whereby the conservatives were granted membership in the Nazi party and all party members who had been arrested were released. The demise of the conservative party passed virtually unnoticed. The Stahlhelm leader Franz Seldte demonstrably joined the National Socialists on 26 April, and on 21 June the Stahlhelm was formally absorbed by the SA.

The smaller democratic parties self-destructed. Only the Centre Party and its Bavarian branch party (BVP) remained. Most of the Reichstag deputies

[72] cravenly begged to be included in the Nazi parliamentary faction, with Brüning and a small group of supporters vainly struggling to remain independent. On 28 March the Catholic bishops, fearing that the state might interfere with the church, made a solemn oath of allegiance to the Nazi state. The Centre Party leader, Monsignor Kaas, was in Rome with von Papen, to discuss details of a concordat with Vatican officials, leaving the party leaderless. Brüning took command on 6 May, but the party had no fight in it and members were leaving in droves. Under the terms of the Concordat priests were forbidden to take part in politics, the Vatican thus distancing itself from political Catholicism. A number of leading figures in the German People's Party (DVP) were arrested and on 4 July the party dissolved itself. The Centre Party followed suit the next day.

To celebrate the victory over the ideals of the enlightenment and the French Revolution, Goebbels chose 14 July, a day of special significance to all democrats, for the promulgation of a series of measures establishing a plebiscitary 'Führer dictatorship'. The compliant Reichstag, whose deputies were now all members of the NSDAP, and which was known to Berliners as the 'world's most expensive glee club', was chosen as the most appropriate forum. The Nazi Party was henceforth the sole legal party. Provision was made for plebiscites, indication perhaps that the 'ideas of 1789' were not yet totally moribund. These plebiscites were designed to be expressions of the people's will, in an acclamation and affirmation of the Führer's charismatic leadership. A law for the compulsory abortion of those foetuses likely to suffer from hereditary diseases, which von Papen had tried to stop, was an alarmingly sinister presage of a murderous racial policy, which had been foreshadowed by the brutal mistreatment of Jews. A law permitting the seizure of the property of those deemed hostile to the '*Volk* and state', coupled with a law removing citizenship from political and Jewish emigrants, further emphasized the regime's determination to achieve the highest possible degree of racial and political homogeneity in the much-vaunted 'racial community'. Victimization and exclusion were seen as the positive virtues of dictatorship, and they made membership of the 'racial community' all the more desirable.

It is a sad fact that Nazi Germany's first treaty with another state was the Concordat with the Vatican. Signed in July 1933 it was modelled on the Lateran Accords with Mussolini and greatly enhanced the status and prestige of Hitler's dictatorship at home and abroad. Pope Pius XI had already praised Hitler's robust anti-Communist stand on 13 March, and had abandoned the Centre Party, thus making the establishment of a one-party dictatorship all the easier. The German bishops now outbid one another in singing the praises of the new Germany. Bishop Gröber of Freiburg, who [73] had played an important role in negotiating the Concordat, proclaimed that he was in total support of the new Reich, and Bishop Berning of Osnabrück was given a seat on the Prussian council of state as a reward for his work on the Concordat. It was an honour, which he gratefully received.

Hitler at first presented himself as a man of peace and on 15 July Germany was party to the Rome Pact in which Germany, Britain, France and Italy pledged to uphold the League Covenant, the Locarno Treaties and the Kellogg–Briand Pact. Then on 14 October Germany withdrew from the League of Nations and the Disarmament Conference amid a frenzied press campaign in which Goebbels' propaganda ministry pulled out all the stops. Hitler announced that he had been obliged to take this step because the refusal to allow Germany military parity with other powers was a grave insult to national honour. He then called for a plebiscite so as to have a show of popular support for this affront to the international community, as well as assent to the fundamental changes that had taken place during the last ten hectic months. The results were spectacular, exceeding the most optimistic expectations. Of those eligible to vote 95.2 per cent went to the polls, of whom 95.1 per cent voted in favour of the plebiscite. Reichstag elections were held at the same time with 39 million of the 45 million eligible voters supporting the 'Führer's list' – the only candidates on the ballot. Since there is no evidence whatsoever that the results were fixed this was a remarkable affirmation of Hitler's charismatic leadership. As one commentator said in the typically convoluted language of the Third Reich, this was 'a miraculous step towards becoming a people' (*Volkwerdung*). It gave Hitler massive popular backing for a more aggressive foreign policy.

The dictatorship was further strengthened with the law 'On the Unity of Party and State' of 1 December, which Goebbels announced made Germany a 'total state'. The NSDAP was said to be 'the upholder of the German idea of the state', with its own jurisdiction and with the distinction between party and state further confused. The most notorious of these party courts, the People's Court in Berlin, began its unsavoury business in May 1934. To underline the amalgamation of party and state two prominent party members, Rudolf Hess as Hitler's second-in-command and Ernst Röhm as the head of the SA, were given ministerial posts.

A law on the Regulation of National Labour of 30 January 1934 applied the 'Führer principle' to all business. Each enterprise was to have a leader (*Betriebsführer*); the employees were to be known as 'followers', who were legally bound to obey orders from above. Four weeks later special interest groups such as the renamed Reich Estate for German Industry (RDI) were

[74] made into state-controlled organizations with executive authority. On the whole labour accepted these measures stoically, even though they had lost so many hard-won rights. There were signs that the economy was on the mend, unemployment was down from 24.9 per cent in 1933 to 13.5 per cent by the end of 1934, the DAF offered a few carrots that helped to forget the sticks, and most workers felt that criticism of the regime's efforts amounted to sabotaging a promising effort to overcome a severe economic crisis.

There was no place in Goebbels' 'total state' for any remnants of Germany's centuries-long history of federalism which, although often derided as hopelessly ineffectual and a hindrance to the creation of a modern nation state, had helped to preserve certain essential liberties and which had served as a model for such progressive constitutions as that of the United States of America. On 24 April 1934 Göring appointed Himmler Inspector of the Gestapo in order to strengthen his hand against Frick. This was the first major step towards creating a national police force, a process that was completed in 1936. Education, which had been a state rather than a federal concern, was centralized under the Reich Ministry for Science, Education and the Edification of the People on 1 May 1934. Bernhard Rust, a former schoolteacher who had been dismissed in 1930 for sexually molesting a pupil and who suffered from a severe mental handicap as a result of a head wound received while serving as an infantry lieutenant during the war, was thought to be the most suitable person to head this important ministry. Goebbels remarked of him that he was 'not quite all there'.

The universities had long been hotbeds of National Socialism, and the ranks of the National Socialist German Students' Association were swelling. In May 1933 they organized an impressive 'Action Against the Un-German Spirit' in emulation of their forebears on the Wartburg in 1817[3]. Bonfires were lit throughout Germany and books and newspapers that were felt not to reflect the spirit of the new age were consigned to the flames. Goebbels attended one such ceremony in Berlin where he addressed the crowd and proclaimed that the intellectual foundations of the November republic were thus reduced to ashes. Heinrich Heine, who had witnessed a similar act of barbarism almost a century before, uttered these prophetic words: 'In the end one burns people wherever books are burnt.'

The British ambassador fondly imagined that the intellectuals would be solidly anti-Nazi. He could not have been more wrong. Victor Klemperer, who lost his university job because he was a baptized Jew, had every reason to confide in his diary in 1936 that the intellectuals were the worst of the lot and deserved to be strung up once this hateful regime had ended[4]. It was not only the students who enthusiastically endorsed the new regime. While the books were burnt thousands of university professors made an open declaration of their devotion to the Third Reich, hoping thereby to further their miserable careers. It was not merely the second rate who lent their enthusiastic support to Hitler's dictatorship. Martin Heidegger, Germany's greatest philosopher, lauded the regime in a speech given in his capacity as rector of the University of Freiburg. He never retracted this shameful oration, though he was later to find kind words for Hitler's nemesis, Josef Stalin. The fact that his works were condemned by Nazi ideologues for being 'scatterbrained', ridden with 'hair-splitting' arguments 'in the worst Talmudic tradition' and that they contained 'no elements useful to National Socialism', left him unmoved[5]. Carl Schmitt, a renowned expert on constitutional law, provided ingenious justification for Nazi lawlessness, rejecting materialism and modernity, presenting politics as an endless struggle between friend and foe, and frantically searching for transcendent values; but he soon fell from grace partly because, unlike the sage of Todtnauberg, he had a wide circle of Jewish friends. Some of his best friends might have been Jewish, but this did not stop him from telling a group of German jurists: 'We need to free the German spirit from all Jewish falsifications, falsifications of the concept of spirit which have made it possible for Jewish emigrants to label the great struggle of Gauleiter Julius Streicher as something unspiritual.' Gerhard Ritter, a historian with impeccably conservative credentials and a highly decorated war veteran, was appalled at the 'cowardice' of his colleagues whom he aptly described as 'riff-raff'. Fifteen per cent of university professors lost their jobs with scarcely a murmur of protest. There was a general dumbing down of university education as a necessary consequence of Nazi contempt for the intellect, 'rowdy anti-Semitism' (*Radauantisemitismus*) and 'rage against the Jews' (*Judenkoller*) were given a tinge of intellectual respectability by entering academic discourse, while institutes of Jewish and racial research provided homes for fanatics, allowing their more sober colleagues to work in relative peace. Walter Frank's Reich Institute for the History of the New Germany in Berlin and the Institute for Research into the Jewish Question in Munich churned out reams of dubious material, and continued to do so when Frank was toppled in 1941 due to squabbles with Rosenberg and Bormann. The Reich Institute's main contribution to scholarship was the assertion that Max Weber's Protestant ethic was not at the root of capitalism, but rather Jewish greed and materialism was. Walter Gross, a 29-year-old doctor and head of the Racial Political Office of the NSDAP, editor of *Racial and Social Political Archives* as well as *The Biologist*, provided the intellectual justification for the 'final

[76]   solution of the Jewish question' which he summed up in his book *The Racial Political Preconditions for the Solution to the Jewish Question*, published in 1943.

The army had every reason to be pleased with the new regime and was prepared to offer its full cooperation. One of Hitler's very first acts as chancellor was to meet with a group of senior officers at the private apartment of General von Hammerstein-Equord on 3 February 1933 to give them an idea of his long-term goals. He certainly did not mince his words. He promised strict authoritarian rule that would rid the country of the 'cancer of democracy', 'exterminate' Marxism and pacifism and once again make Germany ready for war by an extensive rearmament programme and by the introduction of universal military service. In an ominous footnote, which most of his audience appear to have overheard, he spoke of 'radically Germanising' the east by carving out 'living space' (*Lebensraum*)[6]. With their traditional anti-Semitism, their loathing for 'Jewish-Bolshevism', their determination to rearm and to revise the Versailles settlement, they were encouraged by these remarks and from the outset had no principled objection to Hitler's plans for a racist war of annihilation and colonization. For all their snobbish disdain for the vulgar plebeian aspects of National Socialism, they were in broad agreement with Hitler's programme, and most of them remained so until the bitter end. The army was more than happy to get rid of any Jews who were still serving; the only problem was how to decide who was Jewish. According to the army's own statistics 2,000–3,000 'pure Jews' (*Volljuden*) had served in the army during the war along with 150,000–200,000 'half-Jews' and 'quarter-Jews'. Most of them had served in the ranks, but there were many officers and 20 generals among them. In the end only 70 Jews were found still to be serving. No objections were raised to incorporating the swastika in army emblems in February 1934. The generals were delighted. General Ludwig Beck, soon to become head of the General Staff, saw Hitler as the first ray of hope since 1918 and lavished praise on the new regime. General von Fritsch, the army's commander-in-chief, had long called for a concerted campaign against Jews, Catholics and 'Marxist workers', and was delighted to see his wishes fulfilled. It was widely felt in military circles that Hitler's concept of 'racial community' was congruent with the army's vision of a 'fighting community' (*Wehrgemeinschaft*) without which a total war could not effectively be fought. When Röhm's ambition to create a National Socialist army was dramatically ended with his murder in the Night of the Long Knives in July 1934, the army was even more favourably disposed towards Hitler.

As the president lay dying, a law combining the offices of chancellor and president was promulgated in open defiance of the constitution.

Hindenburg died the following day, 2 August 1934, and Hitler was now [77] officially Führer and chancellor. He was thus head of state, head of the government, commander-in-chief of the armed forces and party leader. Blomberg promptly ordered the Reichswehr to swear a personal oath of allegiance to the Führer, rather than to the constitution as had previously been the case. A number of soldiers were thus to suffer severe and genuine pangs of conscience when they contemplated resistance to the man to whom before Almighty God they had sworn total allegiance. Blomberg imagined that this oath of allegiance would guarantee the army's independence. He was soon to find out that the reverse was true.

Hitler had thus consolidated absolute power in the person of a charismatic leader. In this Führer state all checks and balances had been removed, and there were no institutional or legal restrictions on Hitler's sovereign power. Confident of the outcome, Hitler called yet another acclamatory plebiscite on 19 August, in which 95.7 per cent of eligible voters turned out to vote and almost 90 per cent voted to sanction the coup.

The myth was thus perpetrated that the National Socialist 'revolution' was perfectly legal. True, Hitler had become chancellor on 30 January by legal means, but subsequently the law and the constitution had been violated on numerous occasions. A parliamentary republic had been replaced by an all-powerful charismatic dictatorship. Parliament had been rendered powerless and was now nothing more than a forum for the Führer's announcements. The NSDAP was the sole legal party. The time-honoured federal structure had been destroyed and replaced by a centralized dictatorship. The rule of law had been trampled underfoot, the people delivered into the intractable and vicious hands of the various organs of the SS and the special courts. Political opponents and Jews had been murdered, thrown into concentration camps, driven into exile, denied a livelihood and their property had been seized. The murder of the handicapped had begun as the first ominous phase in the eradication of all elements considered to be a threat to the Aryan race and the 'racial community'. The old power elites who had fondly imagined that they could use the 'Bohemian corporal' for their own ends had been reduced to a subordinate position as executants of the Führer's will, and a new elite was firmly in the saddle. Although National Socialism was diametrically contrary to the fundamental principles of the Christian religion, and although Hitler and Goebbels openly stated that National Socialism should be seen as a secular religion, the churches were pusillanimous in their submission to the new regime. Those few churchmen who were unable to salve their consciences were submitted to brutal persecution. For the vast mass of Germans, Hitler was indeed the embodiment

[78] of the struggle for national prestige, strength and self-esteem, of the principle of racial superiority and the struggle to create a healthy 'racial community'. He was a man with a clear mission that every decent German could endorse whole-heartedly. He was a political Messiah who would lift up the nation after the humiliation of a lost war, the injustice of the Treaty of Versailles, and the deprivation caused by the depression. The loss of personal freedom was a small price to pay in order to reach the shores of the promised land.

It was never quite clear what Hitler meant by the term 'revolution' which he banded about with thoughtless abandon. Most of the time for him 'revolution' amounted to little more than the seizure of power; at others it was a call for a permanent revolution, for activism and flux. It was essentially a counter-revolution bent on undoing the work of the republic and claiming a direct link to Bismarck's Germany. At the same time it was directed against the inchoate revolutionary aspirations of party radicals.

The fundamental structural changes in politics and society resulted in similar changes in the mentality of the average German, especially among the young and impressionable. The making of the 'racial community', the struggle to create a people (*Volkwerden*), the destruction of the old class structures that these entailed, were more than the mere effusions of Goebbels' propaganda ministry; they appeared to be realized as fresh opportunities for social advancement within a meritocracy were opened up to the average 'racial comrade' (*Volksgenosse*). The brutal exclusion of the 'other' reinforced a feeling of belonging, which was often combined with the solidarity afforded by a nagging conscience. Hitler's charismatic leadership was further reinforced by a desperate longing for a new beginning, an intoxicating enthusiasm and blind hope. These were to be amply satisfied in a series of spectacular successes, both at home and abroad, that served to reinforce Hitler's aura of omnipotence and omniscience. By 1938 Thomas Mann caustically remarked that: 'Germans identify with Hitler and Hitler with the Germans.' Hitler gloried in his godlike status and said: 'I go on the way that destiny has indicated to me with a sleepwalker's sense of security.'

Once the Enabling Act had been passed Hitler's working methods became even more haphazard. He had never been one to pay close attention to organizational detail, was often reluctant to make decisions, and had relied far too much on his second-rate cronies in Munich, much to the frustration of such exceptional talents as Gregor Strasser and Joseph Goebbels, who built up the party in northern Germany. He kept wildly irregular hours, seldom put anything down on paper, and entertained his entourage with lengthy monologues. When he was not rushing around the country addressing the crowds, laying foundation stones and calling impromptu meetings with sundry officials at unlikely hours, he paid increasingly long visits to the Berghof, his mountain fastness in Berchtesgaden. Officials scurried after him begging for his approval. The result was a confusing polycratic form of governance, which has resulted in some historians arguing that there was a fundamental contradiction between an all-powerful tyrant and an amorphous and unstructured executive, to the point that, in one extreme version, Hitler has been described as a 'weak dictator'[7].

The system was undoubtedly chaotic with one minister securing the highest approval for legislation that contradicted what had already been passed via another ministry, but this all served to strengthen Hitler's authority as Führer, for he alone could reconcile such differences and order the implementation of laws, thus creating the impression of order and consistency. The term 'polycracy' should be used with caution. Hitler delegated responsibility to his immensely powerful satraps but, as can be seen in the case of Ernst Röhm, he would not tolerate any challenge to his authority. In the final stages of the Third Reich Himmler and Göring were instantly dismissed when they tried to go their own way. Those among the high and mighty who fell from grace did not challenge the Führer's omnipotence. In 1940 Julius Streicher lost all his party offices, including that of Gauleiter of Franconia, for broadcasting that Göring was impotent and that his daughter Edda was the product of artificial insemination. He was still permitted to bear the honorary title of Gauleiter and to edit his dreadful hate-rag *Der Stürmer*. Similarly, Josef Wagner, the Gauleiter of Westphalia, was fired in the same year for his continued attachment to the Catholic Church. Wilhelm Kube, president of Berlin and Brandenburg, was relieved of his duties in 1936 for corruption, theft and for announcing that Walter Buch, an 'old warrior', Bormann's father-in-law and the highest party judge, was married to a Jewess. He was reactivated in 1941 to establish an unimaginable reign of terror in Belarus.

Hitler resisted all attempts to bring some order into this confusion and thereby drove the experienced and professional civil service to desperation. His instructions were often deliberately vague, so that his subordinates were left to divine his real intent, or he hesitated until one of his myrmidons decided to seize the initiative. In such a situation there was ample room for power-hungry Gauleiter and Reichsstatthalter to carve out empires where they reigned supreme and could afford blissfully to disregard any consideration of law and established practice, while making sure that they always had a direct line to the Führer, without which they were virtually powerless.

[80] Hitler was bored by the details of domestic politics, so there was considerable scope for ambitious men to establish themselves in positions of immense authority and influence where they could be sure of the Führer's blessing. In National Socialist Germany nothing succeeded like success. Hitler saw the distinct advantage of being a 'hands-off' dictator in that the shortcomings and failings of the regime could be blamed on his subordinates, and thus did nothing to undermine his status as the nation's charismatic redeemer. On the contrary: 'If only the Führer knew' was a frequent response to a series of irritations, injustices and deficiencies.

The longing for a leader who would deliver Germany from all evil was deeply rooted ideologically and psychologically. There was Emperor Frederick I of Hohenstaufen, who as 'Barbarossa' lay buried in the Kyffhäuser mountain and who would rise again to save the country in its hour of need. There were the Parsifals and Siegfrieds in Wagner's operas, which Hitler claimed to love so dearly, although he was often seen to take a nap during performances at Bayreuth and much preferred to relax to recordings of operettas of which *The Merry Widow* was a special favourite. There was the deeply ingrained military spirit of Brandenburg–Prussia, the ideology of the youth movement, and a widespread desire to find a substitute for the monarchy as a symbolic representation of the nation. But it was Goebbels with his superb propaganda machine who transformed admiration for the regime's achievements into a quasi-religious cult of the Führer. 'The whole Volk', he proclaimed, 'is devoted to him not merely through respect, but with deep and heartfelt love, because it has the feeling that it belongs to him. It is flesh of his flesh, blood of his blood[8].' Perhaps only someone who had been educated by Jesuits could be capable of such blasphemy.

Few were able to resist enchantment by this superhuman figure. Erstwhile doubters became devotees, and even those who were critical confessed to finding him difficult to withstand. Hitler himself became totally convinced by his own myth, so that this mean-spirited, cruel and bigoted dilettante became convinced that he was the infallible and ineffable instrument of Providence, with a world-historical mission to fulfil. Even those who today speak of the 'fascination' of Hitler are still under the spell of this despicable megalomaniac.

As early as 1940 the émigré social scientist Ernst Fraenkel described this confusion of rival powers as the 'dual state'[9], and another brilliant colleague, Franz Neumann, analysed how the normative state apparatus gradually dissolved into 'organised anarchy' with its characteristically amorphous dynamic[10]. The dualism was not a clear-cut distinction between party and state, but a highly complex intertwining of areas of competence that led to ever-increasing radicalization both in goals and in methods. The key to the oxymorons 'organised anarchy' and 'amorphous dynamic' lies in Max Weber's insistence that charismatic leadership is not simply a matter of the unbridled will of the leader; it relies on a social structure that provides the organs and the apparatus adequate to carry out the mission. Hitler would have been nothing without his able and willing executors. Much writing on the Third Reich suffers from a Tolstoyan foreshortening, where the individual vanishes behind social structures, historical contingencies and blind economic forces. The bitter struggles for power and the personal rivalries among the myrmidons provide the key to much of what happened in the 12 bewildering years of Nazi rule.

The polycratic system was made up of a series of special ad hoc organizations whose heads enjoyed a special relationship with the charismatic leader. The building of the motorways (*Autobahnen*), the euthanasia programme and the mass murder of the European Jews are examples where special bodies were created whose leaders had no special expertise, but who were appointed solely because of Hitler's trust. They were completely beyond the control of or supervision by the law or any regular government body. Polycratic rule of this sort had to be free from any laws, rules or regulations and thus be fully autonomous. In the dual state these exceptional executive organs existed parallel and usually hostile to the established civil service. The party organizations had the upper hand over the old bureaucracy because they had Hitler's authority behind them. The result was a steady erosion of the power and influence of Germany's highly professional civil service, which was still bound by routine and established norms.

There was also an endless struggle between Hitler's satraps over access to the leader and areas of competence. In 1935 there were 33 Gauleiter, rising to 42 by 1944. Ten of these 33 were also Reichsstatthalter, 5 were state presidents and Goebbels and Rust were also ministers. All of these Gauleiter were from the 'Old Warriors', and their virtually limitless power rested on their closeness to Hitler, who showed remarkable tolerance for their incompetence, venality and corruption. He stuck by them through thick and thin, regarding them as his faithful vassals from the mythologized 'time of struggle' in the 1920s, admiring them for their often unruly activism, and only in extreme cases did he see fit to distance himself from one of them.

Under the Gauleiter came the 827 district leaders (*Kreisleiter*) who acted in a similarly independent, arrogant and self-aggrandizing manner. The same was true of the next in the chain of command, the 21,000 local group leaders (*Ortsgruppenleiter*) who had ample opportunity to make the lives of

[82]   ordinary people miserable. They issued certificates of good conduct for civil servants, for all those claiming social assistance, as well as for students and apprentices. No business could be started without the permission of the party, and during the war it was the party that decided which workers were essential and therefore exempted from military service. The lowliest party official was the *Blockleiter* who kept a close watch on the citizenry and extracted contributions for party membership, the National Socialist People's Welfare (NSV) as well as for Winter Help (*Winterhilfswerk*). These Nazi charitable organizations amounted to little more than state-sponsored mugging, and a large chunk of the proceeds went to finance such worthy causes as the building of Goebbels' luxurious villa in Berlin. Money was also collected on 'Casserole Sundays' whereby the proceeds of a modest one-course meal went to assist needy 'racial comrades'. During the war the Blockleiter issued ration cards, thus giving them further opportunities for harassment, and complaints about these vile little bullies at the bottom of the Nazi midden were legion. By 1937 the party had become a gigantic bureaucratic organization with 700,000 well-paid employees. It nearly trebled in size during the war when the 'golden pheasants', as its gold-braided officials were contemptuously called, found ingenious ways to avoid dying a hero's death for *Führer und Vaterland*. All this left the party head-quarters in the Brown House in Munich virtually powerless, and there was no unified cadre of senior party officials. It was a situation that Hitler had deliberately encouraged, for he had no desire to see his deputy and *de facto* party leader, Rudolph Hess, in any way pose a challenge to his absolute leadership, and preferred to deal directly with local party officials.

Fritz Todt was a typical example of the leaders of the new Germany. He was an engineer who had joined the party as early as 1922. He was not only an energetic member of the 'old guard', he was also a technocrat with considerable organizational ability. His remit as General Inspector of the German Roads was to build the *Autobahnen*, and to build them quickly. He worked completely independently from the ministry of transport and the minister, Eltz von Rübenbach, felt it prudent not to complain at this gross affront to his authority. Nor did he have to worry about any challenge from Robert Ley and the DAF. Having made a success of road building, Todt was promoted to Plenipotentiary for the Building Industry and given the task of constructing the massive defensive works known as the West Wall. He then created in Organisation Todt what amounted to a gigantic construction company. In 1940 he was made Reich Minister for Armaments and Munitions and as such took charge of the entire war economy, independent from the ministry of economics. By the winter of 1941 he realized that the war could not possibly be won, and in February of the next year he was killed in a mysterious plane crash that may have been designed to get rid of a tiresome Cassandra.

Todt's successor was Albert Speer, a young architect who was slavishly devoted to Hitler and who had been given the impressive title of General Inspector of the Capital of the Reich. He drew up grotesquely Pharaonic plans for the rebuilding of Berlin, henceforth to be called 'Germania', a project that became an obsession for Hitler. Speer designed a number of bombastic buildings, including the new chancellery and Hitler's eyrie on the Obersalzberg. He was a ruthless sycophant, blinded by ambition, who in the course of his building operations expelled a large number of Jews from their homes, and who as minister of munitions was directly responsible for the deaths of slave labourers from the concentration camps. He escaped the death penalty at Nuremberg thanks to effusive expressions of remorse, selective amnesia and downright lies. He survived a lengthy prison sentence to become, in the eyes of those whom he had so successfully duped, an example of the 'good Nazi' and even a tragic figure who, as a young man, had made a Faustian bargain and who had lived to rue the day.

Robert Ley as head of the DAF was responsible for such diverse fields as professional training, social policy, housing, medical care and leisure-time activities. He thus infringed upon the competence of a number of other ministries at many points. One such minister was the founder of the Stahlhelm, Franz Seldte, a bone-idle creature who had been appointed minister of labour in 1933. When Goebbels suggested to Hitler that Ley should absorb Seldte's ministry, because even though Ley was a chronic drunk he at least managed to get things done, Hitler refused point-blank. He pointed out that Seldte could be replaced at any time, whereas Ley would then be in a position of such power and influence that it would be extremely difficult to dislodge him.

Early experiments to create National Socialist unions were hastily dropped. Known as National Socialist Works Cell Organizations (NSBOs), they attracted disaffected left-wing elements who had the temerity to try to further the interests of the membership. In the summer of 1933 Trustees of Labour were appointed by the ministry of labour to determine wages, contracts and working conditions. Since these officials were mostly recruited from management they looked after the interests of the employers rather than those of the employees. Robert Ley was obliged to purge the DAF of all those who hoped to create National Socialist unions, and now concentrated on the educational programmes and leisure-time activities run by Strength Through Joy (KdF). This vast organization, founded in November 1933, offered further education courses, theatrical performances, concerts,

[84] sports, holidays at home and abroad, and even cruises. Based on the Italian Fascist *Dopo Lavoro*, Strength Through Joy was an undoubted success, giving the German worker his first taste of mass tourism, even though the emphasis was on strength rather than joy. Admittedly only 17 per cent of those who went on cruises to the Norwegian fjords or to the Azores were from the working class, but by 1939 10.3 million had gone on lengthy holidays and a further 54.6 million on shorter trips sponsored by KdF. Although the KdF holiday camps were highly regimented, the inmates indulged in considerably more sex and booze than was acceptable to the authorities. Workers were thus rendered relatively docile and, although they no longer had any voice in management and most had not regained the standard of living of 1928, they were mostly reasonably content with their lot. In 1939 KdF produced the first 'Kdf Wagen', known after the war as the Volkswagen, but in spite of all the propaganda not a single one was sold to the public during the Third Reich. In November 1933 Gustav Krupp von Bohlen und Halbach agreed that businessmen should be included in the DAF. In the following year the DAF was reorganized with four 'pillars': blue-collar workers, white-collar workers, industrialists and small businessmen. It had 40,000 full-time staff plus 1.3 million volunteers; 1.5 per cent of workers' wages was deducted to cover costs.

In the last stages of the Weimar Republic a Reich Commissar for Voluntary Labour Service had been appointed, and Franz Seldte briefly held this post in Hitler's first government. He was replaced in March 1933 by Konstantin Hierl, formerly a professional soldier and Freikorps leader, a party member since 1927, who was made the Führer's commissioner for labour service. In February 1934 he created the Reich Labour Service (RAD), nominally a party organization, although Hierl was secretary of state first in the ministry of labour and then in the ministry of the interior. In June 1935 labour service was made compulsory and hundreds of thousands of young men and women were obliged to serve for one year. In 1943 Himmler, as minister of the interior, gave Hierl his full independence so the RAD became in effect a separate ministry. The RAD was given responsibility for 'the education of German youth in the spirit of National Socialism, the racial community and a healthy attitude towards work, especially towards manual labour'. Labour service was widely seen as a valuable experience for young people from all walks of life and as a successful attempt to overcome outmoded class prejudice. It was widely admired by the many foreign delegations that visited the new Germany.

In 1933 Baldur von Schirach, who had been very successful in organizing university students in the National Socialist Students' Association, was appointed Reich Youth Leader, in spite of his widely rumoured homosexuality. He set about the systematic organization of Germany's youth from the ages of 10 to 18. Boys from 10 to 14 were to join the German Youth (*Jungvolk*) and then graduate to the Hitler Youth (HJ). Girls from 14 to 18 were to join the League of German Maidens (BDM) where they were trained to be housewives and mothers. Hitler placed Baldur von Schirach under his direct command and frustrated the army's attempts to have a say in how the HJ should be trained. In December 1936 the HJ was made compulsory, so that in theory all young Germans spent eight years in Nazi youth organizations, followed by one year of labour service and two years in the armed forces. Those who distinguished themselves during these eleven years were to be rewarded by membership in the NSDAP. Many managed to find ways to avoid such regimentation and there was a vigorous alternative youth movement, such as the working-class Edelweiss Pirates and the bourgeois Swing Youth, that broke free from this dreary uniformed orthodoxy.

No one accumulated as many offices, state, party or independent from both, as National Socialism's Pooh-Bah, the jovial, hysterically sadistic, maniacally anti-Semitic, morphine-addicted and progressively deranged Hermann Göring. He was president of the Reichstag, Prussian minister of the interior, Prussian prime minister, Reich minister without portfolio, air minister, commander-in-chief of the Luftwaffe, commissar for raw materials and foreign exchange and minister responsible for hunting and the forests. The vegetarian Hitler loathed hunting, as did Goebbels who saw it as an activity fit only for toffs and plutocrats, while the sensitive Himmler thought that it was cruel. When Hitler decided to push ahead with his plans for autarky he made Göring Commissioner for the Four-Year Plan, which gave him absolute power over industry and labour, thus overriding all other ministries. Hjalmar Schacht resigned as minister of economics in November 1937 in protest against the forced armaments programme that was getting Germany into serious economic difficulties, and left the Reichsbank in June 1939, but he meekly remained a member of the powerless cabinet. Schacht was succeeded by Walther Funk, a second-rate stooge and chronic alcoholic who is mainly remembered for fencing the property of murdered Jews. Funk, formerly secretary of state in the propaganda ministry, owed his appointment to Goebbels, who loathed Schacht whom he described as an '*arriviste*' with a 'washerwoman' for a wife, dismissing him as 'a cancerous growth on our politics'[11].

Fritz Todt as minister of munitions soon found himself locked in battle with the Four-Year Plan, and Göring proved no match for him. Speer was also able to preserve the supremacy of his ministry over Göring's, and worked

[86] closely with Fritz Sauckel, the Gauleiter of Thuringia who was made Plenipotentiary for Total War Work, responsible for rounding up labour in occupied Europe. Sauckel's outfit totally eclipsed the ministry of labour, and even Speer had difficulty in getting him to toe the line, since the energetic Sauckel had the Führer's ear.

The rapid growth of various special commissions, agencies and offices gave the Nazi movement a certain hectic dynamic in the early years as Hitler's devoted followers flexed their muscles for a struggle in which only the fittest could survive. With Germany involved in a total war this system of polycratic charismatic dictatorship proved to be hopelessly inefficient, with various agencies locked in battle over areas of competence, and with a complete lack of normative structure or clearly identifiable chain of command. The problem was insoluble without changing the entire system, so Hitler's entourage had no alternative but to muddle through to the bitter end.

The Führer's immediate entourage was also locked in constant struggle to increase their power and influence that depended entirely on how close they were to the source of all power. The chancellery was run by Heinrich Lammers, a professional civil servant who had worked in the ministry of the interior during the Weimar Republic. Since the cabinet virtually never met, he was responsible for coordinating the various ministries, and thus acted as a kind of prime minister. He was given a cabinet post in 1937 and since he had direct access to Hitler and filtered the flow of people and information to him he was in a position of immense power. Lammers also acted upon remarks dropped by Hitler and vested with 'special powers granted by the Führer', issued them as the 'Führer's orders'. He fought a losing battle to keep some order in the administration, but during the war he was pushed aside by the ruthless and radical Martin Bormann, the head of the party chancellery and Hitler's private secretary, who now acted as Hitler's ever-vigilant Cerberus.

The 'Führer's chancellery' was a party organization under Philipp Bouhler, who had joined the party in 1920 with the membership number '12'. This new office was designed as a replacement for the old presidential chancellery, but he had no taste for infighting and never established a position of real power and influence. He did, however, leave his mark by organizing the murder of the handicapped in the euthanasia campaign. Rudolf Hess, an unbalanced lickspittle, as Hitler's party deputy was initially more successful. He was given plenipotentiary powers over the party and the right of political intervention in the workings of the government. This made him powerful enemies among men of much sterner stuff and his position was steadily eroded. Hess created a number of subordinate institutions, which true to form struggled to become independent. The 'Ribbentrop Office'

dealt with foreign political issues until its eponymous boss was appointed [87]
foreign minister in 1938. The Foreign Political Organization of the NSDAP
(AO) under the Yorkshire-born Ernst Wilhelm Bohle was responsible for
Nazi groups abroad, collected intelligence and was involved in clandestine
operations. Both these organizations were immediately locked in a battle
with Alfred Rosenberg's Foreign Political Office to emerge victorious over
the Nazi Party's chief ideologue.

After a few feeble attempts, Hess failed to extend his influence over a
number of other institutions and became increasingly isolated and powerless. He sought solace in the occult and in Rudolf Steiner's anthroposophy.
Hitler poured scorn on the extreme rigidity of his vegetarianism. He was
widely rumoured to be a homosexual, was known in Hitler's entourage as
'Fräulein Hess', and his wife spoke openly and contemptuously of his lack
of connubial accomplishments. When he flew to Scotland his place was taken
by Martin Bormann, who as a political assassin was utterly unscrupulous,
soon establishing himself as Hitler's second-in-command.

By 1938 Hitler decided it was time to make some major personnel
changes and to put some more submissive men in key positions. He was
greatly assisted in this endeavour by Himmler, Heydrich and Göring, all
of whom had their personal grudges against the army leadership. Göring
resented the army for opposing the expansion of the Luftwaffe and nursed
the ambition of becoming commander-in-chief of the armed forces. Himmler
and Heydrich were determined to increase the armed units of the SS and to
challenge the conservative army's position as sole bearer of arms in the
Third Reich. Hitler dismissed the war minister, Blomberg, when it was
revealed that he had unwittingly married a 24-year-old woman who had
once posed for pornographic photographs and who was a registered
prostitute. Hitler, who had acted as Blomberg's best man, was genuinely
outraged that a 60-year-old field marshal had fallen for a floozy. The file
on this delicate matter had been carefully prepared by Himmler and Göring
with prurient delight. They also secured the dismissal of von Fritsch, the
commander-in-chief of the army, on a trumped-up charge of homosexuality. The sole witness against Fritsch was a male prostitute and convicted
blackmailer who perjured himself with staggering incompetence, much to
the embarrassment of Heydrich who was in charge of this sordid campaign.
Fritsch was posted to command an artillery regiment at the head of which
he was killed during the campaign in Poland on 22 September 1939. Hitler
wanted Field Marshal Walter von Reichenau as Fritsch's successor, but
there was considerable opposition to the idea in the army because he was
considered to be too much of a party man. Field Marshal Gerd von Rundstedt
told Hitler 'in the name of the army' that Reichenau was unacceptable. Even

[88] Keitel opposed Reichenau's appointment. Hitler, who had made himself supreme commander of the armed forces, was prepared to compromise. His choice was Field Marshal Walther von Brauchitsch, an outstanding candidate for the post with his brilliant military record, his admiration for Hitler and a passionately Nazi young wife. Hitler had given Brauchitsch financial assistance to help him deal with a messy divorce, for which largesse he was suitably grateful. Brauchitsch was put in charge of a new organization called the Army High Command (OKH). One of his first pronouncements in this new office was: 'It goes without saying that in all circumstances an officer should act in accordance with the principles of the Third Reich.' The foreign minister, Konstantin von Neurath, an old-style conservative who was somewhat concerned that Hitler was forcing the pace and running too high a risk, was also shunted aside and was appointed minister without portfolio – a meaningless title since the cabinet never met.

The new men were utterly subservient to Hitler. Wilhelm Keitel was put in charge of a new organization, the High Command of the Armed Forces (OKW), in February 1938. He was a perfect illustration of Italo Calvino's 'Non-Existent Knight', slavishly carrying out Hitler's commands, soon to be widely known as *Lakeitel* – a play on the German word for lackey. Keitel played an active part in the appalling crimes committed by the army in the Soviet Union and was hanged at Nuremberg for his role in planning an aggressive war. His chief of staff, Alfred Jodl, was an unquestioning but highly competent officer and was Hitler's most influential military adviser. He too was hanged at Nuremberg, but a Munich court cleared his name in 1953. Neurath was replaced by Ribbentrop, also in February. 'Ribbensnob' was universally detested, but he faithfully carried out Hitler's instructions without ever questioning their wisdom. Goebbels told Hitler that Ribbentrop was a 'nonentity' and would be a disaster as foreign minister, but Hitler ignored this intervention and changed the topic to a discussion of the many merits of G.B. Shaw. Most soldiers were disgusted by Blomberg's misalliance and were not sorry to see him go, but they were outraged by the shoddy manner in which Fritsch had been treated. This was the beginning of a rift between a number of officers and Hitler and fuelled the rivalry between OKW and OKH that was to have ruinous consequences on Germany's ability to plan and fight a war.

Employment

For Hitler to ensure his charismatic allure and legitimacy and to extend it far beyond the party ranks to include the entire nation he had to tackle the problem of unemployment, which was by far the most pressing social issue [89] of the day. He knew virtually nothing about economics, and what he did know came from crackbrains like Gottfried Feder with his theory of the 'thraldom of interest', but he had a phenomenal memory, combined with exceptional powers of persuasion. He was also an improviser of genius and had an unshakeable determination to get things done. The captains of industry, with the exception of Carl Bosch of IG Farben, were utterly opposed to the idea of state intervention in the economy, as were his first minister of economics, Alfred Hugenberg, the finance minister Schwerin von Krosigk, a former Rhodes Scholar who studied at Oriel College, Oxford, and the Reichsbank president, Hjalmar Schacht. The opposition could marshal powerful arguments to support their case, the most powerful of which was that a make-work programme, as suggested by the minister of labour, Franz Seldte, would lead to inflation which, given the traumatic effects of the hyperinflation of 1923, would be utterly disastrous.

Hitler simply ignored these objections and lent his full support to Fritz Reinhardt, an old Nazi who had been the head of the NSDAP's Speakers School and Gauleiter of Upper Bavaria, who was now state secretary in the ministry of finance. Under the Reinhardt Programme 1 billion RM of state funds were released in June 1933 in the hope of creating 800,000 new jobs. At the same time the much-publicized autobahn building programme was launched, but this in fact provided for only 250,000 jobs by 1938, at a cost of 3 billion RM. Public housing was encouraged and further helped by interest-free loans of up to 1,000 RM given to newly-weds: one-quarter of the repayments were waived with each child born. The programme started in June 1933 and within 18 months 365,000 such loans had been granted. Needless to say they were given only to racially acceptable couples. Nazi housing policy was less impressive. In spite of a massive propaganda campaign extolling their contributions to the racial community only 310,490 units were built in 1936, whereas 317,682 had been built in 1929, and housing subsidies were significantly reduced. In September 1933 a second Reinhardt Programme, designed to overcome seasonal unemployment, went into effect. A total of 5.2 billion RM were spent on such projects by the end of 1934.

Such Keynesian pump-priming takes a long time to have any noticeable effect, and the Nazis were fortunate in that both the Papen and Schleicher governments had ignored financial orthodoxy and had released substantial amounts of public funds in an attempt to overcome mass unemployment. Even taking into account a certain amount of statistical chicanery and an imaginative definition of unemployment, the results were spectacular. Within one year it was claimed that unemployment had fallen from 6 to

[90]   3.7 million and to 2.4 million six months later. Whatever the true figures, by 1936 Germany was the first industrial nation to enjoy virtually full employment, while the United States of the New Deal still had 24 per cent unemployed in 1939. This had been achieved by make-work programmes, by easing credit restrictions and by a massive rearmament programme. By 1936, when rearmament went into high gear, 10.6 billion RM had been spent on armaments. Above all, the regime's resolve and zeal, combined with the exceptional efforts of Goebbels' propaganda machine, created an atmosphere of confidence. Echoing the language of Fascist Italy, the 'victory' in the 'battle for work' in which 8 million workers had been given a job was celebrated with genuine enthusiasm. It was an amazing achievement for which Hitler is still afforded grudging admiration.

There were a number of factors that made the task somewhat easier. By 1932 the worst of the depression was over and the world economy was beginning the painfully slow process of recovery. Employers no longer had to go through lengthy contract negotiations or worry about strikes and they benefited from what amounted to a wage freeze. As a result profits rose by an average of 36.5 per cent annually until 1939, giving employers ample funds for investment, expansion and for taking on new workers. Wages may have been low, but so too were taxes, subsidized to a degree by the seizure of Jewish property. The exclusion of Jews from the professions opened up opportunities for the ambitious. The 'Aryanization' of Jewish enterprises enabled many an unscrupulous businessman to pick up a bargain. The expulsion of Jews from their homes provided extra accommodation for those in search of somewhere to live. The benefits accruing from the persecution of the Jews resulted in an alarming number of ordinary Germans either turning a blind eye to the regime's moral depravity, or conniving, even to the point of becoming an accessory to mass murder.

On the negative side, recovery was also exceedingly expensive, put a severe strain on the economy and was alarmingly inflationary. The massive investments in armaments helped solve the unemployment problem, but they were all part of Nazi Germany's preparations for a war of conquest and racial extermination. Hundreds of thousands of jobs were also found in the hydrocephalic bureaucracies of the party and the numerous subordinate organizations that mushroomed in the Third Reich, as well as in the rapidly expanding armed forces.

Charismatic leadership is legitimized by its ability to overcome crises, but if it does not have a series of crises to master it will lose its lustre, become routine and eventually sink to the level of a traditional autocracy. Hitler had found radical solutions to the political crisis that plagued the

Weimar Republic and to the economic crisis that had put 8 million out of work. In solving these problems he had built up an enormous capital of popular adulation, but unfortunately this obsessive gambler was temperamentally unable to rest on his laurels. He constantly fabricated crises and his luck held until the winter of 1941, when he suffered his first shattering and decisive setback before the gates of Moscow.

By solving the unemployment crisis Hitler won the support of the vast majority of the working class. By destroying the left-wing parties and the unions he could count on the gratitude of the bourgeoisie. The Concordat reconciled Catholics to the regime, and helped them forget the demise of the Centre Party. The opportunities offered by KdF were eagerly seized. The Olympic Games of 1936 were enormously popular, both at home and abroad. He had a series of remarkable successes in foreign policy. The idea of a 'racial community' as a harmonious meritocracy that would overcome all barriers of class and estate had a very real appeal to millions of Germans who rejoiced in a new-found pride in their country's achievements, and appeared to be at least partially realized, thus silencing serious criticism and making the vast majority of the people into accessories to unspeakable crimes.

Anti-Semitism: the first phase

That anti-Semitism proved to be such a powerful and widely accepted ideology was due to its forming what Shulamit Volkov[12] has called a cultural code: the crystallization point of numerous anti-modern prejudices, deep-rooted fears and existential anxieties that could easily be reinforced by personal dislikes. Jews were seen as the incorporation of all that was threatening and unsettling about progress and modernization, the repository of all that was negative. They stood for liberalism, socialism, Communism and capitalism. They were strangers and outsiders in an age of hypertrophied nationalism where nation and state were seen as identical. They formed a counter-identity, the reversal of values and virtues, by being presented as dishonest nomads, cowardly manipulators behind the scenes, shifty money-grubbers and sexual predators.

German identity was based on ethnicity. Not all Germans lived in Germany, and those who emigrated remained German. But this sense of identity was undermined by an acute state of insecurity after the humiliation of defeat and the imposition of a harsh peace settlement, followed by chronic economic and political crises that appeared to be unmanageable.

Figure 3.1 'The Eternal Jew'

The constructed figure of 'the Jew' thus served as a reverse image for German self-definition, resulting in the depersonalization of the individual Jew who was transmogrified into a distorted propaganda image. Most Germans probably did not know a Jew; those who did regarded 'their Jew' as atypical. Hitler was an exceedingly rare combination of unbridled fanatic and shrewd tactician who knew exactly when to harangue the adulatory crowds and when to retreat into silence, leaving the dirty work to his underlings. He passionately believed that 'the Jew' presented a deadly threat to Germany's health, power and culture, representative of an anti-race devoted to the cult of Mammon and materialism. As early as May 1920 he had made the public appeal: 'Anti-Semites of the world unite!' He combined traditional Christian anti-Semitism, as in such often-repeated remarks as: 'When I struggle against the Jews I am fighting for the Lord', with a national anti-Semitism in his determination to save Germany from what he perceived to be a deadly

„Hier, Kleiner, haſt du etwas ganz Süßes! Aber dafür müßt ihr beide mit mir gehen…"

Figure 3.2   The Jew as paedophile

threat, and racial anti-Semitism with his apocalyptic vision of a fight to the death between Aryans and Jews. He thus combined 'scientific' anti-Semitism that presented the Jews as deadly bacteria that threatened the nation, with 'religious' anti-Semitism, which saw them as diabolical. Above all he managed to convince the vast majority of Germans that there was a 'Jewish problem' that needed a 'solution'. Anti-Semitism was thus presented as something positive, an essential part of a comprehensive programme to build a healthy and powerful nation in which the 'racial community' would live in harmony and enjoy the benefits of a purified and vibrant culture.

As early as 1919 Hitler spoke of his emotional apriority as a 'rational anti-Semitism' that required the 'removal' of the Jews. In the following year he spoke of the necessity to 'kill the bacteria that causes racial tuberculosis'. 'Removal' now implied the physical extermination of a deadly threat. Much of the confusion surrounding these events is the result of words such as

[94] 'destruction', 'extirpation', 'final solution', 'removal', 'resettlement' or 'evacuation' meaning different things at different times; but whatever the term, and whatever the sense, they all implied that large numbers of people would perish in the process.

National Socialism was a system whereby the nauseous obsessions of one man were put into practice. Hitler could rely on the active participation of the like-minded, the tacit support of a vast number of sympathizers and the silence of the indifferent. All were guilty in varying degrees of complicity with his ghastly project. Germans did not become Nazis because they were vicious anti-Semites; they became merciless anti-Semites because they were Nazis. Hitler's obsessive brand of anti-Semitism is outlined in his rambling, discursive, ill-written and unremittingly repetitive *Mein Kampf*, and these noxious ideas remained unchanged until the bitter end. He tells us of how as a young man he first saw an orthodox Jew in a caftan in the streets of Vienna, a city that he described as 'the embodiment of miscegenation' and 'a racial Babylon', capital of a 'racial conglomerate'. He asked himself whether this smelly creature, who was both bodily and morally filthy, could possibly be a German. The answer was an emphatic 'No!' Hitler insisted that the Jews were a race and not a religion, and that religious anti-Semitism was a 'phoney anti-Semitism' that was worse than no anti-Semitism at all. Jews masqueraded as a religious community in order to be tolerated, whereas in fact they formed a state within the state, jealously preserving their racial purity by doing everything possible to avoid exogamy. Since the Jews had no state of their own they not only had no culture, they destroyed the culture of others. Whereas in the Middle Ages buildings such as the great cathedrals were for all eternity, modern man can only build 'Jewish department stores' like those of Wertheim and Tietz. Jews, or as he preferred 'the Jew', were at the root of every imaginable evil. From this it followed that he saw his struggle against the Jews as a moral obligation. Jews were the driving force behind parliamentary democracy since 'only a Jew can praise an institution that is as grubby and dishonest as himself'[13]. Social democracy was Jewish, and stood for the internationalization of capital. It thrived because of the struggle between capital and labour resulting from a 'Judaisation of our *Volk*'[14]. Trades unions were all part of world Jewry's sinister scheme to destroy the economic basis of independent nations. 'Manchester liberalism'[15] was also a reflection of an 'elemental Jewish viewpoint'. International Jewish world finance caused the Great War, and therefore the struggle against international finance was of absolutely critical importance. Share capital was also Jewish, and therefore infinitely worse than private capital. The Soviet Union was a country ruled by Jewish literati and stock exchange bandits.

Marxism was the despotism of 'world Jewish finance'. The press was controlled by Jews and Freemasons and manipulated public opinion; it would therefore have to be brought under rigorous state control. Syphilis was due the 'Judaisation of morals and the Mammonisation of the pairing instinct'. 'Sin against blood and race is the original sin of this world', because Jews are out to seduce German girls in order to destroy the race. Jews had run the centralized war industries, had profited immensely at Germany's expense and had thereby ensured that Germany lost the war. Kurt Eisner's revolution in Bavaria in 1918 was at the behest of world Jewry. It was the Jews who brought 'Niggers' as occupation troops into the Rhineland where they sired a horde of 'Rhineland bastards'. These 'Hottentots and Zulu Kaffirs' were hopelessly inferior. They could be trained so long that they could pretend to be 'lawyers and Wagnerian Heldentenors', but only in the same sense that one could train toy poodles. This was all designed to weaken the race to the point that the Jews would take over, thus completing what they had begun by playing Bavaria off against Prussia, Catholics off against Protestants. Hitler completely rejected the notion of citizenship enshrined in the Declaration of the Rights of Man. Since citizenship could be based only on race and the state's principal function was to strengthen the race, the idea of 'Germanizing' was an absurd illusion. As he put it: 'you cannot turn a Nigger or a Chinaman into a German by teaching him to speak German'.

The Jew was the 'schizomycete of humanity', and since the state for Hitler was a racial rather than a political or economic organism, the Jew had no place within it. A nation could recover from a lost war or from economic disaster, but nothing could ever remedy the purity of the blood. For this reason emphasis on a feeling of racial belonging and a determination to preserve the purity of the blood was the most important part of a good education. Without this purity of the blood Germany would simply provide 'cultural fertilisation' for other countries. The 'racial question' was 'not only the key to world history, but to all human culture'. The purification of German blood was for Hitler also a matter of aesthetics, since 'in a bastardised and niggerish world all idea of human beauty and of the sublime, as well as the vision of an idealised future for humanity, would be lost for ever'. From this it followed that only the racially pure should be allowed to marry, and all those with negative hereditary dispositions, syphilis or tuberculosis, 'cripples and cretins' should be rendered infertile. Hitler summed up his programme thus: 'We have to fight for the security of that which exists and the increase of our race and our *Volk*, to feed our children and preserve the purity of our blood, the freedom and independence of our

[96] fatherland, so that our *Volk* can mature to the point that it can carry out the mission given to us by the creator of the universe.' In order for this to be possible 'the international poisoners of our race must be wiped out' (*ausradiert*).

Hitler seldom resorted to such primitive filth in public and left it to Julius Streicher, the odious Gauleiter of Franconia, to trumpet this loathsome message. Even Goebbels, whose anti-Semitic credentials were impeccable, described Streicher as a 'berserker', a 'fanatic' and 'somewhat pathological', but added that he was a very effective public speaker and shared many of the same characteristics as Hitler[16]. Like many Nazis he had first been a socialist and was the co-founder of the German Socialist Party, joining the NSDAP in October 1922. Streicher and Hitler were in complete agreement in their attitude towards the Jews, but for the moment Hitler felt it prudent not to reveal his real feelings in his public discourse. Fortunately very few people had the stamina to plough their way through the two turgid and repellent volumes of *Mein Kampf*; the few threatening remarks in his speeches gave encouragement to Jew-baiters but were mostly regarded as empty rhetoric. Hitler's meteoric rise to power from 1929 was in no sense due to his ability to mobilize anti-Semitic feelings in Germany and he was mindful to dissociate himself from what Goebbels described as 'anti-Semitic rowdyism', but this in no sense meant any softening of his pathological obsessions. As the unchallenged Führer he was the driving force behind the escalating discrimination, expulsion and mass murder to which the European Jews fell prey. This was not the result of uncoordinated violence by groups of racist extremists, but was state-sanctioned anti-Semitism involving hundreds of thousands of ordinary Germans ready to carry out the Führer's will. At the forefront were the ideologically driven specialists in the Reich Security Main Office (RSHA), eager to execute the Führer's bidding, but they could rely on the full cooperation of the civil service, the judiciary and the military, all the way down to stationmasters and engine drivers.

Much of this was either obscured or unforeseeable during the political manoeuvrings between 1930 and 1932 when Hitler was courting the political and economic elites and was anxious to appear respectable. Anti-Semitism was widespread in such circles, but it was implicit, understated and restrained by the norms of polite social behaviour. There was no place here for the crude, knee-jerk anti-Semitism of *Mein Kampf*. That could be left to the contributors to *Der Stürmer*. Hitler spoke of the *Volk*, of race and of *Lebensraum* while the party basis indulged in violent attacks on Jews and boycotted Jewish shops. In 1930 the NSDAP faction in the Reichstag proposed a range of anti-Semitic legislation, but this attracted little notice.

'Racial hygiene' was, as Hitler never tired of pointing out, at the very [97] core of the National Socialist revolution, for this was the means whereby the race would be purified, the 'new man' created and the 'racial community' achieved. 'Special treatment' was to be used in order to rid the 'racial body' of all that threatened its health and purity, thus fulfilling Hitler's Hegelian prophecy that: 'Our revolution . . . shall end by abolishing history.' From the outset the Nazis spoke of their determination to destroy everything that was deemed to be 'alien to the community' (*Gemeinschaftsfremd*) in order to render the race purer, healthier and stronger. First and foremost all Germans of Jewish descent were to be excluded, although a debate continued as to whether this should include 'half-Jews', 'quarter-Jews', or even 'eighth-Jews'.

Jews were considered the most serious menace, but the mentally ill, the asocial, the carriers of hereditary diseases and Gypsies also presented a serious danger to the healthy 'racial body'. 'Asocials' included a wide range of people such as habitual criminals, tramps, the homeless, beggars, the permanently unemployed, prostitutes and pimps, alcoholics, drug addicts and homosexuals. These were to be sterilized so that their bad genes would not live on to infect the 'racial body'. Some 370,000 Germans had been compulsorily sterilized by 1939, including 2,000 for criminal offences, and to add insult to injury they were forbidden to marry since they would be unable to present the Führer with a child eager to do his bidding. The same treatment was to be meted out on all those with genetically transmittable diseases. Gypsies were damned on three counts: they were deemed to be 'asocial', 'inferior', and 'racially unacceptable' (*Fremdrassig*). German children whose fathers were Black colonial troops serving in the occupation forces, the so-called 'Rhineland bastards', were also to be banned from the 'racial community'. The Gauleiter of Berlin, Joseph Goebbels, declared Jews to be 'asocial', but it was difficult to charge this sinisterly powerful, alarmingly successful and deeply threatening people with 'inferiority'. In the jargon of the day the 'racial body' (*Volkskörper*) had to be saved from 'racial death' (*Volkstod*) by the removal of 'racial aliens' (*Volksfremde*). The first step was to be by sterilization of such undesirables, with experts calculating that 1.6 million Germans needed to be neutered for the programme to count as a success; the next step was to be by mass murder.

Homosexuality was a criminal offence under paragraph 175 of the criminal code of 1871, defined exclusively as anal intercourse between males. In 1929 a Reichstag committee began to debate whether the paragraph should be dropped, but the advent of the Nazis to power put an end to this progressive move. In 1935 the law was extended to all forms of sexual

[98] activity between males, thus opening up a wide range of interpretations. Lesbians were persecuted only in Austria, where paragraphs 129 and 130 of the criminal code condemned their proclivity as an 'unnatural sexual offence'. The Nazis closed a number of lesbian bars and clubs in 1933, but many continued discreetly with the police turning a blind eye. Unlike the Jews, homosexuals were never systematically hunted down and murdered, and there was an extensive and vigorous homosexual sub-culture in the Third Reich. In the early years many homosexuals were attracted by the distinctly homoerotic aesthetic of the 'movement', and a number of prominent Nazis would have been in serious trouble had paragraph 175 of the criminal code been rigorously enforced. The SS began to round up homosexuals after the Röhm affair in 1934, since Röhm was a notorious invert (a fact that the party had hitherto studiously overlooked). A special division of the Gestapo dealt exclusively with homosexuals until October 1936 when a Reich Centre for the Fight Against Homosexuality was founded. In all some 50,000 gay men were prosecuted under paragraph 175 during the Third Reich, more than half between the years 1936 and 1938. Of these about 15,000 were sent to concentration camps where they wore a pink triangle on their overalls. By contrast in West Germany between 1953 and 1965 there were 100,000 prosecutions under paragraph 175, about half of whom were convicted. The fact that homosexuals in the Third Reich were tried in normal courts under a law that remained in force after the war meant that it was virtually impossible for them to claim that they were victims of Nazism.

Exceptions were made for members of the Nazi elite. The club-footed Goebbels fathered six children. The morphine-addicted Göring and the alcoholic Ley were left to their own devices, and no investigations were made into the private lives of Baldur von Schirach, Hess or Funk, who were widely rumoured to be homosexual. Goebbels suffered greatly from the widespread rumours that he was gay, which may well have contributed to his notorious Don Juanism and his demonstrative philoprogenitiveness. In order to get round such awkward anomalies it was decided that sterilization was not necessary provided the subject was mentally sound and of pure Aryan stock. Since Goebbels was no fool and fathered six perfectly healthy children (although it was suggested that some bore a resemblance to Magda Goebbels' lover Karl Hahnke, secretary of state in the propaganda ministry), he was not obliged to go under the knife. Such notable exceptions aside, the Aryan race, the source of all that was creative and dynamic, was deemed to be threatened with a 'biological catastrophe' if drastic action were not taken, and millions were murdered, hundreds of thousands sterilized in a demonic

Figure 3.3   Hitler and Goebbels. The picture was banned from publication because it clearly shows Goebbels' club foot

social-Darwinian attempt to purify the race. Since the National Socialist concept of law was based on the will of the Führer and on the 'healthy instincts of the *Volk*', all those who were excluded from the *Volk* were also outside the law, and could be disposed of however the authorities saw fit.

The murder of 6 million Jews, whom the Nazis claimed were a race, was the most extreme and radical of these measures. Obsessive racial anti-Semitism was a product of the late nineteenth century and took firm root in Germany. It spread rapidly during the First World War and infected all sections of society. In a mad search for scapegoats to blame for a lost war, runaway inflation and mass unemployment 'the Jew' proved to be an excellent candidate. Anti-Semitic extremists with their half-baked notions of biological determinism could count on at least the tacit support of the vast majority of the population with their latent anti-Semitism. Many Germans

[100] were envious of the success of the Jewish community and argued that they were over-represented in the professions: 11 per cent of doctors and 16 per cent of lawyers were Jewish and they were concentrated in Berlin where 45 per cent of Jewish doctors and 40 per cent of Jewish lawyers practised. In 1933 average Jewish incomes in Berlin were between 2,660 and 2,910 RM per year, whereas the total average income was 1,550 RM. Germans averted their gaze when confronted with the more unseemly and gruesome aspects of the Nazi's programme of racial purification. The churches were tainted with traditional religious anti-Semitism and, with a few heroic individual exceptions, showed no compassion towards the Christ murderers: the 'perfidious Jews' of the Good Friday mass. Cardinal Faulhaber of Munich announced in his Advent homily in 1933 that:

> with the death of Christ, Israel was no longer in the service of revelation. They had failed to realise that the moment of visitation had come. They denied the anointed of the Lord, rejected Him, cast Him out of the city and nailed Him to the cross. At that moment the veil of the temple of Zion was rent in twain and thus the covenant between the Lord and His people was ended. The daughter of Zion was dismissed, henceforth restlessly to wander across the face of the earth as the eternal Ahasver.

The persecution of the Jews provides a paradigmatic example of the lawlessness, ideological fervour and ruthless brutality of Nazi tyranny. It was also characteristic of the regime that it should be part of a gradual radicalization and that it should be implemented in a somewhat disorganized way with various power centres within this polycratic system vying with one another.

It began immediately after 30 January 1933 in a typically haphazard manner. It was combination of uncoordinated violence from below with SA yobs going on the rampage, vandalizing Jewish property, beating and murdering their hapless victims, and approval and encouragement from above. Whatever happened was legitimized by the Führer's unchallenged authority and was guaranteed his approbation. To a certain extent it was a case of the tail wagging the dog: the SA ran amok for two months and the government responded with the officially sanctioned boycott of Jewish stores. Similarly, a number of incidents in 1935 were followed by the Nuremberg Laws, and the pogrom of 9 November 1938 came after a series of violent outbursts in 1938. It was followed by a series of further anti-Semitic measures. Thus the basis acted and the leadership reacted. Jews from all walks of life fell prey to this escalation of violence. There was an immediate and

robust reaction against these atrocities from abroad, but this only provoked
the regime to step up its anti-Semitic campaign. The British ambassador,
Sir Horace Rumbold, who reported that Germany was 'swamped' by Jews
and who agreed with a number of foreign diplomats and journalists that
Hitler was a moderate anti-Semite, was appalled at this mayhem, reporting
that this was an alarming case of 'irresponsibility and a frivolous disregard
for all decent feelings which is without precedent'. Goebbels promised that
he would 'teach foreign Jews a lesson' for interfering in German affairs
on behalf of their 'racial comrades'. A Central Defence Committee Against
Jewish Atrocity and Boycott Besetment was formed under Julius Streicher,
who rejoiced in the reputation of being the movement's most brutal, scato-
logical and vicious anti-Semite, whose 'impregnation theory' outlined in
his book *German Racial Health from Blood and Soil* of 1935 was a perfect
example of the deep-rooted sexual anxiety that lay at the root of his anti-
Semitism. He wrote: 'An Aryan woman needs to sleep with a Jew on only
one occasion for her blood to be poisoned for ever. An alien soul will enter
her body with this foreign protein.' Hitler and Goebbels agreed that he
was the ideal man to be given the task of organizing a boycott of Jewish
businesses, doctors and lawyers, to begin on 1 April 1933.

It was not a success. Goebbels was bitterly disappointed at the lack of
popular enthusiasm for his carefully orchestrated demonstration protesting
against 'world Jewry's horror campaign' against the new Germany. People
resented being stopped by SA louts from going to their favourite stores, or
from consulting their doctors, and there were widespread complaints about
the excesses of the Brownshirts. The boycott was called off after three days,
but this by no means meant a reconsideration of Nazi policy towards the
Jews and the boycott continued in areas where party radicals held sway,
regardless of orders from above. From 1933 to 1936 the Nazis concentrated on the persecution of 'Marxists' – all their enemies of the left of
centre. The vast majority of Jews who were arrested in these years were
flung into concentration camps because they were on the left, not simply
because they were Jews. The leadership was determined to rein in the anti-
Semitic rowdies in the SA whose anarchic violence was most disturbing to
the conservative elites, but local boycotts of Jewish shops continued throughout 1933 and 1934, even though they were theoretically illegal.

On 7 April 1933 the Law for the Restoration of a Professional Civil
Service was passed which excluded all Jews. A Jew was defined as someone
who had one Jewish grandparent or parent. Hindenburg insisted that Jews
who had been in the civil service before 1 September 1914, who had served

[102] in the war, or whose father or son had been killed in the war should be exempted. This exception ceased shortly after Hindenburg's death. The same definition of who was Jewish was used for excluding Jews from practising as lawyers, doctors, dentists, dental technicians and accountants. In July army officers were forbidden by Blomberg to marry Jews, while Jewish officers and other ranks were dismissed from the Reichswehr.

On 21 April 1933 a law was passed forbidding ritual slaughter throughout the Reich, but once again the law merely confirmed what had happened in a large number of communes and states. In like manner a law of 25 April 1933 restricted the number of Jewish students in schools and universities, measures which were already in effect in a number of areas.

Most Germans either felt that such actions were a fair punishment for imagined wrongs, or they simply ignored them. Precious few protested, but there was very little active support for behaviour that the solid bourgeois felt to be somewhat uncouth. There was widespread indifference with ordinary Germans showing a shameful disregard for fundamental human rights, and an appalling lack of compassion towards the victims of a terrible crime. It is all the more perplexing that this should happen in the country where the emancipation and integration of the Jews had been so unusually successful. Had not Rabbi Leo Baeck described Germany as witnessing the third golden age of Judaism, following that of Hellenic Judaism in the period before the destruction of the second temple, and that of Sephardic Judaism before the expulsion from Spain? Was it possible to ignore the extraordinary contribution of Jews to Germany's cultural heritage? Did the fact that 33 German Nobel Prize winners were Jewish count for nothing?

In the summer of 1933 things began to settle down somewhat and many German Jews felt that the worst was over. Others were sceptical. Thirty-seven thousand emigrated in 1933, and a further 23,000 in the following year; 16,000 of these emigrants returned to Germany either because they failed to gain admission to another country, or because they met with a hostile reception. A conference held in Evian in 1938 failed to resolve the problem of finding new homes for persecuted Jews, with most countries anxious not to offend Germany and mindful of anti-immigration sentiments at home. Under the terms of the Haavara Transfer Agreement of 1933 Jews going to Palestine were allowed to take most of their belongings with them. The RSHA was strongly opposed to the agreement and did everything it could to frustrate it. The Foreign Office was strongly against encouraging Jews to emigrate to Palestine and objected vigorously to the Peel Commission's report suggesting that Palestine be divided. They felt that a Jewish state would be like the Vatican or Moscow, and become the centre of the world Jewish conspiracy. Hitler did not agree, arguing that anything that helped to rid Germany of Jews was desirable. The Jewish Section of the party's SD suggested that cutting off their means of existence was the best way to achieve this aim, but soon began to be sceptical that enough Jews would be willing to go to Palestine, or would be accepted by the British authorities. Hitler did not concur.

Baeck's optimism was tragically misplaced. This was the beginning of the systematic exclusion of the Jews from German society, a relentless process involving some 1,400 prohibitions and restrictions, some of which bordered on the ludicrous, with the ministry of finance debating at inordinate length the question of whether seeing-eye dogs for blind Jewish war veterans should continue to be tax deductible. It was a campaign of unspeakable baseness that was accepted in silence or actively supported by the vast majority of Germans. Any encouragement that the Jewish community might have got from the failure of the boycott campaign was soon dashed. They were left abandoned by their fellow citizens and with precious little help from the international community. Germans accepted this apartheid out of a lack of moral courage, out of a fear of reprisal, or because of a deeply ingrained anti-Semitism. The depraved ranting of Hitler, Goebbels and Streicher on the threat posed by world Jewry to the Aryan master race met with a shrug or with varying degrees of assent. Precious few realized that Germany was heading towards a moral bankruptcy of incalculable consequence. A community is by its very nature exclusive, and the Nazis set about removing everything that was 'alien to the community', but for the time being the regime felt it prudent to move somewhat cautiously for fear of economic disruption and foreign reaction.

Hitler had no master plan on how to deal with the 'Jewish question'. Even as late as 1935 he talked of expelling the Jews from the trades and professions and rounding them up in certain areas where the German people could look at them as if they were 'wild beasts'. Quite where these safari parks were to be located remained unspecified. In 1933 the SA had unleashed random acts of 'rowdy anti-Semitism' and chicanery. The boycott in April was a further grim warning of things to come. Within a year 2,000 civil servants had been dismissed and about an equal number of artists forbidden to work. Some 4,000 lawyers were no longer allowed to practise their profession and hundreds of doctors and university professors lost their livelihoods. For the moment Jewish businessmen were needed to help the process of economic recovery, but their days were numbered. Even Jewish agencies recommended leaving the country only if an individual was in extreme personal danger. There were some encouraging signs that things

[104] were quietening down. Hitler may have secured himself a position of virtually absolute power, but he was anxious not to alienate foreign opinion and presented himself as a man of moderation and peace. The elimination of Ernst Röhm and the radicals in the SA was a hopeful sign, and the military, industry and the civil service still had some vestiges of autonomy.

Streicher continued to enjoy Hitler's absolute and unconditional support for his rabidly pornographic and sadistic anti-Semitic campaign. In 1934 copies of his revolting magazine *Der Stürmer*, with hideous caricatures of loathsome Jews luring innocent Aryan children, were exhibited in glass cases throughout the land, with the paper's motto, a quote from the nineteenth-century German historian Treitschke, 'The Jews are our Misfortune', on prominent display. School books parroted similar ominous rubbish. In one such text it was asserted that:

1. The Jewish race is much inferior to the Negro race.
2. All Jews have crooked legs, fat bellies, curly hair, and an untrustworthy look.
3. The Jews are responsible for the World War.
4. They are to blame for the armistice of 1918 and the Treaty of Versailles.
5. They caused the hyperinflation of 1923.
6. They brought about the downfall of the Roman Empire.
7. The Jew Marx is a great criminal.
8. All Jews are Communists.
9. Russia is ruled by Jews.

The sinister fears expressed in such caricatures underlay the Law for the Protection of German Blood and German Honour, otherwise known as the Nuremberg Laws of 15 September 1935. They made marriage, sexual intercourse and 'acts analogous to cohabitation' between Jews and non-Jews criminal offences. Prosecution for 'racial defilement' (*Rassenschande*) enabled the Nazis to invade the intimate lives of ordinary Germans. Jewish men were forbidden to employ Aryan women under the age of 45 as domestic servants. Henceforth only those German citizens who had 'German or similar blood' could enjoy full civil rights. The framers of these laws were at a loss how to define who was Jewish, and after lengthy debate decided that a Jew was someone who had 'three grandparents who were racially full Jews', or a practising Jew with only two Jewish grandparents, or someone with two Jewish grandparents who was married to a Jew. Those with only two Jewish grandparents were labelled 'Jewish half-breeds', but for the time being they still retained their civil rights. Radical anti-Semites thought the Nuremberg Laws were a feeble compromise that allowed far too much Jewish blood to threaten the purity of the Aryan race. For all the talk of Jews as a race, the definition was still based on religious affiliation. It did not occur to the hordes of crackpot racial researchers and skull-measurers that there was no other way. Also in 1935 the Law for the Protection of the Hereditary Health of the German People made it illegal for people with hereditary diseases to marry.

The Nuremberg Laws were generally welcomed inasmuch as anti-Semitism appeared to have been taken off the streets and channelled into the law. The regime now concentrated on the elimination of 'rowdy anti-Semitism' which damaged Germany's image abroad, was bad for business and encouraged lawlessness. Heydrich wrote: 'Rowdy anti-Semitic methods must be stopped. You do not fights rats with a revolver, but with poison and gas.' As early as May 1934 he said that the aim of 'Jewish politics' must be 'to force the whole lot of them to emigrate'. Further encouragement was offered when anti-Semitism was played down during the Berlin Olympic Games of 1936 and the showcases with *Der Stürmer* were temporarily removed. Himmler had to be content with a law in June 1936 forbidding Jews to have such truly German names as Siegfried or Thusnelda. This was not seen as a serious hardship. When the Nazi Party's representative in Switzerland, Wilhelm Gustloff, was murdered by a Jew in Davos, a valuable opportunity to mount another pogrom had to be missed. Goebbels was determined not to let another such chance slip through his hands.

Once the Games were over the persecution of the Jews was ratcheted up another notch. A massive attack on Jewish capital and foreign currency holdings was built into the Four-Year Plan, with Göring giving Heydrich responsibility for such actions. A number of businesses were 'Aryanized', in other words sequestered and sold off to non-Jews at bargain basement prices. By 1938 60 per cent of Jewish business had been confiscated. Jews were also forced to pay special taxes and contributions and those still in business were subjected to an ever-tightening boycott. In April 1938 they were forced to make a full disclosure of their assets. Heavy taxes were levied on émigrés' goods and capital, the tax on capital reaching 96 per cent by September 1939. The seizure of Jewish housing might have disrupted the property market with supply outstripping demand, but huge profits were made from Aryanization that were used to subsidize the rearmament programme. In August Jews were obliged to add the first names Sarah or Israel and their passports were stamped with a 'J'; the latter measure being taken at the request of the Swiss government. German Jews thus lost their individual

[106] identity, which was further emphasized by the Nazi habit of referring to the Jews as 'the Jew'. Jews were excluded from all state contracts, no longer had reduced income tax for children and could not own any type of weapon, and in November 1938 Jewish children were forbidden to attend state schools. Hundreds of other discriminatory measures were enforced nationally and locally that served to exclude Jews from civil society and to make their lives utterly miserable. At the same time emigration was made increasingly difficult because the regime hoped to use rich and famous Jews as hostages.

The fresh wave of radical anti-Semitism in 1938 was particularly virulent in Berlin where Goebbels announced that the capital would soon be 'uncontaminated by Jews' (*Judenrein*). He harangued a meeting of 300 policemen telling them that 'law is not the order of the day, but harassment'. During the summer, synagogues and Jewish shops were ransacked and the appallingly venal police chief, Count von Helldorf, cooperated enthusiastically with Nazi thugs. In addition to ordering his men to make the lives of Berlin's Jews as unpleasant as possible, he amassed a considerable fortune by confiscating the passports of rich Jews and selling them back again for up to 250,000 RM apiece. Later he was to see the writing on the wall, joined the conspirators of 20 July 1944, was arrested, tortured and hanged.

A heavy hint that worse was to come was contained in the SS magazine *Das Schwarze Korps* which announced:

> We must intern all those Jews who are still living in Germany and whom the Jewish element has not provided with regular employment, where we will encourage them to do an honest day's work. We must make sure that all other Jews . . . no longer live together with Germans, under the same roof, in the same street, or in the same district. We must gather them together in areas where their activities can be monitored . . . and lastly we must decide to what extent the fabulous wealth of the Jews in Germany should be used by its owners to ensure a decent and productive existence, and how far it has been squirreled away and denied to the German racial community . . . We must take advantage of these assets and use them to make good the economic damage caused by the bellicose propaganda of world Jewry that has forced us to rearm.

The SD now decided upon a policy of 'orderly harassment' (*geordnetes Schikanieren*). This involved local bans on Jews visiting public parks, theatres, cinemas and the like. With very few exceptions Jews were banned from practising medicine, the law and similar professions. In April 1938 Göring ordered a strict boycott of Jewish businesses so that Jews would be 'completely excluded from the economy' and their wealth help further the [107] Four-Year Plan. This placed the Nazis in something of a bind; on the one hand they wanted the Jews to leave Germany, but on the other they had reduced them to such a state of poverty that precious few could afford the cost of emigration. *Das Schwarze Korps* demanded 'the genuine and final end of Jewry in Germany – its total annihilation'. Brute force now seemed to provide a solution to this dilemma. Here Austria, where there had been an orgy of anti-Semitic violence immediately following the Anschluss in March 1938, provided a worthy example.

On 7 November 1938 Ernst vom Rath, a young diplomat serving in the Germany embassy in Paris, was gunned down by a Polish-German Jew by the name of Herschel Grynszpan. It was an act of revenge for the gross mistreatment of his parents by the Gestapo. They were among the 17,000 Polish Jews who were expelled from Germany in October, but many of them were refused entry by the virulently anti-Semitic Polish government. A few lucky ones managed to emigrate to America; some were allowed into Poland but the remainder were interned. Rath died on 9 November, which was also the anniversary of Hitler's putsch in Munich in 1923, and the party leadership was assembled in the Bavarian capital for the annual celebration of the event. On Hitler's orders Goebbels promptly ordered a 'spontaneous expression of popular outrage', and the Gauleiter let loose the SA who went on a nationwide rampage euphemistically known as the 'Night of Broken Glass' (*Reichskristallnacht*). It was a night of shattered lives and broken hopes in which at least 800 Jews were murdered, 200 synagogues burnt to the ground, 7,500 Jewish stores, apartments and houses ransacked. Thirty thousand Jewish men were arrested and thrown into concentration camps. That same night Heinrich Himmler spoke of a war to the death between Germans and Jews. Schacht was ordered to draw up plans for the expulsion of all Jews from the Reich. Hitler put on an astonishing performance, claiming to be outraged by such vandalism and ordering the police chief of Munich to undertake a thorough investigation. Göring sang from the same hymn sheet, saying that he was opposed to the idea of an indemnity payment by German Jews on the grounds that it would cause an unfavourable reaction abroad.

Insurance adjusters estimated that the damage amounted to 25 billion RM, but the money went to the state rather than to those who had lost their property. In addition a special levy of 1 billion RM was imposed on the Jewish community, as if the destruction had been self-imposed. Such large-scale destruction of private property did not meet with public approbation, but neither was there any protest, and few cared about the suffering

[108] Jews. Silent disapproval for the destruction of private property was the order of the day, but there was considerably less concern for those who had lost their lives and their livelihoods. For the SS this was merely the beginning of a new phase in their campaign against the 'racial enemy'. At tho ond of tho month their official journal *Das Schwarze Korps* published an article calling for the 'real and final end of German Jewry', the 'final extinction' of this 'parasitic race'. On 12 November Göring told a group of senior officials that in the event of war Germany would 'first of all settle accounts with the Jews'. On 21 January 1939 Hitler told the Czech foreign minister Chvalkovsky: 'We shall destroy our Jews.' On 30 January he told his captive audience in the Reichstag that another world war would result in 'the annihilation of the Jewish race in Europe'. Thus the pogrom marked a portentous step towards a 'final solution'.

Until the end of 1937 big business had on the whole protected Jews in senior positions in management or on boards of directors and many Jewish-owned banks continued to do business, but this changed dramatically in 1938. Big banks, such as the Deutsche and Dresdner Banks, seized many a lucrative opportunity to take over Aryanized firms in Austria after the Anschluss. With the November pogrom life for Jews in Germany and Austria became utterly intolerable. Some 175,000 of the 550,000 German Jews in 1933 had emigrated by 1938 and 120,000 followed until the outbreak of war. The *Ostjuden* were deported so that in October 1941, when emigration was finally forbidden, about 163,700 people remained. Of these 15,000 went into hiding, most of whom were helped by non-Jews of exceptional courage and moral stamina, and 13,700 survived the extermination camps. One hundred and thirty thousand German and Austrian Jews emigrated to the United States, 51,000 went to Britain and 47,000 managed to evade the British cordon and get to Palestine. Others made their way to Argentina, Brazil, Chile, Australia and South Africa. The 100,000 who went to neighbouring European states underwent unimaginable suffering and precious few survived the ordeal. Other states were shamefully inhospitable. Canada's record is a national disgrace. Switzerland made sure that few stayed permanently and only 1,700 European Jews were granted residence permits.

When the war began there were 185,000 practising Jews left in Germany along with 18,000–20,000 'Nuremberg Jews', plus a further 60,000–65,000 in Austria and 100,000 in Bohemia and Moravia. Almost two-thirds of the Jews in Germany and Austria were able to escape, but in the case of the Germans they had had several years in which to make the decision. The Jews of occupied Europe had no such opportunity.

Eugenics

The Jews were without doubt the most important element in the National Socialist racist equation and Hitler's abiding pathological obsession, but the 'racial body' had also to be rid of other elements that threatened the purity of its blood by means of 'racial-hygienic special treatment': those with genetically transmittable diseases, the 'asocial' who could never find a place within the 'racial community', a vast range of people classified as 'vermin' (*Schädlingen*) that included the insane, the handicapped, alcoholics, habitual criminals, prostitutes, homosexuals and Gypsies. The National Socialists thus combined eugenics with their own particularly venomous form of anti-Semitism and racism in a truly demonic brew. They decided who was 'normal' and 'healthy' and set out to destroy all those who did not meet their criteria.

Eugenics was very much in vogue in the scientific world and was widely seen as a promising means of improving the general level of public health. 'Scientific genetics' had been founded by Darwin's cousin Sir Francis Galton with the publication of *Hereditary Genius* in 1869, and it was he who cooked up the word 'eugenics'. It was Darwinism stood on its head: decisions were

Figure 3.4 Social cost of caring for people with hereditary diseases

to be made as to who should breed and then a suitable environment was to be created in which the offspring could be raised. It was what Darwin had called 'artificial selection'; the eugenicists replied that 'natural selection' had been suspended in modern society thanks to economic, scientific and medical advances so that the 'breeding stock' had become hopelessly degenerate. Society was now burdened with a horde of degenerates: the insane, alcoholics, the bearers of hereditary diseases, vagrants and criminals – criminality being, according to Cesare Lombroso[17], hereditary. In addition there was an army of what in Britain were known as the 'undeserving poor'. In Germany eugenics was an essential component of the ideology behind Ernst Haeckel's immensely popular Monist League that combined a glorification of the scientific outlook, especially in Darwinism, with hostility to Christianity, a passionately romantic cult of nature, particularly for the German landscape, an optimistic, forward-looking obsession with hygiene and selective breeding as well as an emphasis on the 'leadership principle' based on a cell theory in which each cell is subordinate to the body as a whole, all this rigmarole subsumed under the heading of *Lebensreform*. Such ideas had a widespread appeal. In the United States involuntary sterilization was legal in 28 states, where 45,127 such operations were performed between 1907 and 1945. Eugenics was enthusiastically championed by the social democratic Nobel Prize winner Gunnar Myrdal and his wife Alva, and their confused and ultimately well-meaning speculations on race are far from free of prejudice. In the Supreme Court, Justice Oliver Wendell Holmes suggested that three generations of cretins were enough. Segregation in the Jim Crow South was rigorously enforced, in part because of the fear that black men would have sex with white women. L. Frank Baum, the author of the delightful children's book *The Wizard of Oz* (1900), called for the annihilation of Native Indians. Gunnar Myrdal was not quite so extreme; he simply suggested that the 'Negro problem' could be solved by a drastic reduction in the number of Black Americans.

Eugenics thus sprang from a perverse form of Darwinism that was regarded not only as a cornerstone of modern science but also as a kind of substitute religion. Those who should have been eliminated by natural selection survived, so that the genetic material of the naturally strong and superior was threatened by that of the naturally weak and inferior. From this it followed that those of inferior genetic stock should be prevented from breeding, if necessary by compulsory sterilization, in extreme cases by euthanasia. Medicine should thus not only address the health of the individual, but also that of the entire community. The social order was to be conceptualized in biological terms. It was an anti-egalitarian and elitist theory, in a pseudo-scientific guise that fortunately remained a small, if singularly vociferous, group within the scientific community.

The German Society for Racial Hygiene, formed in 1905 under Alfred Plötz, was the first of its kind in the world. He was an appalling Nordic racist who had a powerful influence on Nazi ideology. Hitler gave him the title of professor, and his brother-in-law and co-editor of the journal *People and Race*, Ernst Rüdin, a psychiatrist who drafted the law on sterilization, said of him: 'His religion was the well-being and the splendour of his race.' In 1920 Karl Binding, a law professor, and the psychiatrist Alfred Hoche finally published a 62-page pamphlet which they had been unable to have printed during the war because of the paper shortage, in which they introduced the noxious concepts of 'life unworthy of life' and 'ballast existences'[18]. Such ideas gained a number of converts after a war in which it was widely believed that the best had been killed, leaving the mediocre in command. With a sharply declining birth rate that could only be offset by immigration there was soon talk of the end of European civilization, cultural decay and the decline of the West. When eugenics became mixed with racial theory this confusion between normative social and cultural values and physical and biological values became deadly dangerous.

There was considerable resistance to these ideas from scientists who rightly saw them as a gross perversion of Darwin's theory of evolution, from the churches, which raised serious moral objections, and from social scientists such as Max Weber who delivered a devastating critique of biological racism. Pius XI condemned the practice of sterilization in his encyclical 'Casti Connubii' of 1930. With Hitler firmly in command as a charismatic leader with an interpretative monopoly of a nauseous worldview that mixed the anti-Semitism of Gobineau, Marr and Lanz von Liebenfels with the crudest forms of social Darwinism and eugenics, all restraints were removed. The race was to be renewed, revitalized, purged of all that threatened it, and strengthened so that the strong and beautiful would emerge triumphant. Eugenics gave a pseudo-scientific seal of approval to racist anti-Semitism as both stood for the purging of the 'racial body' of all that threatened its purity.

From the outset National Socialists demanded the compulsory sterilization of the 'inferior' and Hitler told the party faithful at the 1929 Nuremberg rally that he would not permit 'sentimental silliness' to stand in the way of what he called natural selection. This was all summed up in the widely publicized slogan: 'death for those unworthy of life'. In 1933 the radical racists and eugenicists were given absolute freedom to put their ideas into practice, for they could be certain of enthusiastic support and encouragement

[112]   from on high. The Law for the Prevention of the Birth of Children with Hereditary Diseases was included in a raft of menacing legislation passed on 14 July 1933. This was designed to enable the 'decontamination of the racial body' by means of the compulsory sterilization of 'biologically inferior genetic material', in an operation popularly known as a 'Hitlerean' (*Hitlerschnitt*). It has been estimated that approximately 1 million people fell into this category. An alarmingly high percentage of German doctors supported this measure, and pitifully few had any pangs of conscience over this gross infraction of their Hippocratic oath. The churches remained resolutely silent. This was the first step towards converting doctors into executioners, a transmutation which alarmingly few had the ethical courage to resist.

That such a moral collapse was possible was due in part to the deep-seated anxieties that find expression in such a devil's brew of racism and eugenics. The irrational and obsessive fear of 'the Jew' as an all-pervasive threat, a cancer eating away at the heart of society, a bacterium that had to be destroyed, a defiler of German maidenhood and a cultural parasite was all part of an apocalyptic vision of the decline of Western civilization, the menace of a cacocracy of the inferior, the deviant and the racially undesirable, a dysgenic nightmare of racial demise, which could only be countered by a drastic programme of racial selection and renewal. These manic obsessions were all the more lethal because they were dressed up as science, as a tough-minded response to an imminent medical danger. Biology and race were claimed to be the causes of the manifold social problems confronting an advanced modern state. A robust and unsentimental approach was needed to tackle this key issue.

Doctors immediately set to work implementing the July 1933 law and some 360,000 people were sterilized, the vast majority of whom were women. Two-thirds of these unfortunates were classified as 'racially undesirable'. Approximately 1 per cent of fecund German women were sterilized, and one trembles to think what the figure would have been had Germany won the war. Initially those suffering from such disorders as schizophrenia, epilepsy, manic depression and 'idiocy' were selected for sterilization, but very soon social rather than medical criteria were used. Habitual criminals, alcoholics, prostitutes and tramps fell victim of this extensive campaign for 'racial hygiene'. Sterilization was not enough for the more radical eugenicists. In 1935 the German doctors' leader Gerhard Wagner demanded the 'annihilation of lives that are not worthy of living', but Hitler was not yet prepared to give the green light for the mass murder of the mentally and physically handicapped. His former adjutant, SA-Brigadeführer Fritz

Wiedemann, testified that Hitler had made his intention quite clear that in the event of war he would order the killing of the mentally ill on the grounds that they were 'superfluous eaters'. As soon as the war began all such restraint was removed. SS Einsatzgruppen began murdering the handicapped in Poland along with the Jews and soon boasted of some 90,000 victims. In October Hitler issued instructions to the chief of his private chancellery, Philipp Bouhler, and his personal physician, Dr Karl Brandt, to organize the murder of the mentally ill. This order was pre-dated to 1 September 1939, and the ministry of justice was neither consulted nor informed. Even before 1 September 5,000 handicapped children had been murdered. The programme of what was euphemistically called 'euthanasia' was code-named T4 after the address of Hitler's private chancellery Tiergarten 4 in Berlin. The murders, by either lethal injection or gas, began in April 1940. The bodies were then burnt in special crematoria. The expertise gained in T4 was then used to build gas chambers and crematoria in the concentration camps in Poland, beginning in 1941.

Children were the first victims, adults soon followed and hospitals and nursing homes were combed for Jewish patients. The victims' families were told that they had died of natural causes. A crime of this magnitude could not be concealed from the public. Parents of a child who had already had an appendectomy knew that something was seriously amiss when they were informed that a ruptured appendix was the cause of death. People living near a crematorium soon found out the cause of the oily soot on their windows. Else von Löwis, a party stalwart and senior official in the National Socialist Women's Association, a woman described by Himmler as a 'Nordic goddess rather than a human being', complained bitterly to Walter Buch, the foremost judge in the NSDAP and Bormann's father-in-law, about the killings which included epileptics who were perfectly capable of doing productive work. Himmler called a halt to the killings at the asylum at Grafeneck on 19 December 1940, but the last murder had taken place ten days before because the supply of victims from the surrounding institutions had at last run out. The killers from Grafeneck were then sent to Hadamar, near Limburg, where they carried on with their grisly business. Protests were also lodged with the ministry of justice and the minister, Franz Gürtner, made a timorous objection. He died in January 1941 and his successor Franz Schlegelberger was an enthusiastic supporter of euthanasia. The victims' relatives finally persuaded Bishop Count Clemens August von Galen, bishop of Münster, a conservative nationalist who was by no means unfavourably disposed towards the regime, to speak out against this terrible crime and he did so in a number of widely publicized sermons in July and August 1941.

[114] Bishop von Preysing of Berlin had already denounced euthanasia in a sermon on 9 March 1941 and had received a note from Pius XII praising his courageous stand. On 26 June the German Catholic bishops published a pastoral letter condemning the murder of the innocent. Galen's sermons were certainly audacious, but they were neither the first, nor were they unique. Bishop Mehrens had denounced this evil in far more outspoken terms in a sermon given in Hildesheim on 17 August 1941. Bishop Gröber of Freiburg said that 'euthanasia' was simply another word for murder. Goebbels argued that only idiots believed in the Christian religion, and that it was for this reason that the churches were against euthanasia. Hitler, who did not want to risk a confrontation with the Catholic Church in the middle of a war, ordered Action T4 to stop on 24 August 1941. By this time T4 statisticians estimated that 70,273 people had been killed. The bishops' protests thus came painfully late in the day, and by August 1941 the search for potential victims in Germany was bringing meagre results. The bishops also remained silent over the persecution and murder of the Jews and agreed with Cardinal Bertram of Breslau when he argued that any attempt to stand up for the rights of Jews might 'lead to the worst possible interpretations'. The Evangelical Church had been in favour of euthanasia from the 1920s when a Standing Committee for Racial Protection had been formed. This made it virtually impossible for those Protestants who had serious moral qualms over the practice to find any support from their church.

Action T4 continued in the utmost secrecy, in spite of the 'Führer order', accounting for some 150,000 further deaths. It ran parallel to the murder of Jews, since both were essential parts of the programme for racial regeneration that was at the very core of National Socialism. The question has been hotly debated whether this was all part of what Detlev Peukert called a 'pathological form of the development of modernity'[19]. There were a number of doctors and scientists who genuinely believed that what they were doing was scientifically justified, others furthered their interests by jumping on this particular bandwagon, some seized the opportunity to indulge in their perverted instincts, but the vast majority of those working in various aspects of the medical profession were not involved. They were guilty of turning a blind eye, but they did not actively support this appalling programme of 'hereditary health'. Eugenics may be morally repulsive, but it does at least have some scientific basis. Racial anti-Semitism has absolutely no scientific justification whatsoever, and is merely the age-old hatred of Jews dressed up in a pseudo-scientific guise. National Socialist anti-Semitism and eliminatory eugenics cannot be reduced to being due to the pathology of the modern. They were both to a remarkable degree a

lethal mixture of science and superstition, the rational and the irrational, [115]
the modern and the anti-modern.

The Hitler myth and the racial community

In the six years of peace from 1933 to 1939 Hitler enjoyed an ever-increasing popularity from people in every walk of life. He had promised to overcome the political and economic crises and to restore Germany to its former greatness, and he had fulfilled this promise in a series of startling successes both at home and abroad. Small wonder then that the charismatic leader met with the adulation of his enthralled devotees. There was of course a dark side to the regime. The Social Democrats and Communists had been brutally suppressed; the destruction of Jews and those who did not match the National Socialist criteria for the normal and healthy had already begun in a desperate attempt to build a new society. The arts had been brought under strict government control, basic civil liberties had been suspended and any opposition promptly and brutally suppressed. Yet in spite of all these horrors Hitler's hold over the German people was not based on terror. Germany had not been hijacked by an Austrian villain and his gang of thugs as some apologetic historians have suggested. Hitler was seen as the saviour of the nation from the shackles of Versailles, from the threat of Marxism, from economic misery, from the rowdies within his own ranks, and as the man who had made Germany once again a great power. Here was a figure who was larger than life, comparable to Bismarck or Frederick the Great. Few felt that the destruction of parliamentary democracy, of fundamental freedoms and the rule of law was too high a price to pay. The masses were susceptible to seizures of quasi-religious ecstasy, sinking into a mystical trance in which all critical faculties were numbed. As Dieter Rebentisch has pointed out, leading Nazis saw themselves as part of Hitler himself, joined in a kind of mystical union[20]. It left them blind to the fact that Hitler's charismatic leadership depended on a series of successes, and that for this to continue the stakes had to be raised. The great magician was an obsessive gambler whose only play was, as he himself admitted, '*va banque*'. Success blinded him to the risks involved, megalomania clouded his judgement, and the toadies and yes-men who surrounded him reinforced his sense of omnipotence and omniscience.

It is very difficult for us today to imagine what made this Führer cult so irresistible. Instead of a godlike figure we see in Charlie Chaplin's *Great Dictator* or Brecht's *Arturo Ui*, the saviour of the nation appears as the

[116] embodiment of demonic evil, the mass murderer who led Germany to ruin. How different things were then! At the 1936 party rally, his prestige at a new height after the enormous success of the Berlin Olympic Games, he could tell the rapturous crowds 'It is a miracle of our time that you have found me . . . from among so many millions; and that I have found you – that is Germany's good fortune!' Three years later, during his lavish 50th birthday celebrations, he boasted: 'I have overcome chaos in Germany, have restored order and raised the productivity of all sectors of our national economy.' He then listed his successes in foreign and domestic policy and modestly claimed that he, who 21 years ago was an unknown worker and soldier, had done it alone, with the modest assistance of Providence.

It was not only Germans who fell under his spell. On 17 November 1936 readers of Beaverbrook's *Daily Express* were treated to a paean to Hitler written by Lloyd George. The wartime prime minister wrote:

> The old trust him, the young idolise him. It is not the admiration accorded to a popular leader. It is the worship of a national hero who has saved his country from utter despondency and degradation . . . He is as immune to criticism as the king in a monarchical country. He is something more. He is the George Washington of Germany – the man who won for his country independence from all her oppressors. To those who have not actually seen and sensed the way Hitler reigns over the heart and mind of Germany, this description may appear extravagant. All the same it is the bare truth.

None of this would have been possible had there not been something within Germany's political culture that prepared the ground. There was a widespread longing for a great personality who would solve the problems of a state whose political system had failed and whose economy was in ruins. The answer could only be found in the long-standing Prussian-German tradition of the 'revolution from above'. Germany had suffered a devastating setback to national self-esteem in 1919 and felt bitter, humiliated and frustrated. Hitler, with the brilliant assistance of Goebbels' propaganda, managed to transform himself into the incorporation of Germany, the linch-pin of the 'racial community', the embodiment of national hopes and dreams. In doing so he became destiny's child, born to lead the nation to fresh heights of glory, the head of a quasi-religious movement. In *Mein Kampf* he had stressed the vital importance of 'religious belief' and of 'self-sacrifice' for the success of any political movement. He defined National Socialism as an 'apodictic faith', and as a church, while at the same time mocking the Wotan worshippers and armchair Siegfrieds, the 'charlatans, idiots and imbeciles' in the *völkisch* movements, with their runes and old Germanic names, who wanted to replace Christianity with a Germanic religion. He was to have many a confrontation with Himmler who entertained such hare-brained ideas. It was a matter of some regret to him that his views on racial regeneration ran contrary to his belief in the benefits of celibacy. In *Mein Kampf* he wrote: 'I consider those who establish or destroy a religion far greater than those who establish a state, not to mention a party.' Luther, Calvin, Cromwell and Robespierre were singled out for special praise with Hitler adding: 'We are not a movement. We are a religion.' Shortly before being appointed chancellor Hitler made the following announcement: 'I hereby put forward for myself and my successors in the leadership of the party the claim for political infallibility. I hope the world will grow as accustomed to that claim as it has to that of the Holy Father.' Goebbels insisted that National Socialism was nothing without 'absolute conviction – unconditional faith'. Albert Speer was in full agreement and hoped to build a 'secular cathedral' that would be 'basically a hall of worship' for 'without such a cult significance Hitler's ideas would be meaningless'.

Hitler as the central figure in the National Socialist religion was kept deliberately distant, to the point that there was at times a certain confusion between the earthly leader and the Heavenly Father. This was emphasized by the insistence that always he be addressed as 'Mein Führer', by his elaborate ritual of the Nuremberg party rallies in which he acted as high priest, and by presenting himself publicly as the sexless bachelor with no private life, whose energies were devoted solely to the well-being of his followers. For Goebbels, Hitler was first 'an apostle with a mission' but by 1938 he wrote: 'I trust in him as I do in God.'[21] The French ambassador François-Poncet spoke of the 'almost mystical ecstasy, a kind of holy madness' that took hold of the participants at the annual party rally in Nuremberg[22]. They reminded the American journalist William Shirer of the ecstatic ceremonies of the Holy Rollers, and added that these cultic ceremonies 'had something of the mysticism and religious fervour of an Easter or Christmas mass in a great Gothic cathedral'. He noted that the masses looked up to Hitler 'as if he were a Messiah, their faces transformed'.[23] The British ambassador was less effusive, but it was he who described Albert Speer's lighting effects as creating a 'cathedral of light'. From time to time during peacetime Hitler would mingle with the people on 'Casserole Sundays' and present himself to the adoring crowds and dispense his charisma. National Socialism, like the churches, had its calendar: 30 January was celebrated as the day of the so-called 'seizure of power', a Heroes' Memorial Day was held in March, Hitler's birthday on 20 April was followed by the Day of National Labour on 1 May, which was also Mother's Day. The party rally was held in

[118] September, Harvest Festival in October, and 9 November, the anniversary of the Munich Putsch, was celebrated in the 'movement's capital'. As a concession to the Germanic enthusiasts the solar equinoxes were also celebrated, but in a more modest manner,

Not only Hitler, but also the National Socialist vision of a racial community, had enormous appeal, and with the achievement of full employment it seemed to be much more than a distant utopian vision. Could the class conflicts of the past be replaced by social harmony, all obstacles that stood in the way of the talented be removed, and a class society replaced by a genuine hierarchy based on ability? Could a new society be created in which the communal good (*Gemeinnutz*) took precedence over selfishness (*Eigennutz*), and in which the individualism of bourgeois society would be replaced by a determination to serve the common good? The Communist and Social Democratic notion of the comrade (*Genosse*) was now replaced by the 'racial comrade' (*Volksgenosse*), the Marxist vision of a classless society transformed into the racial community. This was a utopian vision which appealed to many a former Social Democrat and Communist and which had a particular attraction to the young. Birth, wealth or even education no longer seemed to be insuperable barriers to social advancement. New opportunities were opened up for those with the determination and the talent, while the fossilized social structures of the past appeared to be dissolving.

This intoxicating vision of a new Germany under an inspired leader did not appeal merely to idealistic youth or alienated proletarians. Many of Germany's finest minds were similarly affected. Heidegger enthusiastically welcomed the new regime and told his students in Freiburg: 'scientific principles and ideas should not rule your being. Today alone the Führer himself is the future German reality and its law.' The poet Gottfried Benn, a physician and enthusiastic eugenicist, saw the Third Reich as a 'vision of the birth of a new mankind, perhaps the very last grandiose conception of the white race'. Carl Schmitt proclaimed that 'the totality of the political must find its form in the total state' and that any who raised objections or who disregarded its authority should be 'destroyed without consideration'. Schmitt's star pupil, E.R. Huber, soon to become Germany's leading constitutional historian, argued that the Führer's authority was above that of the state. The vast majority of the German intelligentsia joined in this shameful chorus, slavishly placing their enormous prestige in the service of Germany's new masters. Constitutional lawyers hymned the praises of the 'total state' and justified the need for an all-powerful Führer. Precious few paid the consequences of this flagrant betrayal of intellectual honesty and elementary moral decency. When pressed they usually attributed their past mistakes to misplaced youthful idealism.

The ideology of the 'racial community' proved to be a powerful opiate. It was widely believed that barriers to social mobility were being removed, that Germany was fast becoming a classless meritocracy. Those who profited from the changes since 1933 all too easily forgot that in this society of equals some were a great deal more equal than others. Jews and the racially inferior were excluded, as were those thought to be bearers of genetically transmittable diseases. Members of the party and of the SS were in privileged positions, while those who expressed any reservations about the regime were rejected.

Names are often badges of belonging. Before 1933 the name Adolf was relatively common and had no particular ideological significance. Thereafter there was a rush to name the newborn after the Führer, reaching a peak in 1934 when 2.5 per cent of newborns were thus named. Thereafter there was a sharp decline due to Hitler's intervention. He feared that his name was suffering from acute inflation. The bizarre feminine forms of Adolfine and Hitlerike were also banned. Henceforth the faithful preferred the name Horst, after Horst Wessel. This name suffered a drastic decline beginning in the fateful year of 1941. Germanic names for boys such as Berthold, Gerhard, Gundomar, Gunnar, Günther, Hildorf, Holger, Lars, Olaf, Otto, Sven, Volker and Volprecht were greatly favoured, as were Adelheid, Berta, Brunhilde, Elfrun, Gerburg, Gisela, Gudrun, Irmgard, Reglindis and Sigrun for girls. Aryans were not forced to give their children any such mildly preposterous names and names such as Karl, Thomas and Peter, or Elisabeth, Johanna and Maria, were still common. After Stalingrad there was a marked decline in the adoption of Germanic names – a clear sign that the ideology was wearing thin and the 'racial community' falling apart.

The Germany of 1933 was still very much a class society in which certain sectors enjoyed special privileges. Although many German historians argue that the country was exceptionally and excessively retrograde in this respect, and that the political and social structure was chronically out of phase with an advanced industrial economy, there is no evidence that Germany was substantially different in this respect from a country such as Britain or France. National Socialism was not a necessary response to such over-determination, but Germany's was a society in which the call for a 'racial community' met with an eager response from those who found the way forward blocked by outmoded and unjustifiable social barriers. It was a situation that was further exacerbated by the depression, which left a whole generation of graduates with no prospect of a career commensurate with

[120] their training, and millions of desperate workers without a job. The National Socialist party was a youthful party, with a youthful dynamism and appeal. In 1933 Hitler at 44 was something of an elder statesman. He was a demagogue of genius who was able to transmit his absolute conviction in the attainability of his lofty goals, thus confirming Nietzsche's adage that people believe in the truth of all that is seen to be strongly believed. The mobilization of this yearning for renewal, for change and for a more equal society was something of a mixed blessing. It was the most powerful factor behind mass support for the NSDAP, but it was also the cause of a serious friction within the party between the rowdies in the SA with their demand for a 'second revolution', and those whom they denounced as 'reactionaries' and 'tin gods' (*Bonzen*). Furthermore, by unleashing a social-Darwinian struggle in which only the fittest among the 'racial comrades' would reach the top, a premium was placed on brutal egoism and moral blindness. This may have been welcomed by many as a break away from outmoded hierarchical structures and conventions, as a death blow to fossilized class society, and as an opportunity to give way to their resentments, but it also amounted to a frontal attack on normative moral values as the authority of parents, schools and the churches was undermined by the imperatives of 'racial common sense' (*gesunde Volksempfinden*) and the Führer's will. The 'racial community' was in constant danger of degenerating into a corrupt free-for-all.

The RSHA was the nerve centre of Nazi tyranny and its staff was typical of the new elite. Most of its members were born around 1905, most had studied at university and many had doctorates. Nearly all bordered on the fanatical in ideological fervour, although there were differences between them over quite what it all meant. None allowed moral scruples to stand in the way of their meteoric careers. The Nazis certainly provided jobs for the boys. There were 700,000 in party employ, 44,500 in the DAF, and tens of thousands more in the various party organizations such as those for women, youth and welfare. None of this amounted to a major change in the social structure. One-third of the officers in the Waffen-SS came from the aristocracy and the upper-middle class, which made it little different from the officer corps of the regular army. As in the case of the RSHA, most of them had university degrees, one third of whom were fully-fledged lawyers. In industry the boss was still very much the boss, but the DAF made him march alongside the employees on 1 May, which misled many a working man into believing that he had been pulled down a peg or two. The leisure-time activities offered by KdF were greatly appreciated, as were the improved facilities provided at the workplace thanks to the efforts of the DAF. This illusion of social equality was enhanced by the compulsory year of labour service which in theory was incumbent on all but which the better-placed could easily avoid. The charitable Winter Help (WHW) for needy 'racial comrades' collected 2.5 billion RM between 1933 and 1939, although it was virtually impossible to avoid contributing. The funds were used for all manner of dubious purposes but it was a concrete expression of solidarity with the less fortunate, as were the 16 million volunteers in the NSV. Hitler presented himself, at least in peacetime, as a leader who did not disguise his humble origins, who was close to his people and who had not lost the common touch. The 'racial community' was certainly not all that it was made out to be, but it was also a great deal more than a myth or an illusion.

Those who were comfortably within the bosom of the 'racial community' benefited enormously in the years between 1933 and 1939, and many who lived through these times looked back on them as golden years. It required exceptional moral blindness and an unflinching egocentrism to enjoy fully the benefits that National Socialism offered, but even those who had serious doubts and misgivings had to admit that life had improved. An extraordinary energy had been released, but very few realized that this social-Darwinian free-for-all, this endless struggle over who had authority over whom, and the hectic quest for new goals, meant that the regime could never settle down and attain a degree of stable normality, and was driven by an inner dynamic to risk all in a desperate gamble which led to its total destruction.

CHAPTER 4

REORDERING SOCIETY
AND THE ECONOMY

The National Socialist State

From the very outset of his political career Hitler stressed the importance of the 'social question', which by 1933 primarily meant unemployment. He knew full well that the popularity of the regime depended on how successful he was in tackling this key issue. Yet while striving to maximize employment he was determined also to address a number of other key issues. First and foremost, with his primitive neo-mercantilist notions and his reliance on what David Henderson, former chief economist at the World Bank, has called 'do it yourself economics'[1], he hoped to make Germany as free as possible from dependence on imports, the ideal situation being one of complete autarky. He was determined to rearm rapidly, even at the cost of economic efficiency and growth. Lastly he never lost sight of his goal of conquering 'living space' (*Lebensraum*) in the east, for which he needed the armaments and by means of which he hoped to achieve the highest possible degree of autarky. In 1931 he told his economic adviser Otto Wagener, head of the NSDAP's economics department, that Germany needed Russia's grain, meat, wood, coal, iron and oil in order to be able to take on the USA. *Lebensraum* meant different things to different people. For Himmler and like-minded Nazi ideologues it involved atavistic dreams of rugged settler colonies, a quasi-religious order braving the harsh elements and breeding a new race of racially pure ascetics. For Hitler this would be Germany's India in which a handful of the racially superior would exploit the natural resources, industrial potential and agricultural produce for the benefit of the master race. An economically independent Germany could then make its bid for world power.

In 1933 Hjalmar Schacht, who had played a major role in the intrigues that brought Hitler to power, was the key figure. He was brought back as Reichsbank president, in 1934 was made minister of economics and in the

following year was appointed Plenipotentiary for Wartime Economics.
He had been brought up in the United States, had excellent connections
throughout the world of international finance, and was widely admired as
the financial wizard who had overcome the hyperinflation of 1923 and
stabilized the mark. A man with such a background and with such extensive
powers did much to promote the erroneous notion in left-wing circles that
in Nazi Germany it was the capitalists that called the shots and had the
party at their beck and call.

Schacht was a Keynesian who set about stimulating the economy by a
dose of deficit spending, while at the same time keeping a close watch
on inflation. Rearmament was financed in large part by an ingenious
scheme cooked up by Wilhelm Lautenbach, a senior official in the ministry
of economics. In May 1933 four large companies, Krupp, Siemens, the
Gutehoffnungshütte and Rheinmetall, pooled their resources and formed
the Metallurgical Research Establishment (Mefo) with a capital of 1,000
million RM. The government paid for armaments orders given to these
four companies with five-year promissory notes, guaranteed by the government, and known as Mefo bills. The government then discounted them, so
that the Mefo bills acted as a form of currency. Mefo bills worth thousands
of millions of Reichsmarks thus fell due in 1938 and the government took
recourse to highly dubious methods in order to pay the bill. Tax relief was
offered in lieu of payment, banks were forced to buy government bonds,
and the government took money from savings accounts and insurance
policies. By 1937 inflation was getting out of hand and the central bank
was no longer able to control the volume of money in circulation, so that the
government used the printing press to meet the cash shortage. In February
that year the Reichsbank lost its independence from the government, which
had been guaranteed by law in 1924, and now took its marching orders
from Hitler. A new Reichsbank law of June 1939 placed the Reichsbank's
board of directors directly under the Führer's control, so that Hitler now
had his hand on the printing press and restraint was cast to the winds. The
amount of money in circulation increased from 5.7 billion RM in 1933 to
14.5 billion in 1939. By 1945 it had reached 56.7 billion. Hitler scorned
any attempt to address this catastrophic situation, saying: 'money should
play no role whatsoever. Guns decide in a crisis situation, not whether bills
of exchange are covered or not.'

Foreign trade was strictly regulated by Schacht's Four-Year Plan of 1934.
The Office of the Four-Year Plan was created with exceptional powers to
coordinate the various ministries and organizations that were responsible
for different aspects of the economy. Stringent controls were imposed on

[124] foreign exchange and prices, imports were drastically reduced and the reserves of foreign currency correspondingly improved. Exchange controls are typical of totalitarian regimes because they make it virtually impossible for the average citizen to travel abroad, or to import foreign books critical of the regime. Capital was funnelled into the armaments industry and denied to sectors of industry deemed to be of secondary importance to the achievement of Hitler's goals. The first steps to achieving the highest possible degree of independence from foreign supplies of raw material were made as early as 1933 when planning went ahead for massive investment in the chemical combine IG Farben to manufacture synthetic motor fuel and rubber.

In spite of all these efforts the economy was soon in serious difficulties. A sharp increase in the importation of iron ore needed for the armaments programme, which was already in high gear, caused a major crisis in foreign exchange and fuelled inflation. Agricultural production was unable to keep up with demand and the serious problem of food shortages could no longer be ignored. In December 1936 Goebbels was told that the food situation was already 'serious' and that there would be severe shortages by the following May. Germany could not afford both guns and butter so that Schacht called for fiscal responsibility, while Göring and the generals refused to make any modification to their extravagant plans.

Hitler had already addressed this problem in August 1936 in a memorandum in which he gave the military priority. He announced that the country had to be ready for war by 1940 and therefore the economy should already be placed on a wartime footing. He offered no suggestions as to how this should be achieved, simply reverting to his old formula that 'fanatical will-power' would overcome all obstacles. A new Four-Year Plan was launched in the following month. For Hitler this was the introduction of a planned economy (*Planwirtschaft*), a cross between unbridled capitalism and a Soviet command economy. It was to place the 'common good' above 'self-interest' (*Gemeinnutz vor Eigennutz*) and as such was designed to reinforce the sense of 'racial community'. Schacht's powers were greatly reduced and General Georg Thomas, head of the army's armaments department, was given exceptional powers as Commissioner for the Four-Year Plan. Göring was put in charge of the Four-Year Plan, thus eclipsing Schacht, and he promptly appointed a Reich Commissioner for Raw Materials and Foreign Exchange to underline the point. Göring's quasi-ministry grew rapidly and soon employed more than a thousand people, most of whom came with practical experience in industry or the military, rather than party hacks. Schacht lost the economics ministry in 1937, but stayed on as president of the Reichsbank until 1939. He continued on as minister without portfolio until 1943, an empty office since the cabinet never met. This proved to be a stroke of good fortune as he was acquitted by the Nuremberg tribunal and resumed a lucrative career after the war. Göring was briefly appointed minister of economics on Schacht's departure, with the result that the Four-Year Plan and the ministry of economics were to all intents and purposes amalgamated, and the ministry became the executive organ of the Plan. None of this did anything to solve the fundamental problems caused by forced rearmament, and in July 1937 Goebbels noted that the shortage of foreign exchange and raw materials was 'serious' and he was obliged drastically to slow down the building of a new radio station in Berlin.

Economic planning in Nazi Germany was typical of the Nazi polycracy, where ministries overlapped and competed, where state and private inter-twined and where much of the work was done by special plenipotentiaries with their 'work groups'. Karl Krauch provides a paradigmatic example of the new type of manager-bureaucrat. He joined IG Farben's board of directors in 1926. Göring called upon him for advice, and in 1938 appointed him Plenipotentiary for the Chemical Industry and head of the Office of Economic Expansion in the Four-Year Plan. He became chairman of IG Farben's board in 1940, and thus until 1945 was head both of Europe's largest chemicals company, the manufacturer of Zyklon-B, and of the state board of control over the industry. Similar dual positions were held by Paul Pleiger, founder of a major engineering company, whom Göring placed in charge of the coal sector and who, along with Krupp, became the only industrialists condemned at Nuremberg for exploiting slave labour. Pleiger's close friend, Hans Kehrl, was a textile manufacturer from Lausitz who was given leading positions in the Four-Year Plan, the Hermann Göring Works and the ministry of munitions. He was also a brigadier-general in the SS and the man responsible for the disposal of the clothing of murdered Jews. Such cases did not result in the submission of the state to the requirements of monopoly capitalism as in Marxist-Leninist mythology, but did mean that the state paid due attention to industry's needs and wishes, while at the same time the state's control over industry was tightened. IG Farben for example prospered, but at the cost of becoming partially nationalized.

As a result of all this confusion there was a series of ad hoc measures rather than an overall plan, with impossible demands being made, such as Hitler's order in November 1938 that the production of armaments should increase threefold. It is truly amazing that so much was achieved during what Richard Overy has judiciously called the 'era of incompetence' before the war economy came under rigorous control, resulting in crippling costs

[126] as well as a horrendous waste of time and effort[2]. Vast amounts of labour and manpower were squandered on mammoth projects such as the West Wall, a largely pointless line of defences against France that employed 400,000 men, consumed a third of the steel allocated for the armed forces and used up 130,000 hectares of valuable agricultural land, thus making autarky an ever remoter prospect. A further major problem was the incessant inter-service rivalry, with Göring favouring his Luftwaffe, and the army and navy struggling to get their fair slice of the cake. The squabbles and rivalries inherent in the Nazi system were such that General Thomas despairingly described the Four-Year Plan as a 'free-for-all'.

There was a long tradition in Germany of what Schacht called 'economic steering' (*Wirtschaftslenkung*). The Reich Statistical Office had been founded in 1872, and from 1924 had been led by an exceptionally talented economist, Ernst Wagemann. By the 1930s it had 2,800 employees at a time when the Soviet planning agency Gosplan had only 400. The German economy had been strictly controlled during the war, and it was widely felt that there were many useful lessons to be learnt that would be valuable in peacetime. Lenin was greatly impressed by German wartime planning, and in turn many German economists felt that there was much to be learnt from the Soviet Union. The Institute for Business Cycle Research, founded in 1925, was based on the work of the brilliant young Soviet economist Kondratiev, who was soon to fall foul of the regime and was murdered in the purges. The Latvian economist Karl Ballod's *The State of the Future*, which was full of praise of the Soviet experiment, was highly regarded[3]. The Nazi economy suffered from all the shortcomings inherent in a dirigiste economy. Credit rationing, price controls and resource allocation involved excessive red tape. The emphasis on investment and armaments rather than exports and consumption led to a chronic lack of foreign exchange, a growing disparity between rich and poor and a crippling deficit. The Reich finances had a modest surplus in 1932, thanks to Brüning's penny-pinching policies. They had a minus of 796 million RM in 1933 and 9.5 billion RM in 1938. The pursuit of autarky was economic madness, although it must be said that at a time of mounting protectionism and shrinking world trade, with a relentless disintegration into national markets and beggar-thy-neighbour trade policies, it did not appear to be quite so grotesque as it does to most of us today, apart from a few out of this world anti-globalizers. National Socialists were by no means alone in ignoring David Ricardo's notion of 'comparative advantage', one of the most brilliant ideas in economics[4], but then had they known of it they would have dismissed it as 'Jewish'. On the other hand, Ricardo had also argued that world trade could not expand indefinitely, and this had made him Rosa Luxemburg's favourite [127] economist, whose ideas she borrowed for her theory of imperialism, which in turn was largely endorsed by Bukharin. Werner Sombart in his influential book *The Future of Capitalism*[5] had preached the 'law of the falling rate of exports', and the revolutionary conservative Ferdinand Fried, editor of the journal *Action* (*Die Tat*), warned of 'The End of Capitalism'. Once again the extremes of left and right were in broad theoretical agreement. The liberal market economy was on its last legs, and massive state intervention was essential. There was also the heavy burden of a history of protectionism in Germany that dated back to 1879 when Bismarck turned his back on a liberal trade policy and caved in to special interests. That the Nazi economy achieved as much as it did is largely due to the efforts of highly professional civil servants like Erich Neumann, who was in charge of all matters pertaining to foreign exchange in the Four-Year Plan, and Friedrich Gramsch, another senior official in Göring's economic empire. These were certainly not apolitical bureaucrats. Neumann, who was an honorary SS-Oberführer, took part in the Wannsee Conference. Gramsch was put in charge of fencing stolen property in the east.

The armaments programme resulted in a dramatic reduction of investment in the consumer goods industry, which fell from 34.3 per cent of industrial investment in 1928 to 18.9 per cent in 1938. Hitler, however, was insistent that both guns and butter should be produced, with the result that Germany never achieved a level of armaments sufficient in depth for the realization of his long-term goals. Nevertheless, right from the very beginning Hitler insisted on the absolute priority of making Germany 'once again ready for war' (*Wiederwehrhaftmachung*). Given that this would involve a complete repudiation of the armaments clauses of the Treaty of Versailles the political risk was very high. Since the cost of this preparation for war rose from 1.5 per cent of gross national product to 23 per cent, the financial burden was staggering. Only half the cost could be covered by fiscal means, and the use of Mefo bills was getting so out of hand that when they matured in 1938 there were no new issues. Henceforth the government went so heavily into debt as to be effectively insolvent. It was a situation that could only be remedied by starting all over again with the introduction of the Deutschmark in 1948.

A remarkable degree of self-sufficiency was achieved. IG Farben's Leuna and Buna works produced impressive quantities of gasoline substitute and artificial rubber. Domestic supplies of ores were increased substantially, and Germany led the world in the production of aluminium until it was overtaken by the United States in 1938. Once again this was all at a staggering

[128]   cost. The state-owned Hermann Göring Works at Salzgitter, managed by Paul Pleiger, mined inferior quality German iron ore in an attempt to reduce dependence on imports that required foreign exchange, but with total disregard for the incredible expense involved. The Leuna and Buna works likewise consumed astronomic amounts of capital. A substantial proportion of these costs were offset by the confiscation of Jewish property, euphemistically called 'Aryanization'. The Hermann Göring Works seized 30 Jewish-owned industrial plants in Austria, including iron ore deposits that were more economical to mine than those at Salzgitter. This plunder continued with the occupation of Bohemia and Moravia, and Pleiger's men followed like jackals behind the victorious Wehrmacht, thus building up a vast industrial empire. By 1940 the Hermann Göring Works was the largest industrial combine in Europe with 600,000 employees.

Agriculture

State intervention in industry, although substantial, pales behind the restructuring of agriculture. National Socialist ideology proclaimed that the German peasant was the pure source of true Aryan blood and as such had to be protected from the exigencies of the market and privileged as a new racial aristocracy to be called National Farmers (*Nährstand der Nation*). Walther Darré, whose head was filled with all manner of racist rubbish, was the high priest of 'blood and soil', and his friend Heinrich Himmler shared his utopian romantic vision. The German peasantry was much taken by this flattering attention, having felt abandoned by the Weimar Republic, and provided substantial support for the Nazis on their way to power. Hitler did not have much time for such hogwash, but he was determined that agriculture should be given every assistance in making Germany self-sufficient so that the appalling hunger of the war years would be avoided in a future war. All the agricultural organizations and associations fell prey to *Gleichschaltung* and were forced into Darré's empire. Some 40,000 agricultural cooperatives were also absorbed. In May 1933 Darré was given the imposing title of Reich Farmers' Leader (*Reichsbauernführer*), and in the following month became minister of food. Although a man of exceedingly mediocre ability, he had thus accumulated a combination of party, state and professional offices that only Göring could match.

All of Germany's 17 million farmers and peasants were forced to join the Reich Farmers' Association (*Reichsnährstand*), which controlled the prices, production and marketing of all foodstuffs. It was a vast bureaucratic apparatus with autocratic farmers' leaders (*Bauernführer*) at various levels down to the smallest village. They were soon locked in battle with the local party officials over their respective areas of competence. The Reich Farmers' Association had its own courts that could impose fines. In accordance with the ideology of 'blood and soil' 1 million hereditary farms (*Erbhöfe*) were created. They were between 75 and 125 hectares (185 to 309 acres), they could not be sold or divided, were to be inherited by the eldest son, and remained under close government control. Only those who could demonstrate generations of racial purity, who were known to be 'honourable' men and who were efficient farmers, qualified for a hereditary farm. Such men were known as 'farmers' (*Bauern*), whereas those who did not meet these stringent criteria were somewhat condescendingly labelled 'agriculturists' (*Landwirte*).

Thirty-seven per cent of all agricultural land was in these hereditary farms by 1939 and the rest could not be bought or sold without special permission. Agricultural land could not be used as collateral for loans, so there was a desperate shortage of capital that made modernization nigh-on impossible. The younger children of hereditary farmers had to be given compensation, thus adding an additional burden. Soon it became apparent that farmers were subjected to a new form of serfdom. The landowning aristocracy still had a powerful lobby in government and in the upper echelons of the officer corps and were excluded from Darré's programme, so that a long overdue programme of land reform was once again postponed. Movement away from the land became a serious problem as the economy recovered and the prospect of better-paid jobs lured workers to the urban areas. Half a million peasants had left the land by 1938. This meant that those who stayed on the land were obliged to work even harder, and the increases in agricultural production between 1933 and 1939 were due almost entirely to the intensification of human labour. Peasants were given a helping hand by the Hitler Youth, the League of German Maidens and the Labour Front, but this in no way offset the chronic loss of manpower. Farmers spent substantial sums on new machinery, but German agriculture remained seriously under-mechanized.

Poor crops in 1934 and 1935 coupled with the red tape and the incompetence of Darré's inflated bureaucracy led to serious food shortages. In 1935 fats had to be put on ration. The situation improved when a trade agreement with Poland was signed later in the year and rationing was lifted, but this brought only temporary relief. By the following year the situation was once again critical. Darré was clearly inept and had to hand over his authority to his secretary of state, Herbert Backe, who was also a

[130] blood-and-soil ideologue but a man better versed in the infighting that prevailed in Nazi Germany. Part of Darré's empire now fell under the aegis of Göring's Four-Year Plan, with Backe in command. Darré finally resigned in 1940 and Backe renamed what was left of the organization the Reich Office for Countrymen. It was an entirely spurious and powerless organization. After Darré's deposition agriculture was controlled by Göring, then by Todt and finally by Speer. Backe's principal contribution was to plan the death by starvation of millions of Soviet citizens. He committed suicide while in jail at Nuremberg.

Agriculture was the sector of the economy most affected by National Socialist ideology. Extravagant promises were made that new farmland would be made available for those peasant farmers who had lost their land to the hereditary farms, and for the siblings of hereditary farmers, but precious little was achieved. Seven million hectares were selected for agricultural consolidation, but in fact only 70,000 hectares were converted. The amount of barren land brought under cultivation was 536,000 hectares, but 650,000 hectares of agricultural land were lost to motorways and training grounds for the military. The Weimar Republic provided 57,300 new farm jobs, whereas the Nazis managed to open up only 22,000 positions, and the flight from the land continued unabated.

Under such circumstances it is truly remarkable that agricultural production increased as much as it did, although there were chronic food shortages and Germany was never able to achieve self-sufficiency. Coffee and fruits were rationed in early 1939, white bread was only available with a medical certificate, coal was rationed and metals were collected with saucepans turned into aircraft. Precious few workers in Germany's industrial heartland could afford meat more than once a week. Visitors from Stanley Baldwin's Britain were appalled at such grim austerity. Such improvements as were achieved were due almost entirely to working longer hours, the intensification of labour and the exploitation of women. Wages were far lower in agriculture than in industry, rose far more slowly and were based on a 12-hour rather than an 8-hour day. The majority of German farmers lived in poverty and most were still on smallholdings, many of which provided insufficient income to feed a family so that the farmer had to top up his income with other work. Many farms had no running water and were without electricity. Precious few could afford a tractor.

In spite of ambitious plans to overcome the yawning gap between town and country, to overcome what Karl Marx called the 'idiocy of rural life' and turn ignorant peasants into valuable 'racial comrades', to abolish the smallholdings and create a race of well-trained and efficient farmers of impeccable racial stock on large and productive farms, precious little was [131] achieved. The most exotic of such plans were drawn up under the aegis of Konrad Meyer, an expert in regional planning and a prime example of a highly efficient and knowledgeable technocrat who was also a fanatical National Socialist, murderous racist and 'blood-and-soil' fanatic. His best known plan, General Plan East, the first version of which dates from February 1940, envisaged the 'evacuation' of all Jews from Poland, along with 3.4 million Poles, and settling 3,345,000 German farmers in the east, most of whom would have to come from the 'Old Reich'[6] as there were not enough people of pure German stock in the east. Meyer then called for the 'transfer', in other words murder, of 34 million Slavs to make way for these settlers. He also drew up plans for the Old Reich, which involved abolishing all smallholdings and a large-scale land reform, plus a consequential programme for the 'racial improvement' of the rural population. It was a plan that combined a perfectly justifiable need to improve agricultural productivity by doing away with holdings that were not economically viable, with perverted racist eugenics, war, plunder and mass murder. After the war Konrad Meyer was obliged to take time out until he was appointed professor for regional planning in Hanover in 1957.

Small business

On their way to power the Nazis made extravagant promises to the craftsmen and artisans, the butchers, bakers and candlestick makers, whom they claimed were the backbone of a healthy economy and whom they were to protect against the cartels and monopolies, the big department stores and the insatiable banks which imposed the 'thraldom of interest' on the little man. The host of Hitler's supporters from this class were much encouraged in the early months of his chancellorship. A boycott was imposed on Jewish-owned department stores. The opening of new branches of such stores was forbidden, and more stringent conditions were placed on the foundation of new enterprises. Life was made so hard for the chain stores that within a few months some were threatened with bankruptcy. By June 1933 the Hertie chain was on the brink of collapse and 14,000 employees were about to lose their jobs. The government with its commitment to overcome unemployment could not afford to allow this to happen, and Hitler reluctantly agreed to bale out the company.

The rescue operation for Hertie marked a critical change in policy towards what was called the 'old middle class', which was also tied in to

[132]   the offensive against the SA which is described in detail later. Their interests were furthered by the National Socialist Commercial Middle-Class
Fighting Group under Adrian von Renteln, who was one of the key figures
in organizing the boycott of Jewish stores along with the SA. When the
boycott was called off Renteln was reined in, and the Fighting Group was
absorbed by the DAF and ceased to have any influence. Renteln was made
head of the German Chamber of Commerce as well as holding a number
of other important offices, but was firmly under the control of the DAF.
During the war he gave vent to his frustrations as Commissar in Lithuania
where he was directly responsible for the deaths of 20,000 Jews in Kovno.
Captured by the Russians he was executed in 1946.

The chain stores' share of total sales steadily increased after 1933 and
in 1940 an additional tax on them was lifted. Correspondingly the number
of smaller stores decreased rapidly. The same was true of the artisanal trades,
which were brought under strict government control. By the outbreak
of war 180,000 small enterprises and workshops had been closed down
in the interests of rationalization and modernization. Hitler's most enthusiastic initial supporters thus paid a heavy price for the forced rearmament
programme.

Contradictions within National Socialism

In spite of these problems in all sectors of the economy, the vast majority
of Germans felt that the regime's economic record was nothing short of
miraculous. In place of 8 million unemployed there was now full employment. No other advanced industrial country recovered from the effects of
the depression with such dynamic speed. The record was so impressive that
few realized that it had been achieved at a crippling cost. Vast amounts
of capital had been squandered on rearmament and on an economically
senseless autarky programme. By 1939 the currency was worthless and the
system could only continue with deficit financing on a staggering scale,
by sequestering Jewish property and by the exportation of inflation to the
occupied countries. Perhaps most dangerous of all was the fact that Hitler's
passionate engagement in job creation, and his fervent celebration of the
victory in the 'battle for employment', further enhanced his position as the
charismatic Führer in whom his followers could have blind faith.

There was a profound contradiction within National Socialism between
the romantic visionaries of 'blood and soil' and the technocrats involved in
building Germany's war machine; between those who wanted to return to

an economy dominated by craftsmen from Wagner's *Meistersinger* and those [133] like Schacht who argued that you could not build tanks and submarines with spinning wheels and folk dancing. It was a fundamental distinction between the exigencies of the efficient and the modern, and wild dystopian dreams. Wherever the bizarre ideas of the likes of Himmler and Darré were put into practice the result was a disaster. The imposition of a neo-feudal order on agriculture resulted in a steep decline of this sector and the absurd attempts to make Germany once again an agricultural society were doomed to failure. Himmler's exotic schemes for populating the 'Eastern Space' (*Ostraum*), which would have entailed murdering 30 million Slavs and converting 14 million 'racially valuable' Ukrainians and Balts into helots for 4.5 million 'armed farmers' (*Wehrbauern*), were further evidence of a complete refusal to face reality. Hitler had precious little sympathy for such anachronistic notions and was far more interested in the economic potential of the Eastern Space than in returning to the days of the Teutonic Knights. Similarly, he thought Himmler's obsessions with Germanic gods and rites, with the search for Atlantis or the Holy Grail, childishly absurd. On the other hand he felt that the Reichsführer's pitiless and murderous policies in the east might well help him realize his plans. Where National Socialist madness was combined with ruthless German efficiency the results were unimaginably horrific, as in the murder of 6 million Jews and millions of others in Eastern Europe and the Soviet Union.

The Third Reich undoubtedly marked a profound change in the political system, in ideology and mentalities, even though there was much in Germany's history that made such changes possible, but in terms of social structure the break was far less abrupt. The first major impact of the regime on the bourgeoisie was the exclusion of all Jews from its ranks. Those who were not affected by this discrimination were either indifferent, or delighted to see the removal of a group which was widely regarded as 'pushy'. The bourgeoisie stood passively by as Social Democrats and others who were less than sympathetic to tyranny were hounded out of office. The destruction of the rule of law, the very foundation of bourgeois society, was passively accepted. Judges and lawyers outbid one another to interpret the Führer's will and make their reading of 'racial common sense' the basis of their rulings. Few seemed to comprehend the anti-bourgeois thrust of Nazi ideology and either distanced themselves in snobbish isolation from the brown-shirted guttersnipes, or wholeheartedly embraced the ideology of the 'racial community'. All this amounted to a shameful betrayal of the lofty ideals of bourgeois society. The free and committed citizen, actively participating in the political process, respectful of legal norms,

[134] mindful of individual rights and freedoms, cast all aside in submission to a charismatic Führer. Academic freedom in research and teaching, the priceless heritage of the German enlightenment, was rejected in favour of racist pseudo science und *völkisch* twaddle. The passive abandonment of hard-won freedoms, the shameful capitulation before a state-sponsored anti-feminism, the appalling acceptance of the exclusion, persecution and murder of minorities, amounted to the moral bankruptcy of a class on whose values modern society was based.

Industrialists, bankers and businessmen longed for an authoritarian solution to the manifold problems that beset the Weimar Republic, and were delighted that the left had been silenced and the unions destroyed. They were indifferent to the fate of their Jewish competitors, associates and lawyers. They profited substantially from the economic upswing, with full employment and consumer confidence high. Average real wages for workers never reached the pre-1929 level even though per capita gross national product rose by 75 per cent between 1933 and 1939. During that same peacetime period the real income of the average entrepreneur rose by a staggering 130 per cent – a cruel comment on the economic reality behind all the nonsense about the 'racial community'. Theoretical collectivism was converted into meritocracy with a Nazified form of Stakhanovism[7] in the Reich Trades Competition held annually to encourage increased productivity. The hero, whether labourer, inventor or industrialist, was emphasized at the expense of the community. Once again semantics disguised reality as when Hitler announced that the German word for economics (*Volkswirtschaft*) implied that it was an 'economy for the people', the material underpinning of the 'racial community'.

National consensus

Apart from a few thousand Jews among their numbers, the captains of industry and top management were virtually unaffected by the change of regime, and the vast majority of them kept their positions after 1945. Most of this economic elite was university educated, and most had doctorates. About 10 per cent came from the working class and had worked their way up from the very bottom. It was a largely self-perpetuating elite, with selection based on nepotism rather than ability. They managed to exclude Nazi hacks from their boards of directors, and were left pretty much to their own devices within their own enterprises. The only somewhat eccentric exception among the Aryan industrial magnates was Fritz Thyssen, who was the only member of the Reichstag to oppose the declaration of war in [135] 1939. He emigrated, bitterly disappointed with a regime he had helped to finance, and his vast steel empire was absorbed by the Hermann Göring Works. Younger recruits to the elite came from much the same background and were easily absorbed, quickly affecting the manners, habits and tastes of their older colleagues. Although they ruled supreme as Works' Leaders (*Betriebsführer*) they were largely dependent on political decisions for the allocation of capital, raw materials and labour, but with substantial profits and a free hand in their own enterprises they were easily able to convince themselves that they were indeed their own bosses.

The educated middle class had suffered terribly during the war, in the hyperinflation that followed it and during the depression. They hoped to win back much of their privileged status in an authoritarian, ultra-nationalistic state and within the much vaunted 'racial community'. In fact they were bitterly disappointed. By 1939 the upper echelons of the civil service were not even close to having the real purchasing power they had in 1928. Two thousand Jews among them lost their jobs, and although that was accepted without a murmur, some found an elaborate question-naire to test their loyalty highly insulting. They lost much of their power and influence and became the silent executants of a dictatorship. Traditional institutions, such as the foreign office, were often disregarded, their work done by special commissions, party organizations or impulsive deci-sions from on high. Their status was uncertain in a polycracy with its indeterminate chain of command, the only constant being the unchallenged power of the almighty Führer. Although bureaucratic routine was upset by Nazi improvisation, the civil service mushroomed. Within ten years the number of permanent officials increased from 750,000 to 1,298,000 and those in lowlier employ from 170,000 to 724,000. This resulted in a water-ing down that further diminished the status of a class of which Hitler was deeply suspicious and openly contemptuous.

Lawyers did well under the new regime. Some 4,000 Jewish lawyers were forbidden to practise, their clients promptly snapped up by their Aryan colleagues. Various paralegals were outlawed, so that all legal matters were the exclusive domain of fully qualified lawyers. Some judges took comfort in the fact that the codes of criminal and civil law remained in effect, others had no compunction in applying specifically National Socialist laws with the utmost severity. Young lawyers who were unable to find a job found no difficulty in finding a position in the grossly inflated bureaucracy, whether in the state, the party, the SS, or the rapidly expanding armed forces. Lawyers were over-represented in the higher ranks of the SS, particularly

[136]   in the Gestapo, the SD and the RSHA, and as such played a critical role in the organization and execution of the 'Final Solution'.

There were 5,500 Jews among the 35,000 doctors. They were soon excluded from the profession, their places taken by eager youngsters. Physicians seemed to find the SS particularly attractive and 3,000 of them joined Hitler's praetorian guard by 1938, but they were not alone in engaging in eugenic and racial research, which was as morally reprehensible as it was scientifically worthless. They too played a key role in the Shoah[8], and it was a doctor who made the life or death decisions on the ramp at Auschwitz, ostensibly on purely medical grounds. The perversion of the honourable professions of medicine and law is among the most abysmal aspects of the regime, and crimes were committed in both that were never adequately expiated after the war, when many a criminal got off scot-free, casting a dark shadow on post-war Germany.

University professors formed the highly respected elite of the educated middle class. There were some 7,200 professors and lecturers and they identified to a shocking degree with a movement that had nothing but contempt for learning and the intellect. Most of them were ardent nationalists who wished to see Germany as the hegemonic power in Europe. They longed for an organic state in which there would be no place for the class struggle. They were violently opposed to the 'cultural Bolshevism' of the avant-garde, and dreamed of a cultural renewal whereby traditional German values and virtues, which were threatened by the corruption of the modern, would be nurtured and thrive. The Nazis quickly purged the academy of Jews and republicans: 3,000 scholars had left Germany by 1939, among whom were 24 Nobel Prize winners, to the inestimable gain of the host countries.

Clerical workers, once seen as enthusiastic supporters of the Nazis, were in fact relatively immune to them and by and large they continued to support centre and left of centre parties. The Nazis set about overcoming the wide differences between white- and blue-collar workers. Average wages for clerical workers were more than twice those of manual workers, but the DAF treated both sectors equally. They enjoyed the same social services and went on the same KdF holidays, but the clear distinction between the two still remained. Each had their own specific social insurance schemes and the Nazis' efforts to level the difference in income and status, which were bitterly resented by the clerical workers, were kept within bounds for fear of serious repercussions and unrest that might endanger the 'racial community'. Clerical workers' discontent was largely assuaged by expanding employment opportunities and prospects for advancement within a rapidly growing bureaucracy.

Figure 4.1   KdF holiday camp

The myth about the enthusiasm of clerical workers for National Socialism is matched with the heroic myth, nurtured by left-wing historians, of the robust and solid opposition of the industrial proletariat. It is quite true that the KPD struggled as best it could against the regime until it was quickly and thoroughly smashed. The SPD were less active, and their opposition was more often than not from a safe distance, but they also had some heroes among their ranks. The Communists and Social Democrats never posed a real threat to the regime, in large part because they clung to the ludicrous theory that Hitler and his followers were marionettes manipulated by sinister capitalists, and were thus totally unable to understand the true nature of the Nazi dictatorship. They had precious few active supporters among a working class that remained docile and faithful to the regime, for all their habitual grumbling and whingeing, until its last few dying months.

After the years of wartime hardship, hyperinflation, depression and mass unemployment, the economic recovery after 1933 seemed to be nothing short of a miracle. The regime benefited from a relaxation of pressure when the low birth rate cohorts of the war years began to enter the labour market, by the reflationary efforts of the Papen and Schleicher governments that were beginning to have an effect, by a general improvement in the world economy, and by imaginative juggling with statistics. The massive

[138] increase in government expenditure helped tackle unemployment, but was to create alarming problems within a few short years. Although average real wages actually dropped during the peacetime years, this was more than offset by the feeling of security that came with a regular wage packet. Increases in gross wages, often the result of working longer hours, were frequently eaten away by increased taxes and contributions such as DAF dues and WHW donations. Even so, in some industries, such as armaments, net wages did manage to reach the 1928 level, and in some instances surpass it. In other sectors, such as consumer goods, there was stagnation, and even where there were modest gains they were soon eaten away by inflation.

Wages may not have risen significantly, and in some cases actually fell, but workers also received a number of significant benefits. Family allowances were greatly improved, as were widows' pensions. Holidays were increased from an average of three days with pay to six, and in some cases even twelve or fifteen. All workers were now covered by health, accident and unemployment insurance and were guaranteed a pension. The DAF's programme Beauty of Work supervised the building of canteens, adequate toilets and showers, made sure that the shop floor was clean and properly ventilated, the works spic and span. Larger firms were required to provide sporting facilities. The wide palette of KdF holidays was greatly appreciated, as were the concerts, plays and exhibitions that they organized. The DAF improved working conditions and services in many enterprises where the old unions and political parties had failed to make any headway.

Prominent Nazis seized every opportunity to stress the dignity and importance of manual labour and the slogan 'Labour Ennobles' met with a surprising degree of acceptance from a working class that appreciated the many benefits the regime had brought them. They overlooked the fact that these were only available to 'racial comrades', or that while they enjoyed greatly improved medical care and preventive medicine, doctors elsewhere were castrating, sterilizing and murdering those deemed to be 'unworthy of life'.

That the Nazis found it relatively easy to win over the working class at least to a passive acceptance, and in many instances to an active support of the regime, is due in large part to the collapse of the labour movement in the final years of the Weimar Republic. The labour unions were crippled by the depression that left them with no powers of collective bargaining. The Communist Party had become a sect, prey to ideological obfuscation, whose voters came largely from the unruly ranks of the unemployed and Marx's despised lumpenproletariat. Support for the Social Democrats was dwindling rapidly, while the leadership was seriously divided and incapable of taking decisive action. Communists and Social Democrats fought one another over ideological issues that bore no relation to a grim reality and were thus incapable of building a common front against Nazism. Communists preferred to march arm in arm with the Nazis, as in the Berlin transport workers' strike, rather than settle their differences with the Social Democrats and face a deadly common threat.

Workers no longer had any representative bodies of their own and were subject to harsh punishments for infractions of the regulations. Those who refused to work overtime could be sent to prison for one year by the labour courts. Several instances of unpunctuality could result in three years in jail. Nevertheless, measures such as the Labour Service orders of 1938 and 1939 that denied certain key workers freedom of movement, or the wage freeze of September 1939, were modified due to workers' protests, stoppages and slow-downs. German workers were thus by no means totally passive, but they resisted only over bread-and-butter issues, while remaining indifferent to the fate of the regime's many hapless victims. Hitler was ever mindful of the consequences of labour unrest during the First World War, and was determined that this should not happen again. A degree of flexibility was needed for loyalty to be preserved.

Workers were initially attracted in ever-increasing numbers to the NSBOs that were designed to replace the unions. They already had 400,000 members by January 1933 as workers abandoned the traditional unions, but they were far too radical for the DAF and after the Röhm Putsch of 1934 they were abolished. This was accepted without protest by a working class that was coming increasingly under the spell of the charismatic Führer. Most put security above freedom and placed their faith in Hitler. Social Democrats welcomed the removal of the Communists who had been their bitterest opponents. Improved working conditions, generous services, opportunities for advancement in a rapidly expanding economy, coupled with efforts to overcome the disparity between clerical and manual workers, all served to make the talk about the 'racial community' seem something much more than mere propaganda. Pride at Germany's successes in foreign policy further enhanced Hitler's status and strengthened working-class loyalty to the regime. Traditional working-class solidarity eroded with the destruction of the SPD and KPD with their unions, press, clubs, youth organizations and educational programmes. It was also threatened by an increasing differentiation of skills and wages with the resulting competitiveness between workers that was actively encouraged by the DAF. At home, working-class families were closely watched by the Nazi Party's cell and block leaders, spied upon by Gestapo informants, and denounced by jealous neighbours.

[140] Class solidarity could not survive in such an atmosphere of suspicion and fear. Allied bombing further destroyed class identity and increased the degree of individualization, thus putting the finishing touches on a complex process that transformed the mentality of the working class.

The aristocracy

One persistent myth is that German aristocrats were from the very outset opposed to the Nazis. Was it not the case that people of such lofty estate had nothing but contempt for the brown-shirted *canaille*? Did not southern Germany's devout Catholic nobility look with horror on the pagan practices of the Third Reich? Were not members of Germany's oldest and most distinguished families prominent among those who opposed Hitler? In fact precious few aristocrats were able to accept a republic which had sent the princes packing, they lost many of their privileges and rights under the new constitution, and the army, which had provided a home for the scions of the Prussian Junkers for centuries, was reduced to a minute force with precious few career opportunities. Aristocrats were among the most violent and extreme opponents of the Weimar Republic, fighting in the Freikorps and in the border guards. One-fifth were members of the German Aristocrats' Association, which was violently anti-Semitic and demanded that its members could demonstrate that their families had 200 years of pure Aryan blood. The aristocracy was further radicalized by the agricultural crisis of 1928 that left many a landowner in dire straits.

Initially there was little in National Socialism that was attractive to the aristocracy, but things began to change in the early 1930s when younger members of the north-German aristocracy began to feel that the Nazis would be valuable allies against the hated republic and against Marxism in all its forms. Together they might be able to build a new, powerful and dynamic Germany. Nazi racial theory was easily assimilated by people obsessed with heredity, with the *Almanac de Gotha* as their studbook, their traditional anti-Semitism and contempt for Slavs. The aristocracy was particularly attracted to the SS, and Himmler welcomed them into the officer corps of his elite order. A quarter of SS generals were aristocrats, about the same proportion as in the regular army in which they were still over-represented as it rapidly expanded until there were 18 million men in arms. At this point the officer corps had become so diluted that the aristocracy hardly counted. The failure of Darré's 'blood-and-soil' campaign and Hitler's determination to achieve the highest possible degree of self-sufficiency in foodstuffs resulted in the protection of the aristocratic estates, an easing of the burden [141] of debt, in addition to which many an aristocrat benefited directly from the confiscation of Jewish property.

There were, however, distinct disadvantages. The republic had already ended aristocratic self-governance in Prussia east of the river Elbe, but now the rural councillor (*Landrat*), once an aristocratic preserve, was replaced by the Nazi farmers' leader (*Bauernführer*), whose extensive powers were bitterly resented. It was the war that finally forced the aristocracy into opposition. The blood toll within their ranks was exceptionally high, with more than 8,000 losing their lives. When it became clear that all was lost they finally decided to act. When the badly bungled, but extraordinarily brave plot of July 1944 failed, the aristocracy paid a heavy price when hundreds were killed. Hitler swore that once the war was over he would destroy the entire caste, and cursed himself that he had not acted sooner against this pack of disloyal snobs. The Red Army seized the estates of the East Elbian aristocracy and forced them into exile. Land reform in the German Democratic Republic (DDR) finished the job. The aristocracy in the west kept their lands and their wealth and were determined to sustain their privileged position.

Women in Nazi Germany

For many years historians largely ignored the female half of the population of Nazi Germany, until feminists sharpened their pens and set to work restoring the balance. The picture that emerged was of a society run by misogynist monsters, brutal machos and mad scientists bent on mass sterilization, in which women were cast into the depths of a gynaecophobic hell, where their only function was to bear a series of warrior children sired by callous patriarchs, to be sent to their deaths on the battlefields of Europe. Subsequent research by cooler-headed social historians reveals a more nuanced picture.

For many women life in the Third Reich was indeed hellish. Jewish women suffered unimaginable horrors, as did the hapless victims of the eugenicists. The wives, daughters and sisters of political prisoners who were punished for crimes committed by male members of the family – a system known as *Sippenhaft* (clan arrest) – should not be forgotten. Nevertheless, the lot of the vast majority of women in the Third Reich improved greatly. Although they were excluded from political power, were underpaid and denied birth control and abortions, their husbands had steady jobs, real

[142] wages were rising, although never to reach the pre-depression levels, and the future looked promising. Married couples were given a loan of 1,000 RM, provided that the pair was eugenically acceptable and the woman stayed at home. A quarter of the loan was written off with each child born. Generous tax relief was given for children, and family allowances were paid with the third child, payments coming from the brimming unemployment insurance fund. Medical services for women were also greatly improved. Five million women visited the new Maternity Schools by 1944, and 10 million women availed themselves of the services of special advice centres. By 1941 there were 15,000 childcare centres run by the Mother and Child Charity (*Hilfswerk Mutter und Kind* – often shortened to '*Muki*'). Pregnant working women were given six weeks of leave with full pay before and after a birth, a policy that was unrivalled anywhere else in the world. Free holidays were also provided for mothers and children. Generous provision was provided for unwed mothers, provided of course that the offspring were of suitable racial stock. Women were appreciative of these measures, and gave the state their grateful loyalty. In spite of all the efforts of the natalists the number of abortions steadily increased and although the birth rate rose from the low depression level and was higher than in other Western European countries, it did not surpass the level of the early 1920s.

If this was no hell for women, it was also no paradise, and there were many negative aspects of Nazi policy towards women. As Paula Müller-Ortfried, president of the Protestant Ladies Aid organization, remarked bitterly in 1933: 'Today one talks an awful lot about the German *Volk*, but one really means German men.' Under ideal circumstances women were to be confined to the home as mothers of racially sound children, all in the interests of eugenics, racial politics and preparation for war. The Führer needed children, and to this end Mother's Day, an American celebration which had been introduced during the Weimar Republic thanks to the florists' energetic lobbying, was made into the central event of the Nazi fertility cult, celebrated with great pomp, ceremony and pathos. The Mother's Service Medal was awarded to those with four children and more, graded according to number of children. Motherhood ceased to be a private affair, and was seen as a public service that helped improve the racial stock and create a genuine 'racial community'. To this end abortions, which prior to 1933 were estimated to average 600,000 annually, were made illegal. Birth control devices were virtually unobtainable, except for Jews and other undesirables. Compulsory abortions were performed on the racially unwanted and the eugenically suspect. A new law on marriage and divorce in 1938 further reduced women's legal rights.

The birth rate increased from 14.7 per thousand in 1932 to 18.6 per [143]
thousand in 1936, but this was the result of improvements in the economy
rather than ideological pressure. The number of women workers increased
sharply, particularly in low-paid and unskilled positions, in spite of the generous loans offered to married women who left the workforce. The greatest
concentration was in agriculture, where 65 per cent of the workforce was
female. At the other end of the scale many women with university degrees
were forced to leave their jobs, and only a very limited number of women
were admitted to institutions of higher learning. There were 20,000 female
university students in 1933; by 1939 the figure had dropped to 5,500.
Married women were weeded out of the civil service and were not permitted to practise law or medicine, nor could they hold senior positions
in education. In 1936 women were no longer called for jury duty on the
grounds that they were constitutionally 'unable to think logically or reason
objectively'.

National Socialist policies towards women were thus profoundly contradictory. Women were to serve the Führer and *Volk* by raising large numbers
of children and tending the family home, rather than going out to work.
On the other hand, with the increasing shortage of labour, women were
desperately needed in the workforce. By 1937 women no longer had to
give up their jobs in order to qualify for the 1,000 RM marriage loan.
Large numbers of women were also employed in the various women's organizations, social services and medical facilities, as well as being needed to
staff the National Socialists' mushrooming bureaucracy. Paradoxically, this
had a liberating effect. Women felt that new opportunities were opened up
for them, that they were making a vital contribution to society and that
their work was appreciated.

The persistent myth that German women, although freed by a pagan
regime from any obligations towards the *Kirche* (church), were still chained
to *Kinder* (children) and *Küche* (kitchen) can be quickly dismissed. As early
as 1936 there were 600,000 more women in the workforce than there had
been in 1933. By 1939 52 per cent of German women between the ages
of 15 and 60 were in regular employment. By contrast, in Britain the figure
was 45 per cent, and in the United States a mere 36 per cent. In Germany
36 per cent of married women and 88 per cent of unmarried women were
wage earners. Women comprised 41 per cent of the workforce by 1940
rising to 51 per cent by the following year, whereas in Britain they made
up only 29 per cent. Hitler persistently resisted attempts to force women to
work during the war for fear that it would have an adverse effect on morale
and lead to a repeat performance of the widespread discontent in 1918,

[144] which he believed was the major reason for Germany's defeat. He refused to allow women's wages to rise so as to equal men's, and soldiers' wives were given generous allowances so as to encourage them to stay at home. Nevertheless, women took on a range of jobs that previously had been exclusively reserved for men. Female bus conductors and readers of gas and electricity meters were paid the same wages as men. Women doing piece-work in the armaments industry were paid on the same scale. The chronic shortage of doctors meant that restrictions on the admission of women to medical schools had to be lifted. In 1933 only 6.5 per cent of doctors were women; by 1944 the figure had risen to 17 per cent. Some 900,000 women were eventually forced to work in 1943, but they came from the ranks of the underprivileged. For all the talk of community, women from higher up the social scale were exempt from labour service, and Nazi Germany thus clearly remained a two-class society. With the men at the front, women had to take on a whole host of new responsibilities and with them an increased autonomy, whether it was by running the family firm, looking after a farm, standing behind the counter, or providing services for the mounting number of refugees and those left homeless due to the bombing raids.

There were 3.3 million members of the National Socialist Women's Association (*Nationalsozialistischen Frauenschaft* – NSF), led by the formidable Gertrud Scholtz-Klink, a slender, blonde, blue-eyed mother of eleven children from three husbands, who was also the head of the German Women's League (*Deutsches Frauenwerk* – DFW) with some 4.7 million members. In addition she was head of the women's section of the DAF. She was thus on paper the most powerful woman in the Third Reich, but she was caught in the glaring contradiction between her vision of German women as submissive wives, mothers and housewives, and as party activists in the NSF and DFW. Scholtz-Klink was unable to find a solution to this fundamental discrepancy, and her remark that the wooden spoon was as powerful a weapon as the machine-gun was somewhat unconvincing. She was further troubled by the contradiction between her own prudish sexual morality, and the racial theories of the party that made no distinction between legitimate and illegitimate motherhood. Scholtz-Klink faced the paradoxical situation of being called upon to mobilize women, who according to National Socialist ideology were apolitical creatures, for political ends. Although well versed in political infighting she was unable to realize her anti-modernist revolution. Hitler, who had no time for plaited hair and blue eyes à la Scholtz-Klink, or for the BDM racial ideal, and who had a large collection of photographs of glamorously alluring film stars and dancers in his Munich apartment, gave her no support. Scholtz-Klink published her

account in 1978 in a book entitled *Women in the Third Reich* which she
defiantly dedicated to the 'victims of the Nuremberg Trials'.

Women were subjected to a great deal of ideological harassment and
discrimination in a male-dominated and misogynist society, but they also
made great gains thanks to generous social policies, and an appreciation of
their contributions to society both at work and in everyday life. Gertrud
Scholtz-Klink might denounce the women's movement as a 'symbol of
decay', Hitler write of it as a product of the Jewish intellect, bent on the
systematic destruction of the Aryan race, and Goebbels announce that women
were being removed from public life in order to restore their essential dignity,
but they were powerless against the pressures of a society stretched to the
limit. In spite of fierce political resistance, the exigencies of a terrible war
were such that women gained a degree of independence that was to fuel
the demand for further emancipation in the post-war years.

Youth

The Nazi Party was a young party, it was the self-proclaimed incorporation
of 'young Germany', and was determined that youth should be thoroughly
indoctrinated with the basic principles of National Socialism and infused
with a fanatical enthusiasm for the national cause. Young men were to be
made, in Hitler's words, 'tough as leather, hard as Krupp steel and swift as
greyhounds'. They were to have the discipline, unselfishness, self-confidence
and obedience necessary for them to become valuable 'racial comrades'.
Loyalty to the regime was youth's absolute priority, above family affection
or religious conviction. They were to become the unconditional devotees
of the godlike figure of a charismatic Führer. The Hitler Youth (HJ) and
League of German Maidens (BDM) were the organizations whose task it
was to create the new German youth. They were converted to state organization in 1936 and all 10–18-year-olds were obliged to go twice a week
for 'duty' on Wednesday and Saturday afternoons. They were also often
ordered to attend propaganda films on Sunday mornings so that they would
not be able to go to church. Ten-year-olds were initiated into the German
Youth (*Deutsche Jungvolk*) on Hitler's birthday on 20 April in a solemn ceremony. At the age of 14 they graduated to the Hitler Youth. The emphasis
was on physical health, on building 'character' and on the inculcation of
basic attitudes deemed essential for a true National Socialist.

The Hitler Youth, which had been founded in 1926, was a relatively
small organization in 1933, with just over 100,000 members. By contrast

[146] the Catholic youth group had over 1 million members. Baldur von Schirach, who had been remarkably successful in organizing university students, was made Youth Leader of the German Reich and immediately set to work with characteristic energy and efficiency to the effect that by 1934 the HJ had 3.6 million members. By 1939 the number had increased to 8.7 million. The Hitler Youth took the Boy Scouts and the various youth groups of the Weimar Republic as a model. They wore a similar uniform, went to camp, sang songs around the campfire, did pre-military training and had various ranks and offices. During the war the Hitler Youth were used to clean up after bombing raids and build defences, and from 1943 all 16-year-olds could be called up to operate anti-aircraft guns and searchlights. In the following year the age limit was dropped to 15, by which time 16-year-olds were being drafted into the Waffen-SS. By the end 14-year-olds were fighting alongside 65-year-olds in the People's Militia (*Volkssturm*).

The League of German Maidens was formed in 1930 with a similar structure. Ten-year-olds joined the Young Girls (*Jungmädel*) and graduated to the BDM at 14. Like the boys they wore uniforms, went to camp and were forced to go on route marches and particular emphasis was placed on physical fitness. They had to put up with a heavy dose of political indoctrination. They were also trained as prospective mothers and were obliged to work in areas that were felt to be suitably feminine. They assisted families with numerous children, did first aid, helped with the harvest and tended the sick. The BDM like the HJ was organized along strictly hierarchical lines, but it did offer opportunities for young women to develop initiative and self-confidence, and was in this sense not quite the grimly repressive organization it has often been depicted. On the other hand, the blind obedience, the contempt for the feeble civilian world, the glorification of war and the racism that was at the basis of the HJ and BDM's philosophy, all too often offset such emancipatory possibilities.

The vast majority of boys and girls accepted the HJ and BDM with passive indifference. There was a small group of fanatical enthusiasts who were promoted up through the ranks, but they were a minority. It was not until the war, when organized German youth was called upon to do life-threatening work, that there was any real resistance to the compulsion, discipline and collectivization of these organizations.

Since the Hitler Youth was in large part designed as preparation for military service it is hardly surprising that HJ leaders were given commissions in the armed services and were particularly welcome in the Waffen-SS. The fanatical stand of the SS division Hitlerjugend, which held up the Allied invasion force by Caen, is a typical example of the blind faith in the Führer that the HJ was so often able to inculcate. Mercifully this was only a small [147] minority, and for most the experience of total defeat, the revelation of the extent of Nazi crimes and the rapid recovery of the West German economy, eradicated most of the evil consequences of this early training.

The wartime economy

The peacetime economy had been to an increasing degree geared towards the production of armaments and to this end investment, raw materials and labour had been regulated to the point that some spoke of a 'peacetime war economy'. Plans were also made for a series of additional measures once the fighting began. At the same time Hitler was convinced that Germany's defeat in the Great War was due in large part to the collapse of morale on the home front. He was determined that this should not happen again, and therefore ordered that the consumer goods sector should not be drastically curtailed and that there should be plenty of butter along with the guns. By 1941 there was a serious shortage of both guns and butter so that talk of a 'peacetime economy in wartime' is far wide of the mark.

Ration cards were printed in 1937 and on 28 August 1939, four days before the attack on Poland, certain basic foodstuffs were placed on ration. Clothing and shoes were rationed in October 1939. In spite of these efforts there was already a serious food shortage by 1940, the harvest that year was very poor, and by 1941 the situation was critical. On 4 September 1939 extra payment for overtime and night shifts was abolished, amounting on average to an 8 per cent reduction in wages. Restrictions on the length of the working day were also lifted. There were widespread protests against these measures, a number of Gauleiter were sympathetic, Göring, Hess and Funk agreed that the working class needed to be appeased in order to avoid a repeat performance of 1918, and the measures were rescinded in the following month. Income tax on the wealthier was increased to 13.7 per cent on incomes over 10,000 RM a year and to 55 per cent on incomes in excess of 100,000 RM per year. The equivalent rates in Britain were 23.7 and 75 per cent.

With the swift defeats of Poland and France there seemed to be no pressing need to force the pace of armaments production. Göring issued a ukase calling for a marked increase in armaments, but this met with an indifferent response from industrialists anxious to return to more profitable peacetime production. Such complacency was due in part to the enormous efforts that had been made in the pre-war years. Germany had managed to produce

[148] 90 per cent of the oil required synthetically, half of it at IG Farben's Leuna works. Synthetic rubber produced at IG Farben's Buna works covered most of the Wehrmacht's requirements. Otto Friedrich, who learnt the trade at B.F. Goodrich and who was on the board of Germany's major rubber company, Phoenix, was appointed by Hans Kehrl, a textile manufacturer who was responsible for the exploitation of the occupied territories, to head the Reich Rubber Office. He did an excellent job and, after serving a couple of years of the 15-year sentence for his crimes, was to have a stellar career in post-war Germany, serving on the board of directors of Phoenix, Daimler-Benz and Siemens, holding a key position in the Flick group, and being appointed president of the employees' association in 1969.

As in the First World War, Germany imagined that the defeated enemy would pay the bill, so that fiscal prudence was thrown to the wind. Overtime payments were made tax-free after the defeat of France. Exotic plans were drawn up for the exploitation of a conquered Europe, euphemistically described as 'large area economics' (*Grossraumwirtschaft*), in which the east would provide the agricultural products and the west industrial goods. Hitler constantly emphasised the need to expand eastwards, not simply to find living space for Aryan colonists and to smash 'Jewish-Bolshevism', but even more importantly to secure the oil and mineral resources along with the agricultural produce without which Germany would never be able to make its bid for world power. This was to be more than a racial war of annihilation; it was also to be a war of plunder and colonization.

Since the National Socialists were determined to spare the 'racial community' from tax hikes during the war and since the 'racial comrades' were singularly reluctant to buy war bonds, remembering all too well how bondholders had lost everything in the First World War, Germany faced a chronic problem of inflation. Unlike Britain, where increased taxes and the extraordinary response to a 'national savings' campaign drastically reduced the amount of money in circulation, Germans had large amounts of disposable income and a shortage of consumer goods. It was therefore decided to export inflation, first by manipulating the rates of exchange of occupied countries and then by encouraging the occupation forces to spend their money abroad. Thus the French franc was devalued by 25 per cent, the Czech krone by 33 per cent and the rouble by 470 per cent, so that the Ukraine was reduced to a barter economy. Deposit boxes held by foreigners could not be opened and the property of 'enemies of the Reich' was seized. All foreign currency in Germany was collected along with all share certificates in foreign currencies. The gold reserves of the occupied countries were plundered, with 53.6 tons of gold taken from France, Belgium and Holland.

The result was an appalling inflation and the devastation of the occupied countries dressed up as legitimate payment for the cost of occupation. In fact such costs were a mere fraction of what was collected. Göring organized the systematic plunder of occupied Europe to provide a Christmas bonus for the 'racial comrades', which was added to the 'occupation costs'. Small wonder then that the French referred to the Germans as *coryphores* (Colorado beetles) and the members of the civilian administration in the east were known as 'Eastern Hyenas'.

Belgium with a population of 8.3 million was called upon to increase revenue from taxes from 11 to 16 billion francs and was forced to hand over its entire gold reserves of 558 billion francs. Holland was forced to come up with 100 million guilders per month between 1940 and 1942. The real cost of occupation was adequately covered by two-fifths of that amount. In addition to such colossal burdens, occupied Europe was ordered to pay a special tax for the 'anti-Bolshevik fight', foreign 'plutocrats' were ferociously taxed, and some enterprises were taxed at rates as high as 112 per cent. By such means Germany extracted 800–900 billion francs from France, and the equivalent of 10 billion marks from occupied Italy.

The 'racial comrades' profited immensely from this ruthless exploitation of occupied Europe and above all from the plunder and murder of the European Jews. Daniel Goldhagen's grossly exaggerated and seriously misguided account of *Hitler's Willing Executioners* at least drew attention to the willing complicity of the average German with Hitler's crimes. It was comforting and convenient to blame all these horrors on a mad dictator, a pied piper who bewitched an entire nation, on the half-crazed racist ideologues, Hitler's brutal paladins, on rapacious capitalists, on the Communist threat, on sadists in the *Einsatzkommandos*, even on the temper of the times, and thus let the average 'racial comrade' off the hook. German troops returned from serving abroad laden with scarce commodities that were denied to the occupied peoples whose economies Hitler was systematically ruining. Even a man like the writer Heinrich Böll, whom no one could possibly accuse of being a Nazi, contributed enthusiastically to this plunder in actions which he subsequently roundly condemned in his impeccably politically-correct post-war novels[9].

German Jews began to be deported in 1941 so that housing could be provided for 'racial comrades' who had lost their homes to Allied bombers. A quarter of a million Jewish homes in France were confiscated and sold, the amount realized sent to the Reich, along with the furniture for the victims of the air raids. Similar treatment was meted out to 3,868 Jewish homes in Belgium, under the slogan 'Jewish property belongs to the *Volk*'.

[150] Property extracted from the 140,000 Dutch Jews brought in 1.5 billion RM from the total of 14.5 billion RM stolen from Holland.

Götz Aly has calculated that the Germans took about 170 billion RM from foreign sources during the war, an amount that was ten times the total Reich revenues for 1938 and which would amount to between 1.7 and 2 trillion euros in today's purchasing power[10]. Between 15 and 20 billion RM was stolen from Europe's Jews in order to help finance Germany's war. Goods stolen from Jews were converted into war bonds in order to appear to be on the right side of international law, since they were technically not robbed. Such awkward creditors were soon murdered, the debt thus nullified. Financial experts, most of whom enjoyed highly successful careers in banking in post-war Germany, encouraged the dispossession of Europe's Jews on the grounds that the measure was anti-inflationary. With perfidious cunning, rampant inflation was blamed on the Jews. Currencies were stabilized when their property was stolen and placed on the market, because the amount of goods relative to the money in circulation was increased. The point was thus proved. The overwhelming majority of Germans profited directly or indirectly from this murder and plunder. Taxes for ordinary Germans were kept remarkably low and the booty was distributed fairly among the less advantaged 'racial comrades' according to the Nazi theory of the unity of racial and social policy and of socio-political appeasement.

Foreign workers were also further exploited by ingenious currency manipulations. Workers from France, Belgium, Holland, Croatia, Serbia, Bohemia and Moravia were paid in marks, but the bulk of the money was sent home at manipulated rates of exchange. In the case of Italian workers the Reichsbank kept the money and the workers' families were paid from credits extracted from the Banco del Lavoro. The families of Polish workers had to be supported by funds from the General Government, a practice that even Hitler thought was scandalous. Polish workers were obliged to pay an additional 15 per cent tax on the grounds that they did not pay any contributions to the WHW or the DAF. Soviet workers had their property seized and sold, the profits going to finance the army of occupation.

Hitler imagined that after the lightning campaigns in Poland and France he would have little difficulty in defeating the Soviet Union. All that was needed, he said, was to kick in the front door and the entire rotten building would collapse. The Wehrmacht was just about adequately prepared for a campaign that would last a few weeks, but was totally unprepared for anything longer. Fritz Todt, a man with exceptional organizational talents

Figure 4.2   The Autobahn was largely a propaganda measure, as the traffic was minimal.

who had built the motorways and the West Wall, whose Organisation Todt (OT) was a gigantic construction company that made extensive use of labour from 'training camps', was appointed minister of munitions in March 1940. He was deeply concerned that Germany's armaments were not adequate to achieve Hitler's ambitious goals. His pessimism increased when the Wehrmacht was halted outside Moscow in December 1941 and 'Barbarossa' had failed. Hitler gave him additional powers and he was able to make a number of significant improvements, but he came to the conclusion that the war could not be won and urged Hitler to make peace. Hitler appointed Albert Speer as Todt's successor in February 1942. He gradually accumulated a position of immense power, totally eclipsing the vain, indolent, drug-addicted and incompetent Göring as an economics tsar, to become

[152] one of the leading figures in the Third Reich, fully implicated in its worst crimes.

Speer believed in rationalization and central planning and was ably assisted by Hans Kehrl whom he appointed head of the armaments and planning office within his ministry. Kehrl drew up detailed production and distribution plans for industry both at home and in the occupied territories. Raw materials were rigorously controlled, the flow of investment capital carefully channelled, production levels set and labour, including hundreds of thousands of slaves from the concentration camps, carefully allocated. This involved ferocious battles with Göring's Four-Year Plan, with General Georg Thomas's War Economics and Armaments Office, with leading industrialists determined to assert their independence, with the Reich commissars for armaments, and with powerful figures in the party such as Bormann, who were committed to the National Socialist doctrine of saving small producers from 'plutocrats' and 'capitalists'. Speer won the day because he made absolutely certain that Hitler covered his back.

Speer's approach was based on Todt's control from the centre by delegating responsibilities to subordinate bodies that were given a degree of autonomy. This in turn was copied from the Italian Fascist corporatist model. These subsidiary organizations were run by managers and professionals, who set about their business untroubled by meddlesome hacks and ideologues from the Nazi Party. Speer recruited a number of talented, ambitious and forceful young men, known contemptuously by the older generation as his *Kindergarten*, who were to pursue highly successful careers in the Federal Republic's booming post-war economy. He also encouraged such exceptional talents as aeronautical engineer Ernst Heinkel, who employed 9,000 workers in 1936, increasing to 450,000 by 1944. Willy Messerschmitt had a similar success and like Heinkel employed slave labour, ordering the compulsory sterilization of pregnant workers. Claudius Dornier built the elegant Do17 light bomber, known as the *Bleistift* (pencil), and was the head of the aircraft section of Speer's empire. Ferdinand Porsche, who had presented Hitler with the first 'KdF car' on the occasion of his birthday in 1938, built tanks during the war, headed the tank section, and made use of 16,000 slave and foreign workers, some in an underground factory where conditions were unspeakably awful. Speer closed down small plants, drastically curtailed the consumer sector, centralized and standardized production and awarded generous premiums to the most productive firms. By such means he was able to achieve a threefold increase in armaments production between February 1942 when he was appointed and August 1944, after which time Allied bombing ruined his chances.

The 'armaments miracle' under Speer must be seen in perspective. It is [153] true that the increases under his aegis were remarkable, even given the fact that he juggled with the statistics and engaged in some highly creative book-keeping, but the level at which he started was amazingly low, with Hitler imagining that he could win swift campaigns on the cheap without a drastic reduction in the consumer sector. Throughout the war the production of consumer goods remained astonishingly high. Taking the 1939 level as 100 it was still 86.1 in 1942, rising to 90.8 in 1943 and slipping back to 85.4 in 1944. In large part this was due to the need to replace consumer goods lost in the air raids and thus to bolster civilian morale. The diversion of industrial production away from armaments into the consumer sector was another major contribution of the bomber offensive to the Allied victory. Armaments production in Germany lagged far behind that of the Soviet Union, the United States and Great Britain. The main reason for this was that much of the industrial plant in Germany was outmoded and unproductive, and the majority of labourers were half-starved slaves and foreign workers whose productivity was necessarily abysmally low. Manufacturers concentrated on quality at the expense of quantity, a serious mistake with a mass army. Armaments production was also seriously affected by the Allied air offensive. After the raids on Hamburg in July and August 1943, which left 30,000 dead, Speer warned that if another six cities were so badly hit the war would be lost. In October 1943 he said that armaments production had been seriously reduced due to the bombing raids and transportation and fuel supplies disrupted. In 1944 Speer admitted that the Allied bomber offensive was 'the greatest lost battle on the German side'.

By early 1944 Germany no longer had access to supplies of foreign ore, resulting in a disastrous drop in steel production. A year later the industrial region of Upper Silesia in the east and the coalfields of the Saar in the west were lost. In July 1944 Goebbels finally got his way and was appointed Plenipotentiary for Total War. He was soon locked in battle with Speer who wanted more industrial workers, while Goebbels wanted men between the ages of 16 and 60 to serve in the militia (*Volkssturm*), women to serve in the Auxiliary Service (*Hilfsdienst*) and boys in the *Werwolf*. Goebbels won the day and Speer, who had already lost the struggle against the Allied air offensive, suffered another serious setback. In March 1945 Hitler ordered the destruction of all industrial plant near the front and the evacuation of the entire population, but this 'Nero Order' could not possibly be carried out. The Gauleiter in the west were unanimous in their verdict that nothing could be done. The Allied advance was so rapid, there was no transport available for refugees, and no one capable of destroying the factories.

[154]   Goebbels thought the whole idea was absurd and noted in his diary on 28 March: 'We issue orders in Berlin that do not arrive any more, and in any case cannot possibly be carried out. I see here the danger of a serious loss of authority.' It is one of the main myths still surrounding the duplicitous Speer that he heroically defied the Führer and countermanded the Nero Order. He merely repeated what Goebbels and the Gauleiter were saying.

    Speer's system was a curious mixture of state control and entrepreneurial autonomy, in which party activists were eager to play a part. Boards of directors were reasonably successful in stopping Nazi functionaries from getting their snouts in the trough, in spite of dire threats of nationalization coming from some lofty quarters. There was never any serious threat that the Nazis would undertake a massive programme of nationalization. Speer relied on elite managers and gave them enough freedom to act to maximum effectiveness within an overall plan. SS-Obergruppenführer Otto Ohlendorf, a brilliant economist who did a tour of duty as a mass murderer in command of Einsatzkommando D before becoming ministerial director in the ministry of economics, let it be known that private enterprise would be encouraged in post-war Germany and that the SS had no plans for large-scale nationalization.

    Speer's armaments miracle only served to prolong the war, there was never the slightest possibility that Germany would be able to turn the tide and the 'wonder weapons' proved worthless. There was, however, a positive aspect to his armaments programme. German industry was modernized, mass production techniques were introduced on a large scale, huge investments were made in the electrical and chemical industries and a new generation of skilled workers was trained. This was to provide solid foundations for the economic miracle of West Germany's post-war revival.

    None of this would have been possible without the ruthless exploitation of 8 million foreign workers, some of whom came of their own accord but most of whom were press-ganged into service for the Reich, and the plundering of occupied Europe and seizure of the property of murdered Jews. By August 1944 Germany had extracted 90 billion RM worth of real value from the occupied areas of the Soviet Union and 85 billion RM from Western Europe, theoretically in payment for the occupation costs. In addition France delivered 3,700 aircraft, 9,600 aero engines and 52,000 trucks. Nineteen per cent of Germany's consumer goods came from the occupied territories between 1942 and 1943.

    Germany spent 614 billion RM between September 1939 and May 1945. Taxes brought in a meagre 185 billion RM and the state's total income amounted to just 276 billion RM. Only a small fraction of the outstanding

338 billion RM could be covered by credits, so the state was lumbered [155] with a colossal burden of debt that was only offset in part by plundering occupied Europe. The state was effectively bankrupt. By 1948, 300 billion RM were in circulation but there was precious little to buy. The German people had to begin again at scratch with the currency reform and the introduction of the Deutschmark on 18 June 1948. Every German was given 40 of the new marks, and 20 more in August. Investments were compensated at a rate of 6.5 DM for 100 RM.

National Socialism and the problem of modernity

One of the most remarkable achievements of the Nazi regime was that it managed to create the illusion that this was a society in which class divisions had been largely overcome and that equal opportunities were there for all to seize. This metanoia was the result not of any fundamental changes in the structure of society, but from the astonishing effects of charismatic leadership. There was a widespread longing for more equality, for a loosening of traditional social restrictions and for greater social mobility. The Nazis played skilfully on these yearnings with their endless references to the 'racial community', by forcing as many people as possible into uniforms, with the phoney egalitarianism of 'Casserole Sundays' and the forced contributions to the WHW. All this was made plausible because the regime managed to overcome the unemployment problem remarkably swiftly and provided almost 2 million jobs in the host of party and state organizations, special commissions and the rapidly expanding armed forces. For those who were comfortably within the 'racial community' life was very much better than it had been in the last stages of a Weimar Republic crippled by the depression and with a political system that had ceased to function. On the other hand, the neo-feudalism of Darré's 'hereditary farms' was in sharp contrast to this feeling of equality and modernity, as was the godlike status of the almighty and omniscient Führer, or the atavistic elitism of Himmler's SS. Hitler's myrmidons with their power bases within a polycratic state were likewise living proof that this was not a society based on equality. The class bias in education not only remained, it was emphasized when school fees for state schools were increased by 30 per cent in 1935. Only families with three or more children were given a free education. The number of children taking the university entrance examination (*Arbitur*) was reduced, and the social composition of the student body remained virtually unchanged.

[156]   It was still exceedingly difficult for children from underprivileged families to gain access to higher education since fees were required and very few scholarships were offered to young and eager National Socialists. The percentage of working-class students dropped from 3.9 per cent to 3.2 per cent, and of those from farming backgrounds from 7 to 5 per cent. Almost 13,000 new university students matriculated in 1933, but only 7,303 in 1939. In part this was due to the lack of adequately qualified university teachers. A third of all professors and lecturers were dismissed, either because they were Jewish or because they were political undesirables. This loss could not be made good by people who were acceptable to the party, and no effort was made to encourage a new generation of university teachers. The number of people with a doctorate who took the examination required for being accepted for a university teaching post (*Habilitation*) fell dramatically between 1933 and 1944 and only 0.21 per cent of them came from the working class. Little effort was made to inculcate these younger lecturers with National Socialist ideology, nor was it necessary to be a party member in order to get a teaching position. The shameful fact is that the vast majority of those who remained comfortably within the professoriate were already in sympathy with the basic tenets of Nazism.

The attempt to create special elite schools was also not a success. The first National Socialist Educational Establishment (Napola) was built in 1933. It was a boarding school designed to train the future elite of the SS and the SA. In 1936 control of the Napolas was taken from the minister of education, Bernhard Rust, and handed over to August Heissmeyer, the head of the SS Main Office who married Gertrud Scholtz-Klink in 1940. A hundred Napolas were planned, but only 15 were built. Nine further such schools were built in 1941. From 1942 to 1944 21 further schools were built, including two in Holland and one in Belgium.

In 1937 Baldur von Schirach as head of the Hitler Youth and Robert Ley in his capacity as the party's educational director opened the first Adolf Hitler School. Ten such schools were eventually built for 600 students. Both the Napolas and the Adolf Hitler schools accepted a higher percentage of students from poorer families than the conventional schools, but their number was so small as to make no serious overall statistical difference. In 1938 Alfred Rosenberg pressed for the creation of National Socialist universities, to be called Order Castles (*Ordensburgen*), but only three were ever built, in the Eifel, Pomerania and Upper Bavaria. They were poorly attended, with 40 per cent of the available places left empty. The students were barely qualified, the instruction of dubious quality, and the majority of graduates found cushy administrative positions at home or in the occupied territories.

The party offered by far the best opportunities for social advancement. The overwhelming majority of the party was recruited from the working class, the peasantry, clerical workers and small businessmen and artisans. It was also very much a young party. Even by 1935, when many opportunists, particularly civil servants, had joined, 65 per cent of party members were under the age of 40. The number of high ranking officers (*Hoheitsträger*), from the Gauleiter down to the block leader (*Blockwart*), rose from 700,000 in 1937 to over 2 million by 1943, thus offering ample opportunity for those of lowlier birth to throw their weight around and make the lives of their 'racial comrades' miserable. Mobility within this cadre was very much restricted since the upper echelons were peopled by the 'old warriors', many of whom had been party members before 1925. They guarded their positions jealously, fending off up-and-coming talent, and could rely on Hitler's virtually unconditional support and loyalty. He largely overlooked the most astonishing degrees of ineptitude, indolence and downright criminality among his satraps. Darré was shunted aside for total incompetence, but suffered no ill consequences. In the latter stages of the war Göring spent most of the year hunting and playing with his electric trains in his vast palace Karinhall. Wilhelm Frick relaxed in his lakeside home on the Chiemsee. Philipp Bouhler, who ran Hitler's personal chancellery, was shunted aside by Bormann and idled away his time for months on end at his country estate in Nussdorf. Competence was not required of the National Socialist elite; all that mattered was absolute faith in the Führer, unconditional loyalty to the party, and a determination to get things done, no matter what and regardless of cost.

The ministers serving in the peacetime years were all from the privileged classes, among them five aristocrats. The only exceptions were Hitler himself and Hanns Kerrl, the minister for religious affairs and also for town and country planning: hence his popular title of 'minister of space and eternity'. The bureaucracy was virtually untouched at the senior level once the very few Jews and republicans were ousted. The Nazis could rely on their absolute loyalty and the vast majority of bureaucrats joined the party, even though they were under no compulsion to do so. The regime thus had a highly efficient administrative machinery at its disposal, and more controversial 'special duties' such as mass murder could be carried out by ad hoc commissions, which unquestioningly and enthusiastically followed the Führer's wishes. Admission to the officer corps of the army was still dependent on the number of people taking the *Arbitur*, the prerequisite for university entrance, along with some other stringent requirements, so that although the army increased about 28-fold between 1933 and 1939 the social

[158] profile of the officer corps did not change markedly, with promotion still based on time-honoured criteria. It was not until 1942 that a whole set of new criteria for selection was introduced which significantly altered the social composition of this elite. Even the SD and the RSHA, the nerve centres of Nazi tyranny, were staffed to a considerable degree by university graduates with comfortable middle-class backgrounds. They would have formed the elite of the Thousand Year Reich, so that bourgeois hegemony would have been thus maintained within a 'racial community', regardless of all the talk about equality.

The Third Reich was so irredeemably Stygian that it took many years before the question could be asked whether there was anything positive that could be said about it. In 1965 the sociologist Ralf Dahrendorf presented the startling thesis that the 12 years of Nazi dictatorship had provided the impetus for a surprising degree of modernization[11]. In 1967 the historian David Schoenbaum developed this theme and made the extravagant claim that there had been a 'brown revolution', resulting in a fundamental change in mental and social structures[12]. These ideas were either rejected or ignored by historians for a good 20 years, and were then revisited in a debate over modernization. This too got bogged down in a theoretical morass, due to methodological shortcomings, and the sheer impossibility of examining a mere 12 years using a theory that is designed to reveal long-term trends.

The question remains whether the Third Reich helped further the process of modernization, or whether it halted or even reversed it. Was this an example of what Jürgen Habermas has called 'radically uprooting modernisation' that threatened the establishment of symmetrical relationships between free and equal citizens? How much of this was by accident, how much by design? Such questions can only be answered if the 12 years of the Thousand Year Reich are examined within their historical context between the Weimar and federal republics, and not taken as an isolated event, a hideous historical accident, or an abrupt caesura. The problem is further compounded by the Janus face of modernization. The horrors of total war, industrialized mass murder, the misuse of science, hypertrophic bureaucracy and propagandistic indoctrination, are all the products of modernization.

A key component of modernization is the change from an agrarian to an industrial society. The Third Reich did not stand in the way of this process, in spite of the initial effects of Walther Darré's half-baked 'blood-and-soil' ideology. As elsewhere in the industrial world, agriculture declined, there was a continued movement from the land to the urban areas, and agriculture

Figure 4.3   Fritz Todt (left), in his capacity as Inspector General of German Roads, with the Gauleiter of Franconia and editor of the anti-Semitic magazine *Der Stürmer*, Julius Streicher, opening a stretch of the Autobahn near Nuremberg

depended increasingly on government protection by means of tariffs and subsidies. Industry continued to expand, largely due to rearmament and war. Government interfered with the economy, entrepreneurial initiative had to bow before government regulations, but the basic structures of a capitalist economy remained unaffected.

An increasing degree of equality of opportunity is another vital factor in the modernization process. Nazi racial policy allowed little room for this democratic notion. The challenges of the modern were to be met by racial selection, not by an open meritocracy. Upward mobility for the 'Aryan racial comrade' was possible through political selection into the upper ranks of the party, by the opportunities that opened up in a rapidly expanding military and a swollen state bureaucracy. The party elite was recruited almost

[160] exclusively from the lower orders. They worked alongside the old elites, and in many instances either co-opted them or pushed them aside. The social policies of the DAF did much to improve the lot of the working class, and lessened, but did not overcome, the distinctions between blue- and white-collar workers.

Hitler, a rudimentarily educated autodidact, had an intense loathing of intellectuals and what he was pleased to call 'hook-nosed intellectualism'. Intelligence for him was empty and sterile, whereas 'all truth comes from belief'. Another favourite notion was that: 'Feelings must push thinking aside.' Words like 'system', 'intelligence' and 'objectivity' were banned from his vocabulary. With such an attitude it is hardly surprising that there was a dramatic reverse to the process of modernization in the area of education. The number of university students sank from 121,000 in 1933 to 56,000 in 1939. In the technical colleges the numbers dropped from 20,400 to 9,500. The percentage of women university students fell from 15.4 to 11.6 per cent, and in the technical colleges the drop was even more dramatic: from 4.6 to 1.9 per cent. The result was a chronic shortage of specialists in all fields.

All this resulted from a profound loathing of intellectuals, a constant theme in *Mein Kampf* and an essential ingredient in the National Socialist worldview. The expulsion of Jewish and politically suspect scholars from the universities caused irreparable damage to German universities, and was of incalculable value to Germany's adversaries. Vital areas of research were neglected, and effort frittered away in such absurd pursuits as 'race research', the hunt for the holy grail, or for Atlantis. The theory of relativity was condemned as being 'Jewish' with 'German physics' as propounded by two Nobel Prize winners Philipp Lenard and Johannes Stark asserting that time and space were absolutes. Doctors, badly needed for public health, set about the forcible sterilization of 360,000 people, mostly women, and castrated 20,000 men. They measured skulls, pickled brains and conducted sadistic research on live subjects, thus perverting medical science in the pursuit of irrational ends.

A great deal of good work was done in spite of all this officially sponsored nonsense. Scientists such as Max von Laue (Nobel Prize 1914), Max Planck (Nobel Prize 1919) and Werner Heisenberg (Nobel Prize 1932) studiously ignored 'German physics' and upheld traditional science. Among the outstanding achievements of German science between 1933 and 1945 were the discovery of sulpha drugs, the establishment of a link between smoking and cancer, the serious health hazards presented by asbestos, certain types of food colouring, pesticides and alcohol. Much of this work was ignored outside Germany, in part because it ran up against the interests of powerful lobbies but also because it could all too easily be dismissed as 'Nazi science'.

The development of democratic processes is also a vital component of the process of modernization, and here Hitler's charismatic dictatorship marked the most dramatic break with the modern. The democratic constitution of the Weimar Republic was torn up, the rule of law cast aside, and Germany became a corrupt neo-feudal free-for-all, in which Hitler's myrmidons skirmished for status and dispensed patronage on their slavish underlings. The 'racial community', which was said to overcome the latent tensions within society, was fundamentally a derisory sham. On the other hand the traditional social hierarchy was delegitimized by this ideology, and many people felt that their longing for a social consensus, which had become acute in the latter stages of the Weimar Republic, had been largely realized in the 'racial community'. Subjective perception, if widely shared, takes on the form of objective fact. Class, in the form of self-perception, could vanish with affective integration into a National Socialist society. It was, after all, a dynamic society that had brought full employment, and with its spectacular successes in foreign policy had restored Germany's prestige in the world. A series of stunning victories up until Stalingrad were further evidence that the National Socialist theory of the master race was based on objective fact. The social state and consumer society, which the Nazis promised would follow upon a final victory, seemed close to realization.

The National Socialists passed a number of measures that greatly benefited the underprivileged 'racial comrades' in what Himmler called 'the socialism of good blood', besides which the efforts of most post-war social democratic parties pale by comparison. Wages might have been frozen, the hours of work increased, but workers were given twice the amount of free time, and were able to enjoy the facilities of KdF during their holidays. Protection for tenants and debtors was significantly strengthened. The feudal remnant of entailment (*Fideikomiss*), the abolishment of which liberals had been demanding for over a century, was finally ended in July 1938. Family allowances were substantially increased and amounted to twice those in Britain or the United States. Taking the 1938 level as 100 they rose to 125 in 1939, 128 in 1940, 156 in 1941 and 196 in 1942. Taxes on low-income families were minimal and when the war began wives were given 85 per cent of their serving husbands' previous income. The only major tax increases were between 1936 and 1938 and were designed to meet the horrendous increase in government expenditure due to the

[162] rearmament programme. These increases were equitably distributed. The tax-free allowance for families was increased proportionate to the number of children. The rich carried the brunt of the burden, followed by the unmarried and the childless. The tax on corporations was increased from 20 to 40 per cent in order to cream off the profits of rearmament and to service a debt that now accounted for three-fifths of total revenue. The number of tax loopholes and write-offs was substantially reduced. Home-owners faced a heavy tax burden that was substantially increased during the war. The luxury hotel Adlon in Berlin was called upon to pay 40 per cent tax on a turnover of 5.7 million RM in 1941, and by 1943 profits were taxed at between 80 and 90 per cent. Blue- and white-collar workers paid no extra direct taxes in wartime, although much has been made of the hardship caused by the wartime increase in the taxes on tobacco, beer, Schnapps and sparkling wine, but these were regionally adjusted. The increase in the price of beer was substantially less in beer-swilling Bavaria, and there was no increase in the tax on wine in the Rhineland to protect the hard-pressed vintners and the local oenophiles. The agricultural sector was spared any tax increases. An attempt to end overtime pay, with the bonus paid by the employer to the state, caused such an outrage that it had to be stopped later in 1939. Pensions for the poor were increased in 1941 and in the same year a universal health-care system was instituted with premiums a mere 1 RM per month. It was free for widows and orphans.

Such benefits were enjoyed only by 'racial comrades'. A Jewish worker at Daimler-Benz who earned 234 RM per month paid 108 RM in tax. An Aryan colleague earning the same amount paid 9.62 RM tax and 20.59 RM in social benefits, contributions to WHW and the DAF. The 'eastern workers' (*Ostarbeiter*) were paid 40 RM per week and were left with 10 RM after tax. Since there was precious little to buy they placed their money in savings accounts which were instantly seized by the Reich.

Churchill's Britain of 'blood, sweat and tears' increased taxation by 335 per cent in a grossly inequitable way, with 85 per cent of tax revenue paid by those earning less than £500 per annum. Unlike the British, lower-income Germans were singularly reluctant to buy war bonds, thus denying the government an important source of revenue. Hitler would not consider such austerity measures and even reversed a ban on household pets, except of course in the case of Jews. Germany's tax burden increased by a mere 196 per cent, the bulk of this increase born by the wealthy, with the regime behaving as if there were no tomorrow, issuing dud cheques, with Hitler, as his conservative opponent Goerdeler said: 'going ever further along the easy path of self-delusion'. The price for such largesse was paid by the occupied countries that were ruthlessly exploited, and by the billions in [163] assets stolen from Jews.

Hitler himself embodied the crisis of the modern. On the one hand he loved aeroplanes and fast cars, announced that he was 'crazy about technology', shared none of his cranky followers' dislike of industry, and mastered the modern means of mass communication; but he also imagined the deadly threat posed by Jewry, which embodied for him all the negative aspects of modernity. Modern technology was placed in the service of essentially atavistic ideological aims, and it was precisely the crushing defeat of these aims that removed so many of the barriers that stood in the way of modernity. The military was destroyed, the officer corps discredited, the East Elbian aristocracy robbed of any influence, all pretensions to the superiority of the German race reduced to an absurdity, and the notion that a charismatic dictator could reach the promised land, by means of a war of conquest and genocide, was finally revealed as a satanic delusion.

CHAPTER 5

THE CHURCHES AND EDUCATION

National Socialism was a secular religion and was seen as such by its leading ideologues. As Hitler put it in August 1933: 'We shall ourselves become a church.' It therefore posed a serious threat to the churches, which in turn were dependent on the state for financial support. Its heathenism, manifested in the adulation of a charismatic Führer, the recitation of the Nazi catechism, the elaborate rituals of May Day, Harvest Festival, the party rally in Nuremberg and the Martyrs' Day on 9 November, the ceremonies marking the summer and winter solstices, and the absurd intent in some quarters on returning to the worship of ancient Germanic gods, were all an open challenge to the Christian churches. The Nazis' leading ideologue, Alfred Rosenberg, was outspoken in his condemnation of the pathetic Christian notion of universal love and was horrified at the Eucharistic Congress in Chicago in 1926 where 'nigger bishops celebrated mass'. Furthermore the profound confessional division within German society was antithetical to the concept of 'racial community'.

Catholics were far more resistant to the lure of Nazism than were Protestants. The former were used to being treated as outcasts and pariahs, certainly since Bismarck's attack on the Catholic Church known as the *Kulturkampf.* In 1932 the Catholic bishops' conference proclaimed that it was not permissible for Catholics to join the NSDAP. Uniforms were not allowed to be worn in church. Many lay Catholics and some courageous priests opposed a regime that was so crassly contrary to basic Christian principles, but most bishops made their opportunistic peace with the Nazis and enthusiastically supported their anti-Communism, blessed Hitler's racially motivated war of annihilation and colonization and remained silent over the persecution of the Jews, although some were finally forced to speak out against the euthanasia programme because of widespread public outrage.

Protestants

The Evangelical Church was divided between those who gave their whole-hearted support to the regime, calling themselves German Christians, and those who believed that Nazism and Christianity were irreconcilable. The German Christians wanted to rid the faith of all its Jewish aspects, whereas most Nazis, understandably feeling that this was impossible, subscribed to a vague form of pantheism, calling themselves 'Germans who believe in God' (*Gottgläubige Deutsche*). Hitler came up with the astonishing idea that Jesus was crucified because he opposed the Jewish attempt to take over the world. Walter Künneth, a young Protestant theologian, called for a 'heart-felt yes to National Socialism' since God had created the Germans as a 'special race' and that race had a 'godly destiny'. Otto Dibelius, a Berlin pastor who was to become a leading figure in the Protestant Church after the war, initially proclaimed the Nazis to be a Christian party, felt that the regime's actions against 'Jewish pushiness' were perfectly justified and argued that the Nazi state was ruled 'in God's name'. Others followed the teaching of the great Protestant theologian Karl Barth, opposing both the regime and the official church leadership and forming a spirited group known as the Confessing Church. This left the Protestant laity in a serious dilemma whether to go along with a leadership that had betrayed the fundamental values and beliefs of the Christian faith, or risk all by clearly identifying with the Confessing Church.

The Nazis were divided over how to deal with the churches. Hitler was characteristically undecided and wanted to avoid an outright conflict. He professed his agreement with Schopenhauer, who wrote that the two greatest scourges of mankind were Christianity and syphilis, but he wanted to put off a final reckoning with the churches until after the war. He laced his speeches with references to God, divine intervention and Christian eschatology, presenting himself as a religious figure with a mission from on high and convincing many that this was a fresh start under an authoritarian regime determined to uphold the basic tenets of the Christian religion. Himmler and Rosenberg were enthusiastic Wotan worshippers, their heads filled with all manner of Germanic rubbish. Goebbels had nothing but contempt for such nonsense, but also wanted an all-out attack on the churches and to replace Christianity with the Führer cult. Small wonder then that the minister responsible for the churches, Hanns Kerrl, had no clear policy and was the object of much derision and complaint. Goebbels complained in 1937 that he hoped to conserve the churches while 'we' wanted to liquidate them, although Hitler still insisted on postponing any such drastic decision.

[166]   For Goebbels the churches were part of a monstrous worldwide conspiracy
that had to be crushed. He wrote in his diary: 'The churches, Free Masons,
Marxists, democrats and Jewry work together hand in hand.'[1] Kerrl fought
back by announcing that 'The Evangelical Church, in accordance with the
divine order of creation, accepts the responsibility for preserving the purity
of our racial identity [*Volkstums*].' Kerrl failed in his attempt to convert
the local evangelical churches into a national church, and when he died
in December 1941 he was not replaced. A significant section of the
Evangelical Church thus managed to avoid *Gleichschaltung*.

How was it possible that so many people, particularly Protestants, were
so easily deluded? A major factor was that Protestantism was clearly identified as the national religion of Germany, while Catholics were regarded as
outsiders whose primary allegiance was to Rome. This was a double-edged
process whereby nationalism took on religious overtones while religion
became identified with the national. Friedrich Schleiermacher, although himself a liberal reformer in the post-Napoleonic age, had given this dubious
undertaking some powerful philosophical arguments and the apparent
approval of the greatest Protestant theologian since Luther. He insisted that
faith and the church should be in harmony with contemporary life and
culture and not be separated from the national project. He argued that the
church should not train its guns on the highly educated who rejected religion, but rather on those whose religious zeal led them to obscurantism,
superstition and mindless ritual. His concern was to save Christianity from
atavistic 'barbarism' while at the same time rescuing science from atheism.
Schleiermacher forged the link between Christianity and nationalism at a
time when nationalism was a liberal and progressive ideology, but as times
changed his liberal theology was converted into national Protestantism. This
tendency reached its apogee during the Great War, when the vast majority
of the Protestant clergy rallied to the ultra-nationalist Fatherland Party,
after the war turning to the right-wing DNVP. Many were attracted by
the court preacher Adolf Stoecker's virulent anti-Semitism, and by Adolf
Hitler's variation on Stoecker's social policy in which concern for the poor
and needy was confused and disguised in the notion of 'racial community'.

The Protestant Church was divided up into 28 state churches and those
who had been longing for a national church seized the opportunity in 1933
to press for the necessary constitutional reform. In April Hitler appointed
Ludwig Müller, an army chaplain from Königsberg, as his plenipotentiary
for the Evangelical Church. Müller set to work and by May 1933 drew up
plans for a Reich Church with a Reich bishop and a national synod and
proclaimed that the appointment of Adolf Hitler as chancellor was evidence

of divine intervention. The German Christians, an extremist group formed [167] in 1926, were even more effusive and called for unconditional support for National Socialism and the introduction of the 'leadership principle' (*Führerprinzip*) in church affairs. Müller became the patron of this group, self-proclaimed as 'Christ's SA'. The German Christians rejected the Old Testament as a 'Jewish book' and were determined to purge Christianity of all traces of Judaism, cooking up all manner of ingenious theories to show that Jesus was not a Jew but a man of pure Aryan stock.

Opposition within the Protestant Church to this craven obeisance to the Nazi regime and deformation of the Christian message began in May 1933 when a small group, which included such figures as Dietrich Bonhoeffer, Martin Niemöller and Friedrich von Bodelschwingh, began to organize. Most of them were ardent nationalists and conservatives, much taken by *völkisch* ideas, and most welcomed the change of regime; but they felt that the German Christians had gone too far and also objected to the idea that all non-Aryans should be thrown out of the church. They stood up for Jewish Christians, but did nothing to help the vast majority of Jews who had not seen fit to be baptized.

Bernhard Rust as minister of education was also determined to bring the Evangelical Church directly under state control and to this end appointed a commissar to head the German Christians. This attempt failed, thanks to the intervention of Hindenburg, but at the church elections in July 1933 the German Christians won 70 per cent of the seats, giving them a majority in all the states except for Hanover, Bavaria and Württemberg. At the first national synod, held in Luther's home town of Wittenberg in September 1933, Ludwig Müller was enthusiastically acclaimed as Reich bishop (soon to be shortened to '*Reibi*' by his many opponents) and immediately surrounded himself with party members. He pledged that he would rid the church of all Jews and Jewish influences. More than a hundred Evangelical theologians were dismissed because of Jewish ancestry. From 1934 the church refused to baptize Jews. In December 1933 the 800,000 members of the Evangelical youth organization were absorbed by the Hitler Youth. Müller enjoyed Hitler's full support and set about rigorously centralizing the church. One by one the state churches were absorbed by the national church and those pastors who resisted his dictatorial measures were arrested, some being sent to concentration camps.

Opposition to Müller grew apace at the parish level, with a third of all Evangelical pastors joining the Pastors' Emergency Association, the origin of the Confessing Church. Its leading spokesman was Martin Niemöller, a humourless authoritarian, fervent nationalist and anti-Jewish former U-boat

[168]   commander, who had been a member of the Freikorps 'Organisation Escherisch', supported Kapp and his putsch, acted as a pall-bearer for Schlageter, voted for the Nazis in 1933 and sent a congratulatory telegram to Hitler on Germany's withdrawal from the League of Nations. But he was also a man who, unlike the German Christians, put Christ before the Führer even though, as Bonhoeffer pointed out, he imagined that he was a true National Socialist. In January 1934 a meeting was held in Barmen that was addressed by the great theologian Karl Barth, who denounced the Reich bishop's flagrant heresies and called for self-governance for what became known as the Confessing Church. The Barmen Synod rejected as false the doctrine that the church could and should recognize as a source of its teaching other events, powers, historic figures and truths as God's revelation, beyond and besides the one Word of God. It rejected the false doctrine that there could be areas of life which belonged to other lords than Jesus Christ, and that there were areas which did not need justification and sanctification through Him. It rejected the false doctrine that the church could permit itself to hand over responsibility for its teaching and its organization to whomever it might wish, or submit to the vicissitudes of the prevailing ideological and political convictions of the day. It rejected the false doctrine that, apart from this ministry, the church could and should have permission to give itself or allow itself to be given special leaders (*Führer*) vested with ruling authority. It rejected the false doctrine that beyond its special commission the church should and could take on the nature, tasks and dignity that belong to the state and thus become itself an organ of the state. The Confessing Synod of the German Evangelical Church declared that it saw in the acknowledgement of these truths and in the rejection of these errors the indispensable theological basis of the German Evangelical Church as a confederation of confessing churches. It called upon all who could stand in solidarity with its declaration to be mindful of these theological findings in all their decisions concerning church and state. It appealed to all Evangelicals to restore unity in faith, hope and love.

Some 6,000 pastors, about a third of the total, joined the Confessing Church. Most were conservative nationalists, but they rejected the *völkisch* rigmarole to which the German Christians had fallen prey. Women were strongly attracted to the Confessing Church and found little that was appealing in the macho posturing of the German Christians. The Confessing Church welcomed women as active participants in church services and discussion groups, and was the first to ordain women.

The attitude of the Confessing Church towards Jews was far from admirable. There was much rubbish talked about 'God's punishment' for

his chosen people, and biblical references were trotted out to show that this
was part of their destiny ordained by the Almighty. There was general agreement that Jews were far too influential and needed to be pulled down a peg
or two. The Confessing Church differed from the German Christians in that
it wanted Jews to be baptized, whereupon they ceased to be Jews, but it was
little concerned with the fate of those that refused to accept the sacrament.

Müller did not have much of a success with his heavy-handed attempt
to centralize the church, and resistance from the individual state churches
grew as the different factions among the German Christians became increasingly antagonistic. The Nazis began to abandon the idea of sponsoring a
coordinated national Protestant Church and turned their attention to undermining the Christian faith, while for the time being avoiding an outright
confrontation with the churches. Hanns Kerrl, a member of the Nazi Party's
old guard and a man remarkably lacking in any obvious ability, was given
the completely new position of minister for the Reich churches in 1935.
He appointed a committee of compliant theologians who promptly issued
the following announcement: 'We affirm the National Socialist effort to
create a new people [Volkwerdung] based on race, blood and soil.' This
distasteful document left the Confessing Church seriously divided. Some
saw no alternative but to go into outright opposition, others formed a
kind of parallel body to Kerrl's henchmen called the Lutheran Council.
The Evangelical Church was thus now divided between the German Evangelical Church Council with Müller as Reich bishop, Kerrl's committee,
the Lutheran Council and the hard core of the Confessing Church. This
left both Kerrl and Müller helplessly at sea. They soon became objects of
contempt and derision for the likes of Joseph Goebbels.

By 1936 the radicals in the Confessing Church decided that it was time
to go on the offensive. They wrote a memorandum to Hitler attacking the
regime's ideology and practice, the neo-heathen Führer cult, the secret
police and the concentration camps. Hitler still hesitated, but the church
elections in 1937 were cancelled for fear that the Confessing Church would
put on an impressive performance. After the Anschluss it was announced
that all Evangelical pastors would be obliged to swear an oath of allegiance
to Hitler. The Confessing Church left it up to individual consciences whether
to take this step. Niemöller was arrested, his principal offence being that he
was opposed to the persecution of baptized Jews, but the court handed
down a very modest sentence, whereupon he was hauled in front of a special
party court and sent to Sachsenhausen concentration camp as a 'prisoner of
the Führer' where he remained until 1945. Goebbels commented: 'I'd like
to see that swine Niemöller put in front of a firing squad.'[2]

[170]   The Confessing Church took a pacifist stand during the Czech crisis, prompting the SS to demand the 'eradication' of these 'politicized pastors'. Kerrl managed to get a couple of bishops to condemn the 'peace liturgy', resulting in yet another deep split within the Evangelical Church. Even though the Evangelicals had powerful support among the conservative elites in the army, the civil service and the judiciary, they refused to speak out against the pogrom on 9 November 1938. This shocking lack of civic courage lost the church much of its remaining moral authority. Hitler did not want to risk an open confrontation with the churches as he prepared for war, and their supine attitude towards the regime gave him no immediate cause for concern. The whole issue could be postponed until after the victory celebrations.

The Evangelical Church's record during the war was even more shameful than that of the Catholic Church. No prominent churchman followed Bishop von Galen's example and spoke out against the euthanasia programme. Evangelical pastors thundered on about the patriotic duty of all the faithful to support Hitler's murderous racist war and the crusade against godless Bolshevism. Jewish Christians, who were now obliged to wear a yellow Star of David, were banned from churches in December 1941, and the few courageous clergymen from the Confessing Church who admitted them were denounced as 'Jewish pastors'. The church went one step further in that it helped the SS with its genealogical researches to trace Jewish blood and to establish the essential certificates needed as proof of Aryan blood (*Ariernachweis*). Although the church was well aware of the fact, if perhaps not the extent, of the murder of Jews it remained silent, with the one exception of a carefully disguised and moderate criticism voiced at the Breslau Synod of the Confessing Church in 1943. This all left a tiny group of remarkably brave people in a painful dilemma. Should they, as Dietrich Bonhoeffer put it, agree to the nation's defeat so that Christian civilization could survive, or should they work for victory and thus destroy the very basis of that culture? Since Lutheran theology did not allow for resistance to the civil authority, there was precious little that they could do except offer passive resistance or go into what Germans call 'inner emigration'[3].

Hans Kerrl died in December 1941 and was not replaced. Instead a somewhat fatuous Spiritual Council was formed. After the attempt on Hitler's life on 20 July 1944 the council ordered that prayers be said in all churches in thanks that the Führer enjoyed 'God's merciful protection' and that He should further protect the Führer and 'give him strength for the great tasks ahead'.

Catholics [171]

Hitler, who was raised as a Catholic, had immense respect for the Catholic Church as an institution, as he frequently remarked in *Mein Kampf,* and had roundly criticized the Pan-Germans for their anti-Catholicism. He had no such understanding of or admiration for Protestantism. At the same time he detested the political Catholicism of the Centre Party and insisted that the churches should not meddle with politics. Mussolini's Lateran Accords of 1929, which banned priests from getting involved in politics, were there-fore an example to be followed. In 1932 the party newspaper *Völkischer Beobachter* called for a German equivalent to the Lateran Accords. In Feb-ruary 1932 Bernhard Rust, who was to become minister of education in 1934, asked whether a similar concordat could be negotiated. The two Catholic political parties still had 89 seats in the Reichstag after the March elections of 1933, and were thus a force with which to be reckoned. Hitler argued in a cabinet meeting on 7 March that the best way of dealing with them was to persuade the Roman Curia 'to drop both parties'. On the next day Vice-Chancellor von Papen sounded out the chairman of the Catholic bishops' conference, the archbishop of Berlin, Cardinal Bertram, to see if there was any chance of reaching a concordat. Cardinal Faulhaber, archbishop of Munich, was in Rome in early March where he was received by the Vatican's foreign minister Eugenio Pacelli, later to ascend the throne of St Peter as Pius XII, and who had been papal nuncio in Germany. He told Faulhaber that the church's critical attitude towards National Socialism had changed considerably and that its anti-Communism was praiseworthy. On 23 March the Centre Party and the Bavarian People's Party voted for the Enabling Act, and thus sawed off the constitutional branch on which they were sitting, Monsignor Kaas, the Centre Party's leader, having been assured by both Hitler and von Papen that a concordat would be reached if his party voted for the bill. On 28 March the Catholic bishops, meeting in Fulda, form-ally withdrew their objections to National Socialism and promised their allegiance to 'legal authority', thus placing the German church solidly behind the regime. Individual bishops repeated that it was the duty of all Catholics to support the regime, and the bishops' conference issued a pastoral letter at the end of June forbidding any further debate about the rights and wrongs of National Socialism. The Concordat was concluded on 20 July.

The Roman Curia paid an extremely high price for the Concordat, both morally and politically. It had abandoned the two Catholic parties in Ger-many that together were one of the few consistent and constant supports of the Weimar Republic, however much they might have moved to the right under Brüning and Kaas. It gave a regime that had already trampled on the law and the constitution, and which was guilty of serious human rights abuses, its seal of approval, thus boosting the prestige of the regime both at home and abroad. It had made significant concessions at a time when such were not strictly necessary, as the example of the Confessing Church clearly showed. Cardinals Bertram and Faulhaber described Hitler's part in negotiating the Concordat as a 'world historical deed' and prayed that God would protect the chancellor. During the election campaign of November 1933 the Catholic bishops urged the faithful to vote for the Führer, thus helping to overcome the reluctance of many Catholics to support these uniformed heathens. Catholic intellectuals busied themselves building bridges between the church and the party, and in early July 1933 the Centre Party and the Bavarian People's Party went into voluntary dissolution.

At first sight it might seem incredible that the Catholic Church should capitulate so easily to National Socialism, but that it should have done so is in large part due to the temper of the times which affected Catholics almost as much as other Germans. There was a deeply ingrained distrust and suspicion of the modern, whether in the form of a capitalism which had resulted in a catastrophic depression, of parliamentary democracy which ended in a rancorous deadlock, of liberalism which was at the root of secularism and moral decay, or of Marxism which was the deadly antithesis of everything for which the church stood. It was all too convenient to see the sinister figure of the Jew behind these phenomena and to attribute the mysterious machinations of international finance, the hair-splitting wrangles of parliamentary debate, liberal secularism and atheistic Bolshevism to 'world Jewry'. The Catholic Church had a fatal tendency to look inward, to entrench itself behind doctrinal rigidity and an authoritarian structure and to pay insufficient attention to the world outside, beyond a broad condemnation of secular modernity. Catholic politicians were so absorbed with church affairs that they overlooked the deadly danger posed when parliamentary democracy and the rule of law were destroyed, imagining that the Concordat was an adequate solution to all major outstanding problems. Another contributing factor was that the church was still traumatized by the *Kulturkampf* – Bismarck's struggle against the Catholic Church – and was determined above all to avoid another such confrontation.

The Nazis had no intention of sticking to the letter of the Concordat and as early as 1934 began to harass the church. Catholic youth organizations were dissolved, Hitler Youth gangs mocked religious processions, and a number of prominent Catholics fell victim to the Röhm purge. In 1935 a campaign was mounted against priests and the religious orders. In addition to trumped up charges of abuses of currency regulations, 274 priests and monks were charged with homosexual offences in a widely publicized campaign to show up the church as, in Goebbels' words, 'a gang of pederasts'. This attack backfired, however, since it was feared that similar scrutiny of National Socialist organizations would reveal an embarrassing number of violations of paragraph 175 of the criminal code, and the hunt was called off on Hitler's orders in October 1936. In March the following year, when there were persistent rumours that the minister of economics Walther Funk was a homosexual, they were silenced by Hitler, who insisted that there should be no snooping into the private lives of his myrmidons.

The Vatican finally reacted in March 1937 with the encyclical 'With Burning Concern' that roundly condemned the Nazis' tyrannical practices. Two hundred thousand copies of the document were printed and it was read from virtually every pulpit in the land. Goebbels felt it best simply to ignore it, and issued instructions that it should not be shown to Hitler. At the same time he mounted a vigorous press campaign against the churches. The German Catholic bishops under the pusillanimous leadership of Cardinal Bertram, a man of whom a senior cleric said: 'He's as cold as a dog's nose', failed to back up the encyclical with a pastoral letter. At the end of 1937 Cardinal Faulhaber of Munich calmly announced that: 'There is no doubt that the Chancellor believes in God. He recognises Christianity as the master-builder of European culture.' The Nazi leadership did not agree with the cardinal. It was torn between those who wanted to step up the persecution of the Catholic Church and those who argued that as Germany was preparing for an eventual war it would be unwise to divide the nation so drastically on the eve of a great test to national unity and determination.

The Catholic Church gave its full and enthusiastic support to Hitler's war. Cardinal Bertram sent his heartfelt birthday greetings to the Führer on 20 April 1940, promising the sincere prayers of all Catholics for 'the people, army and fatherland' as well as 'the state and Führer'. Many bishops were disgusted by such toadyish adulation that did nothing to preserve the church from a renewed offensive by Nazi radicals. On orders from local Gauleiter in March 1941, 120 religious houses were seized and turned into holiday homes for party comrades and a sizeable amount of church property was sequestrated. The German church remained silent when German Jews began to be deported in the autumn of 1941, and Pius XII's lips were sealed. The Pope also refused to condemn the murder by Catholic Croats of 200,000 Orthodox Serbs in which Catholic priests played an active role; but when Archbishop Stepinac, in whose diocese fascist thugs from the

[174] Ustasha were free to murder, rape and plunder, was arrested by Tito's Communist partisans, there were immediate howls of protest from the Vatican. The final act to this shameful dereliction of moral duty came at the beginning of May 1945. When Cardinal Bertram heard of Hitler's death he ordered all priests to read a requiem mass for the Führer.

Education

Hitler went on at some length in *Mein Kampf* on the need radically to change the educational system so as to stress the importance of character, leadership and initiative, as well as emphasizing the fundamental importance of race, but in fact little was changed. The curriculum remained much the same, in part because of the reluctance of teachers to revamp their courses to include racial studies (*Rassenkunde*) or to discuss the latest piece of National Socialist literature, and also because virtually no new textbooks were written that took account of the new worldview. This was hardly a pressing problem since most teachers and texts were in broad accordance with the principal aims of National Socialism. They reflected a conservative, nationalist and authoritarian viewpoint that, although it was reactionary rather than radical in the eyes of Nazi zealots, was not so distinct as to be the cause of any concern.

In the initial stages, Bernhard Rust as minister of education concentrated on weeding out any political opponents within the educational system as well as strengthening the position of the National Socialist Teachers' Association. He soon found himself locked in a battle, typical of the Nazi polycracy, with Baldur von Schirach, Robert Ley and the SS over the elite party schools.

In 1938 all of the remaining private elementary schools were closed, and all children between the ages of 6 and 14 were obliged to attend state elementary schools (*Grundschulen*). The majority of these elementary schools were tiny institutions with only one or two classes, and there was a desperate shortage of properly qualified teachers. A 'Führer order' was issued in 1941 to provide four years of upper classes for elementary schoolchildren that would include learning a foreign language, but it was not put into effect until after the war. After the promulgation of the Nuremberg Laws, Jewish children were taught in separate elementary schools, until these were closed and they were sent to their deaths. Catholic private schools were closed so that the church's influence on the curriculum ended, in spite of the Concordat, and state schools no longer celebrated religious holidays.

Figure 5.1 Hitler, Göring and Baldur von Schirach near Hitler's mountain top residence at the Obersalzberg

The educational system underwent drastic changes during the war when children were evacuated from the urban centres and forced to work during harvest time. This led to further struggles between Baldur von Schirach's Hitler Youth and the ministry of education, because classes ceased when the children were working in agriculture. Education was also adversely affected by the continuing shortage of qualified teachers. New teacher training colleges were instituted that placed greater emphasis on ideological correctness, but admission standards were dropped to the point that it was no longer necessary to have a school-leaving certificate (*Arbitur*) in order to qualify. Most of the pupils in elementary schools went on to trade schools (*Berufsschulen*) and it was possible for the talented to graduate from them to train as engineers, technicians or architects at polytechnics. This was a positive reform allowing for a higher degree of social mobility, as was the

[176] 1938 law that made attendance at trade schools compulsory for all those who did not meet the requirements to enter a secondary school.

There were three types of secondary schools. There were two for boys: one specialized in the sciences, the other in languages, with separate secondary schools for girls. The grammar school (*Gymnasium*) remained as a special form of elite secondary education. The number of grammar schools was greatly reduced, and they only survived in the larger urban centres where they provided an excellent education for the sons of the wealthier bourgeoisie. This did not sit well with the ideology of the 'racial community', but there were powerful interests determined to defend these outposts of traditional privilege and status. On the other hand, the private schools were brought under state control, but all forms of secondary education were fee-paying and therefore beyond the means of the majority of 'racial comrades'. The same was true of the various forms of middle schools that provided education beyond the primary level for those who were unlikely to meet the entrance qualifications for higher education. Jewish pupils were excluded from all forms of secondary school after the 1938 pogrom. As in the primary schools there was little change in the curriculum. Racial studies were not taken seriously, and the history text *Volk und Führer*, published in 1939, did not replace more traditional conservative works. There were of course a number of fanatical Nazis on the teaching staffs of some secondary schools, but they remained a minority and were regarded with a certain snobbish disdain by colleagues and pupils alike.

Educational standards fell drastically during the war as the age for entry into the armed forces was dropped from 18 to 17 and then to 16. Since officers needed to have a school-leaving certificate, and as the need for more engineers and doctors grew, the pass mark was lowered to the point that it became almost automatic. The universities were hotbeds of National Socialism. Students flocked to the National Socialist Students' Association (NSStB). Three hundred professors signed a declaration of loyalty to the new regime on 3 March 1933, and nine days later 700 professors swore allegiance to 'Adolf Hitler and the National Socialist state'. This was no sudden conversion. The majority of the professoriate was in broad agreement with the principal ideas of National Socialism. They had a congruent dislike of the Weimar Republic and all that it stood for. They wished to restore Germany as a hegemonic power in Europe. They had a hearty dislike of 'cultural Bolshevism'. They longed for an authoritarian regime that would reinforce their status as the intellectual elite of the nation. They were also fearful that were they not to toe the line they would lose their jobs. They were equally anxious not to provoke the wrath of the radical student body, and they feared nothing more than the loss of a comfortable pension.

In April 1933 1,684 Jewish and politically undesirable university teachers were removed. Almost a third of all teaching staff was dismissed by 1939 and 3,000 scholars had gone into exile. The natural and social sciences were hit far harder than the arts. That there were a large number of Jews among them is at least testimony to the fact that during the Weimar Republic anti-Semitism had not yet seriously affected hiring policies. There were 3,950 Jewish students in 1932 in the universities. By 1934 there were only 548. The terrible loss of teaching staff was never made good, not in numbers and certainly not in quality. There was virtually no protest at this crass violation of everything for which the university stood. Germany's professors offered their mute and cowardly approbation as the Bavarian minister of education, a primitive member of the 'old guard', announced that it did not matter whether something was true or not, merely whether it served the National Socialist revolution; or when the historian Gustav Adolf Rein called for a 'racial science' infused with 'racial-political intelligence'. Martin Heidegger, Germany's greatest philosopher, as the newly-appointed rector of Freiburg University, refused to allow his Jewish mentor and predecessor, Edmund Husserl, to set foot on the campus and in a formal address on 27 May 1933 announced that the Führer was the 'embodiment of present and future reality', as well as of the law[4].

Precious few professors were prepared to follow Heidegger and make this ontological leap in the dark, or to accept Alfred Rosenberg's ideological hogwash. They admired Hitler's startling successes in foreign policy and they got carried away by talk of the 'racial community', but they felt far superior to the ill-educated Nazi elite with their crude anti-intellectualism and vulgar petit-bourgeois tastes. There were practically no dyed-in-the-wool Nazis among the professoriate and even Heidegger, who continued to wear the party badge on his lapel until the bitter end, felt that Hitler had betrayed his own ideals. The majority of professors were party members. They may not have been fanatics, and may have been denounced by the RSHA as 'passive', but they were loyal supporters of the regime.

The main reason for this lack of enthusiasm for 'the movement' was that most Nazis loathed intellectuals with exceptional passion. The pages of *Mein Kampf* and of Goebbels' diaries are peppered with outbursts against effete academics, dreamers and desk-bound pedants. Julius Streicher, a knee-jerk anti-Semite and pornographic hate-monger, much admired by both Hitler and Goebbels for his fanaticism, poured scorn on the pin-headed professors who were all dwarfed by the Führer's genius. Some academics met

[178] these creatures halfway. The rector of the Berlin polytechnic announced that 'every energetic lecturer belongs in the SA'. Another scholar announced that the 'bookworm and the desk-bound scholar' should be replaced by 'lecture hall heroes, stout soldiers, smartly marching, toughened by life in the camp'. Elsewhere there was an appeal for scholars to pick up a shovel and be toughened by physical labour. An attempt to inculcate young scholars with this martial spirit was made at the end of 1934 when all lecturers under the age of 45 were obliged to attend a lecturers' camp (*Dozentenlager*) for ideological schooling. This programme was not a success, since there was a chronic shortage of lecturers and they were badly needed in the universities. By 1938 attendance at these camps was no longer obligatory. The ideologically committed and the outright opportunists joined the National Socialist Lecturers' Association, whose representatives acted as political watchdogs and as a kind of alternative administration within the universities. They were more of a nuisance than anything else, since the ministry of education tended to support the university administration against them, in the interests of maintaining educational standards at the expense of ideological purity.

The NSStB, having organized the book-burnings in May 1933, hoped to have a voice in university affairs, but instead of that they were obliged to serve the new state by enrolling in the RAD or in the SA as well as spending their fourth semester in work camps. All the traditional student fraternities were converted into a Nazi association by the winter of 1935. A large number of university students lost their lives in Hitler's war, others had their studies interrupted during the many years of war and imprisonment, to continue their studies after 1945 amid the ruins of a defeated Germany.

The Nazis did bring about certain changes in the curriculum and introduced new approaches in certain disciplines. Germany's most distinguished historical journal, the *Historische Zeitschrift*, began a special section on 'The Jewish Question'. The Reich Institute for the History of the New Germany under Walter Frank began the rewriting of German history from a National Socialist perspective. Biology and medicine were chronically infected with racist obsessions and eugenicist fantasies. Johannes Stark, an apostle of 'German physics', was appointed president of the prestigious German Research Association (DFG), but had to be removed because of gross professional incompetence. Max Planck, the father of quantum mechanics and the 1918 Nobel Prize winner, resigned as president of the equally distinguished Kaiser Wilhelm Society (KWG) in protest against the violation of academic freedom. The attempt to make Stark his successor failed miserably and the chemist Carl Bosch, co-winner of the Nobel Prize in 1931 and president of [179] IG Farben, took his place. Bosch was the brother-in-law of Fritz Haber, the 'father of gas warfare', who had won the Nobel Prize for chemistry in 1918 for his work on the synthesis of ammonia from hydrogen and atmospheric nitrogen, thereby overcoming the shortage of natural nitrate needed for explosives. As a Jew he was forced to resign from IG Farben's board of directors in 1933 and died the following year. Bosch stood up courageously for those professors who had been dismissed, but was given virtually no support. He suffered from bouts of depression and died in 1940 a broken man. Excellent work was done within the framework of the Four-Year Plan, but this was almost entirely in the field of armaments, while fundamental theoretical research, an area in which Germany had once excelled, was sadly neglected. The harm done to Germany's universities, much of it self-inflicted, has yet to be made good.

CHAPTER 6

THE ARTS AND PROPAGANDA

Arts and entertainment

The arts played a vital role in Nazi Germany. Hitler, the failed artist and amateur architect, who was hailed as 'the greatest builder of all times', saw his Third Reich as a mammoth aesthetic project. Goebbels was keenly aware of the propagandistic potential of the arts and delighted in the company of artists to the point that he was known as the 'Babelsberg goat', after the film studios over which he ruled with minute and prurient attention. Göring was a hideous caricature of a renaissance prince, plundering the art galleries of Europe for his private collection and showering favours on his preferred artists. The artistic elite in Nazi Germany was handsomely rewarded. They were exempted from military service, lavishly remunerated and showered with all manner of privileges. Their rivals were in exile, imprisoned and banned from working. Some of them were wholehearted supporters of the regime, others were careerists and opportunists; a mere handful used their positions of power and influence to help colleagues who had fallen foul of the regime.

Goebbels' ideal propaganda was such that the average audience would not realize it was being indoctrinated. As he told a group of leading figures in theatre and radio in March 1933: 'Of course propaganda has a purpose, but this purpose must be so skilfully and ingeniously hidden that the message comes across without it being noticed.'[1] This was the fundamental problem. Goebbels wanted a specifically National Socialist art, but it had to be subtle, of the highest artistic quality, and above all easily digestible. As he often repeated, he longed to make a Nazi *Mrs Miniver*, a *Ten Days That Shook the World* or a *Battleship Potemkin*. Leaving aside the question whether great art can ever be reconciled with political propaganda, it was almost impossible to find the right mixture. Most of Goebbels' films were not nearly political enough for Hitler, and outright political polemics and celebrations found little favour among the public. A further problem was that most of the artists of sufficient calibre to walk this narrow line had left the country. As success followed success the task of the propagandists was relatively easy, but after the failure of Barbarossa there were no more victories and Hitler refused to appear on camera for fear that the deplorable state of his health would cause widespread alarm. All the regime had to offer now were appeals to fight on to the bitter end, along with vain promises of miracle weapons that would turn the tide.

The central aim of propaganda was to strengthen the sense of 'racial community' and to give substance to the slogan '*ein Volk, ein Reich, ein Führer*'. Scorn, derision and loathing was poured upon those who were excluded from this elite group: Jews, Marxists, 'plutocrats', the habitually criminal, the mentally and physically handicapped, along with all those deemed to be racially inferior. Since the individual was the antithesis of the communal, National Socialism rejected what the media expert, Professor Emil Dovipat, was pleased to call the 'alien individualistic liberal ideology of Jewish provenance'. Goebbels banned all forms of criticism in November 1936, delivering the German people from the 'egotistical tyranny of the critic', from 'egocentric standards' and opening up the way for a healthy relationship between the arts and the 'racial community'. In 1936 an elaborate exhibition entitled Degenerate Art was opened in Munich and travelled to a number of major cities in the following months. In the same year 17,000 works of art, including paintings by van Gogh, Cézanne and Matisse, were seized, with many of the choicest works ending up in Göring's private collection. In November 1937 a gigantic exhibition was held in the House of Art in Munich of ideologically acceptable art. Another show entitled The Eternal Jew was organized in the German Museum designed to demonstrate the destructive and degenerate nature of Jewry in the arts and the deadly danger it posed to the 'racial community'. The exhibition then toured a number of major German cities and attracted a total of 500,000 visitors. This was followed by the exhibition Degenerate Music in Berlin in the following year. In March 1939, 5,000 works of 'degenerate' art were burnt, away from public view at Berlin's main fire station. In May 1942 an exhibition entitled The Soviet Paradise opened in Berlin. It was a piece of staggeringly crude anti-Communist propaganda that provoked a small Jewish and Communist resistance cell, led by Herbert Baum, to make an arson attempt and to distribute handbills reading: 'Permanent exhibition – NAZI PARADISE – War, Hunger, Lies, Gestapo, How Much Longer?' Twenty-two members of the group were arrested and executed, others were sent to concentration camps without a trial. It would seem that Baum committed suicide.

Figure 6.1   'Degenerate Art' poster

Goebbels knew that he could only succeed if he could get the cooperation of as many as possible of the really talented artists who remained
in Germany, and he was prepared to make major concessions to achieve
that end. Thus the great actor Gustav Gründgens was given a free hand in
Berlin's Staatstheater even though he was well known to be a homosexual.
Richard Strauss and Wilhelm Furtwängler made pacts with the devil, but
like Gründgens helped many of their colleagues, including a number of
Jews. Herbert von Karajan, a shameless careerist of immense talent, needed
no such inducements. He prudently joined the Nazi Party twice, once in his
native Austria and the second time in the Reich. A number of leading artists
lent their support to the new regime, among them the poet Gottfried Benn,
the actors Heinrich George and Werner Kraus, the film directors Veit Harlan
and Leni Riefensthal. Musicians were particularly susceptible to the lure of
the new and included such superstars as Wilhelm Backhaus, Karl Böhm,

Hans Knappertsbusch and Elly Ney. Some, like the artist A. Paul Weber, collaborated after a spell of re-education in a concentration camp. Others cooperated while remaining politically in opposition.

The arts were thus used as a form of indirect propaganda as when Furtwängler conducted the Berlin Philharmonic in a factory canteen under the auspices of the DAF, or when the film star Heinz Rühmann appeared in newsreels dressed in a sergeant's uniform in the cockpit of a military aircraft. In some cases the propaganda was laid on with a heavy trowel as in the film *I Accuse*, a gruellingly sentimental defence of euthanasia, *Jud Süss*, Veit Harlan's viciously anti-Semitic film with sinister sexual undertones, the crude anti-British diatribe *Ohm Krüger*, and finally *Kolberg*, Goebbels' last large-scale production that made a rousing appeal to fight on to the bitter end.

The NSDAP was a protest party that knew what it was against, but had little idea of what it would do should it ever be in power. The party programme had been so watered down as Hitler made his peace with the established elites that it had become little more than a few vacuous phrases. Only a few Nazis had any experience of government, and that only at the state or local level. It is hardly surprising that the first stage of the 'cultural renewal' was to get rid of all those artists who belonged to groups deemed to be undesirable. The arts, in short, were subjected to *Gleichschaltung*. The Law for the Restoration of a Professional Civil Service of April 1933 applied to all those in state employ, including university professors, schoolteachers, musicians in state-sponsored orchestras, actors in national theatres, museum staff and librarians and all members of the illustrious Prussian Academy of the Arts (even though these latter were not even civil servants). A number of important publishing houses and newspapers were closed down by means of the Law for the Confiscation of Communist Assets in May and the Law for the Confiscation of the Assets of Those Hostile to the Race and the Nation in July.

In 1928 the NSDAP's leading ideologue, Alfred Rosenberg, founded the Activist Association for German Culture (*Kampfbund*). It was run by an incompetent and was on the verge of bankruptcy when Hitler came to power. Hans Hinkel, a former Freikorps thug and one of the party's 'old warriors', was appointed director, a man whom his rival Goebbels described as 'an intriguer and a born liar'[2]. Hinkel was an accomplished powerbroker whom Bernhard Rust appointed as special commissar for culture and Göring put in charge of the Prussian state theatres. Like virtually everyone else he loathed the inept Rosenberg, with the result that the *Kampfbund* died on the vine while Hinkel went on to become head of the Reich Chamber of Culture

[184] (*Reichskulturkammer* – RKK), soon to be put in charge of the entire film industry.

In March 1933 Hindenburg appointed Joseph Goebbels as minister for popular enlightenment and propaganda. In June he was given formal powers over the radio, press, theatre, films, art, music and literature, with some exceptions in the case of Prussia that remained in Göring's bailiwick. All those involved in any of these activities had to be registered with the RKK, which was divided into seven divisions, each covering a specific activity such as art or music. Goebbels hunted high and low for distinguished figures to head each of these sub-groups, but he found only one. Richard Strauss actively lobbied to be appointed president of the Reich Music Chamber as well as of the Association of German Composers, ostensibly in the hope of bettering the lot of musicians and composers. Strauss appointed Furtwängler vice-president, though he was soon to be dismissed for championing the music of Paul Hindemith.

Strauss managed to ensure that the royalties paid to composers of serious music, such as himself, were considerably higher than those paid to those who wrote popular music. He also managed to persuade Goebbels to increase the protection of copyright from 30 to 50 years after the composer's death. This was a promising start, but the troubles began when Strauss insisted on remaining in Bavaria at his home in Garmisch, instead of moving to Berlin. He also found it virtually impossible to work with the Nazi bureaucrats in the Chamber, preferring to use colleagues in whom he had confidence. He was almost solely concerned with the well-being of serious composers, in spite of the fact that they formed a very small minority of the members. Even more serious was Strauss' protection of non-Nazi musicians and his refusal to apply the 'Aryan Paragraphs'[3] and dismiss Jews from the Chamber, which would thus deny them a livelihood. Alfred Rosenberg, who was deeply resentful of Goebbels for having pushed him onto the cultural sidelines, was determined to get his own back. Strauss had been collaborating with Stefan Zweig before Hitler came to power. He was writing the libretto for an opera 'The Taciturn Woman' (*Die schweigsame Frau*) and Strauss had somehow managed to get Goebbels' and Hitler's permission to continue working with this prominent Jewish author. Rosenberg mobilized his National Socialist Cultural Association (*Gemeinde*) against Goebbels for thus protecting a Jew and a dangerously modernist composer. Goebbels was now in an awkward situation. He accepted Rosenberg's political objections, but did not wish to risk the scandal of cancelling the première of *Die schweigsame Frau*, scheduled for June 1935. Strauss stuck by Stefan Zweig; their correspondence was read by the Gestapo and forwarded to Goebbels and Hitler. Strauss wrote that 'these are sad times when a composer of my distinction must ask a young whippersnapper of a minister what he can compose and perform. I belong to a race of "waiters and the waited-upon" and am almost envious of my racially persecuted friend Stefan Zweig.' He told Zweig that he was 'miming' the office of president and that he did so only to ensure that worse did not befall. Goebbels felt that Strauss had been shamefully disloyal and demanded his resignation in July 1935. It was said to have been on medical grounds.

Goebbels' struggle with Rosenberg was typical of Nazi Germany and he was soon locked in battle with other powerful rivals over areas of competence. Göring jealously guarded his authority over the theatre in Prussia. Bernhard Rust as minister of education was in charge of the schools, universities and public libraries. Frick as minister of the interior supported local governments and the Gauleiter against the propaganda minister's encroachments. Robert Ley was responsible for the lavish cultural offerings of the DAF. In early 1934 Hitler made Rosenberg responsible for the ideological schooling of the NSDAP. Reinhard Heydrich and the SD, regarding Goebbels' ministry and the RKK as dangerously liberal and permissive, kept a close watch on all forms of cultural activity. Max Amann as head of the NSDAP's publishing house, which controlled almost 80 per cent of the German press, was close to Hitler, having as a sergeant been his immediate wartime superior, and had no intention of taking orders from Goebbels. Otto Dietrich was the press chief of the NSDAP, vice-president of the press division of the RKK and secretary of state in the propaganda ministry. Goebbels said of him: 'He's useless and does nothing', but he also was determined to maintain his independence. Philipp Bouhler was responsible for the censorship of party literature and from October 1934 was head of Hitler's private chancellery, thus enjoying a certain autonomy. Goebbels admired Bouhler for having organized the murder of some 80,000 mentally or physically handicapped persons in the euthanasia campaign. In 1941 Martin Bormann was appointed head of the party chancellery and began to meddle in cultural affairs. In such a situation 'conformity' (*Gleichschaltung*) in culture proved to be an impossibility, and the ensuing chaos reflected the many different interpretations of what National Socialism was all about.

One thing they could agree upon was that Jews and people who were related to Jews (*jüdisch Versippte*) had to be removed and culture rendered purely 'German', but even here the practice was far from uniform. Initially a number of exceptions were made and a Cultural Association of German Jews and a Reich Association of German Jewish Cultural Organizations offered increasingly restricted opportunities for German Jews to maintain

[186]   their cultural identity until the RSHA put an end to all such organizations in September 1941.

Similarly, it took some time for an effective censorship system to be developed. All artistic efforts had first to be vetted by the appropriate department within the propaganda ministry. The works of composers such as Alban Berg, Paul Hindemith, Arnold Schoenberg and Anton von Webern were strictly prohibited. 'Jazz and Negro music' was banned in 1935, and in 1939 a number of other pieces of music were placed on the index. A list of 'harmful and undesirable' books had already been published in 1935 that included the works of all Jewish authors. In spite of increasingly vigilant control and the use of outright terror, a few brave souls provided opportunities for non-conformists. Publishing houses such as Rowolt (until it was taken over by the NSDAP in 1938) and S. Fischer under the inspired leadership of Peter Suhrkamp (until his arrest in April 1944) published the works of distinguished writers such as Peter Huchel, Erich Nossak and Marie Louise Kaschnitz. The *Berliner Tageblatt* (closed down in 1939) and the *Frankfurter Zeitung* (until 1943), along with a number of local newspapers, remained defiantly independent, while the cultural section of papers such as the *Kölnischer Zeitung* resolutely refused to toe the party line.

Some theatres, principal among them Gustav Gründgens' Staatstheater in Berlin, tested the limits of artistic freedom and gave the public outstanding interpretations of the classics. Wilhelm Furtwängler and the Berlin Philharmonic courageously performed works by Honegger, Hindemith, Bartók and Stravinsky. Jazz was immensely popular, especially with the young, and the fact that it was outlawed made it all the more desirable. A number of films were produced that were irreconcilable with National Socialist principles.

Goebbels once said: 'I couldn't care less whether Furtwängler is a National Socialist or not. As far as I'm concerned he can bitch and criticise as much as he likes. He's worth it. After all he's not a political functionary, but an advertisement for our attitude towards the arts.' Himmler, Rosenberg and Bouhler cared very much whether artists were National Socialists or not, and were appalled by Goebbels' lax attitude. This placed great artists like Furtwängler and Gründgens in a very uncomfortable position. They were not Nazis and remained true to their art, but they were also painfully aware that they were working for Goebbels and for the regime without doing anything that was specifically National Socialist, although it should be noted that Gründgens lived in a splendid villa that had been recently Aryanized. Gründgens, whom Karl Zuckmayer described as 'a tightrope walker on the razor's edge'[4], took a certain delight in living dangerously, and although he married Thomas Mann's daughter Erika and then the actress Marianne

Hoppe as a cover, he made no attempt whatsoever to disguise his homosexuality. Berlin audiences were staggered when in his hugely successful performance of *Hamlet* he stepped forward to the footlights to deliver the monologue 'What a piece of work is man!' Reversing the order of the original he declaimed: 'man delights not me' followed by a long pause before saying: 'by your smiling, you seem to say so'.

Goebbels having been outfoxed by Rosenberg over the Richard Strauss affair, realized that he had to watch out and protect himself from further attacks from the NSDAP. The Chamber of Culture had to be made politically orthodox and to this end he appointed three Reich cultural overseers (*Reichskulturwalter*). Two of them, Hans Hinkel and Franz Moraller, were in the classic mould of brutish 'old warriors', whereas Hans Schmidt-Leonhardt was an opportunistic bureaucrat. Together they set about combing out the racially and politically undesirables. The process of 'de-Jewing' had to be stepped up, and all those who 'were inclined to make compromises over the Jewish question and other important National Socialist issues, or who allowed for liberal notions' were to be ruthlessly purged.

The head of the Writers' Chamber, Hans Friedrich Blunck, was an ultra-nationalist who wallowed in ancient Germanic lore and the romanticism of 'blood and soil', but he took a principled stand on the Jewish question, accepting the presidency only on condition that there would be no discrimination against Jewish writers. In this he showed far more courage than Richard Strauss, whose son was married to a Jewess and who was thus Jewish-related (*jüdisch Versippte*). Blunck was eased out in 1935, wrote numerous articles for the *Völkischer Beobachter*, was awarded a gold medal by Hitler personally and posed after the war as an anti-fascist. He was replaced by Hanns Johst, a full-bloodied Nazi, a close friend of Hans Hinkel and author of *Schlageter*, a play he dedicated to Hitler, which celebrated a fascist thug who had been executed for an act of sabotage against the French occupying forces in 1923 to become the 'first martyr of National Socialism'. Johst soon clung to Himmler's coat-tails in abject subservience and oiled his way into Hitler's presence. Although he was a man with no discernible literary talent he was showered with prizes, and Himmler elevated him to the rank of SS-Gruppenführer, the equivalent of a general or an admiral.

Johst was an incompetent, who like Strauss and Blunck preferred the comforts of home, in this case a villa on the beautiful Starnberger See in Bavaria, leaving most of the work to a dutiful secretary and a henchman from the SD, provided by Himmler. The result was that his empire fell apart and all really important decisions were taken by Goebbels personally, leaving the Writers' Chamber as little more than an administrative unit.

By 1935 only four of the original seven Chamber presidents were still in office, but in spite of these changes the ultra-Nazis around Rosenberg were appalled at the number of Jews that were still tolerated, complained about the lax liberal approach to the arts and were horrified when a group of young artists attempted to argue that expressionism was reconcilable with National Socialism. They were greatly encouraged when Hitler gave a speech at the Nuremberg party rally in 1934 in which he roundly denounced the culturally modern, while at the same time denouncing the idealization of a Germanic dream world in a non-existent past.

The man chosen to clean the Augean stable was Adolf Ziegler, a painter of grim technical proficiency who had joined the NSDAP in 1925, and whose lifeless nudes were much admired by Hitler. He mounted a massive campaign against 'degenerate art', which included an exhibition of such works in Munich, and German museums were rid of all that came under the heading of what Hitler called 'cubism, futurism, dadaism etc.' Ziegler's fall from power was as swift as it was surprising. After Stalingrad he realized that the war was lost and plotted with two men prominent in business circles to contact Winston Churchill's son Randolph to discuss the possibility of a separate peace. It was an absurd idea that was quickly unearthed by the Gestapo and Ziegler ended up in a concentration camp. Hitler left him there for a few weeks before ordering his release.

Architecture

Hitler saw the monumental architecture of the Third Reich as the outward expression of the greatness of the times, as 'the word in stone'. The stadium in Nuremberg where the yearly party rallies were held, the colossal buildings in Munich's Adolf-Hitler-Forum, the gigantomanic government offices in Berlin, were designed to impress and to provide a backdrop against which the National Socialist drama would be enacted.

There was nothing original about this architecture. It carried on a style developed during the Weimar Republic and which was echoed in buildings throughout the world. Heinrich Wolff's vast building for the Reichsbank echoed Hans Poelzig's IG Farben offices in Frankfurt, which one critic described, without a hint of irony, as 'a palace for the princes of capital'. It had the same basic unadorned cubic form, and was covered with the same travertine stone. The design was selected by Hitler personally, who thus rejected the exciting modern architecture of Mies van der Rohe, Walter Gropius and Peter Behrens, all of whom had submitted models in the

competition. Stone was to replace glass, massive pillars slender steel
columns, the monumental the light and airy.

Hitler's favourite architect, Ludwig Troost, set the grammar and the syntax
for the new architecture. He was an exceptionally skilled vulgarian with a
keen sense for the theatrical, who managed to combine the modern with
the traditional, the contemporary with the timeless, the dynamic and the
monumental. He had learnt his trade as an interior designer for luxury
liners where he artfully combined the brashly luxurious with decorative
restraint. Troost died in January 1934 and his widow Gerdy said of him
that his buildings had 'eternal value' while being 'monuments to belief in the
movement'. In less pretentious terms he managed to combine the traditional with the contemporary, neo-classicism with the specifically German,
and to place modern building techniques in the service of his essentially
conservative architecture.

Troost's monument in Munich to the 12 who 'fell for the movement' on
9 November 1923, flanked by the party headquarters in the Brown House
and Führer's House, provided an immensely effective setting for the yearly
parade when thousands paid homage to the martyrs. His successor, Albert
Speer, followed in Troost's footsteps and perfected the art of providing
remarkable settings for spectacular mass meetings. Hitler was immensely
impressed with Speer's setting for the demonstration on 1 May 1933, held
on the Tempelhof Field in Berlin, and in the following year gave him the
task of building a stand for the guests of honour at the Zeppelin Field in
Nuremberg, scene of the party rallies. Speer took the Pergamon altar[5] as a
model for what in effect was an altar for the National Socialist cult, with
Hitler as the high priest addressing the faithful from an imposing pulpit.
Speer was also greatly influenced by Max Reinhardt's large-scale theatrical
productions at the Deutsche Theater in Berlin and also by Fritz Lang's films
Nibelungen and *Metropolis*, both of which were among Hitler's favourites
and which he watched in his Berlin bunker in the final days of the war.
The design for the Nibelungen castle in Worms in the film is echoed in
much of Speer's work and in other National Socialist monuments. Here
again the continuity between the aesthetics of the Weimar Republic and
the Third Reich is clearly evident in what Walter Benjamin in 1936 was to
call 'aestheticised politics'.

A number of architects prominent in the Weimar Republic found it relatively easy to adapt to the new style. Wilhelm Kreis' Hygiene Museum in
Dresden of 1930 is a set of unadorned symmetrically arranged cubes with
a faintly ancient Egyptian air. In 1937 he was commissioned to build a
district headquarters for the air force. This time the massive central cube is

[190] adorned with reliefs of fighting and dying heroes, giving the whole the look of a sacrificial altar.

Speer recruited a number of young architects, many of whom were fellow students or acquaintances, who were quick to learn the new aesthetic. Those who had been trained in the Bauhaus turned for inspiration to the Braunes Haus, the party headquarters at Munich known as the Brown House. Fritz Todt, who was responsible for building the motorways (*Autobahnen*), skilfully combined the high-tech modern with the Germanic traditional in an attempt, as he phrased it, to make these motorways 'an expression of the German spirit [*Wesen*]'. His massive reinforced concrete bunkers on the West Wall were state of the art pieces of military engineering, with strong echoes of medieval castles as represented in Fritz Lang's *Nibelungen*, along with a hint of Erich Mendelsohn's futuristic Einstein Tower. Hermann Giesler's Gauforum in Weimar was an artful synthesis of the 'less is more' aesthetic of the Bauhaus with an Aryanized classicism. Thus in the early years a strong element of the Weimar modern is discernible in most of the buildings commissioned by the regime. For this reason most of these young architects were able to pursue highly successful careers in post-war Germany by emphasizing these modernist elements in their work. Hanns Dustmann is an excellent example. He was a talented student of Walter Gropius who was elevated to the post of Reich Architect of the Hitler Youth in 1935 and was responsible for a series of dreadfully twee folkloric neo-medieval buildings. During the war he reverted to a monumental Roman style drenched in the *Götterdämmerung* spirit of the dying Reich. After the war he built the delightfully airy Café Kanzler in Berlin along with some fine high-rises in Düsseldorf and Berlin.

The big change came in 1938 with the building of the megalomanic neo-classicist new chancellery in Berlin. Hitler detested the old chancellery, dismissing it as adequate for 'the administrative offices of a soap factory', and saw the new chancellery as the first building in what was to become 'Germania', the capital of a vast Nazi Empire. Speer fed the Führer's gigantomanic appetite with plans for rebuilding Berlin and converting Linz into a place of pilgrimage for a grotesque Hitler cult. His designs were grossly inflated plagiarisms of well-known classical buildings. Thus the preposterous Great Hall at the end of the north–south axis of the new Berlin was a gargantuan version of the Pantheon, and the Führer Palace was a bizarre mixture of Nero's *domus aurea* and a renaissance palace. Wilhelm Kreis, whose historicist style had fallen into ill favour, was recalled to rebuild the Museum Island in Berlin and came up with designs that looked like Hollywood's version of ancient Babylon. Peter Behrens' plans for AEG's headquarters in Berlin envisioned a gigantic reproduction of a Roman castle. When there was little left of the Reich apart from a pile of rubble, Speer and his associates sought consolation in the architecture of long ago empires, while Hitler, deep down in his bunker, lived in the dream world of a future Germania.

Film

Goebbels was keenly aware of the usefulness of the cinema, both as a propaganda medium and as a means of stiffening morale, and he was also highly knowledgeable about the cinema. He was therefore determined to bring the entire film industry under his personal control. The Reich Film Chamber was formed in July 1933 and began the process of weeding out the undesirables, many of whom, such as Fritz Lang, Billy Wilder, Peter Lorre, Elisabeth Bergner and Max Orphüls had already left to pursue stellar careers in Hollywood and elsewhere. When this process of discrimination and outright terror was completed and the industry 'synchronized', the major film companies such as Ufa, Tobis and Bavaria were placed under direct state control. Goebbels now personally vetted the script, cast and director of all major productions. He also furthered the careers of young actresses, exploiting to the full the possibilities of the casting couch, and giving rise to numerous complaints to Hitler by Himmler and Rosenberg, both of whom loathed Goebbels. He made every attempt to bring Marlene Dietrich back from Hollywood, but his diaries do not reveal whether he had any ulterior motive. Stars, such as the Swedish beauty Zarah Leander or Irene von Meyendorff, benefited greatly from his sponsorship and encouragement. It has recently been suggested that Zarah Leander was a Soviet agent. Whatever the truth of this assertion she was certainly not the non-political artist of her memoirs. She met Goebbels on numerous occasions and had lengthy political discussions.

The 'de-Jewing' of the film industry was entrusted to SS-Obergruppenführer Hans Hinkel, a brutish creature whom Goebbels described as a 'bug' (*Wanze*) but of whose crude anti-Semitism he heartily approved[6]. In 1942 Hinkel married an actress whom Goebbels had sent for a spell to a concentration camp in 1939, by which time he was on much better terms with his superior. He was a close friend of many of the stars, all of whom felt it imprudent to put a word in for him when he was interned after the war.

Fritz Hippler as Reich Film *Intendant* was another important figure. He was widely respected for his technical competence, for his refusal to join in

[192] the intrigues that plagued the film industry, as everywhere else in Nazi Germany, and for his even-handedness. Even though he directed the most obscene of films, 'The eternal Jew' (*Der Ewige Jude*), in contrast to Hinkel his colleagues rallied around him after the war and the Allies gave him a 'Persil Certificate' that washed away his disreputable Nazi past.

Cinema means stars, and Goebbels was quick to realize that they could be put to excellent propagandistic use. Hitler enjoyed the company of the stars, as did Göring who was married to the actress Emmy Sonnemann, who used her new status to meddle in artistic affairs, much to the propaganda minister's annoyance. Hitler gave the actor Emil Jannings and the director Veit Harlan lessons in demagogy, took great pleasure in hearing Heinrich George declaiming suitably nationalistic texts, called upon the Dutch comedian Johannes Heesters to sing a song, and laughed heartily at Heinz Rühmann's innocent gags. Once the war began he had no time for such frivolity, and henceforth Goebbels only met socially with a small group of key artists. Goebbels' casting couch days had already come to an abrupt end in 1938 when he became seriously entangled with the Czech actress Lida Baarova, Hitler putting an end to the affair at the urgent request of the minister's neurotic wife, Magda.

The stars were showered with prizes, medals and titles and given recently Aryanized villas. They were paid handsomely. Emil Jannings, for example, whose obsession with money bordered on the pathological, had a guaranteed annual income of 250,000 RM, even if he never acted. From 1942 Goebbels attempted to cut the stars' salaries, but all in vain, even though actors were forbidden to have agents and had to deal with Goebbels directly. He could afford to give way because most of the films were a huge success at the box office, and also because he needed the stars to sell the openly propagandistic films that otherwise would not have attracted much of an audience. Thus Hans Albers, who specialized in light comedies and musicals, was used in *Carl Peters*, a film extolling the virtues of German colonialism, and another immensely popular actor Heinz Rühmann starred in 'Hurrah, I'm Dad' (*Hurra ich bin Papa*), a paean to the 'racial community' and an urgent appeal to the master race to multiply. Ilse Werner's sex appeal was needed to peddle 'Submarines Westwards' (*U-Boote westwärts*) and Zarah Leander's presence in 'The Great Love' (*Die Grosse Liebe*), a wartime melodrama on the theme of love versus duty, made it one of the most successful German films ever.

Goebbels realized that in wartime people needed entertainment, not outright propaganda, and was given to repeating that 'high spirits are a weapon of war'. Direct propaganda was now mostly restricted to the weekly newsreels, while the virtues of self-sacrifice, self-denial and doing one's [193] duty were extolled in melodramas, musicals and comedies. Stars like Zarah Leander and Heinz Rühmann guaranteed their success and the people responded enthusiastically. Some 450 million cinema tickets were sold in 1938 and by 1941 this figure had doubled to almost 900 million. It was not just light entertainment that attracted the punters. Films packed with such crude and disgusting anti-Semitic invective as *Jud Süss* were immensely popular, attracting audiences of 20 million. Equally aggressive films such as *Die Rothschilds* and *Ohm Krüger* were also huge successes, suggesting that ordinary Germans were sympathetic to the malevolent aims of National Socialism, their post-war assurances to the contrary. There were some dissenting voices. Wilm Hosenfeld was disgusted by *Ohm Krüger*. Witnessing the 'annihilation' of Jews and Poles in May 1941 he wrote that Germany was in no position to criticize British imperial policy[7].

With the notable exception of Leni Riefenstahl's film about the 1934 party rally, *Triumph of the Will*, it was not until 1937, with Veit Harlan's 'The Ruler' (*Der Herrscher*), glorifying the 'Führer principle', that a truly National Socialist film was produced. Hitler had been growing increasingly impatient, repeatedly demanding when the vast amounts of money invested in the film industry were going to bear political fruit. It was Veit Harlan who was to provide the answer, first with *Der Herrscher* and then with the anti-Semitic *Jud Süss* of 1940, and the rousing appeal to hold on until the bitter end in his film on Frederick the Great (*Der Grosse König*) of 1942. This was followed by a series of skilfully crafted political melodramas on various themes between 1943 and 1944: self-sacrifice in 'The Golden Town' (*Die goldene Stadt*), regional patriotism in *Immensee* and fidelity in 'Sacrifice' (*Opfergang*). In 1945 he directed *Kolberg*, a mammoth production showing how Germany would go down to a glorious defeat, but would rise again. These films were both immensely popular and ideologically orthodox. Somewhat surprisingly, only three of the 2,000 films produced in the peacetime years were exclusively anti-Semitic, although many of the others contained anti-Semitic sequences and asides.

Leni Riefenstahl, known as the 'Reich's crevice in the glacier' because of her skiing films, was the most original and influential of all the National Socialist film-makers. She was close to Hitler, Goebbels admired her work, and she worked together with the odious Julius Streicher who financed her film on the Olympic Games. She used Gypsies interned in concentration camps for her film *Tiefland*. Having finished the film they were deported and murdered. As an attractive, self-confident, independent and modern woman she did not fit the National Socialist ideal of womanhood, but in

[194] her propaganda films she produced a classic self-representation of the Third Reich. She made two films of the party rallies: *Victory of Faith* in 1933 and *Triumph of the Will* in 1935. This was followed by *The Day of Freedom – Our Armed Forces* in the same year and two films on the Olympic Games of 1936, finished two years later: *Festival of the Peoples* and *Festival of Beauty*. During the war she embarked on a number of ambitious projects, all of which remained unfinished by 1945. After the war she made absurd attempts to stylize herself as an anti-fascist. Shortly before her death in 2003 at the age of 101 she was charged with holocaust denial. It was a sorry end to a misguided woman who placed her exceptional talents at the service of a criminal cause.

Literature

In March 1933 writers who were members of the Prussian Academy of the Arts were required to sign a declaration of loyalty to the new regime. Thomas Mann's brother Heinrich had already been forced to resign as president of the writers' section of the Academy in February, and Thomas Mann and Alfred Döblin resigned in sympathy. Franz Werfel as a Jew was excluded. Most of those writers inimical to the regime left the country. Precious few protested against this frontal assault on artistic freedom. Their places in the Academy were taken by predictable and mostly long since forgotten nationalist writers. The fiercely independent Ernst Jünger refused to join, arguing that he was still a soldier, having been mobilized in August 1914, and that he could not accept any 'academic obligations'. The poet Gottfried Benn had no such scruples. He agreed to replace Heinrich Mann, wrote the declaration of loyalty to the new regime which all had to sign if they wished to remain members of the Academy, and gave two talks on the radio calling upon intellectuals and artists to submit to the Führer, while denouncing the émigrés as traitors. Benn became intoxicated with Nazi claptrap, fulminating about 'rebirth', 'the realisation of the world spirit' and the necessity to 'breed a stronger race'. Those in power did not appreciate praises from such quarters. Benn was an expressionist and his earlier works were denounced as *Schweinereien*, the perverse products of a sick mind. Hans Johst, the president of the Writers' Chamber, who also had an expressionist past, appealed directly to Himmler to protect Benn. The Reichsführer promptly ordered the SS to stop attacking him, but in 1938 Göring ordered Benn's dismissal from the Chamber, whereupon he returned to work as a doctor in a military hospital where he specialized in the treatment of venereal diseases.

A number of lesser writers failed in their attempts to jump onto the Nazi
bandwagon. Their dubious pasts caught up with them and they were dismissed from the Writers' Chamber. Goebbels had little patience with such
hacks and was determined to win over writers of international status for
the National Socialist cause. One such figure was Gerhardt Hauptmann, the
Nobel Prize winner of 1912. He was a conservative nationalist, co-founder
in 1905 of the Society for Racial Hygiene, who during the Weimar Republic was seen as the embodiment of an open-minded and socially mindful
Germany, the conscience of the nation. This was not the kind of thing that
appealed to the National Socialists, and Rosenberg wanted nothing to do
with him. Hauptmann, like Benn, was much taken by the new Germany,
wrote a hymn in praise of Adolf Hitler, found kind words for *Mein Kampf,*
describing it as 'the really very important Hitler bible', and imagined that
he was witnessing the rebirth of the nation. Goebbels disliked Hauptmann's
realistic dramas, but was prepared to use him for propaganda purposes. The
playwright lavished praise on Hitler's every move in foreign politics with
effusive newspaper articles and radio addresses. His diaries reveal him as
a mean-spirited anti-Semite, even though he attended the funeral of his
patron, Max Pinkus, and wrote a generous obituary for his publisher, Samuel
Fischer, for which he was taken to task in the Nazi press. In spite of his
advanced age he stepped up these efforts during the war and remained an
unrepentant apologist for the regime until the bitter end. He died in 1946
at the age of 83.

The Austrian writer Heimito von Doderer was another distinguished artist
who found much that was admirable in National Socialism. Even though
he was married to the daughter of a Jewish dentist, his diaries show that he
was full of anti-Semitic prejudices and he joined the Austrian Nazi Party in
April 1933. In 1936 he moved to Germany and applied for membership in
the Writers' Chamber, announcing that he was working on a novel *The
Demons* in which he intended to expose the *Theatrum Judaicum* for which he
had an acute eye, thanks to 'the purity of my blood'. The novel did not
appear until 1956, by which time he had rid it of all anti-Semitic content.

Goebbels was determined to have firm control over all aspects of literature
from writers to publishers, booksellers to libraries. He was angered by the
book-burnings of May 1933, which were organized by students and were
not sanctioned by the state, and decided to mount a monster *auto da fé* in
Berlin to show who was in command. The Writers' Chamber was ordered
to draw up a list of books deemed to be 'contrary to the cultural intentions
of National Socialism'. The list was published in October 1935 and was
updated at regular intervals.

[196]   Erich Kästner, author of the international bestseller *Emil and the Detectives*, decided for a complex of reasons to remain in Germany, principal of which was his desire to stay close to his mother to whom he was devoted, even though his books had been consigned to the flames in Berlin. In 1934 his *Flying Classroom* was given the imprimatur, but that was the end of his career in Nazi Germany. In 1936 all his books were placed on the index, but such was the need for foreign exchange that he was permitted to publish abroad. *Three Men in the Snow* was published in Switzerland in 1934 and Kästner made repeated efforts to join the Writers' Chamber, renouncing his waspishly satirical earlier work, only to be repulsed as a 'cultural Bolshevik' who had wallowed in pornography, homosexuality and abortion and who should consider himself lucky not to have been sent to a concentration camp. Nevertheless, Goebbels appreciated Kästner's exceptional talent and in 1941 commissioned him to write the script for Ufa's jubilee film *Münchhausen*, starring Hans Albers. Hitler somehow found out that Kästner was the author, even though he had been given the pseudonym Berthold Bürger. He was promptly placed on the list of forbidden authors.

     Hans Fallada was the author of the hugely successful novel 'What's Up Little Man?' (*Kleiner Mann – was nun?*) which contains a singularly unattractive portrait of an SA man and whose heroine is a resolutely class-conscious Communist. He was arrested by the SA in 1933. Although he never sympathized with National Socialism, he was determined to avoid any further trouble and hastily rewrote the novel, converting the SA man Lauterbach into an apolitical football fan. Two further novels were carefully crafted to be in tune with the times, but contained occasional flashes of savage irony. Goebbels admired Fallada, but was locked in battle with the literary department of his own ministry that took a dim view of this turncoat. His books were a commercial success and he prospered under the National Socialists while making minimal concessions to the regime, but his conscience gnawed at him, assuaged by drugs and alcohol. Somehow he managed to survive under the Communist regime in East Germany, entirely on the strength of his earlier work.

     No one was coerced into singing the praises of the Nazi regime or forced to produce propaganda on its behalf, but those who did so were richly rewarded. Many pursued successful careers in the Federal Republic after the war, often insisting that they were never in sympathy with the Nazis and had either gone into 'inner emigration' or were involved in active resistance. Up until the 1960s the majority of writers in Germany had been active between 1933 and 1945, not a few even before.

Theatre [197]

Hitler's first birthday as chancellor, 20 April 1933, was celebrated with a gala performance of Hanns Johst's play *Schlageter* in the Prussian State Theatre in Berlin. The birthday boy did not appear, his place taken by Hermann Göring who had the pleasure of watching his future wife, Emmy Sonnemann, playing the part of Schlageter's emphatically Aryan spouse. The play, which Johst dedicated to 'Adolf Hitler in loving admiration and unwavering fidelity', is packed with nationalistic pathos and contains the famous lines, often attributed to Göring: 'When I hear the word culture, I release the safety catch of my Browning.' There were 62 different productions of the play in 1933 and 34 in the following season.

By the time of the première of *Schlageter* the process of purging the German theatre of non-Aryans and the politically suspect had already begun. This was the result of pressure from Rosenberg's Activist Association for German Culture, from the 'synchronized' press and from Göring as prime minister of Prussia. The Law for the Restoration of a Professional Civil Service of 7 April 1933, which called for the dismissal of all those of 'non-Aryan descent' or whose 'previous political activities provide no guarantee that they wholeheartedly support the nation state', was rigorously applied to all state theatres. Goebbels applied the law to the commercial theatre when the RKK was formed in July. Henceforth all those who were involved in the theatre, from stars to stagehands, had to be enrolled in the Reich Theatre Chamber. 'Half-Jews', that is to say people with one Jewish parent, were excluded as were 'those with a familial link to a Jew' (*jüdisch Versippte*), unless they were given special dispensation. One exception was Emil Jannings who was fond of saying of himself: 'Where does the Goy get it from? From his *jiddischem mamme*', and provocatively referred to his 'Jewish conk'. It took some time for the cultural life of Germany to be 'de-Jewed'. In February 1937 Goebbels announced that the RKK was finally rid of Jews, but in the following month he discovered to his horror that this was not quite the case. Even Goebbels, whose anti-Semitism bordered on the pathological, felt that the hunt for Jews sometimes got out of hand. He was furious when some over-zealous Jew-baiter found out that Johann Strauss was quarter Jewish and remarked: 'In the end all that will be left of our history will be Widukind, Henry the Lion and Rosenberg[8]. That is a trifle sparse.' Even Hitler admitted to having a soft spot for Mahler's music, remarking that 'Jews can produce quite good stuff by copying others'. Of the 40,000 people working in the theatre about 4,000 were dismissed. Many managed to emigrate. Those who remained were mostly murdered. Precious few survived.

Even Mozart presented serious difficulties to the regime. In 1941 the Nazis decided to celebrate the 150th anniversary of his death by heralding him as a great German. They soon found themselves in serious difficulties. Had not Nietzsche proclaimed him to be 'the last great European' whose cosmopolitan style accounted for his universal popularity? Had he not been greatly influenced by Italian composers? Then there was the Masonic rigmarole of 'the Magic Flute' and the unfortunate fact that his librettist, Lorenzo da Ponte, was Jewish. Performing the operas in German was also a problem because the favourite translations were by Hermann Levy, also a Jew.

Some brave souls defied the new regime. Georg Kaiser's *Silbersee* with music by Kurt Weill premiered in Erfurt, Leipzig and Magdeburg in February 1933. It was a sentimental quasi-socialist piece of escapism that was bound to incite Nazi ire and all three productions had to be cancelled immediately after the première. In Magdeburg the main role was played by the great actor Ernst Busch, a self-proclaimed Communist, who shortly thereafter emigrated. The conductor in Leipzig, Gustav Brecher, was Jewish and also left Germany. Georg Kaiser was dismissed from the Prussian Academy in May, emigrated to Switzerland in 1938 and died a broken man in Ascona in 1945.

The works of most of the major German playwrights were soon added to the index, among whom were Berthold Brecht, Ödön von Horváth, Ernst Toller and Carl Zuckmayer. All works of Jewish authors such as Hugo von Hofmannsthal, Arthur Schnitzler and Carl Sternheim were banned along with anything that had a hint of socialism or pacifism. Henceforth plays had to glorify the race and the nation, underline the need for living space, denounce individualism and democracy, thus upholding the leadership principle. Prime examples of this genre were Wolfgang Möller's anti-Semitic *Rothschild's Victory at Waterloo* and his anti-democratic *The Panama Scandal*.

Carl Niessen, whose speculations about the ancient Germanic theatre interested some of the more extreme National Socialists, prominent among them Heinrich Himmler, insisted that the Germanic *Thing* (pronounced 'ting') was an open air theatre as well as a council chamber. He speculated that, similar to classical Greek drama, the main roles were played by professionals, while ordinary people provided the chorus. Otto Laubinger, who was responsible for theatre in the ministry of propaganda, enthusiastically set about building 'Thing Spaces', modelled on Greek amphitheatres, where open-air 'Thing Plays' would be performed. The Labour Service was ordered to build 20 'Thing Spaces', with 40 more to follow in 1934. Laubinger envisioned a total of 400 open-air theatres, each for between 3,000 and 10,000 spectators: 14 were built by 1935.

The Reich Dramatic Adviser, Rainer Schlösser, ordered 30 writers to [199] set to work on 'cult plays' for these theatres that would combine rousing declamations, dramatic choruses, pantomime, dance and gymnastics. The first such work, Kurt Heynicke's *Play of German Labour*, was performed in a 'Thing Space' in Halle in July 1934. It was about the struggle between capitalists who wanted to close an unprofitable mine and the miners who were determined to keep it open under the slogan 'labour is the heartbeat of the new Reich'. After three hours of class struggle the cast of 1,000 marched in unison and sang the 'Horst Wessel Song'[9].

Richard Euringer's *German Passion 1933* had to be performed in the courtyard of Heidelberg castle because the 'Thing Space' had not yet been completed. It was based on the tasteless analogy between the sufferings of the German people under the Treaty of Versailles, inflation and the Weimar Republic, and Christ's passion. It was not a success. The Heidelberg 'Thing Space' was formally opened in June 1935 when Goebbels watched a cast of 12,000 sing the praises of the *Sacred Fatherland*. This was followed in July by Kurt Heynicke's *The Way to the Reich*, in which an engineer returns to Germany and plans to redirect a river so as to avoid a major flood. A woman, conscious of her responsibilities towards the 'racial community', cedes her claim to a hereditary farm in order to make this possible. The vast chorus underlined the themes of self-sacrifice, duty and struggle.

Laubinger died in October 1935 and Goebbels saw this as an excellent opportunity to put an end to the 'Thing Play' movement. It was announced that a successor could not be found, that suitable writers were not available, and that it had all been carried out too precipitously, with insufficient planning. In November 1935 Goebbels issued orders that the words 'Thing' and 'cult' should no longer be mentioned in the press in connection with the NSDAP. Henceforth the 'Thing Spaces' were used for celebrations of the equinoxes, a spectacle particularly favoured by Himmler, for party events and for classical drama. During the Olympic Games in 1936 Eberhard Wolfgang Möller's *Frankenberg Dice Game* was performed in the 20,000 seat open-air Dietrich Eckhart Stage (now known as the Waldbühne). The play, very much in the 'Thing' tradition, was about the struggle of Protestant peasants against the Habsburgs in 1625. Seven judges delivered the judgement of history and absolved the peasants of all guilt. A knight in black armour, clearly symbolic of Adolf Hitler, rode onto the stage announcing that 'An emperor [in this instance Ferdinand II] who nails his people to the cross, stands condemned for all eternity.'

Berlin was without question the theatrical capital of Germany and unlike in the provinces, where most theatres were owned by the state or

[200]   municipalities, most of the major theatres were in private hands. Max
Reinhardt ran five such theatres, but he along with a number of other
Jewish impresarios left the country in 1933. Goebbels put the well-known
actors Eugen Klöpfer and Heinrich George in charge of the Volksbühne
and the Schiller-Theater respectively. Heinz Hilpert, a highly professional
director, was put in charge of the Deutsches Theater.

The Prussian government was responsible for the Staatstheater, Staatsoper
and Schauspielhaus, and Göring was determined that these should remain
under his control and not be absorbed by Goebbels' ministry. In 1933 Franz
Ulbrich and Hanns Johst had put on a series of appallingly melodramatic
'blood-and-soil' plays in the Staatstheater, all of which were resounding
flops. Then in February 1934, to everyone's surprise, Göring placed one
of Germany's greatest actors, Gustav Gründgens, in charge of Schinkel's
beautiful theatre on the Gendarmenmarkt. Gründgens had triumphed in
1932 in the same theatre when as a young actor he had played Mephisto
opposite the Faust of Werner Krauss, a man whom most critics regarded as
Germany's greatest actor. This was the 'Faust' of the century, with Gründgens
putting Krauss in the shade.

As a well-known homosexual Gründgens was highly vulnerable, in
spite of enjoying the protection of Göring's new wife Emmy. In 1934 he
offered his resignation, alarmed at the homosexual ramifications of the Röhm
Putsch, but Göring refused. In April 1936 he thought it prudent to move to
Switzerland when the press suggested that his decidedly gay *Hamlet* did
not show the necessary 'Nordic qualities'. Again he offered his resignation,
whereupon Göring not only telephoned Gründgens in Switzerland and
pleaded with him to return, but ordered the arrest of two critics who had
suggested that Gründgens was lacking in virility. On his return Gründgens
was given the title of State Councillor (*Staatsrat*).

Goebbels was determined to involve Gründgens in his film projects, but
the actor managed to keep out of the minister's clutches until 1941 when
he was obliged to play the part of Austen Chamberlain in the anti-British
film *Ohm Krüger*. A peevish Gründgens was accompanied to the studios by
a Luftwaffe officer and insisted on being addressed as 'Herr Staatsrat'. He
felt obliged to produce some dubious plays such as *The Seven Years War* in
1937 in which he played Frederick the Great as the state's first servant. In
1941 he played Alexander the Great in a play by the Hitler Youth author
Hans Baumann, but cancelled the production when Germany invaded the
Soviet Union so as to avoid too obvious a connection between Alexander
the Great and Hitler. A production of *Richard III* in 1937, starring Werner
Krauss as an amoral, power-crazed, club-footed political delinquent was an

incredibly daring portrait of the propaganda minister. In the following [201] year Gründgens starred as *Richard II* in which the king's homosexuality was provocatively emphasized.

Gründgens stayed in Berlin in the final stages of the war, was arrested by the Soviets and interned for nine months. He was released owing to the intercession of his Communist colleague, Ernst Busch, whose life he had saved by providing legal assistance when he had been arrested by the Gestapo.

Unlike Gründgens, Heinz Hilpert was directly under the control of the propaganda ministry and suffered accordingly. His production of *The Trial of Mary Dugan* in the Volksbühne was banned on the first night on the grounds that it harboured certain reservations about the death penalty. Ödön von Horváth's *Heavenwards* was instantly struck off the list of forthcoming productions. Among a number of colleagues who were related to Jews, Hilpert was able to protect only the set designer Ernst Schütte whose wife was Jewish. He was unable to engage Erich Engel, a close associate of Berthold Brecht, on a full-time basis, but he was allowed to direct a few shows that were among the most brilliant of the day, including works by Shaw, Calderón, Kleist and Shakespeare. He was also obliged to direct a number of appallingly crude propagandistic plays such as *The Panama Scandal*, a primitive diatribe about the evils of parliamentary democracy, and *Uta von Naumburg* which extolled the superiority of the Nordic over the Roman Catholic.

After the Anschluss Hilpert was put in charge of Max Reinhardt's Josefstadt Theatre in Vienna and also the direction of the Salzburg Festival, which hitherto had been in Reinhardt's hands. Hilpert worked amazingly hard to meet these various responsibilities, directing 80 different plays between 1934 and 1944, his plans being constantly frustrated by the propaganda ministry. His plans for a comprehensive celebration of Gerhardt Hauptmann's 80th birthday came to nothing and in 1943 his immediate boss, Werner Schlösser, ominously accused him of trying to 'escape from the present'. When the theatres were all closed in the final stages of the war he was forced to work in the armaments industry and was then called up in the Volkssturm, from which he was released in April 1945 having suffered a heart attack. He had a successful career in the Federal Republic and died in 1967 aged 77.

Heinrich George, whom Goebbels put in charge of the Schiller-Theater in 1938, was one of the more controversial figures in the Nazi theatre. He had a reputation for being on the left, but he hastily came to terms with the new regime. In 1933 he played the part of a Communist proletarian who

[202]   sees the light and joins the NSDAP in the propaganda film *Quex the Hitler Youth*. This was followed by a series of triumphs in such plumb roles as Goethe's *Götz von Berlichingen*, Judge Adam in Kleist's *The Broken Jug*, Franz Moor in Schiller's *The Robbers* and Pedro in Calderón's *The Judge of Zalamea*. He is probably best remembered for playing the leading role in the ghastly film *Jud Süss*, by which time the erstwhile wild-eyed Communist was clearly identified with National Socialism. He was undisciplined, domineering, manipulative and an ugly drunk, but also an actor of immense talent.

The Schiller-Theater was remodelled on Hitler's orders and opened in November 1938 with a gala performance of Schiller's *Kabale und Liebe*, directed by Heinrich George and with Hitler and Goebbels in the Führer box. The Schiller-Theater under George concentrated on outstanding performances of the classics, but produced more than its fair share of National Socialist dross. The theatre harboured a number of artists with Jewish connections, but this had nothing to do with Heinrich George, who ignored all those who fell foul of the regime. As the director Jürgen Fehling, whose production of Kleist's *Prinz von Homburg* with George in the role of the elector was one of the outstanding productions of the day, said of him: 'I loved him above all other German actors, but in the end he was a blind harpist playing to Nazi idols.' He was arrested by the Soviets in June 1945 and died in the Sachsenhausen concentration camp after an operation for appendicitis.

Painting and sculpture

Although Goebbels had expressed his admiration for the works of Nolde, van Gogh and Barlach in the 1920s, by 1933 he was determined to extirpate the modern and 'degenerate' and return to traditional representative and genre art. In painting this meant going back to the earlier nineteenth century, spiced with the brutal realism of *neue Sachlichkeit*[10], in sculpture a figurative neo-classicism.

As in the other arts there was a fierce debate over the course ahead and a bitter struggle over fields of competence. Rosenberg and his Kampfbund predictably adopted an extreme stance and demanded that all forms of modernist art, including expressionism, should be outlawed. Representatives of the NSStB agreed that the new German art should be 'heroic, epic, Nordic, Germanic, racial, inspired, fundamental, mystical, spiritual, down to earth, and rooted in the native soil', but argued that expressionism was a uniquely German art form that expressed German-ness in an ecstatic and prophetic manner. It was the antithesis of degenerate formalistic French impression-ism and was close to Italian futurism, which was approved by the Fascist regime. This so-called Berlin Opposition argued in their journal *Art of the Nation* that the new art should be based on expressionism, and that the officially sanctioned *völkisch* art was cloyingly kitsch and petit bourgeois. Goebbels, who was always ready to score a point against his rival Rosenberg, and who had a horror of 'party painters', tended to side with the Berlin Opposition.

Rosenberg had some powerful allies in the struggle against expression-ism, chief among them Paul Schultze-Naumberg, an architect who built the Cecilenhof for the Crown Prince, where the Potsdam conference was to be held after the war. He was a friend of Hitler's and the author of *Art and Race* (1929), a ferocious attack on the likes of Picasso and Modigliani, whose works he compared to those of the mentally deranged. As director of the State Academy for Architecture in Weimar in 1930 he began weeding out 'degenerate' art works in what became known as the 'Weimar iconoclasm'. Goebbels described him in 1931 as 'a bit senile, but means well'. Schultze-Naumberg called for an art modelled on late Gothic and old German painting, the German renaissance and late nineteenth-century German genre painters such as Wilhelm Leibl. Hitler put an end to the expressionism debate in a speech to the Nuremberg party rally in 1934 in which he declared war on the enemies of traditional art and lent his support to the Rosenberg line. *Art of the Nation* was banned in 1935 and painting and sculpture had henceforth to accord with Hitler's philistine, blinkered and uninformed notions of art.

This left German artists in an awkward situation. On the one hand the regime called for an art based on racial criteria that had to be both 'time-less' and yet meet international artistic standards. Sturdy Bavarian peasants, distinctly Aryan nudes, sentimental Black Forest landscapes were hardly the stuff to impress the visitors to the 1936 Olympics and henceforth such *völkisch* themes were no longer encouraged. The emphasis now was on art for the monumental buildings and a revival of old media such as tapestry and frescoes, or massive triptychs such as Hans Schmitz-Wiedenbrück's affectively overblown *Workers, Peasants, Soldiers* of 1941.

This triptych is a typical National Socialist cult object. The form is that of an altar painting, the central trinity a soldier, an airman and a marine, sturdy and aggressive Nordic types, their eyes fixed on a lofty horizon. The figures on the wings, an 'Eastern' (*Ostisch*) miner and a 'Palatine' (*fälisch*) peasant leading a cow, are in suitably reverential and subservient poses. The whole is designed to demonstrate the 'racial community', but there is a

[204] clear hierarchy not only of professions, but also of racial types. The military represent the dominant and masterly modern, the miner and the peasant the timeless relations of production.

Landscape was the most favoured art form, whereas the townscapes dear to the artists of *neue Sachlichkeit* were few and far between. Figures in a panoramic landscape were indicative of the close ties between blood and soil, showed the timeless beauty of the fatherland, and stilled yearnings for the good old days. Second in popularity were paintings of peasants, particularly of peasant women, peasant families, village festivals, of sowing and reaping. It was an idealized world without modern machinery, where work seemed to be an effortless acknowledgement of fruitfulness within the context of a conflict-free traditional society.

Third in popularity were paintings of women: sturdy peasant women in traditional attire, elegant bourgeoises in conventional poses, and above all representations of women in their essential role as mothers. Curiously enough there were few paintings of the large families that the Nazis demanded. Artists preferred the traditional theme of mother and child with its obvious Christian overtones. Nudes became increasingly popular during the war and provided ideologically suitable titillation for the brutal and licentious soldiery. The most famous nude painting in Nazi Germany was Adolf Ziegler's triptych *The Four Elements* of 1937, which hung in the salon of the Führerhaus in Munich. Earth and Water are represented in the middle panel. Although Ziegler was popularly known as 'the master of German pubic hair', Mother Earth as the race's vital source is modestly draped. Water is less inhibited, as is Fire on the left, but a rather dreary Wind strategically places an arm across her lap. The uninvitingly realistic painting is life size; the tall, slim and small-breasted figures, which accord with the racial-political ideal of the Aryan, are without the slightest hint of eroticism.

Other famous nude paintings are positively degrading. Ivo Saliger's *The Judgement of Paris* (1939) represents woman as a consumer object to be chosen at will. Paul Mathias Padua's *Leda and the Swan* (1939) is a repulsive symbolic representation of rape and submission. A number of female Nazi function-aries objected strongly to such voyeuristic representations of women as objects, but their protests had little effect in a thoroughly misogynist society.

There were very few paintings of work, with the exception of repres-entations of the 'beauty of labour' with athletically muscular workers effort-lessly churning out tons of steel, seemingly without the use of machinery. Similarly, wartime paintings virtually never show the enemy, and concen-trate on the themes of comradeship, steadfastness, grit and determination in the face of an indeterminate other.

Sculpture played a far more important role than painting in the Third Reich. It was used to adorn the bombastic new buildings and vast public spaces, providing a suitable setting for displays of military might, devotion to the Führer and party solidarity. Many of the leading sculptors of the Weimar Republic were welcomed by the new regime, including Ernst Barlach, until Hitler clamped down on expressionism.

Initially most of these sculptures were hewn from granite or limestone to give the figure sufficient weight and monumentality. These materials fell out of favour by 1937 when bronze was considered the appropriate medium for the new bodily ideal. Naked muscle-bound Aryan heroes, sword at the ready, represented the ideals of courage, fidelity, readiness and devotion to duty. The nude represented the racial ideal and harked back to the classical tradition, giving it a sense of timelessness, whereas the knights in armour of the historicists were anonymous, faceless and abstract symbols of yesteryear.

The Olympic Games of 1936 gave extra impetus to this new aesthetic. Beautiful Nordic bodies were representative of the superiority of the race, standing on guard against the ugly, the degenerate and the racially inferior. Whereas the male nude stood defiantly, encased in the armour of his bulging muscles, the female nude was soft and submissive. Gender-specific roles were thus represented as natural. The much-favoured figure of Nike, the goddess of victory, was a desexualized female proudly representing the apotheosis of male valour and martial ardour.

Arno Breker was the most talented and successful of the sculptors who wholeheartedly embraced the new style. Born in 1900, he lived in Paris from 1927 to 1932 where he became a close friend of Aristide Maillol. He took part in a number of important exhibitions and in 1932 was awarded the Rome Prize of the Prussian Academy that enabled him to spend time at the Villa Massimo. He entered the sculpture competition for the Olympic Games and his 'decathlon athlete' was an enormous success. Thanks to his friendship with Albert Speer he produced a series of monumental sculptures for the new chancellery and for the 1937 World Exhibition in Paris. His colossal figures were designed to represent the 'meta-individual values of race and racial community' and the 'triumph of the strong and healthy over the weak and sickly'. His heroic men were perfect mates for his tender and dutiful women.

Breker was richly rewarded. He was given a vast studio with numerous assistants in Balham near Munich. A huge exhibition of his works was held in Paris in 1942. Hitler proclaimed him his favoured sculptor, gave him a party membership with an artificially early membership number and

[206] showered him with honours. He owed his success not only to the sponsorship of Speer and Göring and Hitler's favourable opinion, but mainly because he satisfied the Nazis' growing taste for gigantic neo-feudal exhibitions of hubristic power and might. After the war he was classified as a 'fellow traveller', largely because he had helped a number of people who had been hounded by the regime. He was much in demand as a portraitist and produced busts of Konrad Adenauer, Ludwig Erhard, Hermann Abs, Jean Cocteau, Jean Marais and Salvador Dali, with whom he enjoyed a close friendship.

Music

Goebbels was keenly aware that music, which he described as 'the most sensual of all the arts', could be used as a subliminal means for the aesthetic representation of power, or as Hitler phrased it: 'Nothing is better suited to make a little whinger shut up than the eternal language of great art.' Small wonder then that Bertolt Brecht should warn Paul Hindemith that 'music is not a Noah's ark in which one can escape the flood'.

The musical tastes of Germany's greatest conductor, Wilhelm Furtwängler, were distinctly conservative and strongly tinged with a nationalist prejudice in favour of German music. He occasionally performed works by Arnold Schoenberg, but he did so with a certain distaste, announcing that he saw himself as an 'usher' who would show the public the great classical masters. This anti-modernism and anti-intellectualism accorded well with National Socialist ideology, and Furtwängler imagined that given his immense status as one of the world's greatest conductors he could come to some kind of arrangement with the regime.

He could agree over the 'National', but had distinct difficulties with the 'Socialist' and objected to the way the Nazis appropriated all that was deemed to be truly German. Things came to a head over Paul Hindemith whose music he admired, but which the Nazis dismissed as 'degenerate'. Furtwängler lost this round, temporarily resigning from all public offices, and Hindemith went into exile in England, where he was held in high regard.

Richard Strauss was 80 years old on 11 June 1944, but initially Goebbels did not wish to have any special celebration of the event. Hitler was furious when he heard that Strauss had refused to allow refugees or people who had lost their homes in the bombing to stay in his large house in Garmisch, telling the NSDAP district leader that he had 'nothing to do with the war'. Furtwängler sent a telegram to Hitler pointing out that to snub Germany's greatest living composer in this manner would create an extremely bad impression abroad. Hitler, who had enormous respect for the conductor and his 'national attitude', even ordering a special bunker to be built for him so that this national treasure could survive the war, gave way. At the same time the SD kept a close watch on him, and towards the very end of the war he was in real danger.

Furtwängler's attitude towards Jewish musicians was curiously ambiguous. He needed first-class musicians and felt that exceptions to a generally acceptable and 'respectable' anti-Semitism could be made in their case. On the other hand in his post-war memoirs he described the great German-Jewish conductor Bruno Walter, who was forced to emigrate, as 'an American conductor of German descent'. At least that was better than Richard Strauss who described him as 'a slimy little bastard'. Even Hitler was prepared to make certain concessions. He received the baritone Ludwig Hofmann in the royal box at Bayreuth in spite of the fact that he was Jewish, and got quite frisky with a delectable blonde Jewess, the wife of the singer Max Lorenz, ignoring thereby Winifred Wagner who adored Hitler unconditionally. Max Lorenz stood by his wife and announced that he would refuse to sing were he forced to divorce her. The marriage remained intact.

The composer Werner Egk fell foul of the denazification process and was justly condemned for 'having helped weave the cultural curtain behind which the concentration camp ovens smoked', whereupon he defiantly demanded that his sentence be doubled if the Allies could prove any connection between his professional work and the crimes committed in the camps. This was a grotesque denial of any connection between theory and practice, of Nazi ideology and Nazi crimes. His highly successful opera *Peer Gynt*, premiered in 1938, was greatly admired by both Hitler and Goebbels, even though Egk used musical quotations from 'degenerate' composers such as Stravinsky, Kurt Weill and Hanns Eisler, mixed with quotations from 'God Save the King' and Offenbach's famous cancan as a musical background for the world of the trolls. Egk subsequently argued that this was an act of resistance, a homage to outlawed musicians, but the trolls are represented as Jewish-Bolshevik subhumans, intent on pursuing their selfish, materialistic and destructive designs. Thus the composer stigmatized their music as 'degenerate'. There could be no such pseudo-ambiguity about his setting of Hans Fritz Beckmann's Hitler Youth hymn 'The March of German Youth'. Egk's real name was the suspiciously Jewish-sounding Meyer and he based his curious pseudonym on his wife's name. She was Elizabeth *geborene* (née) Karl. It was widely rumoured that it really stood for 'a great composer' (*ein grosser Komponist*).

The composer Hans Pfitzner with Strauss and Furtwängler formed a troika of distinguished musicians whom the Nazis were determined to use to advertise the cultural superiority of the New Germany. Pfitzner in no sense approached Strauss' genius and owed his status in Nazi Germany in large part to the fact that composers of greater talent had felt obliged to leave the country. His was a deliberately backward-looking and reactionary music, but his opera *Palestrina*[11] was admired by critics as discerning as Thomas Mann and Ernst Bloch and is still occasionally performed. He was deeply implicated in the Nazi regime and enjoyed a particularly close relationship with Hans Frank, the murderous head of the General Government of Poland. Frank supplied Pfitzner with ample quantities of red wine, in return for which the composer dedicated a chillingly jaunty Polonaise to his oenophile patron. Pfitzner sent his friend a consoling telegram when he was condemned to death by the Nuremberg Tribunal. He was an ultra-conservative anti-democrat rather than a convinced Nazi, a conventional rather than a fanatical anti-Semite.

The Nazis had distinct difficulties with the vexed question of tonality. Atonality was condemned as the destructive work of 'the Jew Arnold Schoenberg' and thus the product of the 'Jewish spirit', but Richard Wagner, for whom Adolf Hitler professed to have limitless admiration, had begun the liquidation of tonality in *Tristan und Isolde* and Richard Strauss frequently strayed from the path of the strictly tonal. Provided that the composer was not Jewish, and provided that there was no hint of 'Jewish-Bolshevik' flavour or intent, 12-tone techniques were permissible. One such composer was Paul August von Klenau, who was involved with the Schoenberg circle and who for a time was married to a Jewess. He used a duodecaphonic system to produce lightweight and easily digestible music that critics could defend as conventionally tonal. Klenau defended his opera *Michael Kohlhaas* (1933), based on Kleist's novella, as testament to the German love of justice, a significant episode in Germany's 'racial destiny'. No ideological objections were raised, but the opera was not a success. It simply was not any good, and Germany's discerning opera-goers were not impressed.

Winfried Zillig was another of Schoenberg's students who had a successful career in the Third Reich as musical director of the Reich Gau Opera House in Posen. He composed three operas, which although written in the 12-tone manner had distinct tonal elements and the subjects were well attuned to National Socialism. *The Sacrifice* (1937) dealt with Captain Scott's ill-fated polar expedition. Although the critics waxed lyrical in its praise the opera folded after four performances due to what one critic described as its 'icy polar atmosphere'. Zillig later insisted that it had been closed down by the propaganda ministry because it was felt to be anti-Nazi. There is no evidence that this was indeed the case. Similarly, the composer argued that his librettist, Reinhard Goering, committed suicide as a protest against Hitler, thus converting Captain Oates's epic sacrifice into an anti-fascist remonstration, and the National Socialist Winfried Zillig into a hero of the resistance. At least this tactic secured him a successful career in the Federal Republic, where he championed the new music.

Music was an ideal means of propaganda abroad, for it was a demonstration of Germany's outstanding cultural achievements without being specifically National Socialist. It was also used to boost the morale of the troops. Furtwängler refused to conduct in the occupied countries, but he agreed to conduct the 'St Matthew Passion' in Florence in May 1939 and made an exception to his self-imposed rule when he gave a gala performance in Prague in November 1940, making up for this lapse by defiantly opening the concert with Smetana's nationalistic 'The Moldau'. The Berlin Philharmonic gave numerous performances in occupied Europe under such distinguished conductors as Hans Knappertsbusch, Eugen Jochum and Hermann Abendroth. After one such concert two simple soldiers told Knappertsbusch: 'If we didn't know what we were defending, old Mozart and Beethoven would tell us.' A sailor told him: 'Richard Wagner knew very well that the German spirit would conquer the world.' Thus a brutal war of aggression was transformed into the heroic defence of German culture.

All artists who decided to stay in Germany in spite of their reservations about the National Socialist regime had to tread a narrow and perilous path between opposition and collaboration, peril and corruption. For some the price was too high. Fritz Busch, the brother of the great violinist Adolf Busch, was dismissed from his position as musical director of the Dresden State Opera in March 1933 as a result of an underhand political intrigue. Suffering from the delusion that the rule of law still existed in Germany, he was determined to fight back. He was given the opportunity to conduct in Bayreuth in place of the anti-fascist Toscanini. It was a tempting offer, but Busch refused, rejoicing in the realization that at least he had the freedom to choose. Göring tried to persuade him to come to Berlin, but Busch told him that he would not take a position recently vacated by a Jewish colleague, whereupon Göring warned that he had means to force him to accept. Busch replied that a *Tannhäuser* conducted in such an atmosphere would be 'the most boring thing you ever heard in your life'. Soon he received an offer from Buenos Aires which he readily accepted and where he stayed, taking Argentinian citizenship in 1936. Busch's colleague Erich Kleiber, musical director of the Berlin State Opera, was a champion of Alban

[210] Berg's music but fell foul of the regime when he performed the *Lulu Suite* in 1934. He also moved to Buenos Aires and became a citizen in 1938.

Some composers, such as Karl Amadeus Hartmann, opted for 'inner emigration' by consigning their compositions to the desk drawer. One such work, Hartmann's concerto for violin, originally entitled 'Mourning Music'[12], is a harrowing commentary on the horrors of war and a sadly neglected masterpiece. Others like Boris Blacher were daringly defiant. His *Alla marcia* of 1934 is written in 3/4 time, music to which it is impossible to march, a protest against militarism and war. Other forms of protest were even more daring. In February 1945 the Czech Philharmonic performed Smetana's tone poem *Má Vlast* ('My fatherland'), a hymn of praise to the Hussites and the Czech struggle for independence, a distorted theme from which is quoted in the Hartmann concerto. A critic who wrote a glowing account of this patriotic masterpiece was arrested and trampled to death by two members of the Gestapo, Müller and Aurich, on the express order of SS-Obergruppenführer Karl Hermann Frank, Henlein's[13] former deputy and minister of state for Bohemia and Moravia.

Design

There was more to the Third Reich than terror and totalitarianism, propaganda and the construction of ideology. There was also a daily life that, for the vast majority of 'racial comrades', went on much as before. Everyday objects were not invested with a deliberate intent to manipulate or control, and therefore need to be analysed in a subtler manner than that of the earlier polarities of form and function, tradition and fashion, the mass-produced and the hand-made. There never was a specifically Nazi style of design, and no other art form was more hybrid, over-determined or more influenced by the classic modern. The notion of 'designer' did not exist in the Third Reich, so that the vast majority of products are anonymous, and the regime paid scant attention to the problems involved in finding a 'racially appropriate' theory of design.

The question is therefore how far was this heterogeneity an expression of individualism within the collective, of 'inner emigration' or even of resistance. The dominant design in 1930 for aeroplanes, motor cars, furniture and household appliances was technological, streamlined and slick. Favoured materials were steel, glass, synthetic materials and leather. These were objects of what the cultural critic Siegfried Kracauer called 'pleasurable practicality', representative of modernity, progress, speed and the triumph of technology. Motor racing was the most popular sport for the Nazis and the star driver Bernd Rosemeyer, who was killed in a crash, rivalled Horst Wessel as Nazi Germany's pre-eminent sacrificial victim. Such smooth, aerodynamic and politically innocent design presented no problems for the National Socialists; all that was needed was to take it out of its former context in order to make it of service to the new regime.

The Bauhaus in Dessau was the source of inspiration for such modern design, but it was vilified by the Nazis as 'Bolshevik'. In 1932 Anhalt had a coalition government under a National Socialist, Alfred Freyberg, who ordered the closure of the Bauhaus in September. Freyberg had commissioned a report on the Bauhaus by Paul Schultze-Naumburg, head of the architecture school in Weimar, who was one of the founders of the Deutsche Werkbund that sponsored traditional arts and crafts, and who was well known for his intense dislike of the Bauhaus, based more on political than on aesthetic differences.

The Werkbund was an influential institute for arts and crafts that counted among its members such prominent representatives of the modern as the architect Mies van der Rohe, the last director of the Bauhaus. It survived under the Third Reich as a loose association, having been first absorbed by the RKK. Initially a number of powerful Nazis were determined to smash the Werkbund, denouncing it as a collection of pernicious parasites, but Schultze-Naumburg, who was a party member and member of the Reichstag, managed to appease the hotheads in Goebbels' ministry and hastily adapted to the new conditions.

This did not prove very difficult because 1933 was not an abrupt caesura in matters of design and the Nazis had already given their seal of approval to works that were very much in the Werkbund tradition. These were to include the 'people's products' such as the 'people's radio' (*Volksemfänger*). Other such products were on the drawing board, including a 'people's refrigerator', a 'people's motorboat', a 'people's gramophone' and a 'people's piano'. Although these inexpensive consumer goods sound distinctly National Socialist, the concept dates back to the Weimar Republic. The design for the people's radio dates from 1928.

The design of everyday goods was neither specifically fascist, nor was it uniquely German. The National Socialists tolerated designs from dubious institutions such as the Werkbund or the Bauhaus in order both to appear modern and to gain international acceptance, but there were still certain areas with a distinctly National Socialist semiotic. SS-Oberführer Benno von Arent was an ex-soldier and mercenary who had been a car salesman, designer and architect; he had directed a salacious nude show at the Nelson

[212] Theatre in Berlin, and tried his hand at dress design. He joined the NSDAP in 1931 and the SS in the following year. In 1933 he formed the NS Theatre Designer's Association and was appointed Reich Plenipotentiary for Fashion as well as Reich Set-Designer (*Reichsbühnenbildner*) from which came his nickname 'Reibübi'. He was responsible for the choreography and the decoration for parades, party and public events as well as designing uniforms, medals and badges for the SS and the armed forces. His gigantic open-air displays with a uniformed cast of thousands were powerful expressions of National Socialist ideology and demonstrations of the awesome power of a militarized 'racial community'.

Typography was the subject of heated debate. Initially the Nazis adopted the slogan 'Germans write German' and used various forms of 'gothic' (*Fraktur*) type. Other standard forms of type (*Antiqua*) were denounced as foreign and alien. During the war it became obvious that people in the occupied countries had great difficulty in reading 'gothic' script. Some ingenious expert came up with the idea that *Schwabacher*, a form of gothic type, had been invented by a Jew and was known as *Judenletter*. Gothic was now racially suspect and henceforth *Antiqua*, known as 'new standard German', was adopted in the schools and for party publications. *Fraktur* type was still widely used because of the chronic lack of lead for new type.

Advertising was also a field in which the aesthetics of the Weimar Republic were able to continue. Here the Austrian graphic designer, photographer, typographer and exhibition designer, Herbert Bayer, was a key figure. He had been head of the printing and advertising section of the Bauhaus and worked in the Dorland Studio in Berlin, one of Germany's leading advertising agencies, until he left for the United States in 1938. He did a lot of outstanding work for industry and was hired by the propaganda ministry to celebrate Germany as a modern and technologically advanced country.

Bayer encouraged a number of talented young designers who also worked in the Dorland Studio. Hein Neuner had been Lászlo Maholy-Nagy's assistant at the Bauhaus before moving to Berlin with his brother Hannes. The brothers also worked for *Die neue Linie*, which was by far the most modern of Germany's cultural magazines, and also for *Joy and Work*, a propaganda magazine distributed in 44 countries. They were particularly skilled at photomontage and developed a photographic aesthetic that remained valid long after the war. Kurt Kranz also worked alongside Bayer and the Neuner brothers. He was also a product of the Bauhaus and remained true to its aesthetic, producing outstanding designs for commercial advertising and for *Die neue Linie*. He had a successful post-war career in advertising and put his skills to the service of the Cold War.

The organization Beauty of Work was formed on the auspicious day of 30 January 1934. It was under the KdF office of the DAF and was under Albert Speer's formal supervision. The new office was responsible for such things as the design of furniture, cutlery and dishes in canteens, for adequate lighting and ventilation in the workplace, and for propaganda films for workers. Objects produced under its auspices were in the tradition of the Werkbund's unadorned simplicity.

The most famous piece of design in the Third Reich is undoubtedly the Volkswagen, although it was given the name by the Allies after the war. Hitler christened Ferdinand Porsche's car the 'Strength Through Joy Car' (*KdF-Wagen*) on 26 May 1938. It was designed as an affordable vehicle for the average 'racial comrade', who paid 5 RM per week for a KdF savings coupon and was placed on a waiting list. Since the car was to cost slightly under 1,000 RM it would have taken about four years to save sufficient funds. KdF collected 286 million RM in this manner and not a single car was delivered to private individuals. The money was used to build 55,000 vehicles for the army. Only 700 civilian versions of the car were built by the time the war ended and these were for the exclusive use of party

Figure 6.2   The 'KdF car' (later Volkswagen) was only available to the public after the war

functionaries. Hitler is said to have played no small part in its design, saying: 'It should look like a beetle. One only has to look at nature to see how it uses streamlining.' Goebbels was impressed by the technology, but thought the design was 'lacking in embellishment'. The Soviet Union had made a temptingly generous offer to Porsche in 1932 to build a mass-produced car, but he had opted to stay in Germany.

Far more sinister than the 'bug', which after all only went into civilian production after the war, was the 'people's radio' which Goebbels used as a means of direct propaganda for what he called 'affective mobilization' and over which the Führer's voice was heard in millions of homes. The name sounds sinisterly racist within the context of Nazi Germany, but in fact the Dutch firm Philips put a 'People's Radio' on the market in 1931. The simple bakelite casing with just a hint of art deco had been designed by Walter Maria Kersting in 1928, and the workings were called 'VE 301': '*Volksempfänger*' plus 30 January for the date Hitler came to power. In 1938 it was adorned with an eagle with a swastika in its claws. This bastardized product was inaugurated in 1933 and 12.5 million sets were sold by the outbreak of the war. Some might dismiss the VE 301 as 'Goebbels' snout', but to all too many for all too long it was the tabernacle of a Führer cult.

Cabaret

Goebbels was well aware of the political value of light entertainment but he wanted nothing to do with the cheeky cabaret, the naughty shows and the jazz of the deliciously decadent 'roaring twenties', the world of Sally Bowles and *Cabaret*. Most of the outstanding performers from the heyday of Berlin's nightlife were arrested, were silenced or left the country, their places taken by second-rate purveyors of beer garden kitsch, such as 'Herms Niel'[14], composer of such demanding works as 'Tschingta Tschingta Bummtara'.

Hitler preferred operetta to opera, Lehár to Wagner, and frequently took a nap, or on one occasion signed death warrants, during performances at Bayreuth. He enjoyed light farces set among peasant families and Heinz Rühmann's comedies such as *Quax the Bush Pilot*, which he saw ten times. He was a fan of Mickey Mouse and admired Eleanor Powell's dancing. Karl May's westerns were his favourite reading material. He had no time for cabaret, which he claimed was in the hands of 'Jewish monkeys' who were paid vast sums of money for their 'filthy drivel'. His own sense of humour was infantile. His personal photographer tells us that his favourite joke was: 'Why does a swan have a long neck? So that it doesn't drown.'

Germany's entertainers became cogwheels within Goebbels' propaganda machine, most of them blissfully ignorant of the essential part they played in strengthening the Nazi regime. Goebbels pointed out that all art is political and that the political effect of light entertainment relied on the artists being unaware of the political consequences of their work. Goebbels' favoured artists, such as Zarah Leander, Marika Rökk, Rosita Serrano, Heinz Rühmann and Johannes Heesters, were richly rewarded, granted all manner of privileges and showered with honours. Precious few concerned themselves with the fate of those colleagues who for racial or political reasons were persecuted by the regime, comforted by the thought that what they were doing had nothing to do with politics.

Theo Lingen, a brilliant comic whose immense nose excited the interest of the practitioners of 'racial science', stood by his Jewish wife and step-daughter and courageously helped his persecuted colleagues. The Austrian actor Hans Moser, one of Hitler's favourite actors, also managed to save his Jewish wife, to whom he had been happily married for 25 years, along with her daughter. By contrast Heinz Rühmann, Germany's most popular film star, divorced his Jewish wife in 1938, but at least helped her to escape to Sweden. He shamelessly furthered his career by buttering up Goebbels at every possible opportunity and made a cute little film about the propaganda minister's children that he presented to the proud father as a birthday present. Heinz Rühmann's representations of witty and cheeky little characters were enormously popular and he was in great demand on the radio request programme for the armed forces *Wunschkonzert*. His songs 'That Won't Scare a Sailor' (*Das kann doch einen Seemann nicht erschüttern*) and 'Don't Be Afraid Rosemarie' (*Keine Angst, keine Angst, Rosemarie*) symbolized the determination to hang on and fight to the bitter end.

Goebbels was a competent pianist who at times altered the tunes as well as the texts of popular songs. He was even prepared to allow an element of jazz, hitherto dismissed as 'Negro-Jewish' music, especially for radio programmes directed against Britain, which featured such ditties as 'Mister Churchill, You Will Loose [*sic*] This War.' At the end of 1942, when the fortunes of war turned against Germany, he sponsored a competition for 'optimistic popular songs'. Songs that dealt with the pain of parting, marital infidelity and unfulfilled longing were banned outright. The Swedish diva Zarah Leander starred as the plucky wife of a simple soldier in 'The Great Love' (*Die grosse Liebe*) in which she sang two songs by Michael Jary which became immensely popular: 'It's Not the End of the World' (*Davon geht die Welt nicht unter*) and 'I Know That a Miracle Will Happen' (*Ich Weiss, es wird einmal ein Wunder geschehn*). Marika Rökk sang the idiotic grin-and-bear-it song: 'Don't Look Here, Don't Look There, Look Straight Ahead and Don't Worry, Whatever Happens' (*Schau nicht hin, schau nicht her, schau nur geradeaus, und was dann auch kommt – mach dir nichts daraus*). Ida Wüst, one of the great cabaret stars of the Weimar Republic who jumped on the Nazi bandwagon, recommended that: 'One Must Take Life As It Is.' Sometimes such efforts misfired. The song 'Everything Passes, Everything Is Left Behind' (*Es geht alles vorüber, es geht alles vorbei*) soon got a second line 'Including Hitler and His Party' (*Auch der Hitler, und seine Partei*).

Among the most successful of the purveyors of a good mood in trying times was a handsome young Dutchman, Johannes Heesters, the Third Reich's matinee idol. He became a major star when he appeared in the film *The Student Prince* opposite Marika Rökk. In 1938 he starred in *The Merry Widow*, Hitler's favourite operetta. The Führer was in the audience and told Heesters that he was 'the best Danilo I have ever seen'. Heesters played an active role in Nazi Germany, collecting money for WHW, appearing on *Wunschkonzert* even after the invasion of his native country, giving a gala performance to the SS-Leibstandarte Adolf Hitler and in May 1941 paying a visit to the concentration camp at Dachau where he was shown the sights by the commandant, SS-Hauptsturmführer Alex Piorkowski, accompanied by a group of press photographers. Heesters rewarded his host in Dachau by entertaining the SS guards. In 1978 he described Dachau as a 'typical barracks', similar to a camp for the Hitler Youth or the Labour Service. In 1993, by which time it was well known that hundreds of his colleagues had been murdered, he had the gall to claim that although a number of artists had been sent to Dachau, all of them survived. He died unrepentant in 2005, his passing greatly mourned.

Unlike Heesters, Lale Andersen, world famous for her singing of 'Lili Marlene', refused to endorse Nazi crimes. She turned down an offer to take part in a trip to entertain the troops in Poland that included a visit to the Warsaw ghetto, whereupon she was placed under surveillance. When a letter to a Jewish actor in Zürich was intercepted she was forbidden to perform. Only when the BBC reported that she had been sent to a concentration camp did Goebbels lift the ban in order to counter the enemy's propaganda.

'Lili Marlene' was an untypical cabaret song in that its sentimental morbidity was in sharp contrast to the frivolous jollity and carefree optimism of most songs aimed at the soldiery. Its irresistible melody sugared the pill and made it the most popular song of the war. It was as popular with the Allied armies as it was in Germany. Hitler described the song as 'magic'

and Göring made his little daughter Edda sing it on a weekly newsreel.
Goebbels loathed it, describing it as 'a tearjerker with the whiff of a corpse'.
After the German defeat at Stalingrad he banned the song, fearing that it
would have an adverse effect on morale. 'Lili Marlene' was not a product of
the Nazi tin-pan alley[15]. The words had been written by a German soldier
in 1915. It was set to music in 1938 by Norbert Schultze, a highly gifted
composer of operas, film music and popular songs. Lale Andersen's record-
ing was unnoticed until August 1941 when it was used as the signature
tune for the German forces' radio in Belgrade and became an instant hit.

Lale Andersen was the pseudonym of Liselotte Wilke, née Bunnenberg,
who left her artist husband and children and had a successful career in Berlin
as a cabaret singer, performing songs by Brecht, Tucholsky and Kästner.
She remained loyal to her Jewish friends and never identified with the
Nazi regime. Norbert Schultze by contrast became one of the most prized
defenders of the home front. He had written a song in 1939 entitled 'Bombs
on Poland', but the Polish campaign was over so quickly that it was no
longer relevant. The song was given a new text and appeared as 'Bomben,
Bomben, Bomben auf Engeland', sung by a robust male chorus with a rousing
brass accompaniment and broadcast daily. Henceforth 'Bomben-Schultze'
was in great demand, composing marches for Rommel's Afrika Korps, for
submariners and Army Group Kleist, music for the pro-euthanasia film
'I accuse' (Ich klage an) as well as Bismarck and Kolberg. In June 1941 Goebbels
ordered him to write the music for a song for the campaign against the
Soviet Union, 'Führer Give the Order, We Shall Follow You!' (Führer befiehl,
wir folgen dir). The propaganda minister lent a hand in the composition and
suggested that it should be preceded with a theme from Liszt's Les Préludes.
This bombastic work was finished in time for it to accompany the launching
of Barbarossa on 22 June. After the war 'Bomben-Schultze' had the gall to
claim that his grisly marches were not his but were the product of the times
and that he had merely written music while others did the killing.

Comedians had a difficult time in the Third Reich, where laughter about
the high and mighty was not appreciated. Even the Bavarian comic, Weiss
Ferdl, who was an enthusiastic supporter of the Nazis as early as 1922 and
a close friend of Hitler, got impatient with the restrictions imposed upon
his freedom of speech. Karl Valentin, Germany's greatest comic, retired when
his film The Inheritance was banned for its 'predisposition for wretchedness',
remarking: 'I say nothing. I'm allowed to say that aren't I?' Werner Finck,
the brilliant Berlin comic whose cabaret Katakombe was a constant thorn
in Goebbels' side, opted for open defiance. In 1932 he had said: 'Parades
will be held in the first weeks of the Third Reich. Should these parades be

[218] hindered by rain, hail or snow, all Jews in the neighbourhood will be shot.' With Hitler in power Finck announced: 'We were closed yesterday, open today. If we are too open tomorrow, we will be closed the day after.' In 1935 Goebbels ordered the Katakombe to be closed and Werner Finck was sent for a spell of re-education in a concentration camp. On his release he continued to perform in cabaret and on film, his irrepressible wit a constant irritant until he was finally silenced in 1939, whereupon he volunteered for military service to stay out of trouble. His career resumed with great success in 1945, and his routine about his experiences in the Wehrmacht was a superb settling of accounts.

CHAPTER 7

THE SA, SS AND POLICE

The SS

The brown-shirted Storm Section (SA) was founded on 3 August 1921. Organized by Captain Ernst Röhm, its officers came mostly from Captain Hermann Ehrhardt's murderous gang Organisation Consul (OC), the rank and file from various paramilitary groups in Bavaria. It specialized in political murder, beating up anyone who dared heckle Hitler in his beer hall meetings, terrorizing the infant NSDAP's opponents and parading truculently through the streets of Munich. The SA was closely associated with the local army (Reichswehr) units, which trained them in basic military skills. From the outset the SA was fiercely independent, resentful of any control by Hitler and the party. Hitler put Hermann Göring, a highly decorated air ace, in charge of the SA in 1923, hoping thereby to rein in Ehrhardt's men, and selected a small gang of thugs as his personal bodyguards. Their uniform was field grey with black ski caps and a death's head badge. Shortly thereafter Ehrhardt broke with Hitler and withdrew his men from the SA. Hitler renamed his bodyguard Adolf Hitler's Raiders (Stosstrupp Adolf Hitler) and placed it under the command of Joseph Berchtold, a dwarfish stationer who was deputy party treasurer.

The Stosstrupp was banned after the comic opera Hitler Putsch of November 1923 and Göring and Berchtold fled to Austria. While Hitler was in prison at Landsberg Ernst Röhm built up a new paramilitary organization on a national level called Vanguard (Frontbann) whose patron was Hitler's co-conspirator, General Ludendorff. Röhm was determined to keep his organization completely separate from the party and was thus on a collision course with Hitler, who decided to found a rival organization that would be utterly loyal to him. In April 1925 he ordered his chauffeur, Julius Schreck, to recruit a bodyguard. Schreck found eight former members of the Stosstrupp in a Munich beer hall, Torbräu, and gave them the title

[220] Protection Squad (Schutzstaffel – SS). He then ordered every local party group to select 10 'healthy and well-built' men as an SS unit, with 20 in Berlin. By Christmas there were almost 1,000 members.

Berchtold returned from his Austrian exile in 1926 and Hitler put him in charge of the SS. At the same time he appointed a soldier of fortune, Captain Franz Pfeffer von Salomon, head of the SA in the hope that he would bring the organization under control and keep a close eye on the north-German party dissidents. The SS was placed formally under the SA and Berchtold was given the impressive title of Reichsführer-SS in the hope that he would swallow this bitter pill. Berchtold was outraged and handed in his resignation whereupon his deputy, Erhard Heiden, was put in charge of what was still a minute organization. By 1928 there were only 280 members who did little but sell the party daily, the *Völkischer Beobachter*. It kept going thanks to its iron discipline and its self-image as the elite guard of a new Germany. On 6 January 1929 a new Reichsführer-SS was appointed: the 28-year old Heinrich Himmler.

Himmler had first met Röhm in 1922, on whose recommendation he joined the paramilitary group Reich Flag (*Reichsflagge*) which joined forces with Hitler in his ill-fated coup. Thereafter Himmler joined Ludendorff's National Socialist Freedom Movement that was effectively run by Gregor Strasser, an organizational genius who realized that he could make good use of this unemployed poulterer. Himmler played an active part in Strasser's Reichstag election campaign in 1924, racing around Bavaria on a motorcycle, haranguing the crowds with lurid denunciations of Jews, Freemasons, Communists and bankers. The National Socialists won almost 2 million votes and sent 32 deputies to the Reichstag. Hitler was released from prison in December 1924 and immediately set about rebuilding the NSDAP. Himmler joined the party in August 1925 and worked as Strasser's secretary. He remained in Bavaria when Strasser moved to Berlin and did Hitler's bidding with slavish devotion. Hitler rewarded his loyal myrmidon with a series of promotions. By 1927 he was deputy Reichsführer-SS.

Himmler had exceptional organizational talents, but he was also a fanatical ideologue, his head stuffed full of half-baked 'blood-and-soil' racism, Germanomanic rubbish and an unbounded admiration for Henry the Fowler, the tenth-century scourge of the Slavs, whom in moments of crisis he would ask for advice. Himmler envisaged an agricultural state, in which virtuous peasants rejected the degenerate values of the city and lived lives of diligent simplicity. In the belief that he was chosen to re-educate the German people, he bought a farm on which he hoped to train this brave new breed. Alas there were no takers, but it did not take long for Himmler to find the reason for his failure. Farmers were poorly paid, townspeople paid exorbitant prices for agricultural produce, and the profits from this unequal exchange went into the pockets of world Jewry. 'International Jewish capital' had to be destroyed and, emulating the Fowler, Himmler believed that Germany's destiny lay in the east where Slav 'subhumans' were to be driven out and agricultural settlements founded for the younger sons of the peasantry, who then would no longer be obliged to seek their fortunes in the urban cesspits.

A group known as the Artamanen entertained equally outlandish views and Himmler signed on, rising to the rank of Gauführer in Bavaria. Among his new associates were Rudolf Höss, the future commandant of Auschwitz, and Walther Darré, an Argentine German, an old boy of King's College School, Wimbledon, author of a highly regarded article 'The Pig as a Criterion for Northern People and Semites' and of the canonical *On Blood and Soil*[1]. Darré showed Himmler that race was the key to overcoming the agricultural crisis and that all influences harmful to 'Nordic blood' had to be extirpated: wishy-washy humanism, Christianity with its ludicrous message of universal love, Freemasons and above all the Jews.

When Himmler was appointed head of the SS on 6 January 1929 he was determined to put the ideas he had learnt from Strasser and Darré into practice with the SS as the National Socialist vanguard. This was a critical year in the history of a party that was still on the lunatic fringe, Hitler having failed to make any significant inroads, the party riven with internal factions and power struggles. In such a situation Hitler needed a group that was utterly devoted to him rather than a bunch of rune-scribbling Wotan worshippers. Himmler, without losing any of his new-found ideological fervour, willingly accepted the challenge. To most 'party comrades' (PGs) the idea that this gauche creature, a failed chicken farmer in charge of a mere 280 men who were subordinate to the SA, would succeed was patently absurd. Gauleiter Forster of Danzig once said of him, 'if I looked like Himmler I wouldn't say a word about race'. Himmler ignored such mockery and set about building a praetorian guard, selected according to rigorous racial principles. Former Freikorps officers who had little in common with the low-class bar-room brawlers in the SA flocked to the SS. Among such recruits were Erich von dem Bach-Zelewski, a former professional soldier and later mass murderer, Count Wolf-Heinrich von Helldorf, who was to become the hugely corrupt police president of Berlin, Karl-Friedrich von Eberstein, Helldorf's wartime adjutant, who became head of the Bavarian police, and Udo von Woyrsch who was to lead an Einsatzkommando and become chief of the SS and police in Saxony. Then

[222] came a second wave of recruits, men who had failed to find suitable employment in the depression years, many of whom were university educated and often with doctorates. The SS counted 1,000 men by December 1929, 2,727 by December the following year. It was still a minute organisation compared with the 60,000–100,000-strong SA.

Disregarding Pfeffer von Salomon's strict orders to the contrary, Himmler began to lure promising men away from the SA. In order to avoid serious conflict between the two organizations Hitler separated them. The SS remained formally subordinate to the SA, but the SA was no longer permitted to issue orders to the SS. Then on 7 November 1930 Hitler made the SS into a party police force. Its task was now to bring order and unity into a fissiparous collection of proletarian thugs in the SA, blood-and-soil fanatics, Wotan-worshipping illuminati and sour-grapes socialists. Some party members like Strasser argued for an alliance with the Soviet Union against the Versailles system, while others like Rosenberg called for a crusade against this 'Judaeo-Bolshevik' state. Goebbels still thought of Hitler as a prevaricating petit bourgeois. In the north the Strasser brothers, the organizational wizard Gregor and the left-leaning ideologue Otto, along with Joseph Goebbels, dreamed of a social revolution, while in Munich Hitler tried to find a middle way between various madcap schemes on a wide spectrum from revolution to reaction. Hitler temporarily squashed the north-German opposition in 1926 and won Goebbels over to his side, but left-wing Nazism lived on in the SA and was to be revived during the war. Otto Strasser in Berlin was unrepentant and had the support of the local SA. Goebbels also continued to hanker after the 'socialism' in National Socialism, although he knew that this could only be achieved with Adolf Hitler, never against him.

When Hitler went on a right-wing tack with the Harzburg Front and the Young Plan referendum, discontent in the SA grew apace. Otto Strasser stepped up his attacks on the 'reactionaries' in Munich and Goebbels began to have serious doubts about Hitler's leadership. Hitler relied on Kurt Daluege, head of the SS in Berlin, to crack down on the disaffected northerners. He was a specialist in garbage disposal, a man of such limited intelligence that he was known to the Berlin rowdies as 'Dummi-Dummi'. His network of informants revealed that the Berlin SA was little more than a criminal organization that recruited hit men from the swelling ranks of unemployed lumpenproletarians, and was virtually indistinguishable from the Communist equivalent in the Red Banner. Inasmuch as it was political it harboured deep resentments against the fat cats in Munich whom it plotted to overthrow, chanting the popular slogan 'Adolf has betrayed the proletariat!'

Walter Stennes, the deputy Higher SA Leader (OSAF) in eastern Germany, made himself the spokesman of the disaffected. With the support of a number of prominent figures he demanded that SA leaders should be allowed to stand for election to the Reichstag, that the influence of the Gauleiter should be reduced and that SA men should be paid when guarding party meetings. Hitler ignored them. No SA men were on the party list for the 1930 elections in which the NSDAP made its decisive breakthrough. The Berlin SA leadership resigned and refused to help Goebbels with the election campaign. Goebbels sought the protection of Daluege's SS against the SA, but on 30 August the 'Stennes men' stormed the Gau headquarters, overcame the SS, ransacked the offices and Goebbels reluctantly had to appeal to the police, whose Jewish chief, Bernard Weiss, he delighted in subjecting to scurrilous attacks. He then fled to Munich where Hitler was on the verge of a nervous breakdown, but the following day Goebbels pulled himself together, returned to Berlin and assured the SA that he would grant most of Stennes' wishes. The situation was defused, but Hitler, knowing all too well that Stennes was likely to strike again, appointed Dr Leonardo Conti, later to become Reich Health Leader, to keep close watch on him.

Pfeffer von Salomon had clearly lost control and the SA had become too independent, so he had to be removed. Hitler appointed himself head of the SA while waiting for Ernst Röhm to return from Bolivia where he was acting as a military adviser. During this time he demanded that every SA man make an oath of allegiance to him personally. Stennes was soon locked in battle with Röhm, who was determined to bring the SA under close central control, and on 1 April 1930 Stennes unleashed an open revolt against Hitler that spread throughout Brandenburg, Mecklenburg, Pomerania and Silesia. The mutiny soon ran out of steam and Hermann Göring was ordered to set about purging the SA of Stennes' followers. The SS had won another round against the SA and had given further proof of its utter loyalty to the Führer. In 1933 Stennes was arrested by the SS, but Göring, who was now locked in battle with Himmler, secured his freedom and arranged for him to travel to China, where he served as commander of Chiang Kai-Shek's bodyguard.

Under Himmler's aegis the SS concentrated on the collection of information on party members, political opponents, Freemasons and Jews. This was the province of Department 1C under SS-Sturmführer Reinhard Heydrich, an ice-cold and highly intelligent former naval officer who had been cashiered following a breach of promise suit involving the pregnant daughter of a director of IG Farben. He joined the NSDAP in 1931 with the

[224] membership number 544,916. His department was soon to be renamed the Security Service (SD), the party's own secret police.

Hitler had overcome the Stennes revolt and placed his friend Röhm in charge of the SA, but the brown-shirted thugs were still restless. A major problem was the outrageous homosexual behaviour of the leader and his immediate entourage. Walter Buch, who was responsible for 'cleansing operations' in the party and who in 1934 was to be appointed supreme party judge, decided that since Hitler denied that there was any proof of Röhm's sexual proclivities, in spite of a mound of incriminating evidence, the only solution was to murder him. The plot was hopelessly bungled, was partially revealed to the press, and further discredited the SA. Himmler's SS stood by, a ruthless and puritanical band, eagerly awaiting the moment of reckoning with the brutal rowdies in an SA led by an outrageous group that openly flouted paragraph 175 of the criminal code.

Himmler still played a subordinate role in 1933 and had to suffer the indignation of seeing Göring, who loathed the prissy little Bavarian, appoint his underling Kurt Daluege police chief in Prussia. Himmler promptly sent Heydrich to Berlin to keep an eye on Daluege but he was kept at arm's length, whereupon Heydrich returned to Munich, his mission having failed. The National Socialists were now in power, but there was no consensus about what was to be done beyond the destruction of democracy and the creation of a 'totalitarian state' that no one was able precisely to define. There followed a unseemly struggle between the Nazi satraps, each representing a different inchoate vision of the future, with the intense factional infighting of various party organizations parallel to a functioning state apparatus inherited from the republic, the whole confusing polycratic structure ultimately held together by a charismatic Führer as the final authority. Himmler remained in Munich as police chief where he assiduously uncovered real or imagined plots to assassinate the Führer, thereby fuelling Hitler's paranoid fears. Hitler did not trust the Reichswehr men who guarded the chancellery and replaced them with 120 SS men under the command of a vicious, beer-swilling Bavarian, Josef ('Sepp') Dietrich. In September 1933 this group was given the title of SS Personal Standard Adolf Hitler (Leibstandarte-SS Adolf Hitler), the first unit of what was to become the Waffen-SS, a National Socialist army.

In April 1933 Himmler took over the Bavarian political police and during the summer he created a number of SS police units called Special Commandos (*SS-Sonderkommandos*), later named Political Stand-by Groups (*Politische Bereitschaftsgruppen*) which assisted local police chiefs in hunting down political opponents and keeping the SA in some sort of order. Their first concentration camp was founded in a former munitions factory at Dachau, near Munich. Here Himmler's SS bullied, tortured and murdered their victims in a secluded spot, far from the sensitive gaze of the German public, which was often somewhat upset by the open violence of the SA. SS-Oberführer Theodor Eicke, a sadistic Alsatian who had recently been released from a psychiatric hospital for the criminally insane, was placed in command. Under the motto 'tolerance equals weakness' he organized the concentration camp guards, in 1936 called the SS Death's Head Units (*SS-Totenkopfverbände* – TV), which he infused with a passionate hatred for all those in their charge. In July 1934 he was put in charge of all the concentration camps, most of which had been run by the SA. His title was now Inspector of the Concentration Camps and Leader of the SS Guards. It was an impressive title, but his was a small office consisting of five police officers and eight SS men. He was Himmler's immediate subordinate and the bitter rival of Heydrich, who was determined to include the concentration camps in his police empire. Eicke moved on in November 1939 and was replaced by his chief of staff, SS-Obergruppenführer Richard Glücks, a man chiefly remembered for having later organized the recycling of human hair from the victims of the death camps.

Himmler, ably assisted by the Hessian lawyer SS-Scharführer Werner Best and by Heydrich, set about planning a nationwide police force to replace the 16 state police organizations, which he claimed were full of 'people with criminal records and Marxists'. The major obstacle in his way was Hermann Göring, who also wanted to create a unified police under his command. As acting minister-president of Prussia he had appointed Dr Rudolf Diels, a highly cultured and well-situated official in the Prussian ministry of the interior who was not a party member, with the task of converting Section 1A of the police headquarters in Berlin, responsible for political intelligence, into the core of a nationwide secret police. The result of Diels' efforts was the formation of the Secret State Police Office (*Gestapa*) with offices in a former art school in the Prinz-Albrecht-Strasse 8. The new police force was soon known popularly as the Gestapo.

Göring might have been formally in charge in Prussia, but the anarchic and sadistic SA took the law into its own hands, unleashing an orgy of violence, thus openly challenging his rule. Diels was determined to put an end to this chaotic situation. First his Gestapo men raided the SA headquarters and released a number of prisoners who were close to having been tortured to death. He then closed down most of the 'wild' SA concentration camps in Berlin. A number of SA hoodlums were put on trial. Diels also set out to rein in the equally unruly SS, but here he was much less successful.

His main contestant was Arthur Nebe, one of the few genuine Nazis in the Gestapo, a crude and murderous creature who delighted in quoting Balzac's Vautrin, a criminal who became police chief of Paris and who was fond of saying: 'I'll either become someone really important, or I'll be hanged.' Nebe was egged on in his attacks on Diels by Hans Berndt Gisevius, a devious character who was later to join the resistance. The two men were in close contact with Himmler and began to spread the rumour that Diels was a closet Communist. Göring failed to give Diels sufficient support while Himmler kept up the pressure. In November 1933 a compromise was reached when Diels was appointed SS-Standartenführer, but by now it was clear that his days were numbered.

After the Reichstag elections in November 1933 Wilhelm Frick as minister of the interior was determined to put an end to the federal system. The police forces would thus necessarily have to be amalgamated. Göring was able to ensure that the ministry of the interior did not take control of the Gestapo, so that Frick now looked to Himmler, who was still a relatively minor figure in comparison with Göring, to take over the various police forces over which the minister would retain overall control. By January 1934 Himmler was in charge of all secret police agencies in Germany, with the exception of those in Prussia and Schaumburg-Lippe. Göring fought to maintain control over the Prussian police, but faced with growing opposition from the SA he decided to reach a compromise. While still refusing to place the Prussian police under the Reich ministry of the interior he accepted Heydrich as head of the Gestapo and Nebe took over the state crime squad. Diels was shunted off to Cologne as regional president.

Ernst Röhm and the SA felt that they had been betrayed by Hitler in 1929, when he had made an alliance with the old elites by joining in the campaign against the Young Plan referendum. As chancellor he had left the military, industry and the civil service virtually untouched. The SA demanded that these reactionaries should be swept aside in what they called the Second Revolution. Röhm's particular concern was to create a new National Socialist army, based on the SA. General Walter von Reichenau, Blomberg's right-hand man in the Reichswehr Ministry, a man who in wartime was to prove himself to be a murderous anti-Semite and racist, was determined to frustrate this ambition and to bring the SA under the control of the army. To this end in May 1933 he negotiated an agreement between the army, the SA and the 1 million strong veterans' organization Stahlhelm (Steel Helmet) whereby the SA and the Stahlhelm were to be amalgamated and placed under the control of the Reichswehr ministry, thus forming a reserve army. Other right-wing paramilitary groups were also to join the SA. Röhm skilfully maintained control by dividing this greatly enlarged SA into three groups, with the 500,000 original SA men plus 314,000 from the Stahlhelm forming a core group known as the Active SA. Röhm was appointed minister without portfolio in December 1933 and promptly demanded control over the defence of the eastern frontier. The following February he wrote a memorandum suggesting that the SA be made responsible for national defence and that the Reichswehr should merely be responsible for training, whereupon Werner von Blomberg, one of the few generals at this stage who were utterly devoted to Hitler, appealed to the chancellor. Röhm was for Hitler the closest thing to a friend, whom he addressed with the familiar '*du*', and Hitler was also sympathetic to the SA's spontaneous radicalism, but he also knew that he would never be able to achieve his foreign political goals without the experts in the regular army. He was also concerned that only 1 million of the 4 million members of the expanded SA were party members and thus subject to party discipline. In any such awkward situation Hitler was temperamentally incapable of making a clear-cut decision and called for a compromise. On 28 February 1934 he invited the leaders of the army and the SA to meet in the Reichswehr ministry and treated them to an impassioned speech calling for cooperation. An agreement was reached whereby the Reichswehr was reaffirmed as the 'sole bearer of arms' in the Third Reich, while the SA was made responsible for pre- and post-military training. Goebbels was disgusted at Hitler's characteristic prevarication and did everything he could to bring about Röhm's downfall.

Röhm invited Blomberg to his headquarters for brunch, and shook hands over a glass of sparkling wine. Blomberg and his entourage left, but the wine continued to flow. A drunken Röhm referred to Hitler as 'an absurd little lance corporal', denounced him as 'disloyal' and announced that he had no intention of respecting the agreement. He thundered on about Hitler in the following days, insisting that 'Adolf's nuts'. SA-Obergruppenführer Viktor Lutze, the provincial president and police chief of Hanover, was appalled at this behaviour and decided to take action. First he went to see Rudolf Hess, who had no idea what to do, then he went to Berchtesgaden and told Hitler what was going on. Once again Hitler prevaricated, muttering that they would have to wait and see how things developed. Poor Lutze then met Reichenau, who shared Goebbels' opinion of the Obergruppenführer. The general was delighted, telling an associate that Röhm would soon be replaced by the 'harmless' Lutze. He was a man of whom Goebbels said 'good old Viktor is extremely stupid'.

[228]   Reichenau had already been plotting with Reinhard Heydrich, who was determined to liquidate Röhm and his closest associates. It took some time and effort to persuade Himmler of the need to act, for Himmler was Röhm's close friend ever since the early days in Munich, but he needed to mend fences with Göring if he were to gain control over the Prussian Gestapo. He was prepared to sacrifice a friend for such a rich prize. Heydrich set about collecting evidence against Röhm, but precious little was forthcoming. Undeterred, he ordered Theodor Eicke to plan the assassination of Röhm, using his Death's Head unit in Dachau, and to draw up a list of all those who were to be murdered. Reichenau promised the Reichswehr's logistical support. A number of prominent figures drew up hit lists of undesirables and sent them to Heydrich.

The conspirators were highly alarmed when they learnt that Hitler and Röhm had met, agreeing to table further discussion and giving the SA one month's leave, whereupon Röhm went to Bad Wiessee for a cure. How could Heydrich now claim that Röhm was plotting a *coup d'état* when he was in a health farm and his cohorts were on holiday? It was clear that although Röhm was a major problem for Hitler, it was one that he was unwilling to tackle head-on. Now Göring, Himmler, Heydrich and Reichenau offered a solution, but still he hesitated. Then, on 17 June Vice-Chancellor von Papen made a sensational speech at Marburg University, written for him by Edgar Jung, an ultra-conservative Calvinist lawyer, whose inchoate notions of 'revolutionary conservatism' were based on the muddle-headed speculations of the Austrian sociologist Othmar Spann, whose *On the Sociology and Philosophy of War*[2] Hitler had extensively cribbed when writing *Mein Kampf.* It was a powerful expression of conservative opposition to Hitler. Men who had colluded with the Nazis in the belief that they could control and manipulate him had finally realized that they had made a disastrous miscalculation. The speech drew a firm line between conservative authoritarianism and 'the unnatural totalitarian aspirations of National Socialism'. It denounced the lawlessness, brutality and the 'semi-religious materialism' of those who claimed to be in the vanguard of the 'German Revolution'. The 'permanent revolution from below' had to be brought to an end. Papen, who failed to realize the full implications of Jung's argument, was close to a somewhat absurd group of conservatives who hoped, on Hindenburg's death, to restore the monarchy in the person of SA-Gruppenführer Prince August Wilhelm, the son of the former Kaiser, popularly known as 'Auwi'. Goebbels made sure that details of Papen's speech did not appear in the press, and Hitler decided to visit Hindenburg so as to assess his state of health and test his reactions to the Marburg address. Hindenburg let it be known that he thought it essential to restore law and order and argued that there was no place for extremists in the new Germany. Hitler understood this to mean that if he wished to retain the support of the generals after Hindenburg's death, in what was likely to be a matter of months or even weeks, he would have to deal with the SA.

Bombarded with incriminating evidence, the vast majority of which was fabricated, Hitler finally decided to act. He ordered Röhm to call a meeting with all his leading officers in the Pension Hanselbauer in Bad Wiessee on Sunday 30 June 1934 that he intended to address. Hitler personally arrested Röhm early that Sunday morning while he was still in bed. Then he discovered SA-Obergruppenführer Heines, the police chief of Breslau, in bed with a handsome blonde 18-year-old Obertruppenführer, a scene that was embroidered by Goebbels into a 'disgusting and sickening' example of an unspeakable perversion. All six prominent SA men in Bad Wiessee were bundled off to Stadelheim jail where they were executed that evening by SS-Gruppenführer Prince Josias zu Waldeck und Pyrmont and six NCOs under the command of Sepp Dietrich, who could not stomach the sight of the executions and had to leave before all were dead. Hitler was still reluctant to have his old friend murdered, so that Röhm was temporarily spared. At 10 a.m. Hitler phoned Goebbels from Munich, who passed on the codeword 'hummingbird' to Göring. This was the signal for Himmler and Heydrich to start their bloodbath.

A number of old scores were settled that day. The former Bavarian prime minister, von Kahr, was murdered as was a prominent Catholic layman, Erich Klausener, and Papen's speechwriter Edgar Jung. The former chancellor General von Schleicher was shot along with his wife and his close associate General von Bredow. Gregor Strasser was dragged off to the Gestapo headquarters in the Prinz-Albrecht-Strasse and shot. A music critic by the name of Dr Wilhelm Schmidt was gunned down, having had the misfortune of being mistaken for the SA leader Ludwig Schmitt. A Catholic priest, Father Stempfle, who had helped to correct the many grammatical errors in the manuscript of *Mein Kampf,* was also gunned down. As in the case of Klausener this was a warning to other Catholics to keep out of politics. In Silesia several Jews were killed for the amusement of the Gauleiter. There were a number of other cases of mistaken identity among the roughly 200 victims of this Nazi St Bartholomew's. Himmler and Göring finally managed to persuade Hitler that Röhm had to die. He was shot by Eicke on 1 July, having turned down the opportunity to shoot himself. At 4 a.m. on 2 July Hitler ordered the killing to stop, just before SS-Gruppenführer Karl Schreyer was to be shot.

A fifth of the NSDAP's 203,000 political officers were purged after the July coup. Thirty SS and party members were tried for rape, murder and theft. The 21 murderers were acquitted on the grounds that they had been 'provoked'. Three rapists were sent to jail, not for rape but for 'racial contamination'. In the following years a few leading Nazis, virtually all of whom were irredeemably venal, fell from grace. Among them were such prominent figures as Streicher, Josef Wagner and Wilhelm Kube.

Although the state had now degenerated to the level of a criminal organization, there was widespread approval of the bloodbath. A cabinet meeting was hastily called on 3 July and cobbled together a law justifying the 'emergency measures' needed to meet 'treasonable attacks'. Carl Schmitt opined that: 'The Führer protects the law from the worst forms of abuse when he uses his position as leader to create the law in his capacity as supreme judge.' He was later to extend this highly questionable definition of the law in the lapidary injunction that 'the will of the Führer is the highest law'. In October 1935 Hans Frank, in his capacity as chairman of the Association of National Socialist German Jurists (BNSDJ), expressed much the same idea when he stated: 'Formerly we were in the habit of saying: is this right or wrong; today we must pose the question accordingly: what would the Führer say?'

Most Germans were relieved that the SA with their brutal activism had been brought under control by Hitler's decisive action, forgetting that law and order could not be restored by murderous disregard for the law. Even though two prominent generals had been slaughtered, the Reichswehr was delighted. Blomberg cravenly thanked Hitler for his 'soldierly determination' and 'exemplary courage' in dealing with these 'traitors and mutineers'. Lieutenant Count Claus Schenk von Stauffenberg was relieved that 'a suppurating boil has been lanced'. Hitler had overcome all opposition within the Nazi movement and had taken a further giant step on the way to dictatorship. The alliance between Himmler and Göring was sealed in blood. The SS had triumphed over the SA which was now in the servile hands of Viktor Lutze who, when in his cups, would swear to get his revenge on the SS for its treatment of the SA. He was pensioned off in 1941 with a golden handshake worth 154,000 RM. He did not have long to enjoy his retirement because he was killed soon afterwards in a car accident.

There was widespread relief that the plebeian bullyboys in the SA had at least temporarily been reined in and that Himmler's black-uniformed elitist guard was now in control. Whereas the original SS had been made up of ex-servicemen, 'old warriors' from the early days of the party and unemployed university graduates, there were many lofty aristocrats among the 'March fallen'[3]. The Hereditary Grand Duke of Mecklenburg, the Hereditary Prince zu Waldeck und Pyrmont and the Princes Christof and Wilhelm of Hesse were already members, but now they were joined by the Prince of

Figure 7.1   Göring and Himmler enjoying a joke

Hohenzollern-Emden and members of such illustrious families as von Rödern, Strachwitz, von der Goltz and von Alvensleben. In 1938, 18.7 per cent of SS-Obergruppenführer (the equivalent of an army general) were aristocrats, roughly the same proportion as in the army. Further 'reactionaries' entered the SS when the bulk of the monarchist ex-servicemen's organization, the Kyffhäuserbund, was also incorporated into the SS. University graduates continued to flock to the SS. Among these highly-trained technocrats and social engineers, who were fired by an ideological fervour and determined to build a new and dynamic society, were such remarkable figures as Otto Ohlendorf, who was both a brilliant economist and a mass murderer, Walter Schellenberg, the ruthless counter-espionage specialist, and Reinhard Höhn, the RSHA's legal expert. A number of officers left the Reichswehr to join the SS-Verfügungstruppe (Auxiliary Troops, the forerunner of the Waffen-SS), formed in August 1938 as a 'standing army in war and peace'. This gave the officer corps of the military units of the SS a quite different flavour from that of the old rough and ready sergeant-major types like Sepp Dietrich.

In order to emphasize that the SS was a social as well as an ideological elite, Himmler gave a number of prominent figures honorary commissions with the right to wear the dashing black uniform designed by SS-Oberführer Benno von Arendt. Among those so honoured were the state secretary in the foreign office Ernst Friedrich von Weizsäcker, the Gauleiter of Danzig, Albert Forster, the Sudeten German leader Konrad Henlein, and Hitler's secretary Martin Bormann.

A number of prominent businessmen joined the Friendship Circle of the Reichsführer SS, among whom were Friedrich Flick, Albert Vögler of the Vereinigte-Stahlwerke, the Cologne banker Baron Kurt von Schröder, and for a while Hjalmar Schacht. Whole companies joined the Circle such as the Reichsbank, the Deutsche Bank, the Dresdner Bank, the Norddeutscher Lloyd, the Hamburg-Amerika-Linie (HAPAG), IG Farben and the foodstuffs company Dr. August Oetker.

Himmler was also able to incorporate some elite riding clubs into the SS, but this created a number of problems. The horsemen were successful in competitive show jumping and brought fame and glory to the SS, but they were mostly conservative nationalists who were sadly lacking in the National Socialist spirit. The old guard condemned them as reactionaries and demanded that they be brought in line. When 11 horsemen refused to take the SS oath of allegiance to Hitler they were sent to a concentration camp. SS-Reiterführer Baron Anton von Hohberg und Buchwald was summarily executed when caught passing on information about the SS to the Reichswehr and SS-Obersturmbannführer Count Hans-Viktor von Salviati was executed for plotting against Hitler.

While actively recruiting new members, the SS also set about weeding out undesirable elements from its ranks. Sixty thousand men were dismissed between December 1933 and December 1935, among them alcoholics, homosexuals, those who were unable to meet the rigorous racial criteria, a number of old street-fighting types and men deemed to be lacking in ideological fervour. In spite of all these efforts the SS was far from being ideologically and socially unified and contained numerous disparate and conflicting interests. Himmler therefore ordered the Main Race and Settlement Office (RuSHA) to work out a set of racial criteria for admission to the SS. Hauptsturmbannführer Professor Bruno K. Schulz, a specialist in 'empirical genetic prediction', came up with an absurd five-point scale, at the top of which was 'pure Nordic' and at the bottom 'crossbreeds of extra-European extraction'. Only those in the top three categories could be admitted to the SS. Candidates therefore had to be at least from a 'harmonic mixture' of 'pure Nordic' and 'mainly Nordic or Palatine' with a slight touch of 'Alpine, Dinaric or Mediterranean' elements. Himmler imagined that by such means the leading positions in the state would be held by blonde men (one is tempted to say 'like Hitler') and that within 120 years the Germans would once again be a pure-blooded race. Candidates then had to meet certain criteria for a suitable bodily stature before beginning their novitiate on 9 November, the anniversary of Hitler's beer hall putsch. The new recruit was given his service card on 30 January, the day Hitler became chancellor, stylized as the 'seizure of power'. On 20 April, Hitler's birthday, he swore allegiance to the Führer 'unto death'. Then the candidate had to learn the SS catechism with such questions as: 'Why do we believe in Germany and the Führer?' to which the answer was: 'We believe in Germany because we believe in a God Almighty, who has sent us our Führer Adolf Hitler.' The candidate had also to obtain the Reich Sports Medal. At no point was there an intelligence test or any assessment of intellectual ability. The young man then had to spend a year in the army or in the RAD before returning to the SS. If the report on this obligatory year was good he would become a full member within a month. On 9 November he made another oath that he would marry 'solely according to racial and hereditary criteria' and only with the permission of the Reichsführer or the RuSHA.

Befitting this new brotherhood, Himmler built his Camelot in Haus Wewelsburg near Paderborn with a round table for 12 of his chosen knights. This vast complex, on which he spent more than 12 million RM, was just one of a series of bizarre places of pilgrimage serving the SS cult where historical romanticism was mixed with the occult, heathen rites with pseudo-Christian ceremonial for Himmler's 'National Socialist order of Nordic men and the kinship community bound together by oath'. This weird conglomeration of hare-brained notions with a heavy admixture of pixilated racism, along with a venomous and fanatical nationalism, did not add up to a coherent doctrine with which Himmler's order could identify. SS men found the ideological schooling of the RuSHA insufferably boring and found any excuse to absent themselves. Hitler had little patience with all this pseudo-Germanic twaddle and never visited the suite reserved for him at Haus Wewelsburg.

Himmler expected his SS men to marry between the ages of 25 and 30, the intended having passed an extensive test to determine whether the fiancée was of good racial stock, with no history of hereditary diseases in the family. A lengthy questionnaire had to be filled out, which included questions such as whether she was 'comradely or bossy, thrifty or spendthrift, homely or hectic and obsessively tidy'. Senior officers had to trace the family back to 1750 for any trace of undesirable blood. Many SS men ignored all this tiresome and time-consuming rigmarole and were dismissed for disobeying

[234] orders. Soon there were so many infractions that the rules had to be relaxed and a number of men were reinstated. Church weddings were frowned upon and all senior officers had to renounce the church, declare themselves to be 'believers in God' and be baptized, married and buried according to neo-pagan SS rites. Himmler, the stern and puritanical grand master of the new order, was disgusted by Christmas, which he associated with 'the deadly danger of "cosiness"' (*Gemütlichkeit*), and in its place celebrated the 'Yule Festival'.

Himmler's efforts to turn the SS into a pagan order were largely unsuccessful. Sixty-nine per cent of Totenkopf men and 53.6 per cent of the Verfügungstruppe proclaimed themselves 'believers in God', but two-thirds of the General SS remained affiliated to the two major churches. He was equally unsuccessful in persuading his men to propagate. Although he called for families of four children by 1939 the average SS family had only 1.1 offspring, well below the national average. He encouraged his men to impregnate unmarried women of good racial stock, the children to be discreetly born in SS Lebensborn clinics. Precious few took the hint, but with abortion a criminal offence Aryan women who wished to conceal a pregnancy could avail themselves of the excellent services of Lebensborn.

Many found Himmler's attacks on the Christian churches and on bourgeois morality highly offensive. The number of civilian SS supporters dwindled drastically and many of the best SS officers left to join the army. The SS was in danger of falling apart for lack of suitable men in leading positions, but it was saved when the neo-pagan cult of the Germanic gave way to a more appealing activism. Dr Werner Best, the SS legal expert, summed up this attitude thus: 'Fighting is essential and eternal, the goals are contingent and change with time. Therefore success is not important . . . the level of morality is not determined by the content, by the what, but by the how, by the form.' Himmler's definition was less complex: 'the word "impossible" does not exist in our vocabulary!' With morality reduced to 'heroic action' with all moral and ethical restraints removed, the way was open for the SS to become the unconditional instrument of a murderous dictatorship.

Reinhard Heydrich is a paradigmatic example of the power-obsessed, non-ideological man of action typical of the upper echelons of the SS. He had no patience with Himmler's neo-pagan mumbo-jumbo, and despised the Reichsführer-SS for his racial fantasies and ludicrous esoterica, even going so far as to describe this fine specimen of Germanic manhood as 'a typical Jewish lout'. He was appalled by Himmler's narrow, philistine, petit bourgeois family life and his wife Lina described Frau Himmler as 'XXXL knickers'. Heydrich was far from idolizing Hitler and never understood Himmler's slavish adulation of the Führer. He was an excellent violinist as well as a superb athlete, who arranged for the Jewish champion fencer, Paul Sommer, to emigrate to the United States and also provided papers for a Jewish Olympic fencer from Poland, but he was a man virtually without human feeling, emotionally empty, without friends and who saw in his wife little more than a convenient outlet for his insatiable sexual yearnings. None mourned him when he was assassinated by Czech SOE operatives in May 1942. Sepp Dietrich delighted in the news of his demise, loudly proclaiming: 'Thank God the little bastard's kicked the bucket!' For all his reservations about his superior, Heydrich realized that he needed Himmler's protection and treated his boss with exaggerated subservience, but Himmler also knew that he needed Heydrich, whom he feared for his superior intelligence and unbending temperament.

Heydrich's career began in Munich where he built up the Bavarian political police (*BayPoPo*) that energetically hunted down the enemies, or supposed enemies, of the new regime, bundling them off to Dachau in such numbers that the Bavarian commissar (*Reichsstatthalter*) Ritter von Epp and Wilhelm Frick as minister of the interior felt compelled to complain to Himmler. He followed Himmler as he took over all the separate police forces in Germany, but his SD was still a minute organization, a mere 100 men in the autumn of 1933, deeply resented by the police and never likely to become an instrument adequate for Heydrich's ambitions. The various secret police forces such as the BayPoPo were a quite different matter. These were manned by seasoned professionals, whom the pragmatic Heydrich could easily turn into loyal upholders of the Führer's dictatorship. Heydrich felt that the party had outlived its usefulness. It had provided the mass support that had made Hitler's rise to power possible; now it was little more than a nuisance with its factional squabbles, its obsession with ideological nit-picking and its utopian demands. A highly professional police force with a light ideological dusting should replace the NSDAP as the main pillar of the new state. Heydrich studiously ignored the fact that many policemen were not party members and were ideologically suspect. All he demanded was loyalty and professional competence. The bull-necked Heinrich 'Gestapo' Müller, the scourge of Bavaria's Communists, son-in-law of a prominent member of the German People's Party (DVP), a church-going Catholic and known to be excessively parsimonious with his contributions to the Nazi 'Casserole Sunday' collections, was deeply suspected by the Gauleiter of Munich, but followed Himmler's orders with icy efficiency as head of the Gestapo from 1939. The murderous Arthur Nebe from the Berlin police's drug squad was another example of the skilled professional who saw the SS as the police force of the future.

The Gestapo was a separate organization over which the police had no control. It was devoted to hunting down the enemies of the regime, whom Heydrich insisted were busily at work, even after the destruction of their organizations. For him the sinister machinations of 'world Jewry', 'world Freemasonry' and the 'political priesthood' were all the more dangerous since they were now hidden underground. At the core of the Gestapo was Section II comprising five divisions under SS-Obersturmbannführer Reinhard Flesch, one of the tough professional policemen from Munich. Heinrich Müller was made responsible for combating Marxism. He was nothing if not thorough. Almost one-third of the 60,000 Communist Party members who remained in Germany were prosecuted by 1935. Franz Josef Huber, who had once described Hitler as an 'Austrian deserter', as well as a 'jumped-up nobody and unemployed housepainter', looked out for 'reactionaries, the right-wing opposition and the churches'. Another section dealt with abortions, homosexuality and miscegenation (*Rassenschande*), a further one with business and the labour movement, a final department was responsible for issuing arrest warrants and sending the guilty to concentration camps, while Dr Karl Hasselbacher kept an eye on religious sects and Freemasons.

The Gestapo was a law unto itself. As Werner Best phrased it: '[the police never acts] contrary to the law as long as it acts according to the rules laid down by its superiors, all the way up to the highest authority. The police acts legally as long as it carries out the will of the leadership.' Some brave souls tried to uphold the rule of law and investigate cases of torture and murder in the concentration camps, but rarely with any degree of success. When they did manage to secure a conviction, the guilty party was usually pardoned by Hitler. Scholars like Carl Schmitt called upon public prosecutors to become 'legally creative assistants to the leader's will', rather than be 'cramped by the normative and base judgments resting exclusively on the facts', and to cease to be 'slavish followers of the letter of positivist law'.

Wilhelm Frick as minister of the interior and Franz Gürtner as minister of justice made half-hearted attempts to keep the Gestapo within the bounds of the law. They were motivated more by concern over their dwindling authority than by their commitment to the rule of law, but they were no match for Göring, Himmler and Heydrich. Himmler was given the title of Reichsführer-SS and Chief of the German Police in 1936 and Frick had to make do with the meaningless addition of 'in the Ministry of the Interior'. This meant that Himmler was formally under Frick and thus had abandoned the ambition of attaining ministerial rank, but in practice his power was greatly enhanced and he now had control over all aspects of policing. He never even bothered to have an office in the ministry of the interior. Heydrich was made responsible for the Security Police, the Gestapo and the Criminal Police (Kripo), while Kurt Daluege, whom Frick had hoped to put in charge of the police rather than Himmler, was responsible for the routine police work of the Security Police (Sipo), the gendarmes and the communal police forces. Shortly thereafter Heydrich's political and criminal police forces were united under the Sipo rubric, while Daluege's men were now called Order Police (Orpo).

Heydrich's legal experts, Werner Best and Reinhard Höhn, set about redefining the concept of law. Best pronounced law to be the expression of the Führer's will. Höhn claimed that neither the state nor the individual were legal entities, but merely means by which the aims of the *Volk* could be attained, aims that were set by the Führer. The individual thus had no legal recourse and was delivered up to the Sipo's despotic caprices. Heydrich did all he could to bring the concentration camps under his control, but Himmler, who was determined not to let Heydrich become so powerful as to pose a threat to his own position, continued to support the sadistic Theodor Eicke as head of the concentration camps and of the Totenkopfverbände. Heydrich also made little headway against Kurt Daluege who, although he was weak, idle and Heydrich's intellectual inferior, was stiffened by his legal expert Werner Bracht, who skilfully exploited the many organizational anomalies, personal rivalries and legal confusions to keep Heydrich at bay. Heydrich's position was further weakened by the bitter rivalry between Arthur Nebe's Kripo and Heinrich Müller's Gestapo. The Kripo was respected by the public, whereas the Gestapo was both feared and disliked. Müller could count on Heydrich's support, but his Gestapo was a relatively small organization when compared with the Kripo and was often remarkably incompetent in contrast to the professionals in the Kripo. The Gestapo was chronically understaffed, with only 20,000 members by 1939, and were it not for the disagreeable tendency of the German public to tell tales out of school would have been distressingly short of victims. Enthusiastic informants are, sorry to say, an all too familiar figure throughout German history. As the patriotic poet Hoffmann von Fallersleben, the author of '*Deutschland, Deutschland über alles*', wrote some 100 years before: 'The greatest scoundrel in the land/Is and remains the informer.' One shocking example is that of Saarbrücken, where 69.5 per cent of cases of treason and high treason, both of which bore mandatory death sentences, were the result of denunciations. Heydrich complained bitterly about such behaviour

[238] because the vast majority of cases were for base personal motives rather than out of idealism or love for the regime.

Heydrich decided to make up for the deficiencies and unpopularity of the state secret police, the Gestapo, by building up the party's secret police force, the SD, that was still a minute organization whose precise function was virtually unknown. The organization was particularly appealing to young intellectuals, fired with a vision of a new society, who were appalled by the primitive power-hungry party bosses and the vapid piffle spouted by the party ideologues. They were determined to set the mini-Hitlers to rights, correct mistakes and put the party on the path of National Socialist virtue. Otto Ohlendorf, who was born in 1907, was a prime example of this new breed of highly intelligent, critical and ambitious young National Socialists. As an economist at the Institute for World Business in Kiel he was sharply critical of the muddle-headed state-socialist, dirigiste and collectivist notions of the party left, and had been cross-examined by the Gestapo for his heterodox views. He was then introduced to Professor Reinhard Höhn who, much to his surprise, told him that the SD was looking for constructively critical National Socialists to set the party to rights. Other young intellectuals followed suit, many through Höhn's connections in the academic world, and formed the core of a dynamic intelligence service that was free from the bureaucratic spirit that was beginning to ossify the Gestapo. Heydrich as an enthusiastic reader of thrillers took particular delight in this new organization, to the point of copying his British homologue and referring to himself as 'C' in the files.

The revamped SD was divided into three main sections, responsible for organization (Dr Wilhelm Albert), enemies of the regime (Professor Dr Franz Six) and foreign countries (SS-Oberführer Heinz Jost). Germany was divided into seven sectors, each with two or three subdivisions. The SD relied on an army of mean-spirited people eager to denounce their neighbours and of informants (*V-Männer*), the vast majority of whom were not even party members and who were often unaware that they were working for the SD. By 1937 the SD employed 3,000 full-time personnel and 50,000 informants.

'C' was not content with keeping a close watch on the nation's pulse with detailed reports on public opinion, a kind of Gallup poll which has proved a useful source for historians, he was also concerned with active propaganda. To this end he published a weekly newspaper *Das Schwarze Korps* as the official organ of the SS, edited by SS-Standartenführer Gunter d'Alquen, the political editor of the *Völkischer Beobachter*. The new journal with its 24-year-old editor was a sensation and within four years was selling 750,000 copies. Along with venomous attacks on Jews and the churches, which sank to the level of Streicher's *Der Stürmer*, there were scurrilous attacks on the complacency of the bourgeoisie, and defamatory articles on shortcomings in the civil service and indolent party officials. Gunter d'Alquen thus achieved his aim to create a journal that attacked a regime that he felt was relapsing into a self-satisfied torpor and was losing its revolutionary élan. The paper was sharply critical of Nazis who smashed the windows of Jewish stores in Munich in 1935, saying that the 'Jewish question' was a serious matter that could not be solved by hooliganism. It attacked Nazi judges who based their judgments on the 'sound instincts of the people'. It warned against too broad a definition of 'enemies of the people' and attacked the hordes of wretches who denounced their fellow citizens to the Gestapo, while at the same time doing its fair share of denunciation by passing critical letters to the editor on to the police. Initially the editor had ready access to the information collected by the SD and thus had an invaluable archive at his disposal, but soon the alliance between Heydrich and d'Alquen began to fall apart. Heydrich became increasingly critical of d'Alquen's hectic demagogy, defamatory fervour and blank refusal to accept any censorship.

Heydrich was now in a very awkward situation. The *Schwarze Korps* had proved to be something of a sorcerer's apprentice, while at the same time a bitter rivalry was developing between the SD and the Gestapo over areas of competence. In 1937 Heydrich tried to settle the problem by giving each distinct jurisdictions. In practical terms this meant that the SD would be relegated to simply dealing with what in typical Nazi jargon was called 'worldview' (*Weltanschauung*). The highly educated and dialectically agile SD men were determined to fight back. The SD had become more and more involved in espionage and thus came up against the professionals in military intelligence (Abwehr). Admiral Wilhelm Canaris, a hypochondriac believer in astrology who was besotted with his two wire-haired dachs-hunds, was a close friend of Heydrich, with whom he had served on the training ship *Berlin*. As head of counter-intelligence he had made a deal with Werner Best in December 1936 in which he agreed that since he had no military police under his command the Gestapo should take care of all executive matters. But this did not deal with the problem of the meddle-some amateurs in the SD, who were interfering with the Abwehr's work abroad.

The SD had forged papers purporting to show that Marshal Tukha-chevsky, the master strategist who introduced the notion of the 'operational' level and developed the defensive strategy of 'deep operations', was

[240] plotting against Stalin. These were passed on to Moscow via the Czech president, Beneš, an incurable busybody. Tukhachevsky was arrested and executed and Stalin began an extensive purge of the military leadership. Although there is still much mystery surrounding this episode, Heydrich imagined that he had thus decapitated the Red Army, when in fact he had almost certainly been the guileless tool of Soviet intelligence. For Canaris this affair was a clear breach of his agreement with Werner Best and he was determined in future to make sure that the SD kept its nose out of foreign intelligence.

Himmler and Heydrich had issued strict instructions that the SD should not meddle with the internal affairs of the NSDAP, but Reinhard Höhn and his amanuensis Otto Ohlendorf imagined that they could change the party's course by using their detailed reports on public opinion to attack the collectivist ideas of Robert Ley and Walther Darré, which they condemned as 'Bolshevik', and the absolutist and caesaristic notions of Carl Schmitt, which they considered to be 'Fascist'. Ohlendorf collected a vast amount of information on the economy and in a detailed memorandum entitled 'The Economy in the National Socialist State' argued that the excessive pace of rearmament was causing an intolerable strain on the economy and that small businesses were being driven against the wall, while large enterprises had excessive control over prices and wages, thus stifling individual initiative. He argued that National Socialism should seek a middle way between the extremes of unbridled American capitalism and a Soviet planned economy.

Höhn was greatly impressed by this report and made Ohlendorf head of Section II.2 that was responsible for collecting information on all aspects of life in Germany. These reports showed that there was deep public dissatisfaction with the arrogance and megalomania of the party grandees, with the corporatist ambitions of the DAF, the government's spendthrift attitude, and the overwhelming influence of big business. Then Höhn made the mistake of attacking Professor Walter Frank, head of the Reich Institute for the History of the New Germany and of the Institute for the Study of the Jewish Question, and tried to infiltrate SS scholars into these organizations. Frank fought back, ably seconded by Julius Streicher who loathed the SD, dug up an anti-Nazi remark made by Höhn years before and thus secured his dismissal. Shortly thereafter Himmler temporarily suspended Ohlendorf, a know-all whom he had once described as imagining himself to be a 'knight of the National Socialist grail' and whose intellectual superiority he found increasingly grating, arguing that his criticisms of the party were a serious breach of procedure. Ohlendorf requested to leave the SD, but Heydrich did not wish to lose a man whose professional brilliance he admired and with whose ideas he was in broad agreement. It was not until 1938 that Ohlendorf was seconded to a National Socialist trade organization, but he still put in a couple of hours a day as head of his old section in the SD.

The Höhn–Ohlendorf affair put the role of the SD in question and Heydrich's position was rendered extremely precarious with the Fritsch scandal, which led to a serious conflict between the army and the Gestapo while revealing the incompetence of Heydrich's men who had been led by the nose by a small-time previously convicted male prostitute, swindler and blackmailer. Hitler's adjutant, General Friedrich Hossbach, a singularly able and forceful officer known as 'the last Prussian', and Admiral Canaris drew up a memorandum calling for Fritsch's exoneration and rehabilitation as well as substantial personnel changes in the upper echelons of the SS, including Himmler, Heydrich and Best. The army leadership had no stomach for such a confrontation, even though there was widespread outrage at the way Fritsch had been treated. Himmler ordered the little crook, Otto Schmidt, to be shot and shuffled a few of the officers concerned with this unfortunate affair, including his top pursuer of homosexuals, SS-Standartenführer Josef Meisinger, who subsequently made a career for himself as a notorious mass murderer in Poland. Admiral Canaris and his chief of staff, Major-General Hans Oster, were determined to assert the supremacy of military intelligence over the amateurs in the SD, and became ever more involved in political intelligence.

In order to strengthen his hand after the humiliation of the Fritsch affair and against the army's pretensions, Himmler decided to combine the SD and the Gestapo in a common security service. In June 1938 he circulated a memorandum calling for the Orpo to be absorbed by the General SS and for the Sipo to amalgamate with the party's SD. For the SD this was a serious setback in that this elite group would become watered down with men who were not in the SS and many of whom came from the rival Gestapo. In 1939 of the 20,000 men in the Gestapo only 3,000 were members of the SS. Heydrich saw this as an excellent opportunity to break the links between the SD and the NSDAP so that the SD could become a state organization, financed by the state rather than as previously by a parsimonious party, but still retain its special unbureaucratic and unconventional organizational structure.

SS-Brigadeführer Walter Schellenberg, an unremittingly ambitious officer from the SD's main office, was given the task of drawing up an organizational chart for the restructured SS and police. He proposed that a

State Protection Corps, made up of the SS and police, should work side by side with a Reich Security Service comprising the SD and the Sipo under a Reich Security Main Office, which in turn would have Reich Security Inspectorates throughout the country under which would be Reich Security Divisions. The SD was not to be absorbed by the Sipo, but was to retain its 'unique character'.

Rudolf Hess and the NSDAP had no intention of allowing the SD to slip out of their hands and therefore vigorously opposed Schellenberg's proposals. Himmler, unsure of Hitler's position, was not prepared to fight it out with the party, so that the end result was an unhappy compromise. The Reich Security Main Office (RSHA) which was instituted on 27 September 1939 was divided into six sections: Section I for organization and law; Section II for ideological investigation; Section III for domestic intelligence; Section IV for tracking down enemies of the state; Section V for criminal investigation and Section VI for foreign intelligence. The SD, which had officers in a number of these sections, was still a separate party organization and would have atrophied had it not been for the energetic efforts of Otto Ohlendorf and his associates. Even so it became largely concerned with foreign intelligence and then with forming the murder squads, the Einsatzgruppen. The departure of the legally-minded Werner Best with his obsession with due procedure removed the last restraint on Heydrich's organization, which now became an instrument of uncontrolled terror and mass murder on an unimaginable scale.

The RSHA and the foreign office

The SS had become actively involved in foreign affairs in 1936 when yet another institution was formed that challenged the monopoly of the foreign office. From 1931 the NSDAP had a foreign organization (AO) under the forceful leadership of the Yorkshire-born Ernst Wilhelm Bohle, a man whom Goebbels described as 'one of our most competent people'. Bohle became so powerful and independent that foreign minister von Neurath felt it prudent to appoint him state secretary in the foreign office in the hope of reining him in. Bohle was also locked in battle with Alfred Rosenberg and his Foreign Political Office as well as with the theoretically independent Association for Germans Abroad (VDA). Hitler was so distressed with these rivalries that he ordered Hess to create an umbrella organization within the party that would be responsible for all matters concerning Germans living abroad. The result was the Ethnic German Coordination Office

(Vomi) under Otto von Kursell, a third-rate artist, professor in the Berlin Academy and 'old warrior', who proved to be singularly ineffective. Hess then handed the problem over to Himmler who chose SS-Obergruppenführer Werner Lorenz to come up with a solution. He was a charming back-room intriguer, an ex-officer, landowner and connoisseur of the good life, who was to become a mass murderer, and father-in-law of the press baron, Axel Springer. His People's Association for the German Race Abroad (VBA), formed in 1937, soon became yet another rival group in the Nazi hornets' nest.

Himmler was closely associated with Ribbentrop as early as 1932. Ribbentrop was given the rank of SS-Standartenführer, and Himmler was a frequent guest at Ribbentrop's luxurious villa in Berlin, purchased with his wife's money. She was the daughter of the owner of Henkell Sekt in Wiesbaden, for whom Ribbentrop had worked as a commercial traveller. Himmler furthered his friend's career by financing his special office for foreign affairs, yet another rival organization to the foreign office, which was soon to employ a number of SS men who, when Ribbentrop was appointed foreign minister, were to enter the foreign office. A number of officials in the foreign office were honorary SS officers, including Erich Kordt, who was also a principled opponent of the regime.

Squabbles over areas of competence were soon to lead to a breach between the two 'du' friends. During the Sudeten crisis a number of foreign office officials, including the German envoy in Prague, Ernst Eisenlohr, were opposed to annexation. Hitler therefore excluded the foreign office and relied on the SS foreign political experts to deal with the Sudeten German leader, Konrad Henlein. Heydrich, who felt that Henlein was not wholeheartedly devoted to the Führer and was pursuing his own personal agenda, wanted to depose him and was thus at cross-purposes with Himmler. Heydrich's suspicions were largely justified, but after the Anschluss Henlein realized that his ambitions were unrealistic. Aware of the intrigues against him, he decided to take the bull by the horns, met Hitler in Breslau and complained bitterly about the SD's intrigues. Hitler promptly ordered the SD to keep its nose out of Sudeten German affairs. The SS smoothed the waters by appointing Henlein to the rank of Gruppenführer.

Undeterred by these problems, Hitler ordered SS-Gruppenführer Wilhelm Keppler, who was also a state secretary without portfolio in the foreign office, to head an SD mission to Slovakia to urge the prime minister, Jozef Tiso, to declare independence. Once again the mission was bungled, the SD had to resort to sabotage, blowing up a chocolate factory in Bratislava

[244] to create a political crisis that resulted in a ham-fisted intervention from the repellent Gauleiter of Vienna, SS-Gruppenführer Josef Bürckel, but it ended to Hitler's satisfaction and he decided to give the SD the honour of firing the first shots in his war.

It began with an absurd and badly bungled mock attack by SD agents dressed as Polish soldiers on a German radio station at Gleiwitz. Command and control was so incompetent that the operation could not be called off in time when Hitler changed his mind at the last moment, and it was launched on 26 August with an attack on a customs house. 'Gestapo' Müller intervened at the last moment, but after an exchange of fire. Undeterred, the plan was launched once again on the evening of 31 August. The entire operation would have been a piece of comic opera, had not a number of concentration camp inmates been murdered to provide some corpses (known in typical SS jargon as 'preserves') to add a touch of verisimilitude.

Ribbentrop further undermined the professional diplomatists in his ministry by permitting the RSHA to appoint police attachés to Germany's diplomatic missions. In addition the heads of SD missions in foreign countries were given diplomatic status. The net result was a reversion to a situation analogous to that of Wilhelmine Germany when the military attachés had direct access to the 'All Highest' and frustrated the efforts of the foreign office. SD officers were every bit as contemptuous of the 'ink pot men' in the diplomatic corps as had been the soldiers, and they frequently complained to Hitler about their pusillanimous behaviour. The SD also undertook hare-brained schemes to assassinate Stalin, depose Franco, involve the Argentine government in an alliance against the USA and bring the fascist Iron Guard to power in Romania.

Ribbentrop was determined to fight back, but in a situation so typical of the Third Reich he had a weak hand. Hitler had issued a ukase on 3 September 1939 placing all civilian and party officials abroad directly under the head of mission, but he also gave his blessing to the SD's special escapades. In October Walter Schellenberg, head of counter-intelligence in the RSHA, was busy feeding false information to two remarkably gullible British agents in Holland, Captain Sigismund Payne Best and Major Richard H. Stevens, who ignored the warnings of their Dutch colleague Dirk Klop. Ribbentrop protested to Hitler about this operation, but was firmly put in his place and meekly submitted. Then on 8 November an attempt was made on the Führer's life in Munich. A bomb was exploded in the Bürgerbräukeller where Hitler was to celebrate the anniversary of the Munich coup of 1923. Hitler left the building early and the bomb killed seven of his supporters.

Hitler was convinced that this was the work of the British Secret Service and ordered that Payne Best and Stevens should be kidnapped, to be put on trial at an appropriate moment. Schellenberg pulled off this gross violation of international law on the following day when Payne Best, Stevens and Klop were dragged across the border at Venlo. He was rewarded with the Iron Cross first class and a dinner in the chancellery, but he knew perfectly well that his victims had nothing whatever to do with the attempt on Hitler's life and he did not hesitate to say so. The RSHA agreed with Schellenberg, for it was perfectly clear that it was all the work of Georg Elser, an apprentice carpenter and watchmaker. Hitler insisted that it was a conspiracy masterminded by the British secret service, but a panic-stricken Himmler was unable to find any accomplices to what was clearly the work of one man. Elser was arrested and placed in solitary confinement in Sachsenhausen and Dachau. He was intended to play a key role in a show trial after the war, but Himmler ordered him to be shot on 9 April 1945. After the war Martin Niemöller and Otto Strasser defamed his memory by claiming that he was an SS man, acting under orders. He was a lonely man of socialist sympathies, who clearly saw that Hitler was intent on plunging Europe into war, and had the courage to act.

Hitler was furious with Himmler for failing to find Elser's co-conspirators and the RSHA thus suffered a severe setback, much to Ribbentrop's satisfaction. The next round between Himmler and Ribbentrop was fought in Romania. General Jon Antonescu was a caudillo of the traditional type who as such was enthusiastically supported by the German foreign office. The RSHA saw the fascist Iron Guard, which initially supported Antonescu, as analogous to the NSDAP and supported their bid for power in January 1941. Antonescu appealed to Ribbentrop for help and was promptly told that Hitler said that he should give Horia Sima and the Iron Guard the same treatment Hitler had given to Röhm and the SA. The SD frustrated Antonescu by smuggling Horia Sima and his closest associates out of the country. Ribbentrop complained bitterly to Hitler that the SD was sabotaging the Reich's foreign policy. Hitler ranted and raved about the 'black plague' that he would 'rub out', thus encouraging Ribbentrop to order Heydrich to respect the agreement of 3 September. He then further frustrated the SS by appointing prominent SA officers as ambassadors to Bratislava, Bucharest, Budapest, Sofia and Zagreb. Ribbentrop's triumph came too late. Foreign policy became increasingly unimportant as the war progressed. Occupation policy was what now mattered, and it was here that Himmler's men were to reign supreme.

[246] The SS and Germany's eastern empire

Himmler first put his thoughts on the future plans for Eastern Europe on paper in a memorandum dated 28 May 1940. The 'racially valuable' elements should be extracted from the 'racial mush' in Poland. The Jews would be 'snuffed out' (*auslöschen*) by being expelled to Africa 'or some colony'. The Polish elite would be wiped out, the remainder given 4 years of schooling, taught to count up to 500, write their names and learn to obey their German masters. They need not be taught how to read. Himmler at last saw the chance to realize his dream of creating a new Germany based on settlements of 'armed peasants' with an austere agrarian economy, the SS version of the Morgenthau Plan, with a colonized Poland as the 'fountain of youth in which German blood can be permanently renewed'. Himmler's friend Walther Darré had failed to realize his atavistic 'blood-and-soil' project because of the exigencies of a modern industrial state whose resources were needed for rearmament. Similarly Himmler's efforts at a 'racial reparcelling' in Bohemia and Moravia were frustrated by the need to integrate Czech industry into Germany's rearmament programme. Poland was a different matter. Although Hitler did not share Himmler's outlandish dystopian vision, he did agree that Poland should be reduced to helot status and that the Polish elite should be liquidated. To this end he ordered the SD to form units of special troops (Einsatztruppen – ET).

Five Einsatzgruppen, each made up of four Einsatzkommandos of 100–150 men, followed behind the army and immediately set to work murdering tens of thousands of the Polish elites. By the end of September 1939 Heydrich boasted that only 3 per cent of the Polish leadership remained alive. In addition to the Einsatztruppen, SS-Brigadeführer Gottlob Berger, one of Himmler's most devoted underlings, widely known as 'General Confusion', was given the task of bringing the Ethnic German Defence Units under the aegis of the SS. They acted mainly as auxiliary police, but in Danzig and West Prussia where they were led by Himmler's adjutant, SS-Oberführer Ludolf von Alvensleben, they indulged in an orgy of bloodshed. Alvensleben, scion of an ancient and distinguished aristocratic family, was a sadistic brute who wrote to Himmler: 'As you can well imagine, Reichsführer, my work gives me enormous pleasure.' Alvensleben's men were ill-disciplined hoodlums whose indiscriminate slaughtering appalled some of the more sensitive 'ethnic Germans' (*Volksdeutsche*) and even Heydrich, who was more concerned about discipline than human life, complained about these 'unruly acts of revenge'.

In mid-September 1939 Himmler ordered SS-Obergruppenführer Udo von Woyrsch, another of Himmler's aristocratic favourites who had tasted blood in the Röhm Putsch, to take over command of Einsatzgruppe V with orders to murder all Jews living in the Kattowitz area and to drive 500,000 Jews out of Danzig, West Prussia, Posen and Upper Silesia into German-occupied Poland, known as the General Government. The army objected to Woyrsch's activities, largely because he was beyond its control, and the struggle over areas of competence between the army and the SS began to escalate. Gauleiter Forster of Danzig was determined to break free from army control, went straight to Hitler and obtained an order placing Danzig and West Prussia under his command. Forster's rival, Deputy Gauleiter Arthur Greiser, was given the province of Posen, renamed 'Wartheland'; Silesia was the province of another rival, Gauleiter Josef Wagner; the remainder of Poland was named the General Government under the command of Hans Frank. The country was thus no longer under military control and the way was open, as Hitler put it to Keitel, for the SS to rid Poland of 'Jews, Polacks and riff-raff'. Law was now in the hands of the RSHA, which appointed the Higher SS and Police Leaders (HSSPF) who filled the power vacuum, with control over all police and SS units and answerable to Himmler alone.

The army commander in the east (*Oberost*) General Johannes Blaskowitz, a pastor's son, was determined to resist Himmler's encroachments and collected evidence of the atrocities committed by the SS in the area under his command. He sent a strongly worded memorandum of outraged complaint to the army's commander-in-chief, Field Marshal Walter von Brauchitsch, a man who was a devoted National Socialist, but who was regarded by most of the leading Nazis as woefully ineffectual, and who was deeply resented in the army because he was the replacement of the much admired Fritsch. He forwarded the paper to Hitler on 18 November. The Führer launched into a tirade against Blaskowitz, denouncing his concerns for due process as 'childish' and pouring scorn on his 'Salvation Army attitude'.

Blaskowitz continued to collect evidence of murder, rape, plunder and the obscenely brutal mistreatment of Jews, and fancifully reported that his soldiers regarded the activities of the SS in Poland with 'disgust and hatred'. Himmler was beginning to consider the need for some damage control when Hans Frank went to see Hitler in February and demanded that the troublemaker Blaskowitz be removed. Hitler complied: Blaskowitz and the bulk of the army in the east moved west in preparation for the invasion of France. Nothing now stood in the way of Himmler, who began an ambitious ethnic resettlement programme in Poland for 120,000

[248]   Germans from the Baltic States, 136,000 from Soviet-occupied Poland and 200,000 from Romania. Thousands more came from Yugoslavia and Slovakia. The 'people without space' had long been shown to be a 'space without people' inasmuch as there was a desperate shortage of workers in both industry and agriculture. Himmler delegated the task of coordinating the massive programme of remigration to a diligent economist, SS-Gruppenführer Ulrich Greifelt, a former opponent of the Nazis and one of numerous 'March fallen', and to SS-Obergruppenführer Werner Lorenz and the Vomi. This latter organization had initially been directly under Hitler's personal command, but Himmler was able to persuade the Führer that the task ahead was so daunting that it had best be left to his SS, whereupon he was given the additional grandiose title of Reich Commissar for the Strengthening of the German Race (RKFDV). His remit was to encourage Germans living abroad to return to the Reich, to combat 'racially alien elements' that endangered the 'racial community', and to create settlements for returning 'racial comrades'.

Jews and Poles were driven out of those areas annexed by the Reich: East Prussia, Danzig-West Prussia, Wartheland and Upper Silesia. Their property was to be seized by the RSHA and allocated to those settlers who had been vetted by the Race and Settlement Office, but things did not run smoothly. Gauleiter Albert Forster in Danzig refused to allow men from the Vomi to requisition large parts of the city to provide accommodation for Baltic Germans. Alfred Rosenberg, himself a Baltic German, complained loudly about the administrative incompetence of the Vomi that left thousands stranded and bitterly angry with the SS. Erich Koch, who earned a well-justified reputation as the most brutal of all the Gauleiter, a pillar of the Evangelical Church who was to be condemned to death for the murder of 400,000 Poles, but who lived on in a Polish prison to the age of 90, chased Himmler's surveyors out of East Prussia. The Main Trustee Office East of Göring's Four-Year Plan seized industrial and urban property in former Poland, while Himmler's office had to make do with agricultural land. Himmler's old associate and now rival, Walther Darré, had switched allegiance to Göring, who secured for him some say over the redistribution of rural property.

Himmler concentrated his efforts on the expulsion of Poles and Jews from the newly incorporated provinces. His Central Migration Office in Łódź was responsible for the expulsion of 1 million Poles to the General Government by 22 June 1941, by which time 200,000 Germans had been settled. Industry was entirely in German hands, but 80 per cent of artisans were still Polish. With his obsession with classification Himmler ordered ethnic Germans to be sorted out into four categories:

1. Proven racial activists.
2. Passive ethnic Germans who have at least a 50 per cent mastery of the language.
3. People of dubious ethnicity.
4. Opponents of the NSDAP who were of German descent.

Poles were similarly classified into those who could be 'Germanized' and those of pure Slavic stock. One hundred thousand Poles were pronounced to be Germans, 1 million were placed in the ethnic German categories 1 and 2, and 2 million in categories 3 and 4.

The expulsion of a million people from the new provinces not only seriously disrupted the economy by robbing industry and agriculture of manpower, but also at the same time created enormous problems in the General Government which was running desperately short of food. Himmler was bombarded with complaints from the Gauleiter and from the army's economics experts, Greifelt's efforts were frequently sabotaged and a frantic battle ensued between Hans Frank and Himmler. Frank wanted to make the General Government into an exemplary colony with a thriving economy, but his efforts were seriously undermined when Himmler's men shipped a million Poles and hundreds of thousands of Jews from the new German provinces to his fiefdom. His problems were compounded when Himmler ordered 30,000 of the 90,000 ethnic German settlers back to the Wartheland. SS units went on the rampage in the General Government hunting down real and imagined partisans, terrifying the peasantry, thus swelling the partisans' ranks. Frank bombarded Hitler with complaints, while Himmler concentrated on toppling the governor.

Frank, whose corruption, craving for splendour and delusions of grandeur were proverbial, nearly came unstuck when the details of his wife's insatiable appetite for furs and jewellery were revealed, along with his own enthusiasm for plundering religious art from Poland's churches. Frank was hauled up in front of a tribunal that included Himmler, Bormann and Lammers. He was forced to make certain concessions to Himmler, but he returned to Cracow unrepentant and determined to get his revenge. As a lawyer and head of the NSDAP's legal office, he toured German universities giving a series of lectures in which he warned against the lawlessness and violence of the SS, the dangers of a police state and the need to uphold the rule of law. 'Brutality', he said in Munich with staggering hypocrisy, 'is not the same as strength . . . I say that one is strong when one does not have to fear the law.' This was all too much for Hitler who dismissed Frank from all party offices and as minister without portfolio, and in August 1942

Frank offered his resignation from the post of general governor. Hitler, who obviously had a certain respect for Frank's courage in speaking his mind and his indubitable abilities, refused to accept his resignation and he stayed in office in his splendiferous palace in Cracow until his career ended on the gallows in Nuremberg.

Himmler had called some of his paladins, chief among them HSSPF SS-Obergruppenführer Erich von dem Bach-Zelewski, to a meeting at Wewelsburg in January 1941 where he unveiled what became known as the 'General Plan East'. Thirty-one million people were to be 'resettled', a euphemism for killed, so as to solve the chronic food shortages that would follow an invasion of the Soviet Union. Fourteen million Slavs would be permitted to remain in the area west of a line from Leningrad to Briansk, but they would have to be 'Germanized' within 30 years. Eighty-five per cent of the 20 million Poles, along with 65 per cent of Ruthenes, would be shipped off to Siberia. Some 2.4 million Germans would be settled in an area thus cleared of the racially undesirable. In subsequent discussions it was agreed that this vast area should be divided up into three districts: 'Ingermanland' to the west of Leningrad, 'Gotengau' in the Crimea, and the Memel-Narev area in which the German settlers would live an austere life in 'armed villages'.

The 'Jewish problem'

The first attempts within the SS to develop an internal policy towards the 'Jewish problem' were entrusted to SS-Untersturmbannführer Leopold von Mildenstein who was put in charge of the 'Jewish Department' II.112 of the RSHA. As a popular travel writer he had written a series of articles in the autumn of 1934 in Goebbels' newspaper *Angriff* entitled 'A Nazi Travels to Palestine'. The series was a great success, sales boosted by a free offer of a medal with a Star of David on one side and a swastika on the other. Mildenstein was full of praise for the young Zionist pioneers and argued that the SD should support the Zionists, help assimilated Jews become 'self-conscious', encourage dissimilation and persuade German Jews to emigrate to Palestine. This accorded well with those SS intellectuals who strongly opposed the brutal hooliganism of the SA and the *Schwarze Korps* proclaimed: 'The time will soon come when Palestine can once again welcome its long lost sons. They shall be accompanied with our best wishes and those of the state.'

The SD actively encouraged Jews wishing to emigrate to Palestine, but they were only partially successful in their efforts. Of the 270,000 Jewish emigrants from Nazi Germany only 50,000 went to Palestine, partly because of the immigration restrictions imposed by the British authorities. The SD found Mildenstein's unconventional approach to the 'Jewish problem' highly suspect and was not impressed by the results. When he was shunted off to the foreign office in 1937, Section II.112 was handed over to SS-Sturmbannführer Herbert Hagen who came to rely on his unquestioningly obedient and untiringly industrious assistant, Adolf Eichmann, who had studied Zionism with his customary pedantic thoroughness, and in 1936 had published an SS internal pamphlet on 'The Zionist World Organisation' in which he pointed out a fundamental contradiction within the SD's support for Zionism. Germany would solve its own 'Jewish problem' by shipping the Jews to Palestine, but there was the danger that Palestine would become a powerful Jewish state that would seek revenge on Germany on behalf of 'world Jewry'. Eichmann, Hagen and Otto Ohlendorf were worried that the British mandate authorities might not be able to stop the formation of a Jewish state in Palestine that might accord citizenship to those Jews remaining in Germany. Henceforth the SD kept a closer watch on the Zionist Association in Germany (ZVfD) and the Zionist organization Hechaluz[4]. Through the intermediary of the representative of a German news agency in Jerusalem, Eichmann made contact with a senior official in the Haganah, Feivel Polkes, whom he invited to Berlin in 1937. Polkes was determined to promote Jewish immigration to Palestine and to this end established contacts with the British, French and German secret services. His main request of the Germans was that currency restrictions on Jewish emigrants should be relaxed.

With Heydrich's blessing, Hagen and Eichmann accepted Polkes' invitation and travelled to Palestine, arriving in Haifa in October 1937 only to find their entry barred. The British had declared a state of emergency because of an Arab nationalist uprising. The meeting therefore had to take place in Cairo. Hagen reported back that 'nationalist Jewish circles' welcomed Nazi Germany's 'radical Jewish policy' in that it was an incentive to emigration to Palestine. Eichmann was more sceptical, but he emerged as the rising star. After the Anschluss Himmler and Heydrich promoted him to the rank of SS-Untersturmbannführer and made him responsible for Jewish emigration with an office in Vienna. His remit was to seize Jewish property and to expel Jews.

Eichmann, ensconced in the charming Rothschild palace in the Prinz-Eugen-Strasse, became intoxicated by his new powers, surrounding himself with a bunch of unspeakable louts who were soon to distinguish themselves as among Nazi Germany's most repulsive butchers. The major problem facing Eichmann was that the majority of Austria's 300,000 Jews were desperately poor and could not come up with the security required by host countries. He set about solving this problem by seizing the assets of wealthy Jews and by demanding contributions from Jewish communities abroad. By late autumn 1938 he could proudly report that within 18 months 150,000 Jews had been expelled from their native country.

This approach to the 'Jewish problem' was altogether too mild and humane for radicals within the Nazi party. Julius Streicher's *Stürmer* called upon the countries of Europe to join together in an all-out war on the 'world enemy number one'. This developed into an escalating confrontation between Streicher and the SD. On the one hand there were those who believed implicitly in the claim made by 'The Protocols of the Elders of Zion' that the Talmud encouraged every imaginable crime against non-Jews; on the other, those who knew the 'Protocols' to be a forgery, that the Talmud contained no such injunctions and who, for the time being at least, were prepared to cooperate with the Zionists. The Polish government gave the radicals ample opportunity to strengthen their hand when on 6 October 1938 it demanded that all Poles should get a special stamp in their passports, which were only available in Poland, by the end of the month. Failure to do so would render the passport invalid. The German government promptly ordered the arrest of 17,000 Polish Jews living in Germany. They were bundled into trains and sent across the border, but the Polish authorities only permitted 2,000 of these unfortunates to enter the country, among them the literary critic Marcel Reich-Ranicki. This was the immediate background to von Rath's murder and the pogrom of 9 November 1938.

The cruelly named 'Night of Broken Glass' was the work of Hitler, Goebbels and the SA. Himmler and Heydrich first heard of it when it was well under way. Himmler was opposed to the pogrom, not for any sympathy for its victims, but because he saw it as an attempt by Goebbels to take over responsibility for the 'Jewish question' and to sabotage the SD's pro-Zionist policy. Heydrich, Otto Ohlendorf and SS-Obergruppenführer Karl Wolff, the SS liaison officer with Hitler, were in full agreement with their superior. Goebbels could count not only on Ribbentrop's support, but also on that of Hitler. That was decisive and Himmler knew he had lost this round. All he managed to do was to persuade Hitler to order Goebbels not to meddle with 'Jewish politics', which was now Göring's province. Göring handed the question over to Heydrich who appointed SS-Standartenführer Heinrich 'Gestapo' Müller to head a Reich Central Office analogous to Eichmann's in Vienna. Some 78,000 Jews emigrated from Germany in 1939, and Eichmann moved on to Prague were he secured the expulsion of 30,000

Jews from Bohemia and Moravia. Heydrich's men continued to work with
Zionists, but the British drastically reduced the number of immigrants
to Palestine after the violence between Arabs, Jews and the mandate
authorities. The Jews responded by strengthening their armed force, the
Haganah, and forming an intelligence service, the Mossad le Aliyah Bet,
whose agents recruited illegal immigrants. The SD negotiated with Mossad
agents behind Ribbentrop's back, for the foreign minister was utterly
opposed to encouraging Jewish emigration to Palestine, as were the
diplomatists in his ministry, the NSDAP and the AO.

This bizarre alliance between the SS and the Zionists designed to frustrate
the British blockade necessarily ended with the outbreak of the war. An
Allied victory was now the only way to save Germany's Jews. Responsibility for the 'Jewish question' now passed out of the hands of the SD,
which had shown a certain degree of restraint, into those of the Gestapo,
which was the unquestioning executive of the Führer's will. Eichmann, who
replaced 'Gestapo' Müller as head of the Central Office, was a perfect
example of this new type of blindly obedient manager, who, when
appointed head of Section B4 (Jewish affairs, eviction) of department IV
(Gestapo) in the RSHA, had no idea that he was about to become a notorious mass murderer, but he was ideally suited for his new role.

Eichmann and his associate, the SD officer responsible for Bohemia
and Moravia, Walter Stahlecker, still believed that emigration was the best
solution to the 'Jewish problem'. Since German Jews could no longer be
shipped to Palestine, they suggested that a 'Jewish reservation' should be
carved out of occupied Poland. The two men travelled to Poland and
decided that the area around Nisko, a small town on the San to the south-
west of Lublin, was an ideal spot. This marked a drastic dehumanization of
emigration policy. Partially voluntary emigration to Palestine in cooperation with the Zionists was now to be replaced by forcible deportation to
an area from which the original inhabitants would be violently expelled.
Austrian Jews were transported to Nisko from October 1939.

Eichmann's 'Jewish reservation' in Nisko was short-lived. Hans Frank
objected vigorously to Göring, arguing that mass immigration to the General
Government was placing an intolerable strain on the economy, and it
was stopped in April 1940. Eichmann now took up the foreign office's
Madagascar project with his customary finicky fervour, but his dreams of
becoming governor of a Jewish colony in Africa were soon dashed and the
RSHA concentrated on preparations for a racist war of annihilation and
colonization in the east. Heydrich called for 'real men' to volunteer as commanders of the Einsatzgruppen, but initially only the ambitious lickspittle

Arthur Nebe, who had put his expertise at the service of the T4 murderers, stepped forward. The moody Otto Ohlendorf, who had twice refused to serve in the east and who had fallen foul of Himmler, gave way with some reluctance. SS-Brigadeführer Dr Otto Rasch eventually saw this as an excellent opportunity for promotion, and Walter Stahlecker, an opponent of Heydrich who had been posted to the foreign office after a brief tour of duty in Norway, saw this as a chance to get back into the RSHA.

Arthur Nebe (Einsatzgruppe B) and Otto Ohlendorf (Einsatzgruppe D) were the only section heads of the RSHA to play a major direct role in the mass murders in the Soviet Union. Franz Six, head of Section VII (ideological enemies of the regime), briefly served as commander of a special force designated to deal with occupied Moscow before returning to his studies of witchcraft and the 'idea of the Reich'. The rest remained in Berlin and left the actual killing to others. The men were recruited from all branches of Himmler's SS and police empire: from the Gestapo, Kripo and SD, the Orpo and the Waffen-SS. They were an odd bunch, ranging from men with two doctorates to ordinary policemen and including Nazified intellectuals, senior civil servants, lawyers, an opera singer and a Protestant pastor along with interpreters, mechanics and cooks. In all there were between 3,500 and 4,000 men. These were no 'desk-top' practitioners[5] of industrialized murder, but intelligent, well-trained professionals driven by ideological fervour. They were killers who occupied places somewhere along the continuum from psychopath to technocrat. Those who had no stomach for this grisly work could leave without dire consequences. Nebe's adjutant, SS-Hauptsturmführer Karl Schulz, resigned in October 1941 and lived to become chief of police in Bremen after the war. Rasch, having ordered the notorious massacre at Babi Yar near Kiev in September 1941, began to crack up, went on leave and never returned to his post. Nebe, although an energetic and enthusiastic mass murderer who seized every opportunity to undertake yet another massacre, was also clearly unable to stand the strain and was posted back to Berlin. Although he eventually joined the 20 July conspirators and was executed for his treasonous activities, he continued to be closely involved with a number of murderous operations in the Soviet Union, even as late as 1944. SS-Brigadeführer Eberhard Herf requested a transfer, saying: 'To be quite honest, I'm utterly fed up with the East.' The request was turned down and Herf was executed in Minsk in 1946. Martin Mundschütz from Einsatzkommando 12 in Ohlendorf's Einsatzgruppe D had a nervous breakdown after participating in a number of mass executions. This resulted in nothing worse than his mates calling him 'an Austrian limp-dick'. He was sent back to Austria with no punishment and

resumed his duties as a policeman in Innsbrück. As Professor Six sardonic-
ally remarked, no one was shot for asking for a transfer.

The Reichsführer was also somewhat squeamish. He witnessed a mass
murder in Minsk in August 1941 and found the experience most upsetting.
He bemoaned the 'unnecessary suffering' of victims and felt that it put an
impossible strain on the troops. HSSPF Erich von dem Bach-Zelewski
pointed out to Himmler, with a note of derision: 'Reichsführer – that was
only a hundred.' Karl Wolff, Himmler's personnel chief and liaison officer
with the Führer, remarked that it served him right and showed him what
he was asking of his men. Wolff's conclusion was that industrialized mass
murder in concentration camps was the most expeditious and humane way
of dealing with the 'chosen race', as well as benefiting IG Farben with which
he had excellent connections. Eichmann was also revolted by the killings
he witnessed. Franz Stangl, the commandant of Treblinka, claimed that he
had to brutalize prisoners in order for his men to do the job without too
many qualms. His wife provided a cosy space for him to relax and escape
from the gruesome truth that he was directly responsible for 400,000
inconceivably pitiless deaths. Thanks to the help of the Vatican he escaped
justice until 1970, to die in prison less than a year later. Claudia Koonz has
pointed out how, in like manner, conventional family life enabled such people
to divorce what they did from what they were. In a world of murderous
hatred women like Frau Stangl could provide the illusion of normality,
affection and even of love, thus becoming accessories to crime on an
unimaginable scale.

These brutal murderers saw themselves as the heroes in a new type
of warfare, overcoming all weakness to serve the higher good. Himmler
solemnly announced in his speech in Posen in 1943: 'Most of you know
what it means when 100, 500 or 1,000 corpses lie side by side. To have
gone through that and, with the exception of a few signs of human weakness, to have remained reputable has made us tough. This is a heroic page
in our history that has not been written and will never be written.' SS-
Standardenführer Paul Blobel, who was the officer in charge of the massacre at Babi Yar, a violent alcoholic who was posted for his total lack of
discipline, proclaimed during his post-war trial: 'I must say that our men
who took part in this suffered far more psychologically than those we had
to shoot.' His last words were: 'Discipline and devotion to duty have brought
me to the gallows.'

A number of Einsatzkommandos had been formed in the summer of 1940
in preparation for the invasion of England, but they were disbanded in
September. There were initially three Einsatzgruppen in preparation for

[256] Barbarossa, one to be attached to each army, each divided up into a number of Einsatzkommandos. A fourth Einsatzgruppe under Otto Ohlendorf was added later to operate in Bessarabia and the Crimea alongside 11th Army and the Romanians. The EKs were trained in the Border Police School in Pretzsch castle, where they were lectured on the manifold evils of Communist functionaries and the baneful influence of Jews on Stalin's Russia. They were instilled with the belief that this was a 'war of worldviews' in which no holds were barred and in which conventional moral considerations had no place.

While the Einsatzkommandos had already set about their grisly work with grim efficiency, Himmler was made responsible for policing the occupied territories in July 1941. He appointed three HSSPFs in the Soviet Union to correspond with the three Army Groups: Hans Adolf Prützmann in Riga for the North, Erich von dem Bach-Zelewski, of whom Himmler said admiringly 'he waded through a sea of blood', adding that he was 'sharper and even more brutal than Heydrich', in Minsk for the Centre, and the chronically alcoholic Friedrich Jeckeln, a highly proficient murderer, but who proved incompetent in dealing with the partisans and had to be replaced, in Kiev for the South. In the summer of 1942 Gerret Korsemann was appointed HSSPF in the Caucasus, soon to be dismissed for cowardice, a disgrace that saved his life. He died in Munich in 1958.

The HSSPFs recruited volunteers (Hiwis) in the Baltic States and the Ukraine, an assortment of sadists, misfits and psychopathic riff-raff who set about seriously challenging the Einsatzkommandos in the mass murder stakes. Jeckeln proudly reported that his Hiwis had killed 44,125 people in August 1941, most of whom were Jews. By the end of 1942 there were 14,953 Germans in the SD and police in the Soviet Union, enthusiastically supported by 238,105 Hiwis.

The army was also deeply implicated in mass murder. Field Marshal Walter von Reichenau told his 6th Army that they were 'the bearers of an inexorable racial idea' and that they must fully understand the 'need for the harsh but justified expiation of Jewish subhumans'. The commanding general of XXX Corps built a concentration camp for hostages. His example was followed by 124 and 266 Infantry Regiments, as well as the 72 Armoured Light Infantry (Panzerjäger). Local army commanders were so persistent in their requests that the Einsatztruppen should 'liquidate' the Jews in the areas under their command, insisting that they were a dangerous source of disease and supporters of the Soviet partisans, that SS-Sturmbannführer Kurt Lindow from the RSHA Department IV A1, responsible for the 'special treatment' of Soviet prisoners of war, complained bitterly that the SD was being treated as if it were the 'Wehrmacht's executioners'. The army for its part was grateful for the work of the Einsatzkommandos dealing with 'partisans', an umbrella term which soon came to include Jews, 'Asiatics', Gypsies and any other group that was felt to be objectionable. The tally for HSSPF Jeckeln's operation against partisans in February and March 1942, code-named 'Malaria', was 389 partisans shot, 1,774 suspects killed and 8,350 Jews liquidated. The wholesale slaughter of Jews was carried out under such imaginative codenames as 'Hornung' (an ancient Germanic term for February), 'Harvest Festival' and 'Chicken Farm'.

The mass murderers in the Einsatzkommandos were not particularly well received by the Nazi overlords in the east, men like the General Commissar for Belarus, Wilhelm Kube. He was an 'old warrior' and his anti-Semitic credentials were impeccable. He had written an article in which he claimed that: 'Plague, consumption and syphilis are for human beings what the Jews are to the white race . . . Whoever sullies his race, and thereby our people, by miscegenation must be rendered infertile . . . Those who carry the plague must be exterminated.' Kube's brutality in Belarus was such that he was killed by a partisan in Minsk in September 1943. But in the meantime there was a shortage of labour and he needed Jews to make up the shortfall. Kube also objected to murdering German Jews who had served with distinction in the war, and condemned the practice of burying Jews alive as an 'unqualified *Schweinerei*'. Heydrich was unimpressed and replied that Kube must have better things to do than worry about 'Jewish bellyaching'. SS-Obersturmbannführer Dr Eduard Strauch, a sadistic alcoholic who admitted that his men 'get really turned on' by executions, who was Sipo and SD commander in Minsk, was outraged by Kube's lily-livered approach to the Jewish problem, and argued that the only explanation for his behaviour was that he was almost certainly himself a Jew.

Kube and Strauch fought it out. Strauch appealed to Himmler who referred the matter to Rosenberg as the minister responsible for such matters. Kube allied with Reich Commissar Hinrich Lohse, who also detested Himmler. Both men objected to the mass murder of 'partisans', not for any sympathy for the innocent Jewish victims, but largely because thousands of guiltless peasants who were badly needed to work the land were indiscriminately slaughtered. There ensued a struggle so typical of Nazi Germany between these powerful satraps that was only ended when a partisan dressed as a chambermaid placed a bomb under Kube's bed.

[258] Industrialized mass murder

Mobile gas chambers, first used to murder psychiatric patients, were sent to Chelmno, near Łódź, at the request of Arthur Greiser, governor of the Wartheland, which he intended to turn into a model province free of Jews and with the churches put firmly in their place. This grisly work began in December 1941, but the method was not at all efficient. The victims were supposed to die within 15 minutes, but it sometimes took hours and they were often buried alive. Eichmann was sent to see what was going on and was absolutely appalled by what he saw. Unable to stand the sight he returned to Berlin and reported to 'Gestapo' Müller that an alternative method had to be found. Even Goebbels thought that this method was 'somewhat barbarous', while heartily approving of the proposal that 60 per cent of the Jews should be killed, the remaining 40 per cent put to work.

Himmler turned to Dr Ernst Grawitz, the SS Reich Doctor and president of the German Red Cross, for advice on how to kill some 2.5 million Polish Jews quickly and efficiently in Action Reinhard, appropriately named after Heydrich. The good doctor recommended Police Commissioner Christian Wirth, a cold-blooded expert on the use of poison gas, who had gained considerable experience with T4. Wirth set to work with HSSPF Odilo Globocnik in Lublin, the man whom Himmler put in charge of Operation Reinhard, about which he said: 'If the following generation turns out to be so cowardly and feeble as not to be able to understand our noble and necessary work, then National Socialism will have been all in vain.'

Wirth thought that mobile gas chambers were worthless and instead built permanent structures, disguised as 'inhalation and bath rooms'. The first of his death camps was built in Belzec in March 1942, on the railway line from Lublin to Lvov, with the capacity of murdering up to 15,000 victims per day. A second camp was built in Sobibor on the Ukrainian border with a death capacity of 20,000 each day. A third was built at Treblinka, 120 kilometres north-east of Warsaw with 13 gas chambers able to kill 25,000 people every day. Gas chambers were also built in the concentration camp in Lublin, known later as Majdanek, in the autumn of 1942.

Wirth's rival in this unspeakable venture was SS-Hauptsturmbannführer Karl Fritzsch, a diminutive creature affectionately known as 'Speck', the commander of the 'protective custody camp' in Auschwitz in Upper Silesia. Whereas Wirth used the exhaust fumes from diesel motors, Fritzsch experimented with Zyklon B, an extremely powerful insecticide. The rival methods were put to the test. SS-Obersturmbannführer Kurt Gerstein, a devout Christian and expert on prussic acid, the principal ingredient of Zyklon B, travelled to Belzec with Eichmann's deputy, Rolf Günther, to report on [259] their relative merits. Wirth suffered an appalling embarrassment. The diesel motor refused to start, the terrified victims waited in the gas chamber for 2 hours and 49 minutes, according to Gerstein's stopwatch, until it was repaired, and 32 minutes passed before they were all dead. Fritsch was delighted at his rival's humiliation and Rudolf Höss, commander of the concentration camp at Auschwitz who also found the firing squad method somewhat unseemly, ordered Zyklon B to be used.

Mass murder could now go ahead on a hitherto unimaginable scale, disguised as 'resettlement', but Heydrich was worried that some feeble creatures would try to save those Jews that were needed for work, and would not bother to look for alternative sources of manpower. Once again a battle raged between the army's armaments experts who wanted to keep Jewish workers alive, and Himmler who was determined that there should be no exceptions. Himmler got the better of the weak-willed Keitel, the head of OKW, who ordered that the Jews should be replaced by Aryans and sent to the death camps, in spite of the protests of General Baron Curt von Gienanth, the army commander in Warsaw, who insisted that the Jewish workers were irreplaceable. The fate of the Polish Jews was now sealed. For all the talk of the clean and even 'humane' new method of mass murder, acts of unimaginable cruelty and savagery were committed by a minority of sadistic brutes in the SS and the Hiwis. Even Höss, shortly before he mounted the gallows, felt that the 'Final Solution' had been wantonly cruel, and came to the astonishing conclusion that it had done 'a disservice to the cause of anti-Semitism'.

The pedantic and prim Himmler insisted that his SS men should be men of honour with unsullied reputations. Eight hundred cases of murder and corruption were investigated, 200 went to trial. Karl Koch, the commandant of Buchenwald, Hermann Florstedt, commandant of Lublin, Hermann Hackmann, commander of the protective custody camp at Lublin, and Hans Loritz, commandant of Oranienburg, just to name the more prominent, were executed for murder. By April 1944 Himmler realized that these trials were startling evidence that the SS had fallen woefully short of its lofty ideals and was rapidly falling into ill repute and even ridicule. There was also something bizarre about condemning the murderers of Jews to death for murdering Jews. Corruption was so widespread in the Third Reich that precious few would have emerged unscathed from a serious investigation. The Reichsführer now ordered those who were guilty of misdemeanours to step forward. Their pardon would be automatic, their honour restored. These were astonishing acts of denial, a cruel, hideous and obscene tribute paid

[260] by vicious hypocrites to universal and immutable standards of morality. Mass murderers imagined that they could remain decent and honourable as long as they resisted the temptation to use babies as clay pigeons, or take them by the legs and smash their heads against a wall, and return to their loving wives and relax after a hard day's work by playing a Beethoven sonata.

The SS industrial empire

Once again the murder machine was slowed down because of the need for labour. This time the initiative came not from the army but from within the SS. In February 1942 the administration of the concentration camps was effectively handed over to the Main Administrative Office for Business and Commerce (WVHA), at the head of which was the despotic and finicky SS-Obergruppenführer Oswald Pohl, a man without experience in either commerce or industry, who had worked his ruthless way upwards through the German Red Cross. Pohl's experts saw the inmates of the concentration camps as a valuable source of labour, which could be worked to death and instantly replaced by the new arrivals. The mass murder of political and racial undesirables could now continue alongside large-scale industrial enterprises such as the German Oil and Quarrying Company, in small workshops and in agriculture. Some 600,000 undernourished slaves worked 11 hours per day in appalling conditions, the whole operation under the command of the egregious Albert Speer as minister of munitions. Others were employed in the SS Eastern Industrial Company (Osti), part of Pohl's vast empire that included a brush factory in Lublin, a furriery in Trawniki and an armaments factory in Radom. The enthusiasts for the 'Final Solution' were violently opposed to the idea of keeping all this 'racial bacteria' alive. As one HSSPF put it: 'Eastern industry! The very word "industry" makes me want to puke!' The WVHA was now on a collision course with the RSHA, and the first round went to the exterminators. Osti's Jews were ordered to the death camps. SS-Hauptsturmführer Max Horn, Pohl's chief accountant and head of Osti, a man who announced that he would turn the Łódź ghetto into a concentration camp, complained bitterly that deprived of Jewish labour his enterprises were unable to function. Pohl had the support of most of the HSSPFs and was determined to fight back, while Eichmann pursued his murderous designs with a pathological zeal that makes a mockery of Hannah Arendt's shop-worn concept[7] of the 'banality of evil'. The SS was not made up of dull and conscientious paper-pushers and blindly obedient soldiers, and given the degree of conceptual laxity in National

Socialism there was a wide margin of choice that left room for selective [261] compliance.

Pohl was in command of a vast organization responsible for the administration and provision of the Waffen-SS, for the 20 concentration camps and 165 work camps and for the manifold SS industrial and commercial enterprises. The German Oil and Quarrying Company had a turnover of 14,822,000 RM in 1943, the German Armaments Company, which ran all the enterprises in the concentration camps, 23,204,032 RM. There were a number of other enterprises run by the SS, including the German Experimental Institute for Nutrition and Catering, which was devoted to Himmler's hobbyhorses of vegetarianism and herbal remedies, a furniture factory in former Czechoslovakia, a sawmill in Linz, cement works and a porcelain factory in Poland. By 1944 Pohl's organization controlled 75 per cent of Germany's mineral water production. An attempt to take over the British-owned Apollinaris company failed owing to the resistance of the department of industry and commerce, whose insistence on due procedure frustrated Himmler's predatory designs.

The WVHA had two main subdivisions. Section W (commerce and industry) was the province of Dr Hans Hohberg, an accountant with no political ambitions. Section C (SS and police buildings) was under SS-Obergruppenführer Dr Hans Kammler, a ferociously ambitious engineer who was responsible for building the gas chambers at Auschwitz. In August 1943 he was put in charge of a special staff under Albert Speer to supervise the production of fighter aircraft and the V weapons. He took special pride in personally designing the launching ramps for the V1. A slave army laboured away in frightful conditions in underground factories building the much-vaunted 'retaliatory weapons' which were given top priority and Himmler's enthusiastic endorsement.

The SS thus had a vast commercial and industrial empire, but it was one that had to be constantly defended against the claims of the military, from Albert Speer's armaments ministry, as well as the ministries of economics and finance. Many a round was lost, and the SS was never able to achieve its aim of turning Nazi Germany into an SS state. It faced a number of powerful rivals. The army was happy to let the SS do its dirty work, and frequently acted as partners in unspeakable crimes, but it zealously fought to preserve its autonomy and vigorously resisted any attempt to encroach on its authority. The SA under Viktor Lutze looked for opportunities to get its revenge on the SS. The ten powerful commissars in the east were united in their antipathy towards Himmler's men. Hinrich Lohse in Ostland loathed the SS, which he compared to the Soviet GPU, and frequently crossed swords

[262] with them. Erich Koch in the Ukraine, the most brutal and corrupt of the lot, wanted to get rid of them when their criticisms threatened to cramp his style. Koch had a powerful ally in Martin Bormann, who had ready access to Hitler, so that Himmler was eventually constrained to order the SD to stop reporting on Koch's myriad misdemeanours.

NSDAP versus SS

As the war turned rapidly against Germany the Nazi Party became increasingly powerful, largely due to Martin Bormann, Hitler's Cerberus, who made sure that the SS leadership had only limited access to the Führer. The SS had a distinct distaste for the crude 'old warriors' in the upper echelons of the party, not to mention the place-seekers and scrimshankers in the lower ranks. Himmler was given to saying that order would be restored to Germany only when the last of the Gauleiter was hanged from a lamppost. The SS newspaper *Schwarzes Korps* delighted in mocking the NSDAP and the Gauleiter, but one word of complaint from Bormann and Himmler panicked, for he knew with what authority he spoke. Himmler was greatly indebted to Bormann over a delicate private matter. He had an affair with his secretary Hedwig 'Bunny' Potthast and Helge, their first child, was born in 1942. Himmler was far too conventional and cowardly to divorce his wife, whom he had married in gratitude for her having robbed him of his virginity at a relatively advanced age. He decided to set up a separate establishment for 'Bunny' and their child, but the incorruptible Himmler was virtually alone among the leadership in having virtually no money. Bormann provided him with 80,000 RM from party funds with which he bought a house in Bavaria. 'Bunny' was now the neighbour of Bormann's wife Gerda and they soon became friends. Himmler was soon reduced to playing second fiddle to Bormann, bitterly resentful that he no longer had unlimited access to Hitler, and began to complain that the Führer did not treat him with due respect and consideration.

Even without Otto Ohlendorf, who was off in the Crimea murdering 90,000 innocents, the SD's 'Reports from the Reich' continued to savage the party leadership. There were screams of protest from the Gauleiter, the Reich Commissars and from Bormann who complained about the 'Cheka methods' of the SD who were poking their noses into the internal affairs of the party. Goebbels, of whose increasingly jejune propaganda efforts the SD reports were sharply critical, condemned their reports as 'defeatist'. The circle of those who were given the reports to read steadily diminished and

Bormann forbade party members to cooperate with the SD. Bormann was clearly winning a war of attrition when another war came to an end.

The SS was also riven with internal divisions and rivalries, between the various branches of this vast organization, between departments within each branch and between factions within the departments. The authority of the HSSPFs was constantly challenged by those nominally under their control. Some of these rivalries bordered on the comic, as when SS-Gruppenführer Gottlob Berger complained of an HSSPF: 'The Hereditary Prince zu Waldeck doesn't like me. I can't think why.' Others were a great deal more serious. Himmler was fundamentally a weak yes-man who had no stomach for a fight with his fellow paladins, contenting himself with writing letters to his subordinates calling them to order at the slightest sign of excessive drunkenness or megalomania, warning them to follow the Führer strictly, and not to allow themselves to be bossed around by their young wives. In 1943 Himmler appointed a brilliant statistician, Dr Richard Korherr, to examine administrative shortcomings within the SS. He met with fierce opposition from all quarters and earned ferocious slaps across the face from SS-Obergruppenführer Hildebrandt, head of the RuSHA, who denounced the unfortunate man as a blackguard and threw him out of his office. Korherr complained to Himmler, but got no support. He gave up this fruitless task and returned to statistical analysis in a special SS institute in Regensburg.

The Waffen-SS

When Hitler became chancellor Sepp Dietrich's bodyguards were moved to Berlin and given the title SS Staff Guards. Some additional men were added a few months later and they were renamed the Berlin Guard Battalion. Since Sepp Dietrich was profoundly ignorant of military affairs their training was entrusted to 9 Infantry Regiment, stationed in Potsdam. Their commander's incompetence was a matter of no concern to Hitler, because he enjoyed Sepp Dietrich's garrulous company and his men, renamed Personal Standard (*Leibstandarte*) Adolf Hitler (LAH) at the 1933 Nuremberg rally, were intended to be asphalt soldiers, entrusted with purely ceremonial functions.

Two companies of the Leibstandarte were sent to Bad Wiessee and carried out the executions of prominent SA men at the Stadelheim jail in Munich on 30 June 1934. Others were executed in the LAH's barracks in the former cadet school at Berlin Lichterfelde. Himmler was rewarded for this sterling service by being permitted to form three SS battalions, called

[264] SS Auxiliary Troops (*SS-Verfügungstruppe* – SS-VT), their arms to be taken from the SA. The Wehrmacht was highly alarmed, seeing this as a direct threat to its unique position, and Hitler thought it prudent not to allow the new formation the artillery, engineers and other units needed to form a self-sufficient division.

Himmler knew that he could not entrust the SS-VT to an inept, swash-buckling other-ranker like Sepp Dietrich and persuaded Paul Hausser, a suave, sardonic, recently retired general with a distinguished war record to take over command in 1934. Hausser set about training the SS-VT using the Reichswehr as a model. In his eyes they were first and foremost to be military professionals, masters of a time-honoured trade, rather than some new-fangled National Socialist force. New battalions were soon formed: the 1st SS Regiment (Deutschland) in Munich, the 2nd SS Regiment (Germania) in Hamburg, and the Leibstandarte in Berlin was expanded to become a motorized infantry regiment. In October 1936 Hausser was promoted to the rank of SS-Brigadeführer with the impressive title of Inspector of the Auxiliary Troops.

It is hardly surprising in an organization such as the SS that Hausser's position was challenged from all sides. Sepp Dietrich as a rough and ready Bavarian did not intend to allow himself to be bossed around by a haughty Prussian like Hausser. Local SS potentates were determined to resist any encroachments on their powers of command. Ideological fanatics pointed to Hausser's singular lack of zeal for the National Socialist cause. There was constant friction with the regular army, which dismissed the SS-VT as 'Pleasure Troops' (*Vergnügungstruppe*). It was not until 1938 that Dietrich allowed Hausser to begin giving his LAH rudimentary military training. An even more serious problem for Hausser was that a number of young officers were determined to ensure that the SS-VT was not merely a carbon copy of the Reichswehr with different cap badges. For them it was to be a revolu-tionary National Socialist army in sharp contrast to the stuffy, snobbish and conservative Reichswehr.

At the head of these young Turks was Felix Steiner, who had commanded a machine-gun section as a young lieutenant on the Western Front, and who believed that small detachments of storm troopers were the key to success in a future war. As commander of the Deutschland regiment Steiner was soon in conflict with the traditionalist Hausser. He had little time for LAH's obsession with parade-ground drill and concentrated on exercises in the field and physical fitness. Unlike the Reichswehr his men were given camouflaged uniforms and were armed with light machine-guns rather than carbines, and entire regiments were organised as storm troops. He was

determined to break down the strict divisions between officers, NCOs and
men, stressing comradeship and mutual respect. The officer cadet school of
the SS-VT only accepted men who had served in the ranks for two years
and unlike the Reichswehr paid little attention to scholarly achievement.
By 1938 only 40 per cent of officer cadets had passed the school-leaving
certificate (*Arbitur*).

Before long Steiner became the *de facto* head of the SS-VT and Himmler's
favourite, even though he resolutely refused to marry and would not leave
the church as was required of all senior SS officials. His main problem was
that neither officers nor men were of sufficient quality to put his innova-
tions into effective practice. The SS-VT was infused with National Socialist
ideology, saw itself as an elite, was fired with enthusiasm and *esprit de corps*,
but as a potential fighting force it was clearly inferior to the Reichswehr.

As part of the reorganization of the armed forces after the Fritsch-
Blomberg affair Hitler decreed that the SS-VT be a standing army, separate
from the Reichswehr and the police, a party organization under his direct
command. This move was welcomed neither by Hausser nor by Steiner.
They were military professionals who did not want to be seen as members
of a party army. For all their disagreements they were much closer in spirit
to the Reichswehr than to the ideologues in the NSDAP. While they adopted
Reichswehr uniforms and tried unsuccessfully to have ranks analogous to
those in the regular army, Himmler forced officers to serve terms in other
SS units so as to be infused with the same SS spirit as the concentration
camp guards, the SD, the killer squads and racial researchers. Young men
in the SS-VT were infused with National Socialist ideology thanks to the
Hitler Youth and to the political instruction that went along with military
training. They were impatient with the Haussers and Steiners who had
little patience with such rubbish, and it was the old guard that was soon to
have the upper hand.

In August 1939 Hitler placed the SS-VT under the OKH. Deutschland,
Germania and the Leibstandarte fought in the Polish campaign, but they
did not fight well. Pluck, dash and derring-do proved to be no substitute
for skill and good staff work. The resulting casualties were unacceptably
high. A partial answer was that the SS-VT would have to be expanded and
formed into divisions so as to have their own artillery support. The man
responsible for recruitment was Gottlob Berger, a garrulous, slippery and
self-important Swabian version of a Nazified Uriah Heep, who was in charge
of the development office in the SS Main Office. He first managed to wrest
the Totenkopfverbände (TV) from military control and then used a decree
that permitted the SS-VT to be topped up by men from the TV. Fifty

thousand men from the General SS were to be transferred to the TV and thence to the SS-VT. By such means Berger hoped to form three or four SS-VT divisions. Hitler gave the go-ahead and the new SS army was renamed the Waffen-SS.

The Deutschland, Germania and Der Führer regiments were combined into a division soon to be called Das Reich. The loathsome Theodor Eicke, whose hatred of the officers of both Reichswehr and Waffen-SS bordered on the pathological, combined the excess units of his Totenkopf thugs with policemen from the Orpo to form the Waffen-SS Division Totenkopf. The Leibstandarte remained a separate regiment, but was to become a division in 1942. Berger thus expanded the 18,000-man SS-VT into a 100,000-man Waffen-SS.

The Waffen-SS fought with the same fanaticism, irresponsible disregard for superior orders and for human life in the campaign in the west in 1940. SS-Obersturmführer Kraas from the Wehrmacht was appalled at the irresponsible and rash approach to warfare of the Waffen-SS. General Hoepner, a ferociously anti-Semitic crusader against Bolshevism, but also a soldier of the old school, who was dismissed from the army in January 1942 for insubordination and who was executed in 1944 for his part in the 20 July plot to assassinate Hitler, condemned Eicke for having the 'mentality of a butcher'.

Eicke also had his opponents within the Waffen-SS who saw this primitive amateur as a threat to their image as an elite. His Totenkopf division was guilty of a number of atrocities in the campaign in France, including the murder of 100 British prisoners of war, and had illegally requisitioned transport and weapons. He had also made himself somewhat absurd by publishing the names of senior officers in his division who had contracted venereal diseases, and Himmler thought it necessary to issue him with a reprimand. Eicke was unbowed and complained that the campaign against him was 'Marxist' and an insult to the 23 officers and 370 NCOs and men who had died under his command. He died unmourned in a plane crash in the Soviet Union in February 1943.

Hitler, who until the winter of 1941 reckoned with a short war, did not want to antagonize the Wehrmacht and therefore did not agree to any further increases in the Waffen-SS, seeing it more as an armed police force than as soldiers. Berger, who had become head of the SS Main Office in 1940, and as such was responsible for recruitment, enlargement and the ideological training of the Waffen-SS, was not going to accept these restrictions meekly. He cooked up an astonishing plan to recruit 1.5 million 'ethnic Germans' (Volksdeutsche) living abroad into the Waffen-SS, securing Himmler's approval in August 1940. Ethnic Germans who were [267] unwilling to volunteer for service in the Waffen-SS were persuaded to do so by bands of local Nazi thugs under the command of an 'ethnic leader' (*Volkstumsführer*). Towards of the end of the war, service in the army or Waffen-SS was made compulsory. By 1945 some 310,000 'ethnic Germans' had served in the Waffen-SS, many of them in the Florian Geyer division.

Having recruited the 'ethnic Germans' Berger began to look elsewhere for promising material. His recruiters found 125,000 volunteers in Western Europe who were given ideological and military training at Sennheim in Alsace. In early 1941 the Waffen-SS Viking division was formed with young men from Belgium, Denmark, France and Holland. The senior officers were German. Some 200,000 recruits came from the Baltic States, Ukraine and Russia along with Muslims from the Balkans. Himmler's elite Germanic army had become a pan-European force that even included Slav subhumans and devotees of an alien religion. Eicke's Totenkopfverbände was integrated with the Waffen-SS in April 1941. Units of the Waffen-SS were seconded to the Einsatzgruppen. Hans Bothmann's killers who operated the gas chambers at Chelmno joined the Waffen-SS as did their colleagues in Auschwitz and Sachsenhausen. A special unit of the Waffen-SS was responsible for crushing the uprising in the Warsaw ghetto. The Waffen-SS also sponsored a band of habitual criminals and poachers, commanded by a convicted paedophile, Dr Oskar Dirlewanger, which committed such shocking atrocities in the Soviet Union in the pursuit of partisans that even an SS court was called upon to investigate. From 1941 there was a Waffen-SS within the Waffen-SS. One was fully integrated with the Wehrmacht, the other was directly under Himmler's command, with SS-Obergruppenführer Kurt Knoblauch as chief of staff, which hounded down Jews and partisans.

The Waffen-SS was guilty of a number of appalling crimes. The Viking division murdered 600 Jews in Galicia in July 1941, ostensibly in retaliation for Soviet atrocities. In the summer of 1943 units of the Prince Eugen division murdered all the inhabitants of the Serbian village of Kosutica when it was reported that there was a sniper in the church tower. Men from Das Reich laid waste to the village of Oradour-sur-Glane in June 1944 when the Maquis captured a Waffen-SS officer. In August men in the Hitler Jugend division under the command of the 34-year-old SS-Brigadeführer and Waffen-SS General Kurt Meyer, known as 'Panzermeyer', murdered 64 British and Canadian prisoners of war. The Wehrmacht was guilty of similar crimes, but they were better concealed.

The Waffen-SS sustained extremely high casualties, partly because of unimaginative leadership and partly because the Wehrmacht frequently allotted them particularly dangerous tasks. The first generation of young fanatics and idealists bled to death on the battlefields in the Soviet Union, to be replaced by frightened conscripts who had no desire to seek a hero's death for Führer and fatherland. Press-gangs combed the schools and RAD camps, forcing all those over 1.65 m to 'volunteer' for the Waffen-SS. Sixteen-year-olds were sent to the front with inadequate training, where they came under the command of inexperienced officers and NCOs, resulting in even higher casualty rates. Even the leaders of the Waffen-SS, the Dietrichs, Haussers and Steiners, were beginning to doubt that victory was possible and their faith in Adolf Hitler began to weaken. Hausser ordered his II SS-Panzer Corps to break out of the encirclement at Kharkov in February 1943 in defiance of Hitler's order to stand and fight. The Leibstandarte and Viking divisions ignored orders from their superiors in the Wehrmacht. Himmler was often at loggerheads with senior officers who saw themselves first and foremost as soldiers and who had little time for ideological niceties. He required them to be the 'fanatical and dedicated executants of the National Socialist worldview and the ideas of our Führer Adolf Hitler'. This fell on deaf ears. Some divisions did not even bother to give the troops ideological instruction. As one informant told the SS Main Office in October 1943: 'It makes me want to puke. All this talk about the "SS spirit" is a pile of shit. It's nowhere to be seen.' Steiner's artillery commander, SS-Standartenführer Herbert Gille, yelled at the divisional ideological officer with the unfortunate name of SS-Obersturmbannführer Ernst Fick: 'The wearing of a brown shirt is frowned upon in the aristocratic 5th Artillery Regiment. I shall send a de-bagging squad to your room.' Steiner himself greeted his men in the Viking division with 'Heil!' rather than 'Heil Hitler!', was critical of the treatment of Russians as 'subhumans' and referred to Himmler as a 'slovenly romantic'.

After the failed attempt on his life on 20 July 1944 Hitler declared war on the traditional officer corps of the Wehrmacht. Goebbels wrote in his diary that it was a pity that Röhm was a homosexual and an anarchist, since it would have been much better to have shot a few hundred generals on 30 July 1934 and to have established a National Socialist army. Hitler ordered Himmler, who had been appointed commander-in-chief of the reserve army, to form 15 new divisions and Himmler was determined that these should form the core of an ideologically schooled National Socialist People's Army. The new units of this 'revolutionary army' were to be given such racially correct designations as Volks-Grenadier-Divisionen and Volksartilleriekorps, but it was far too late for such an ambitious scheme. At the same time the SD investigated the Wehrmacht, looking for defeatists and doubting Thomases, while special SS units strung up [269] deserters. Half a million new recruits were found and sent to the front after a brief training. Their contribution to the defence of the Reich was minimal.

Heinrich Himmler's decline and fall

On paper Himmler was the most powerful man in the Reich after Adolf Hitler. He commanded the SS, the police and the Secret Service. He controlled an extensive economic empire covering a range of activities from armaments to mineral water. He was in charge of racial policy and was responsible for the coordination of the National Socialist movement in the so-called Germanic countries. He was minister of the interior and commanded the reserve army. In reality his power was dwindling in spite of these impressive titles, as he was gradually pushed aside by Bormann, the man at Hitler's side. In the final stages of the war the defence of the Reich was gradually being taken over by the party, of which Bormann was the administrative head. The first step in this direction was taken by the megalomanic Erich Koch. The Red Army had obliged him to end his reign of terror in the Ukraine and he returned to East Prussia where with customary brutality he forced children, the aged, the halt and the lame into a People's Militia (*Volkssturm*), armed them with a primitive anti-tank weapon (*Panzerfaust*) and ordered them to dig in and fight to the death. Koch overrode the army commander General Reinhardt, as well as the local SS. Bormann and Hitler were impressed and ordered the Gauleiter to follow Koch's example and form units of the Volkssturm. On 18 October, the anniversary of the Battle of the Nations at Leipzig in 1813 in which Napoleon was defeated, Hitler formally inaugurated the Volkssturm. Himmler was formally entrusted with its organization, training and equipment, but Bormann had overall political control.

Bormann used his influence to ensure that his ally Goebbels was appointed Plenipotentiary for Total War in July 1944. This meant that Goebbels controlled all aspects of domestic affairs, Bormann the party and Himmler was left only with the SS and the reserve army. In December Goebbels was made responsible for manpower in the armed forces, thus further diminishing the Reichsführer's authority. Bormann further clipped Himmler's wings by securing his appointment to command the remnants of 19th Army between Karlsruhe and the Swiss frontier, which was given the imposing title of Army Group Upper Rhine.

Whilst Himmler was busy playing soldiers in his headquarters in the Black Forest, some of the more important rats were abandoning ship and joining the Bormann faction. These included Dr Ernst Kaltenbrunner, a cruel second-rater with a heavy dose of Austrian charm whom Himmler had appointed head of the RSHA so as not to have another Heydrich, and SS-Gruppenführer Hermann Fegelein, 'Hitler's brother-in-law' and SS liaison officer. Thanks to Bormann, Kaltenbrunner was a frequent guest at Hitler's headquarters and took orders directly from the Führer, thus bypassing the Reichsführer. Berger and d'Alquen urged Himmler to return to Berlin and fight back against the Bormann clique, but he was so entranced by his soldierly role that he paid no heed. He proved to be a disaster as a military commander, just as Bormann and the Wehrmacht had hoped. His attempt to regain Strasburg was a failure, and his troops were forced back across the Rhine. Having failed in the west, Hitler against the vigorous protests of the chief of the general staff, Colonel-General Heinz Guderian, gave him command of Army Group Vistula to the north of the massive Soviet salient from Königsberg to Frankfurt-an-der-Oder to Cracow. Himmler was unable to master the situation and retreated to an SS hospital run by an old friend, Karl Gebhardt. Guderian managed to replace him by General Gotthard Heinrici, commander of 1st Panzer Army. Himmler's military career thus came to an inglorious end.

On 21 April 1945, the day after his 56th birthday, Hitler ordered Steiner to mount an offensive against the Soviet flank. With only 10,000 men against 100,000 he knew this was suicidal and refused to move. Hitler collapsed when he heard of Steiner's disobedience. Keitel as head of OKW, Jodl his chief of staff, Krebs acting as the army's chief of staff and Heinrici all tried to persuade Steiner to attack, knowing full well that although it would not save Germany from defeat it might save their demented Führer from further humiliation. He was even offered promotion to field marshal, but he obdurately refused to the bitter end. Hitler knew that the war was lost and ordered his young bride to leave Berlin. She refused.

On 28 April Hitler was told that Himmler was negotiating with the western Allies. Hitler took some time to recover from the news, then ordered the newly-appointed Luftwaffe Field Marshal Baron von Greim to arrest the Reichsführer. Hermann Fegelein, Hitler's brother-in-law, was charged with desertion in that he had left the bunker without permission, was wearing civilian clothes and was party to Himmler's efforts to end the war. He was shot in the courtyard of the chancellery. That the man whom Hitler had called 'my Ignatius Loyola' had deserted him was the final straw. Two days later Hitler committed suicide.

Himmler continued to live in a fantasy world, planned a new government and a new party, but no place was found for him in Admiral Dönitz's
government. He was arrested on 23 May by the British Military Police,
was quickly identified and managed to avoid the hangman's noose only by
biting on a cyanide capsule. A number of his cohorts followed his example,
among them Odilo Globocnik, the Reich medical officer Ernst Grawitz,
who oversaw the inhuman medical experiments in the concentration camps,
and the Reich health leader, Dr Leonardo Conti, another murderous physician. Others such as Höss, Kaltenbrunner, Ohlendorf and Seyss-Inquart were
executed by the Allies. Some like Eichmann vanished, to be tracked down,
brought to trial and executed, while others vanished altogether. The vast
majority were given mild jail sentences and lived comfortably in the
Federal Republic of Germany. Reassuring themselves that they had simply
done their duty, their consciences were untroubled.

CHAPTER 8

FOREIGN POLICY

When the major war criminals stood for trial at Nuremberg they were charged with the 'formulation or execution of a common plan or conspiracy to commit, or which involved the commission of, crimes against humanity'. The 'common plan' was for an aggressive war on the continent of Europe and a bid for world domination. The various crimes against humanity, of which the mass murder of the European Jews was the most flagrant, were deemed to be consequences of this war of conquest. The prosecution thus focused its attention on the estimated 45 million victims of Hitler's war, rather than the 6 million Jews who were murdered in the Shoah.

This seems somewhat surprising today when the Shoah is seen as the distinctive horror of National Socialism, the unimaginable crime at the very heart of the system in which its true nature was revealed. In fact it was not until the 1970s that the rather unfortunate term 'Holocaust' was widely used until it became the central theme of the historical examination of the Third Reich. Earlier studies concentrated on the origins of the war and emphasized Hitler's plans and intentions to the point that a whole group of historians were later to be labelled 'intentionalists'. They argued that Hitler was determined to have a war, and from the outset ruthlessly set about its planning and execution.

It was not until the late 1960s, in large part because of the impact of the trial in Jerusalem of Adolf Eichmann, that a number of historians pointed out that from at least as early as *Mein Kampf* Hitler envisioned this as a war not only for 'space', but also for 'race'. Some even went so far as to suggest that race was the principal motive behind the war for space, that Hitler launched a conventional war in order to be able to carry out his murderous racialist designs. They could point to Hitler's speech before the Reichstag on 30 January 1939 in which he said:

Today I shall once again be a prophet: if international Jewish financiers in Europe and abroad should succeed once again in plunging the nations into a world war, the result will not be the Bolshevising of the earth, and thus the victory of Jewry, but the annihilation of the Jewish race in Europe.

While it is true that the Shoah could never have happened on such a scale had not so many Jews had the terrible misfortune to live within German-occupied Europe, it is also true that it was 'space' and not 'race' that was uppermost in Hitler's mind between his appointment in 1933 and the invasion of the Soviet Union in 1941. In *Mein Kampf* he insisted that first of all the German nation must be set in order and then fight to win back the lost provinces. For this it was vitally necessary to 'forge the sword', since the sword alone would decide the future. He poured scorn on the popular idea that Germany's problems could be solved by 'inner-colonization', by developing the potential that existed within the nation's borders. Since this was a pernicious idea it was obviously of Jewish origin. Building up Germany's industrial base in order to pay for imports of food would result in a dangerous dependence on foreign markets. Colonies abroad were a serious mistake. They were costly and led to unnecessary foreign entanglements. Grabbing new land was the only answer. That land could only be in Eastern Europe. In his 'Second Book' of 1928 he insisted that the borders of 1914 were unsatisfactory from a national, military and territorial point of view, and that merely to return to them would be a crime. Clearly this would almost inevitably mean war and thus: 'The sword must stand before the plough, the army before the economy.' Hitler insisted that *Lebensraum* could be carved out only in the east. It was a phrase cooked up by the geographer Friedrich Ratzel and which found its way into popular school texts around the turn of the century, to be revived in 1927 by National Socialism's leading philosopher, Alfred Rosenberg, who proclaimed it to be the key to a future foreign policy. Hitler was a dedicated, obsessive and determined warmonger who passionately believed that it was only in war that mankind could realize his highest potential, discover his true nature, and reach the highest level of achievement. Hitler's appointment as chancellor made a European war virtually inevitable. As he had promised, he set about restoring national unity, strength and determination with the creation of the 'racial community'. He set in train a forced rearmament programme that led to severe economic dislocations that could not be rectified without a successful war in which the vanquished would foot the bill. His foreign policy was carefully designed to place Germany in the most advantageous position possible for fighting a successful war. The naming

[274] of weapons provides a clue to his ultimate goals. A bomber developed in the mid-1930s was called the 'Ural Bomber'; the long-range Me264 of the late 1930s was christened the 'America Bomber'.

Germany and Italy

One of the most contentious foreign political issues in the early years of the Nazi movement was that of South Tyrol. This part of the former Austro-Hungarian Empire with a sizeable German-speaking population was awarded to Italy in the peace settlement. The NSDAP as a nationalist party demanded that it should be part of a new greater Germany and an article to this effect was included in the party programme of 1920.

Hitler soon began to have second thoughts about the South Tyrolian issue, and felt that an alliance with Italy was of such importance that it was worth sacrificing the interests of the Germans who lived in the area. In *Mein Kampf* he argued that South Tyrol could be won back only by force, thus ruining any possibility of an alliance with Italy, and trotted out the lame argument that Jews were behind the agitation for its return so as to ruin any chances of a pact between Germany and Italy. Hitler devoted a considerable amount of space to the issue in his 'Second Book', describing South Tyrol as a 'bridge of understanding' between Germans and Italians. He argued that Italy's need for 'living space' would inevitably lead to conflict with France, and that an alliance with Italy would make possible the defeat of France and the return of Alsace-Lorraine, leaving Germany in a strong position to pursue a 'large-scale territorial policy'. Hitler then argued that the party programme be changed to demand the return of Alsace-Lorraine rather than South Tyrol. This was the one exception to his insistence that the party programme should never be changed or modified.

Hitler's obsession with the need for an alliance with Italy did not sit well with a number of 'party comrades' (PGs). Goebbels, for example, was appalled by the idea and in February 1926 described it as 'ghastly', accusing Hitler of being a 'reactionary' and confiding in his diary that he no longer believed unconditionally in him[1]. In 1928 he referred to the Italians as 'swine' and to Italy as 'a tiny state with a big mouth'.

Although Hitler greatly admired Mussolini and imagined that he could emulate him in Bavaria in 1923, he had argued in favour of an alliance with Italy even before the March on Rome. It was his conviction that Germany desperately needed allies that led him to make an exception to his belief that 'all those who belong to the German race are equally sacred to it'. But many obstacles stood in the way of an alliance between the two fascist dictators. First and foremost was the issue of Austria. Hitler was determined to absorb Austria, and one of his first acts in foreign policy was to impose a fine of 1,000 RM in May 1933 on any German wishing to visit Austria, thus delivering an almost mortal blow to Austria's vital tourist industry. Mussolini wanted to keep Austria as a buffer state between Germany and Italy and was determined that the swastika flag should not be planted on the Brenner Pass. He regarded the Danube basin as Italy's hinterland and was worried that with Austria absorbed by Germany the area would soon become prey to German economic interests. Hitler had nothing but contempt for an independent Austria and needed Austrian industry, agriculture, manpower and the reserves of the national bank to help Germany achieve autarky. Once the unemployment problem was overcome Germany faced a shortage of manpower both in industry and in its rapidly expanding armed forces. Anschluss with Austria would open the door to the markets of south-east Europe as well as greatly enhancing Germany's strategic stance against Czechoslovakia. Most Germans shared Goebbels' contempt for the 'Macaronis' and Nazi philosophers pointed out the differences between National Socialism, which stressed the vital importance of the race, and Fascism, which was based on the worship of the state, which for orthodox Nazis was a purely artificial construct.

Hitler wanted an alliance with Italy, but not at any price. He not only turned down Mussolini's proposals for disarmament point-blank, but also withdrew from the League of Nations, leaving Mussolini in an impotent rage. Hitler met Mussolini for the first time in Venice on 14 June 1934. It was not a great success. Hitler told the blatant lie that he was not in the least bit interested in an Anschluss with Austria. This did not impress Mussolini who said that he had no intention of withdrawing his support for Dollfuss' government. Mussolini roundly denounced the Anglo-German Naval Agreement of June 1935, largely in an effort to maintain good relations with France. When the Austrian Nazis murdered Dollfuss on 25 July, almost certainly without Hitler's consent, he promptly ordered four divisions to be deployed along the Austrian border, denouncing Hitler as a 'murderer' and the Nazis as 'barbarians'. Whether or not Hitler was complicit in the assassination of the Austrian chancellor, he decided to go softly on the question of Anschluss, while never losing sight of it as his long-term goal. Mussolini set store by the Stresa Front, formed in April 1935 in which France, Britain and Italy expressed their determination to uphold the Locarno Treaty of 1925 and to stand together against Germany's violations of the Treaty of Versailles; but it was a toothless affair that was soon to fall apart

[276] when Italy launched its attack on Abyssinia, which had long been in the planning.

In December the British foreign secretary, Sir Samuel Hoare, travelled to Paris where he worked out the details of a plan with Laval for a proposed settlement of the Abyssinian crisis. It was suggested that Italy should annex a substantial part of the fertile plains of Abyssinia with a largely Muslim population; the emperor would remain with his Christian subjects in his mountain kingdom and be given a corridor to the sea to the port of Assab in Eritrea. The British government accepted the subsequent Hoare–Laval Plan, but public opinion was outraged that a government elected on a platform of support for collective security was giving way to brutal aggression against a backward, impoverished and innocent nation. The plan showed that Britain and France's support for collective security was ineffectual, and the League was further discredited. The Stresa Front was now in ruins. Britain had backed down when threatened by Mussolini and had shown extraordinary ineptitude throughout the crisis, lacking any consistent policy except a desire for peace at almost any price. Hoare was obliged to resign and was succeeded by Anthony Eden, who merely pulled faces at the dictators. In May 1936 the king of Italy was proclaimed emperor of Abyssinia and was recognized as such by the German government, which had initially lent support to the Abyssinians. Emperor Haile Selassie, whom Britain, France and the League had been both unwilling and unable to save, settled into exile in Bath. Mussolini boasted that the 'greatest colonial war in history' was the foundation stone of a new Roman Empire. The Italian people rejoiced at such a splendid victory, and at the glittering prospects that lay before them. Hitler congratulated Mussolini on his magnificent achievement.

The repercussions of the Abyssinian invasion left Mussolini disillusioned with Britain and France and much more sympathetic towards Germany. He appointed his son-in-law, Count Galeazzo Ciano, foreign minister in June 1936, a man well known for his favourable opinion of National Socialist Germany. Italy and Germany both intervened in the Spanish Civil War, which began in July, entering a military dialogue on how best to help the Nationalist cause. On 1 November 1936 Mussolini made the insubstantial claim that an 'axis' now existed between Rome and Berlin around which all European states committed to 'cooperation and peace' might collaborate.

The Axis was a figure of speech rather than a reality, but Mussolini told Göring a couple of months later that he was prepared to drop the '*guardia al Brennero*', but he expected to be consulted should Germany make a move against Austria. A string of high-level German visitors to Rome in the spring and summer of 1937 sounded out Mussolini on the level of his commitment to Austria. The Duce visited Germany in September and was given a lavish reception. The Italian delegation remained silent about Austria, from which their hosts correctly inferred that they were no longer prepared to support Dollfuss' successor, Schussnigg. In spite of Göring's repeated assurances that Mussolini would be consulted, he was kept completely in the dark and only asked for his consent immediately before the invasion. He swallowed this bitter pill and gave the go-ahead. Hitler at least kept his word that he would never forget Mussolini for his compliance and stood by him to the bitter end, in spite of his utter contempt for Italy and the Italians. He was also prepared to reassure Mussolini that he had no designs on South Tyrol, much to the disgust of some of his followers.

Mussolini's supine attitude over the Anschluss reduced Italy to a virtual satellite of Nazi Germany, a fact underlined in July 1938 with the adoption of a 'Race Manifesto' designed to eliminate any major ideological differences between Fascist Italy and National Socialist Germany. The Germans never bothered to consult their closest ally and Italy was left virtually isolated, receiving precious little from Berlin apart from marching orders. Italy's attempts to assert its sovereignty, such as the invasion of Albania and Greece, or its attempt to oust the British from North Africa, were pathetic demonstrations of independence that ended in disasters, from which the Germans felt obliged to extricate it. Mussolini was briefly to appear as a master statesman who had brought the Germans, British and French together at Munich, thus saving Europe from war in 1938, but this was soon shown to be an illusion and left Hitler infuriated that he had been denied his war.

Little was changed by the bombastically and inaccurately named 'Pact of Steel' between Germany and Italy, signed on 22 May 1939. Mussolini imagined that with Germany now a formal ally he would be consulted before Hitler made yet another startling move. He hoped for a long period of peace during which Italy would be able to recover from its costly engagement in the Spanish Civil War and managed to convince himself that he would be able to restrain Hitler from going to war. All this in spite of the fact that the Pact committed Italy's armed forces to support Germany, even in a war for which Germany alone was responsible. The ink was hardly dry before Mussolini realized what he had done and desperately tried to wriggle out of this irresponsible obligation. The Germans continued to ignore the Italians and turned a deaf ear to Mussolini and Ciano's pleas for a few more years of peace. At the end of August 1939 Mussolini told Hitler that Italy was unable to meet its treaty obligations, and Hitler reluctantly accepted

Figure 8.1 Hitler welcomes Mussolini at Kufstein prior to the Munich Conference in September 1938

that he would have to take on the western democracies alone. Italy now lamely announced that it was 'non-belligerent' rather than 'neutral' and was thus still committed to the Axis and might possibly join in the war at a later date. On 10 June 1940, with France clearly defeated, Mussolini finally decided to act and declared war on Britain and France. Publicly Hitler was effusive in his expressions of gratitude to his gallant ally. Privately he had nothing but contempt for a nation he regarded as a greedy scavenger out to profit from Germany's victory. Italian setbacks in North Africa and Greece further strengthened Hitler's contempt for the Italians. He had needed Mussolini's acquiescence in the Anschluss, but thereafter Italy was more of a hindrance than a help. He still admired Mussolini, but treated the Italians with utter contempt, regarding them as suitable only for second-rate cannon fodder.

South-east Europe

Hitler genuinely desired an alliance with Italy, but most of Germany's actions were antagonistic to Italy: the murder of Dollfuss in 1934, the Anglo-German Naval Agreement, the supply of arms to Abyssinia and above all its determined attempt to increase its economic and political influence in south-east Europe. Mussolini's capitulation over the Anschluss merely served to encourage Germany's ambition to play a hegemonic role in south-east Europe, an area seen as a key component of what the Nazis were pleased to call 'large area economics' (*Grossraumwirtschaft*). From a slightly less ideological perspective, figures such as Hjalmar Schacht felt that a set of bilateral agreements with countries in the region could help overcome at least some of the difficulties Schacht addressed in his 'New Plan'. Göring had far more ambitious schemes for close economic ties with south-east Europe that would benefit Germany's forced rearmament programme.

Germany's first step in the region was to sign a trade agreement with Hungary in February 1934. The motive was as much political as economic, for Hungary was a major revisionist country that Germany hoped to stiffen against the Little Entente. General Ludwig Beck soon began talks with the Hungarian General Staff on how best to weaken the Little Entente and drew up plans against Czechoslovakia, France's strongest partner in the region. In May 1934 a trade agreement was signed with Yugoslavia and in March 1935 another with Romania, the other two members of the Little Entente. The French foreign minister Jean Louis Barthou, the only European statesman who was fully cognizant of the danger posed by Nazi Germany and who was determined to meet the challenge head-on, kept a close eye on Germany's intentions in the area. His successors were less vigilant. In 1937 the French premier, Camille Chautemps, informed the German government that France would not stand in Germany's way in south-east Europe. After Munich France abandoned the Little Entente and only made half-hearted attempts to repair the damage when Britain decided to take a firmer stand after the 'Prague coup', when German troops marched into the Czech capital.

The British government had been every bit as spineless as the French and had even encouraged Germany to extend its influence in south-east Europe. The historian E.H. Carr, then serving in the Foreign Office's Southern Department, argued that since Germany was going to expand in any case, this was an area where Britain's interests were least affected. Chamberlain warmly seconded this view and giving Germany a free hand in south-east Europe was a key component of economic appeasement. Fortunately not all the officials in the Foreign Office were appeasers like Carr. Orme Sargent, head of the Central Department, warned that it would be extremely dangerous simply to write off countries in central and south-east Europe, but his Jeremiads went unheeded. Britain missed ample opportunities to strengthen its position in the region when Germany failed to live up to its side of the bilateral agreements, leaving its trading partners singularly disgruntled. Germany paid for imports either with blocked accounts or by

[280] barter. Yugoslavia was thus stuck with warehouses full of Bayer aspirin when the war began. By 1939 Germany was the hegemonic power in the Danubian basin, having pushed Italy and Czechoslovakia aside, with Britain and France having made an ignominious and dishonourable withdrawal.

Britain

Hitler initially saw Italy as a promising partner in a war against France, but soon became disillusioned. He believed that Italy's need for space was bound to bring it into conflict with Germany's implacable enemy. In *Mein Kampf* he wrote that France was the principal beneficiary of the peace treaties that had made it the hegemonic power on the continent. The French, with their lax attitude towards the dangers of *métissage*, were gradually becoming negrified, a process of bastardization manipulated by Jews to destroy the nation. It was a country in which the Jews controlled the stock exchange and which 'because of its close association with the aims of the Jewish world conspiracy, presents a lurking danger to the continuing existence of the white race in Europe'. He believed that France was waiting to advance to the Rhine, and was only restrained because of Britain's concern that this would further upset the balance of power. A war with France was necessary not only to remove Germany's deadly rival and threat to the racial stock, but also to provide cover to the rear for a war of conquest in the east. Hitler delighted in repeatedly quoting Schopenhauer's remark that 'Africa has its monkeys, Europe its French'.

Hitler had no such animus against Britain, a country which in the custom of the day he insisted on calling 'England' and for which he had considerable admiration. Along with Italy it was Germany's most likely and desirable ally in a war against France. In *Mein Kampf* he argued that an alliance with Britain was essential to protect the rear when Germany advanced east. The cost of such an alliance would be high, and was one that many German nationalists were reluctant to pay. Germany would have to give up all claims for a return of its colonies, eschew any naval ambitions and avoid any conflicts on the international markets by concentrating on a policy of autarky; but it would be worth the price. He argued that there would have been no war in 1914 had Germany and Britain been allies.

Much of this was repeated in Hitler's 'Second Book', where Britain's enemies were listed in order of importance as France, the Soviet Union (usually called 'Russia') and the United States. Britain would raise no objections to Germany's expansion in Europe, provided that its concerns elsewhere were addressed. Imperial Germany had made the disastrous mistake of building a battle fleet that was bound to alienate Britain. Hitler greatly admired the British Empire as an example of the 'race value of Anglo-Saxonism'. He was later to argue that the Raj showed how a chosen handful from a racial elite could hold down hundreds of thousands of the racially inferior. This was an example to be followed in Germany's eastern empire. On the other hand, whereas Italy had taken some positive steps in the right direction, in his perverted and tortuous view Britain was still engaged in a life and death struggle with the Jewish threat, and only when the British emerged victorious would an alliance with Germany be possible. Hitler insisted that: 'The ultimate goal of the Jewish struggle for survival is the enslavement of productively active peoples.' The British failed to realize that the Jews manipulate nations into going to war. Their aim was 'denationalisation and bastardisation' and the destruction of the national intelligentsia. For Hitler the only comfort was that since the Jew was a parasite his ultimate victory would result in his own death. By the time Hitler came to power he was keen to reach an understanding with Britain. Should this prove impossible there was a convenient group who would take the blame. In 1934 he told a British journalist that he regarded a war with Britain as a 'racial crime', the implication being that were this to happen it would be due to the nefarious devices of world Jewry.

The international situation in 1933 was ideal were Germany to pursue a revisionist policy. The powers were seriously weakened by the ravages of the depression. Collective security was in ruins with the Japanese invasion of Manchuria and the subsequent feeble response of the League of Nations. Reparations had effectively been ended with the Hoover Moratorium, and Brüning had been within an inch of removing the military restrictions placed on Germany by the Versailles treaty. For the moment Hitler decided to tread softly on the foreign stage while he established his dictatorship at home, at the same time revealing his wild dreams of conquest to a select audience. His first announcement of his long-term goals was made behind closed doors to a group of leading generals on 3 February 1933. He certainly did not mince his words. He promised strict authoritarian rule that would rid Germany of the 'cancer' of democracy, 'exterminate' Marxism and pacifism and make Germany once again ready for war (*Wiederwehrhaftmachung*) by rearmament and the introduction of universal military service. France was the only possible impediment to his plans and it remained to be seen whether it had statesmen enough to attack Germany, in alliance with its eastern satellites, before the country was ready to pounce on its hereditary enemy. In an ominous footnote, which most of his audience seem to have overheard, he spoke of 'radically Germanizing' the east in order to carve out 'living space' (*Lebensraum*). The generals with their traditional anti-Semitism, their loathing of 'Jewish-Bolshevism', their determination to rearm and to revise the Versailles settlement, were uncouraged by these remarks. For all their snobbish disdain towards some of the more vulgar aspects of National Socialism, they were in broad agreement with Hitler's programme and were fully complicit in his crimes, most of them remaining so until the bitter end. Publicly Hitler reassured conservatives at home and foreign governments by retaining the aristocratic career diplomat of the old school, Konstantin von Neurath, as foreign minister along with his secretary of state Bernhard von Bülow. The diplomats seemed to have been unaware of or to have ignored Hitler's alarming message to his generals and did not think that the new government meant a radical change in course. They imagined that it would be possible to pursue a somewhat more aggressive policy than that of Stresemann, whereby Germany's position would be strengthened by rearmament, an Anschluss with Austria, and the restoration of the lost colonies.

Hitler's first major public address on foreign policy was made in the Reichstag on 17 May 1933 and was cynically reassuring. He promised to respect all international treaties and obligations, and called for a peaceful revision of the Versailles settlement. This was in part a response to Prime Minister Ramsay MacDonald's appeal for worldwide disarmament, as well as an attempt to undo some of the damage to Germany's reputation abroad caused by the Enabling Act in March and the boycott of Jewish stores in April. Most of Britain's political elite was hoodwinked by this performance, and there were very few who saw through the rhetoric. Prominent among them were Winston Churchill, who in 1930 predicted that the Nazis would come to power and that they were hell-bent on going to war, and the British ambassador in Berlin, Sir Horace Rumbold, who stressed Germany's expansionist ambitions. Even Neville Chamberlain referred to Germany as 'a bully' and the Defence Requirement Committee listed Germany as Britain's most likely enemy.

For all the anti-Marxist rhetoric, and while Hitler was busy murdering Communists at home, Germany signed a credit agreement with the Soviet Union on 25 February 1933, and a friendship and non-aggression treaty on 4 April. Hitler decided to notch up the pressure when on 14 October the German government took the British and French proposal at Geneva, that Germany should be given a four-year trial period before reaching a general agreement on disarmament, as an excuse to leave the League of Nations. This was an enormously popular move in Germany, where the

League was seen as little more than an instrument whereby the victorious [283] powers upheld the *Diktat* of Versailles. Once again Daladier failed to react to this provocation that was clearly contradictory to Hitler's assurances that he was a man of peace. Hitler's next move was to inform the French government in December 1933 that he defined disarmament as Germany's right to rearm up to France's level. Meanwhile Joachim von Ribbentrop, Hitler's adviser on foreign policy, was sent to London in November where he met Stanley Baldwin and relayed a message from Hitler that war in the west was unthinkable and that Germany's ambitions lay in the east.

Hitler as appeaser

Hitler's next move was a surprising non-aggression pact with Poland on 16 January 1934 that marked a radical departure from the pro-Soviet and anti-Polish policy of the Weimar Republic since Rapallo. Chancellor Joseph Wirth had seen Rapallo as an important step towards 'finishing off' Poland. Gustav Stresemann, the architect of 'fulfilment' who was anxious to improve relations with France, had let it be known that he had every intention of winning back Danzig, the Corridor and Upper Silesia. German and Soviet staff officers planned a joint attack on Poland and downed vast quantities of vodka in toasts to the destruction of a country that Hans von Seeckt said should be like a drop of sweat between the mighty hands of Germany and Russia. None of this seemed to be of much interest to Hitler, whose ambitions went far beyond merely returning to the frontiers of 1914. He set his sights on a vast empire in Russia and regarded the Polish question as secondary. A number of leading Nazis, centred around Gregor Strasser, were sharply critical of this view and argued that Russia did not even border on Germany, and that cooperation with the Soviet Union should remain the basis of a revisionist eastern policy. Hitler was firmly opposed to the idea of an alliance with the Judaeo-Bolshevik hordes and rejected this idea out of hand.

Konstantin von Neurath, Hitler's first foreign minister, along with his secretary of state, Bernhard von Bülow, believed that an understanding with Poland was neither possible nor desirable. Rumours circulated in Berlin that Poland, with its superior armed forces, might attack Germany. Such gossip was fanned and used in the political intrigues against Papen and Schleicher, but had no basis in fact. Hitler ignored the foreign office's position paper on policy towards Poland and was determined to continue playing the role of a man of peace while he established his dictatorship. He told the Polish government that he wished to postpone the entire question of frontier revisions and that all such rectifications would be achieved by peaceful means. The Poles saw no alternative to signing the Non-Aggression Pact, but they had every reason to be suspicious. They felt abandoned by their French sponsors and believed they had no other choice, even though Hitler pointed out that the treaty did not mean that there would be no frontier changes between the two countries. The pact was valid for ten years and shortly afterwards a trade agreement was reached which helped Germany to overcome a chronic shortage of certain foodstuffs.

The foreign office and the military were appalled by Hitler's attitude towards Poland as was Hjalmar Schacht, the Reichsbank president and minister of economics, but Hitler made no attempt to reassure them that he regarded the pact as a strictly temporary measure designed to weaken France's anti-German alliance system. Göring was sent on a visit to Poland in January 1935 where he reassured his hosts of Germany's peaceful intentions and even suggested the possibility of a joint attack on the Soviet Union. Hitler's emphasis on rearmament and his success in re-establishing Germany's status as a great power enabled the anti-Polish elites to swallow Hitler's heterodox policy towards Poland.

Hitler continued to appease Poland until late 1938 and during this time it was Poland that put the most strain on relations between the two countries, voting in the League of Nations for a resolution condemning Germany for introducing compulsory military service. After the Munich agreement Hitler agreed that the Czech town of Oderberg should be awarded to Poland, thus causing much grumbling in the usual quarters. That was his last magnanimous gesture. Henceforth he concentrated on winning back Danzig.

The Soviet Union

Hitler's early appeasement of Poland was dictated by his elemental hatred of the 'Judaeo-Bolshevik' Soviet Union. Initially Hitler had toyed with the idea of an alliance with Russia, but by 1922 he was committed to carving out *Lebensraum* in the Soviet Union and was utterly opposed to the Treaty of Rapallo. Many leading Nazis had considerable sympathy for the Soviet Union. Goebbels, for example, announced in 1924 that Communists were absolutely right to hate the bourgeoisie and that Russia was the country of the future. Two years later he felt that Hitler's idea of an alliance with Britain and Italy aimed against the Soviet Union was 'ghastly' and that

Hitler was a 'reactionary'. Hitler constantly harped on the theme that the [285] Soviet Union was run by Jews and had to be destroyed; then the racially inferior Slavs could serve their German masters who would exploit the vast natural and agricultural resources of their eastern *Lebensraum*. Goebbels and other Nazis, who saw much to admire in the Soviet Union, gradually came round to share Hitler's views, even though they supported joint action with the KPD when tactically convenient. By 1933 hostility to Communism in all its forms permeated the Nazi movement and was a major source of its general appeal.

Businessmen had benefited from close trade relations with the Soviet Union during the Weimar Republic and the military took great delight in drawing up plans for the destruction of Poland with their Soviet colleagues. Now they were worried that the new regime would destroy this valuable partnership. Neurath, with his virulent hatred of Poland, insisted that close ties with Russia were essential, but Hitler ignored his foreign minister and simply said that with regard to the Soviet Union it would be 'business as usual'. The Treaty of Berlin of 24 April 1926 was renewed in May 1933, but military exchanges dwindled away to nothing while trade relations deteriorated.

Hugenberg's unfortunate outburst about Germany's need for *Lebensraum* at the World Economic Conference in London in June 1933 was a welcome excuse to oblige him to resign from the cabinet, but it reinforced Moscow's concerns that relations with Germany were entering a new and dangerous phase. In November 1933 Marshal Tukhachevski, the deputy war commissar, sang the praises of the Reichswehr, but this met with little response, and Stalin gave a speech warning that forces hostile to the Soviet Union were busy at work in Germany. On 30 January 1934, the first anniversary of the 'seizure of power', Hitler, who had decided to step cautiously in foreign affairs while he established his dictatorship at home, told the Reichstag that he was anxious to promote international understanding and was determined to strengthen the common interests of Germany and the Soviet Union.

France

Some diplomatists were shrewd enough to see behind the front of Hitler the peaceful revisionist. Prominent among them was André François-Poncet, France's astute ambassador in Berlin. He warned Edouard Daladier, whose government was appointed at much the same time as Hitler's, that the German chancellor was something quite new, who would not be content with simply recovering the frontiers of 1914. Daladier, a Provençal who as mayor of Carpentras earned the nickname 'the lion of the Vaucluse', but who proved far from leonine in foreign affairs, disparaged this tiresome Cassandra and responded by sending a special envoy, Fernand de Brion, on a secret mission to Berlin. Hitler expressed his fervent desire to cooperate fully with France and asked only for an expeditious solution to the Saar problem and the right to a modest level of rearmament. Brion returned to Paris with a glowing account of his talks. Unfortunately most statesmen were equally taken in by Hitler's assurances of his peaceful intentions, while he insistently stepped up his preparations for war. Hitler was a master dissembler, often hiding his intentions from even his closest associates to the point of appearing an indecisive ditherer while waiting for the moment to strike and startle the world with yet another radical measure.

Daladier's appeasement of revisionist Germany set a regrettable precedent and it was unfortunate that he was to return to power at a critical moment in international affairs. In 1934 French foreign policy was in the hands of Jean Louis Barthou, one of the few historians who were also first-rate politicians. He was determined to stand up to Germany, which with the Röhm Putsch in June and the assassination of Dollfuss in July was beginning to show its true face. Barthou did his best to improve relations with Britain and Italy, so as to strengthen the Versailles system and leave Germany diplomatically isolated. Tragically Barthou was assassinated by a Croatian terrorist in Marseille along with King Alexander of Yugoslavia, who was on a state visit to France, on 9 October 1934. This proved to be an irreparable loss. The Stresa Front of 1935 was a pale reflection of the Barthou spirit, and without his guiding hand was an ineffectual affair.

Hitler was fortunate to have Barthou out of the way when he prepared for the Saar plebiscite, held on 19 January 1935. Laval was now in the Quai d'Orsay, a slippery character who was utterly opposed to the use, or even the threat, of force and who entertained a sneaking admiration for dictators. He reversed Barthou's policies, moved away from Britain and France's Eastern European allies and let the Germans know that France had no real interest in the Saar. François-Poncet relayed the Flandin government's assurance that France was not concerned by Germany's rearmament programme. At an Anglo-French meeting in London in February it was agreed that Germany should be permitted to rearm and the fond hope was entertained that Germany would then be willing to join a mutual security system in a revamped Locarno. Hitler was thus given positive encouragement to pursue a more vigorous revisionist policy.

Hitler's first major foreign political triumph was in the Saar where 91 per cent of the electorate voted in the plebiscite to return to Germany, in spite of massive anti-fascist propaganda in this largely working-class area. The Saar was overwhelmingly Catholic and the faithful were greatly encouraged by the Concordat and did not wish to be part of godless France. On 16 March 1935 Hitler introduced conscription for an army of 300,000 men, to be increased at some as yet unspecified date to 550,000. Britain and France were dimly aware that they had seriously misjudged Hitler and joined with Italy in April to form the Stresa Front. From the outset this was without any real substance. Britain deserted in June by signing a naval agreement with Germany. Shortly thereafter Mussolini ordered the invasion of Abyssinia and the Stresa Front was left beyond repair.

Germany worked long and hard to get a naval agreement with Britain. Ribbentrop, who had been given the risible title of Reich Plenipotentiary for Disarmament, was back in London in November 1934 where he met the foreign secretary, Sir John Simon, and Anthony Eden to whom he repeated Germany's offer of a naval agreement. In February 1935 Hitler invited Simon and Eden to visit Berlin on 7 March to discuss the Anglo-French communiqué on disarmament. Three days before the delegation was due to arrive the British government published a White Paper on defence that called for a substantial increase in expenditure for the armed forces, said to be a direct response to Germany's increasingly belligerent attitude. Hitler, buoyed up by his recent triumph in the Saar plebiscite, feigned an indisposition and cancelled the visit and on 10 March Göring announced the formation of the Luftwaffe, the German air force that was expressly forbidden by the Treaty of Versailles. On 15 March the French National Assembly approved an increase in the term of military service from one to two years. The following day Hitler announced the introduction of universal military service.

Simon and Eden were eventually admitted to the presence on 25 March and were treated to a series of monologues, most of them on Hitler's favourite topic of the menace of Bolshevism, and were scarcely able to get a word in edgeways. When they did eventually manage to register a complaint they were shot down in flames. Sir John Simon protested at Germany's flagrant breach of the disarmament clauses of the Treaty of Versailles, whereupon Hitler perkily enquired whether Wellington had raised similar objections when Blücher arrived on the field of Waterloo. These initial soundings were treated with deep suspicion by the British government, but soon attitudes began to change. Britain was seriously concerned with the threat to the empire posed by the Japanese and was anxious to reach a settlement in Europe so as to be able to concentrate on the Pacific theatre. Hitler, who had no pressing naval ambitions and who was prepared to violate any treaty he made, was determined to get an agreement with Britain so as to isolate France, make a further dent in the Versailles system and assuage British concerns about the introduction of conscription in March.

Joachim von Ribbentrop, an insufferably ill-mannered former sparkling-wine salesman, whose boorish behaviour soon earned him the sobriquet 'von Brickendrop', who had wangled an aristocratic title by getting adopted by an aunt and who lived in great style on his wife's money, was sent back to London to do a deal. Hitler, a socially gauche petit bourgeois, imagined that Ribbentrop was a true gentleman and a man of the world. The British government did not take kindly either to him or to his demand for Germany to have a free hand to destroy the Soviet Union, while graciously allowing Britannia to rule the waves and concentrate on the empire. Ribbentrop remained persistent and finally on 18 June 1935 an agreement was reached whereby the ratio of British to German surface fleets was fixed at 100 to 35. Submarines, Hitler's favoured naval weapon, were not included. Hitler was delighted and proclaimed this to be his 'happiest day'. He was soon to refer to Ribbentrop as a 'second Bismarck'. Others were less enthusiastic. He reminded Paul Schmidt, Hitler's interpreter and a keen observer of human frailty, of the dog on HMV records. Goebbels wrote: 'He is an utterly repulsive bloke who has no friends at all.'

Hitler hoped that this was the first step towards an alliance with Britain that would put an end to the system of collective security. In August he told Goebbels that his aim was to achieve 'an eternal alliance with England' as well as good relations with Poland, in preparation for 'the great historical hour' when Germany would expand eastwards. In fact it was the closest that Germany was ever to get to Britain; all Ribbentrop's ham-fisted efforts as ambassador came to naught and he developed what Goebbels called a 'blind hatred' towards his host country. The British were unwilling to abandon their commitment, however half-hearted, to multilateral diplomacy and to the League of Nations, but they were also eager to seize the opportunities offered on the German market and to avoid a costly rearmament programme by pursuing a policy of détente. Many influential figures in the City, principal among them the governor of the Bank of England, Montagu Norman, deluded themselves into believing that economic appeasement would strengthen the hands of imaginary moderates among Hitler's paladins, and that war could be avoided. Of course Hitler had no intention of allowing economic considerations to dictate his foreign policy, and

exploited financial and commercial links with Britain to the benefit of his
rearmament programme.

With such a feeble response from the Versailles powers, Hitler decided to push ahead with his plan to remilitarize the Rhineland, thus fulfilling the military's fondest wishes and effectively putting the boot into the Locarno Pact. France had negotiated a military assistance pact with the Soviet Union in May 1935 that was finally ratified in February the following year. France had made this move in response to the introduction of universal military service in Germany. The Soviets imagined that this was the beginning of a mighty anti-fascist coalition and to show their earnest intent joined the League of Nations. In fact it was a feeble alliance, fraught with all manner of ideological differences and conflicts of interest. Hitler seized this welcome opportunity offered by the spineless Laval government, denounced the pact as a flagrant breach of the Locarno accords and ordered German troops into the Rhineland on 7 March 1936. Blomberg, the minister of war, was somewhat nervous about French reactions to this daring move, but von Neurath had nothing but contempt for the French government, a feeling that was shared by Hitler. The British were equally feeble with their response. There was talk of Hitler merely tending his own backyard, and the main blame was placed on the French for failing to reach an agreement with their neighbour.

Hitler had told his generals on 3 February 1933 that it remained to be seen whether France had any statesmen ready and willing to stand up to Germany's ambitiously revisionist policies. Barthou had given him pause to think, but now he knew there was nothing to fear. Following the unfortunate example set by the British, successive French governments continued to appease Germany, not only politically but also economically. Germany was dependent to a considerable degree on supplies of iron ore from France to meet the needs of the armaments programme that had been stepped up drastically in 1936. Even Leon Blum's Popular Front government imagined that France might oblige Germany to make certain concessions in return for economic assistance. It was only when the Germans marched into Prague in March 1939 that some began seriously to question the benefits of economic appeasement.

By 1936 rearmament, which had cost 9 billion RM since 1933, was placing an intolerable strain on the economy. A series of poor harvests resulted in an increased need for food imports. Fats had been placed on ration in 1935 and were taken off again after the trade agreement with Poland. Hitler, who was determined to keep up the pace of rearmament, threw economic caution to the winds, ordering that domestic sources of

[290] raw materials should be exploited and synthetic rubber and petroleum
produced so as to reduce reliance on imports. He dismissed all concerns
about the staggering cost of autarky, imagining that it could be met with
the rich booty acquired in a war of conquest. In August 1936 he demanded
that the country be ready for war within four years and that a series of
swift campaigns would result in 'an increase in *Lebensraum* and thus of raw
materials and foodstuffs'.

Emphasis on autarky resulted in a chronic worsening of the foreign
exchange situation, prompting Schacht and the foreign office, which was
pro-Russian and anti-Polish, to press for improved trade relations with the
Soviet Union. Hermann Göring as head of the Four-Year Plan enthusiastically seconded this initiative and encouraged discussion with the Soviet
trade mission in Berlin. The German embassy in Moscow was also instructed
to encourage trade relations and was told not to let political considerations
stand in their way. Negotiations for a trade treaty were broken off when
German troops marched into the Rhineland, but Göring was determined to
reach an agreement, making his half-brother Herbert a special envoy with
a remit to conclude a commercial treaty. All this effort came to nothing
because of Germany's refusal to export military equipment and share technical
information. At least the two sides were still talking, even though they
supported different sides in the Spanish Civil War, and in spite of the
Anti-Comintern Pact with Japan, Italy, Hungary and Spain, to say nothing
of the Soviet Union's alliances with France and Czechoslovakia.

In the following years Hitler gave vent to frequent disquisitions on the
urgent need to find a satisfactory solution to Germany's 'space problem'.
On 28 January 1937 Blomberg revealed to Goebbels plans for an attack on
the Soviet Union, Czechoslovakia and Lithuania in alliance with Italy. The
propaganda minister hoped that Germany would seize the first favourable
opportunity to put this plan into action. In February Hitler told Goebbels
in apocalyptic terms that he expected a 'conflict' within five to seven years,
in which Germany would either be victorious or cease to exist. On 5 November 1937 he called a top-level meeting in the chancellery attended by
von Neurath, Blomberg and the commanders-in-chief of the army, the navy
and the air force, von Fritsch, Raeder and Göring. They were treated to a
four-hour monologue which Hitler announced should be taken as his testament in the event of his death and which has survived in a memorandum
written by Colonel Hossbach, Hitler's stiff, aloof and reticent army adjutant,
who was soon to be fired for his open support for Fritsch and the OKH. It
began with a rambling discourse on such pet topics as race, social Darwinism
and geopolitics, on the need to strengthen the 'racial mass' and to carve out

Lebensraum. None of this could be achieved without recourse to force. First [291] there would be an Anschluss with Austria, then Czechoslovakia would be attacked. Germany would have to be prepared to go to war with both France and Britain should they decide to intervene. One month later General Alfred Jodl, chief of staff in the OKW, wrote that when Germany was fully prepared Czechoslovakia would be attacked and the 'space problem' would be solved, even if Britain or France intervened.

The army leadership was fundamentally in agreement with the aims of the Nazi regime, but tried to preserve a degree of independence. The officer corps was unsympathetic to the attempt by the Nazis to have an absolute monopoly over the ideological training of German youth. Relations between the army and the SS were becoming increasingly strained. In turn the SS felt that the officer corps was stuffy, conservative, snobbish and reactionary. There was also some concern in the upper echelons of the army that Hitler was prepared to risk going to war before the country was adequately prepared. Many leading Nazis, chief among them Goebbels, felt that the army was far too independent and risked becoming a state within the state. It was also felt to be sadly lacking in ideological fervour and was chronically infected with monarchical tendencies. Hitler overcame some of these problems with the dismissal of Blomberg and Fritsch and the creation of OKW and OKH in 1938, but serious tensions still remained within the military and between the armed services and the party.

The Anschluss

Austria was now the first item on the foreign policy agenda, although as late as December 1937 Hitler was still opposed to the idea of an invasion, even though the Austrian Nazis were straining at the leash, and Ribbentrop and Göring were urging him to take action. At the end of January 1938 the Austrian police discovered evidence of a Nazi plot to murder the German ambassador, von Papen, and provoke such a degree of repression that the Germans would feel obliged to intervene. Papen persuaded the Austrian chancellor, Schuschnigg, to visit Hitler at the Obersalzberg. Schuschnigg told one of his associates that a psychiatrist would make a more suitable visitor, but he was encouraged by the invitation to make some significant concessions to the Nazis, appointing them to the Council of State, ending discrimination against 'moderates' in the party, and promising to improve relations with the Reich. Hitler, encouraged by such obvious signs of weakness, agreed to talk to Schuschnigg.

[292]   The meeting took place on 12 February. The Austrian chancellor was treated to an extraordinary performance by Hitler, who modestly described himself as 'perhaps the greatest German in all of history'. Surrounded by his generals for maximum effect, he gave the unfortunate Schuschnigg a couple of hours to accept an agreement whereby the Nazis would enter the government and be given the ministry of the interior. Schuschnigg lamely protested that he could not act on behalf of the president, but he signed a protocol and was given three days to deliver a signed agreement.

Schuschnigg did little to win support for Austrian independence in Britain and France, and let it be known that he did not want anything to be done which might provoke Hitler. The French felt powerless; the British ambassador in Berlin, Henderson, a man whom Goebbels described as 'habitually idle' but well disposed towards Germany, implied that his government would not object to an Anschluss. Hitler still hesitated, hoping that further concessions could be wrung from the Austrians without armed intervention, and told his impatient followers in Austria that he wanted the 'evolutionary course to be taken'. Schuschnigg's announcement on 9 March that there would be a plebiscite for 'a free, German, independent, social, Christian and united Austria' with the voting age raised to 24, so as to exclude a large number of youthful Nazi sympathizers, prompted him into immediate action. Hitler was almost hysterical with rage when he heard of this move and, convinced that the plebiscite would result in a major victory for Schuschnigg, ordered the military to prepare for an invasion, although he still hoped that violence could be avoided. Seyss-Inquart, the Austrian Nazi minister of the interior, was ordered by Hitler to resign if Schuschnigg refused to call off the plebiscite. When the Austrian chancellor gave way under this pressure, Seyss-Inquart was ordered to demand his resignation and his own appointment as chancellor. Schuschnigg appealed to Britain and France for help, but since none was forthcoming he handed in his resignation. President Miklas stoutly refused to appoint Seyss-Inquart, whereupon Hitler ordered the invasion of Austria. During the night of 11/12 March Miklas capitulated, but it was too late to stop the invasion. Göring provided the pretext by dictating a letter on behalf of Seyss-Inquart asking the German government for help. The risks were minimal. The German government knew, in part because of the excellent work of Göring's bureau of investigation in the air ministry, which had tapped the telephones in foreign embassies, that neither Britain nor Italy would lift a finger in support of Austria and that France, which was without a government, would not do anything without British backing. Schuschnigg, who stayed on as a caretaker chancellor, broadcast to the nation on the evening of 11 March, announcing that the army would not resist and that Austria was giving [293] way to brute force.

The invasion was a hastily improvised affair, beginning in the early morning of 12 March, and was bloodless. German troops were welcomed by enthusiastic crowds, and on the following day Hitler returned to Vienna in triumph. While Nazi thugs terrorized Vienna's Jews and looted their property, Hitler decided to reduce Austria to a province of the Reich. Austria promptly ceased to exist and became a German province known as the Ostmark. The Reichsmark replaced the Austrian schilling, and overnight Austrians had to learn to drive on the right-hand side of the road like the Germans. In a further plebiscite 99 per cent of those voting supported Hitler's settling of scores with his native country. This cheap and spectacular victory silenced most of the critics of Hitler's change of course and of personnel in the previous months, even in the armed forces, and was a triumph for Göring who had goaded the hesitant Hitler into action. Hitler's motives for swallowing up Austria were entirely ideological. *Mein Kampf* begins with an impassioned call for an Anschluss, and this remained his first priority in his quest for space, but it was Göring as head of the Four-Year Plan, egged on by Paul Pleiger, director of the Hermann Göring Works at Salzgitter, who had his eyes on Austria's iron ore deposits, foreign exchange reserves and manpower, who forced the pace.

With German troops stationed in Austria Czechoslovakia was left dangerously vulnerable and south-east Europe was open to German economic penetration, with the Italians fondly imagining that they would be partners in this profitable enterprise. Britain and France failed to respond to the Anschluss, even though it was a flagrant breach of the peace treaties, regarding it as simply an internal affair. Neither country had any sympathy for the Austrians and both were relieved, as Neville Chamberlain said, that this awkward question was now conveniently 'out of the way'.

Czechoslovakia

Hitler shared the traditional Austrian contempt for the Czechs, although in 1941 he told Goebbels that he admired their skill and intelligence and was greatly impressed by the Skoda works. Czechoslovakia was the one functioning democracy in Eastern Europe and as such was deeply offensive to Hitler. Moreover, the country harboured over 3 million 'racial comrades' in the Sudetenland whom Hitler was determined to bring home. This ambition seemed perfectly reasonable to Britain and France, even though

[294]   Czechoslovakia was a key player in the collective security system and a
vital link between France and the Soviet Union. Hitler was reassured by
the fact that they had raised no objections to the annexation of Austria.
Henderson assured Hitler that there was no ill will between Britain
and Germany, adding that all difficulties were the work of 'Jews and
anti-Nazis'.

At the end of March 1938 Hitler ordered the Sudeten German leader,
Konrad Henlein, to step up the pressure on the Czech government and
began to talk of war in the near future. The military leadership was highly
alarmed. They pointed out that Czechoslovakia had excellent frontier defences, a first-rate armaments industry, powerful allies and a creditable army.
Ribbentrop also urged caution, but Hitler refused to listen and one by one
the doubters capitulated to the Führer's indomitable will. Goebbels mounted
a massive campaign against Czechoslovakia in August 1938, describing
the Czechs as 'a shitty race'[2]. Keitel put the final touches on 'Case Green',
an attack on Czechoslovakia to take place not later than 1 October 1938.

There was widespread violence in the Sudetenland throughout the
summer of 1938 and on 15 September Prime Minister Neville Chamberlain
flew to Munich and told Hitler that neither Britain nor France had any
objection to parts of the Sudetenland being handed over to Germany.
Hitler, taken aback by Britain's willingness to abandon an ally, decided
to take a firmer stand when he met Chamberlain one week later at
Bad Godesberg. Having told both the Poles and the Hungarians that he
supported their claims against Czechoslovakia, he threatened Chamberlain
that he would go to war if all his demands were not immediately granted.

War now seemed inevitable. Czechoslovakia and France mobilized their
armies. Hitler moved seven divisions up to the Czech border. The opposition in Germany moved into action. Not only did they fear that Britain and
France would go to war in defence of Czechoslovakia, but they also knew
that the Sudetenland presented a formidable military obstacle. General
Ludwig Beck had resigned as chief of staff in August in protest against
Hitler's risky policy. Now Colonel Hans Oster, chief of staff in military
counter-intelligence, and Carl Goerdeler, the former mayor of Leipzig,
contacted British politicians and begged them to take a firm stand against
Hitler. Prompted by Mussolini, who was ever eager to play the role of '*peso
determinante*', Hitler with singular ill will agreed to meet the British and
French prime ministers in Munich on 29 September 1938. Without consulting either Czechoslovakia or the Soviet Union, Chamberlain and Daladier
agreed that all areas in the Sudetenland where the Germans were in the
majority should be handed over to Germany between 1 and 10 October.

At first sight Munich seemed to be a triumph for Hitler. He had gained an important industrial area, rich in natural resources and with a skilled workforce. Czechoslovakia had been abandoned by its allies, had lost its frontier fortifications and was left virtually defenceless. But he had been denied the crisis that he needed in order to 'wipe Czechoslovakia off the map' and he was outraged that the vast majority of Germans saw Chamberlain and Daladier as heroes who had saved Europe from war. Hitler asked: 'How can I go to war with a people like this?' and on 10 November, the day after the pogrom inappropriately known as 'The Night of Broken Glass', he gave a lengthy speech to representatives of the press, ordering them to desist from all talk of peace and to steel the people for war in the near future. Goebbels thought that Munich was a triumph, but Hitler told him that it was a miserable failure.

Britain and France continued to appease Hitler even though the pogrom in November 1938 was ample demonstration of his depravity and in spite of the relentless pressure placed on Czechoslovakia. In December France and Germany agreed that they would consult one another on all matters of mutual interest and Hitler assured Daladier that he had no designs on Alsace-Lorraine. In typical manner at the same time Hitler ordered the High Command to draw up plans for an attack on France in collaboration with the Italians, while state secretary Ernst von Weizsäcker told the new French ambassador, Robert Coulondre, that France's ally Czechoslovakia was in the German domain and that its destiny lay in Germany's hands. In his Reichstag speech on 30 January 1939 Hitler made it clear that he was hell-bent on war and that there would be no turning back. It would be a war that would lead to 'the destruction of the Jewish race in Europe' and the creation of a vast German empire, purified of all alien racial elements.

Already in the previous October Hitler had issued instructions for the destruction of Czechoslovakia and for the occupation of the Memel (Klaipéda). The Slovak president, Monsignor Jozef Tiso, was enjoined to declare Slovak independence and on 14 March he complied. He did so with considerable reluctance since he did not want to play the role of a Slovak Seyss-Inquart. That day the Czechoslovak president, Emil Hacha, travelled to Berlin in a desperate attempt to save his rump state. Hitler ranted and raved to such an extent that the poor man collapsed and had to be revived by Hitler's personal physician, Dr Theodor Morell, a man of dubious professional skill, but a dab hand with the needle. Hacha was then told that if he did not hand the state over to Germany it would be invaded, whereupon the shattered president put his signature to a document placing his unhappy and betrayed people 'confidently into the hands of the Führer of the German

Reich'. German troops crossed the border that night and the following day Hitler was met by a silent, sullen, tearful and crushed crowd. He spent a miserable night in the Hradcany Palace in Prague where all that could be provided for the vegetarian teetotaller was ham and Pilsner. He took u uip ot the latter and declared it to be far too bitter. History does not record whether he ate the ham. A few Germans were rounded up to welcome him, but he was glad to return to Berlin where he was received as the conquering hero.

One week later German troops occupied Memel, German territory that had been awarded to Lithuania under the terms of the peace treaty. Hitler arrived in Memel aboard the *Deutschland* after a voyage during which he was much troubled by seasickness.

Poland

Poland was now obviously in Hitler's sights and the Nazis in Danzig kept up the pressure, raucously insisting that the city be returned to the Reich, even though it was a free city under the aegis of the League of Nations and not an integral part of Poland. Ribbentrop sent a note to the Polish government demanding Danzig, an extraterritorial railway line and motorway through the Corridor. In return he promised Poland free access to Danzig, a frontier guarantee and an extension of the Non-Aggression Pact for a further 25 years. Hitler then suggested, knowing full well that he would meet with a blunt refusal, that Poland join the Anti-Comintern Pact, participate in an attack on the Soviet Union, and annex the Ukraine. Poland's vulpine and devious foreign minister, Colonel Jozef Beck, rejected the German offer in November 1938, again in January 1939 and finally in March.

It now appeared as if Romania might be next on Hitler's hit list. On 17 March 1939 the Romanian minister in London, Virgil Tilea, a 43-year-old suave, anglophile graduate of the London School of Economics, informed the British government that Germany had issued an ultimatum demanding that the Romanian economy should be subordinated to the interests of the Reich, and he urgently asked Halifax what his government would do if Hitler made good his threat. London immediately informed Paris, Moscow, Warsaw, Athens, Ankara and Belgrade, asking for their reactions. The replies were all much the same: it all depended on what the others did. On the following day the Romanian foreign minister, Grigore Gafencu, a close friend of King Carol II and a man who elevated the Romanian penchant for fence-sitting to a high diplomatic art, announced that there was not a word of truth in Tilea's alarmist tale. This was a somewhat optimistic gloss on the German-Romanian trade negotiations, which were designed to secure German control over Romania's oil and a dominant position in the economic life of south-east Europe. Even if Tilea was being unnecessarily alarmist, the mere suggestion that Germany might corner the Romanian oil market was enough to cause grave concern in Paris. The French foreign office began to imagine a sinister plot against Romania in which Poland would try to stop Hitler from pressing his demands over Danzig and the Corridor by encouraging him to go for the riches of Romania, which would provide the fuel for the German armed forces, which could then be unleashed against the rest of Europe.

Prompted by the French and by a Soviet suggestion for a meeting with Britain, France, Romania and Poland to work out a common strategy, the British government proposed a joint declaration with the Soviet Union, France and Poland that discussions would be held about the appropriate action to take if the political independence of any European state was threatened. King Carol of Romania spoke of threatening troop movements in Hungary and Bulgaria and the possibility of war. For the British the key to the whole situation was Poland, a country that was considered militarily far more significant than the Soviet Union, with a common border with Germany, and without which no help could be given to Romania, since neither the Poles nor the Romanians wanted anything to do with the Soviets.

Colonel Beck disliked the idea of the Polish government signing a joint declaration with the Soviet Union, and countered the British proposal with the suggestion that there should be a secret Anglo-Polish agreement. The Poles had every reason to look for allies. German pressure on Danzig was a constant irritant; the annexation of Memel threatened its security and raised the possibility that Danzig might be for Poland what the Sudetenland was for Czechoslovakia. The Foreign Office had already begun to think that Hitler had serious designs on Poland, and that he had to be stopped by offering a guarantee to Poland. The problem was that a secret agreement would not have the slightest deterrent effect. British concerns were heightened when Ian Colvin, the young Berlin correspondent of the *News Chronicle* and a man with close ties to British intelligence, reported to Halifax and Chamberlain that General Ludwig von Beck, who had resigned as chief of staff in August 1938 in protest against Hitler's war plans, was in his pocket, from whom he had learnt that Hitler intended to attack Poland in the immediate future. This information, coming from the opposition within the German armed forces and which was heavily spiced for maximum effect, coupled with Tilea's warnings, indicated that Poland and Romania would go the way of Czechoslovakia, and that Hitler would then attack in the west, unless Britain and France took decisive action to stiffen both countries.

On 31 March 1939 Chamberlain announced in the House of Commons that if Poland's independence was threatened and if it offered armed resistance, Britain and France would 'lend her all support in their power'. It seemed that Britain had undergone a minor revolution in foreign policy, and Chamberlain's critics were momentarily silenced. Then it was pointed out that the term 'independence' was hopelessly vague, unlike 'territorial integrity', and was open to interpretation. Furthermore, the guarantee would not apply if the Poles showed 'provocative or stupid obstinacy'. The constitutionality of Chamberlain's guarantee was also highly questionable. Four days later Beck visited London where he downplayed the threat from Germany, refused to consider closer relations with the Soviet Union, and remained silent over Danzig. The British extended the interim guarantee to Poland, encouraged by Beck's assurances that it was unlikely ever to be invoked, and expressed their determination to press ahead with the finalization of a pact, which would include France.

On 3 April Hitler ordered OKW to draw up plans for 'Case White', the invasion of Poland, and to be ready for war by 1 September. On 20 April he celebrated his 50th birthday with a massive military parade in Berlin. A week later he rescinded the Non-Aggression Pact with Poland of 1934 and the Anglo-German Naval Agreement of 1935. The following day he rejected President Roosevelt's appeal for world peace in a relentlessly derisive speech.

Britain and France now pursued a twin-track policy. They prepared for a war that now seemed almost inevitable, while still frantically trying to preserve the peace. This merely fuelled Hitler's contempt for Britain, which he petulantly announced was run by a bunch of Jews, and therefore left him no alternative but to fight it out. Some Nazi ideologues announced that Britain's incomprehensible behaviour was due to the English being the lost tribe of Israel and that Chamberlain should be awarded the medal 'Pour le Sémite'. Hitler proclaimed France to be 'degenerate', 'decadent' and 'pacifist'. Chamberlain never realized the disastrous consequences of his disreputable foreign policy, and in 1939 announced that Hitler would not start a world war over Danzig. Daladier had no intention of dying for Danzig and told his cabinet as late as August 1939 that a deal could still be made with Hitler. On 28 August 1939 the British government offered to guarantee a negotiated settlement between Germany and Poland. This was a matter of great concern to Hitler, who admitted to his generals that he [299] was fearful that some '*Schweinehund*' would negotiate a settlement and that he would be stuck with a second Munich.

On 11 August 1939 Hitler met Carl Burkhardt, the League of Nations' commissioner in Danzig, telling him that Russia was his main enemy and that he could not understand why the West failed to realize this simple fact. This being regretfully the case he would feel obliged to reach an agreement with the Russians, defeat the West and then attack the Soviet Union. Less than a fortnight later, on 23 August, the world was shocked with the signing of the Molotov–Ribbentrop Pact. That this was obviously a purely temporary expedient was clear to Hitler's entourage. His Luftwaffe adjutant, Nicolaus von Bredow, reported that in the autumn of 1939 he frequently heard Hitler express his determination to attack the Soviet Union. The generals were delighted with the pact, welcoming the idea that they were once again allies of the Soviet Union as they had been in the Weimar Republic.

The Ribbentrop–Molotov Pact

From 1933 Stalin had kept his options open. He hoped to maintain contact with the Germans with trade talks and communication between the Red Army and the Reichswehr, while at the same time attempting to build an effective system of collective security against the Nazi threat. As Germany's anti-Soviet propaganda grew increasingly strident, collective security became a pressing concern. Stalin abandoned his ideological principles and decided to protect the Red Revolution with traditional balance of power politics, playing one set of capitalist states off against another in what would amount to a revival of the Triple Entente. The Germans were genuinely perplexed by Stalin. Hitler insisted that he was insane, 'otherwise one cannot explain his bloodthirstiness'. Goebbels noted in his diaries in 1937: 'Stalin is shooting again. A sick man. Brain defect.'³

In April 1939 the Soviet commissar for foreign affairs, Litvinov, proposed a mutual security pact with Britain and France. He had no illusions about Germany. In June 1938 he had cautioned:

> Germany is striving not only for the restoration of rights trampled underfoot by the Versailles Treaty, not only for the restoration of its pre-war boundaries, but is basing its foreign policy on unlimited aggression, even going so far as to talk of subjecting all other races and peoples to the so-called German race.

[300] No reply was forthcoming by 3 May when Litvinov, the champion of collective security and a Jew, was replaced by Stalin's boot-faced hatchet man, Molotov. The Soviets had ample reason to doubt the West's determination to stop Hitler, and dissension between London and Paris on the susceptibilities of Poland and Romania about an understanding with the Soviet Union did nothing to persuade them otherwise. In spite of Hitler's 'Prague Coup' in March, which had so alarmed Stalin, the response from both London and Paris was dilatory, half-hearted and offhand. There was an exchange of notes throughout the summer that led to nothing. Finally a relatively low-rank Anglo-French delegation went to Moscow, travelling on a slow merchant vessel rather than by air. This lack of any sense of urgency was underlined by the fact that the British delegation had no written powers to negotiate, and the French were not authorized to sign any agreement. The British delegation was led by Admiral Aylmer Ranfurly Plunkett-Ernle-Erle-Drax, Britain's leading naval strategist, a man with no political experience, who was given instructions to begin military discussions and to stall until a political agreement was reached. These unpromising talks began on 12 August and two days later Marshal Voroshilov asked the only really pertinent question, one which hitherto had been studiously avoided: would Poland and Romania allow Soviet troops on their territory? When Colonel Beck was asked about this ticklish question his response was that this would amount to yet another partition of Poland, adding with a characteristic flourish: 'With the Germans we risk losing our liberty. With the Russians we lose our soul.' By 19 August Stalin realized that an agreement with Britain and France was out of the question and that he would have to seek an agreement with Germany that would at least give him time to prepare for a war that he felt was virtually inevitable. Unfortunately, he seriously miscalculated the time when Germany would turn the tables on him.

The Soviets had sent out some feelers to Germany in April and May 1939, but Hitler was still somewhat suspicious. On 23 May he told his Generals that he intended to attack Poland in the near future and that he needed to make sure that the Soviet Union did not become party to a guarantee to Poland. He was encouraged by the fact that negotiations between London, Paris and Moscow were obviously going very badly, and at the end of the month cautious moves were made towards the Soviet Union. These contacts continued in June and July, but it was not until the end of the month that the Germans made a definite move. The foreign office was all in favour of an agreement with the Soviet Union, which they thought would be in the tradition of the Convention of Tauroggen, the

Reinsurance Treaty and Rapallo. Dr Julius Schnurre, the Wilhelmstrasse's economics expert, invited Astakhov, the Soviet chargé d'affaires, and Barbarin, a senior trade official, to Ernest's, a fashionable Berlin restaurant serving Baltic specialities, where he let it be known that Germany saw no real reason why there should not be an understanding between the two countries since Britain, not the Soviet Union, was the main enemy. Astakhov agreed that such an understanding was desirable and added that the Soviet Union accepted Germany's claim to Danzig and the Corridor. These sentiments were repeated a week later to Astakhov by Ribbentrop, who with his unfailing ability to get hold of the wrong end of any stick was somewhat concerned that the Moscow talks with Britain and France might make some progress. By the middle of the month the Germans offered a 25-year non-aggression pact, which Ribbentrop said he would sign at any time after 18 August. The Soviets played for time, demanding a definition of spheres of influence and stressing the need for thorough preparation. On 20 August Hitler sent a telegram to Stalin almost begging him to receive Ribbentrop by the 23rd at the latest. Twenty-four hours later Stalin's reply came, to the immense relief of the Germans. Ribbentrop, whose frenetic diplomatic travelling had inspired the British humorous magazine *Punch* to give him the title of 'The Wandering Aryan', flew immediately to Moscow.

The signing of the pact in the early morning of 24 August was accompanied by a mammoth and bibulous banquet. Stalin told Ribbentrop, who was the first minister of a foreign power whom he had received personally, that Britain should not be allowed to rule the world, but warned him that it would be a formidable adversary. Ribbentrop assured his host that the Anti-Comintern Pact was aimed against Britain and not the Soviet Union. Stalin reassured his guest that he would never betray his new partner.

The pact did not contain the usual escape clause found in other Soviet non-aggression pacts, and thus applied even in the event of German aggression against Poland. Soviet claims to Polish territory, to the Baltic States and to Bessarabia were acknowledged in a secret protocol. Germany and the Soviet Union would thus meet face to face on the Narev, Vistula and San, in a subsequent agreement also on the Pissa. Astakhov, who had done so much to bring about this agreement, but who had presciently warned Molotov that the Germans could not be trusted further than their limited ability to spit, and that they were likely to break any agreement whenever it suited them, was recalled to Moscow, flung into prison and murdered in 1941.

[302] War

Hitler assembled his generals at the Obersalzberg and told them that the Nazi-Soviet pact would make it impossible for either Britain or France to give Poland any assistance and that Poland was now helpless. He then gave orders for the invasion of Poland to begin on 26 August. The Polish-German customs talks were abruptly halted when the German delegation made a series of totally unacceptable demands. On 25 August Hitler made a 'large, comprehensive offer' to Henderson in response to the passing of the Emergency Powers Act and the ratification of the Anglo-Polish Treaty, which included cooperation with the British Empire and disarmament talks in return for a free hand in Danzig and the Corridor. On the same day he ordered a postponement of the invasion in the hope that Polish obduracy would give him an excuse to invade.

Chamberlain told the Swedish industrialist Birger Dahlerus, whom Göring had engaged as an intermediary, that Britain might be prepared to accept German control over Danzig, but not over the Corridor, which he suggested might be placed under international control. On the evening of 28 August Henderson downed half a bottle of champagne and, thus fortified, lost his temper with Hitler and launched into a denunciation of the perfidies of German foreign policy. Hitler was relatively unruffled and said that the British proposals were interesting. The Polish government dug in its heels. Mussolini told the British Ambassador on 31 August that Italy would remain neutral and proposed what looked like a second Munich, but Hitler told the Italian ambassador, Attolico, that the die was cast and that Poland would be invaded at 4.45 the following morning. On the dot the battleship *Schleswig-Holstein* opened fire on the Polish garrison on the Westerplatte near Danzig while Stuka dive-bombers swooped down on the city. Europe was once again at war.

Hitler was a daring gambler, driven by certain obsessions, but he was also a master tactician who skilfully exploited all those chance opportunities that were offered to him. He did not have a blueprint for foreign policy, but he was driven by a fanatical anti-Communism, a virulent racism, a determination to carve out *Lebensraum* in the east and by the conviction that war was an end in itself, a means by which the country could be kept vigilant and strengthened, the weak weeded out. He did not deviate from his course, disregarding public opinion and remaining true to his ideological principles. Everything moved so rapidly and unexpectedly, too much depended on so many contingencies for there to have been a detailed master plan. How these obsessions were to be realized and in what order remained open.

Would it be with Britain against the Soviet Union, or initially with the Soviet Union against the West; with Poland against the Soviet Union, or vice versa? The permutations are almost endless. The situation was also complicated by the number of key figures who made important decisions in foreign policy, including Göring, Ribbentrop, Rosenberg and Schacht. None of these paladins was ever able to act independently from the Führer's will and Hitler, for all his vacillations and hesitations, his indifference to certain issues and his hasty improvisations, was firmly in charge of foreign policy. On occasion he may have been influenced by others, but all the great decisions were his and his alone. The end result was the horror of war and genocide on an unimaginable scale, the memory of which continues to plague a damaged world. As Hitler accurately predicted, the end result would be 'world power or annihilation'. Fortunately for us all, Hitler's *va banque* gamble failed and the Third Reich was buried beneath the rubble.

CHAPTER 9

THE SHOAH

The invasion of Poland marked a new and terrible phase in what the Nazis called 'Jewish politics' (*Judenpolitik*) within the context of the quest for living space, the racial reordering of the east and the foundation of the Great Germanic Reich. As the prospect of ever achieving this dystopian goal grew increasingly dim the anti-Semitic and anti-Bolshevik aspects were emphasized to the extent that Hitler could proudly proclaim in his political testament, dictated on the eve of his suicide, that he had at least made the Jews atone for the war which they had provoked. He may not have achieved his aim of forcing 45 million people behind the Urals, but at least he had almost managed to leave Eastern Europe virtually 'cleansed of Jews' (*Judenrein*).

Jews had not only to be removed from the east to make way for Aryan settlers, they also had to be eliminated in the rest of Europe, since they were the embodiment of all that was wrong with the modern world and a deadly threat to the purity of the Germanic race. As a result of this crazed vision 6 million Jews were rounded up, shot, gassed or sent to one of the six death factories. Millions of Slavs were also murdered, but the sheer impossibility of the undertaking, combined with the tenacity of the Red Army, frustrated General Plan East which called for the slaughter of an excess population of at least 30 million.

Many ingenious and some thoughtless explanations have been put forward in an attempt to account for this seemingly inexplicable crime. Were Germans for centuries prey to an 'eliminatory anti-Semitism', waiting for a regime that would remove all restraints on this murderous intent? Or did a group of doctors, geneticists, biologists and lawyers come to the conclusion, on the basis of their expertise and scientific knowledge, that the German race would be rendered healthier by a systematic ethnic cleansing? Others have put forward the idea that conditions in the east under German occupation were so chaotic and the food shortage so chronic that men on the spot took it upon themselves to seek a radical solution in mass murder. Those historians who believe that the Final Solution was the result of long-term planning and intent have been challenged by those who speak of a process of 'cumulative radicalization', caused by a number of structural imperatives and individual decisions. The first group, often called 'intentionalists', argue that the answer lies ultimately in Hitler's vicious anti-Semitism as adumbrated in *Mein Kampf.* Those in the 'structuralist' camp insist that this industrialized mass murder was not ordered and controlled from the centre, but resulted from decisions by local officials and SS commanders who were ever eager, in Ian Kershaw's felicitous phrase, to 'work towards the Führer' and who acted according to the changing fortunes of war. The resulting debate became increasingly acrimonious, exaggerated and ultimately tedious, both sides overlooking the immense complexity of the motives behind this most monstrous of crimes committed by Hitler's Germans.

The structuralists tend to overlook the fundamental importance of ideology as the motive force behind National Socialist policies. Blinded by the search for functional or material causes they discount the indisputable fact that thoughts frequently determine action. Radical biological anti-Semitism was at the very heart of Hitler's worldview and of all those who were held in his charismatic sway. Race was the clue to world history and to political action, in much the same way as class was to Karl Marx. The Aryan race was seen to be in mortal danger from a sinister international Jewish conspiracy that involved both international finance and Bolshevism. Intentionalists, most of whom argue that Hitler made this momentous decision in the spring or early summer of 1941, place too much emphasis on Hitler's decision-making, and discount the role of his subordinates within a polycratic structure.

Adolf Hitler was the incorporation of National Socialism, he was the final authority for the determination and interpretation of its ideology, and he was ultimately the one who turned theory into practice. Without his fanatical anti-Semitism the Shoah would never have happened. The charismatic Führer was the source of all power; his was the definitive sanction for all actions. None of his satraps and minions could ever have carried out mass murder on such a scale without his approval and encouragement. This does not mean that the hundreds of thousands actively involved and the millions of those who tacitly approved were simply carrying out orders, and were thus the innocent instruments of his demonic will. Charismatic leadership is a two-way affair and wholly dependent on the approval and willingness of the masses. There were instances of spontaneous violence

[306] and brutality, but the intricate planning and execution of the Final Solution was done in the name, according to the will and was seen as the work of the Führer. Anti-Semitism was at the very heart of National Socialism, the fundamental principle on which the new society was to be built, and it was precisely this deadly state-sponsored anti-Semitism that was the unique defining feature of Hitler's tyranny.

This does not necessarily mean that Hitler was planning the mass murder of the European Jews in the early 1920s, but this was still the logical consequence of the sulphurous fulminations of *Mein Kampf*. From the outset he insisted that the Jews were a deadly danger to the Germanic race and to European civilization and that they had to be 'removed'. Quite how this was to be done remained an open question. He toyed with various schemes of forcible emigration, shipping the Jews off to Madagascar, or rounding them up in a 'reservation' somewhere in the east. The road to Auschwitz may have been twisted, but it ended there. If the Jews really posed such a deadly threat then they had to be ruthlessly exterminated. In Hitler's eyes the Jews were the source of all that was evil in the modern world and he believed that it was they who had plunged the world into war. As Goebbels reported in his diary, he announced to a group of Gauleiter in characteristically pseudo-religious terms in December 1941:[1] 'He [Hitler] prophesied to the Jews that if they were ever again the cause of a world war, it would result in their extermination. That was not an empty threat. The world war is here; the extermination of the Jews must be the necessary consequence. The question is to be tackled without sentimentality.' The ultimate horror was the outcome of the work of ideological frenzy, immoral planners, fanaticized mass murderers, anti-Semitic radicalism, institutional constraints and personal rivalries, economic interests and military limitations.

Poland

The RSHA prepared for the invasion of Poland by forming Section IIP for Polish affairs under SS-Obersturmbannführer Germann, while Otto Ohlendorf established Judenreferat II.112 to deal with Polish Jews. As a result of a decision made at a top-level conference in July 1939, four Einsatzkommandos were formed based on Vienna, Oppeln, Breslau and Dramburg in Pomerania, and were told that they might soon see service in the Ukraine. A fifth was added shortly afterwards in Allenstein. They were largely made up of men chosen from SS and police units and followed closely behind the victorious Wehrmacht as it marched across Poland. They were ably assisted by units of the Secret Field Police (Geheime Feldpolizei – GFP), which was the military equivalent of the Gestapo and was directly under the command of OKH. It was a matter of pure chance whether a policeman was drafted to the GFP or to the Einsatzkommandos, and their tasks were virtually identical, except that the GFP were not primarily concerned with murdering Jews, although they were happy to round up Jews and hand them over to the Einsatzkommandos. The Field Gendarmerie Division (FGA), also under OKH, was the military equivalent of the Order Police. The Auxiliary Police Battalion 101 proudly claimed to have killed 83,000 people in Poland between 1942 and 1943, most of whom were Jews.

The initial remit of the Einsatzkommandos was to collect material on Jews, Catholics and Freemasons, but on 7 September Heydrich told the heads of the Gestapo, Kripo and SD that the Polish elites would have to be 'rendered harmless' and that Poland would become a German protectorate. On the following day he announced that the 'aristocracy, sky pilots [*Popen*] and Jews' must be killed. Some 30,000 representatives of the Polish elite were promptly thrown into concentration camps where, in Heydrich's words, they were 'rendered harmless'. The formation of Jewish Councils (*Judenräte*) and the expulsion of Jews to the General Government began on 7 September 1939; on 20 September Hitler told the commanding generals that Polish Jews would be driven out of those parts of western Poland that were to be annexed by the Reich and that the Jews would be herded into ghettos. Heydrich repeated this on the following day, ordering all Jews to be rounded up and forced into ghettos in the larger cities. This was a major task in which the army was more than willing to cooperate. He added ominously that this measure would 'make subsequent measures easier'. The Sipo and the SD were formally under army command during the Polish campaign, but Himmler's orders to them were simply not passed on to the military authorities, and the SS acted like maddened mercenaries. The Einsatzkommandos committed acts of wilful and pointless sadism from the outset, and bore no resemblance whatsoever to the systematic, scientific, bureaucratic and banally evil murderers to be found in some versions of these terrible events. Some army units also ran amok, somewhat to the alarm of the generals who were concerned about preserving military discipline. OKH and the SS were soon on a collision course. No solution was found in Poland, but the Wehrmacht was able to ensure that the SD and Sipo did not follow behind the troops during the attack on France.

A number of Germans living in Bromberg/Bydgoszcz (the estimates range from 150 to 1,000) were murdered by Poles, provoking ferocious reprisals in which units from 4th Army joined in with the murderers in Einsatzgruppe

[308]   IV. Himmler issued orders that all *franc tireurs* should be executed. They
were generously interpreted and the Einsatzgruppen indulged in an orgy
of slaughter. Little distinction was made between Jews and *franc tireurs*
and these indiscriminate killings were enthusiastically supported by those
Germans living in Poland organized in 'self-protection units', as well as
by units of the Wehrmacht. The commander in Poland, General Johannes
Blaskowitz, wrote two memoranda condemning the behaviour of the
Einsatzkommandos, but in general the military leadership was either
pathetically weak or shamefully compliant, so that Himmler and Heydrich,
certain of Hitler's support, could do whatever they liked in Poland.

In October about half of German-occupied Poland was formally incorporated into the Reich; the remainder was called the General Government,
designed as a reservoir of helots to serve the master race. Hitler appointed
Himmler Reich Commissar for the Strengthening of the German Race
(RKFDV) with the remit to expel all Poles and Jews from the area recently
annexed by Germany: 325,000 Poles were deported, their property stolen,
and they were replaced by Germans from the Baltic States and Volhynia by
the end of 1940. Hundreds of thousands of 'protected' Poles[2] were shipped
off to work in armaments factories in Germany or on the land – some
voluntarily, others forcibly. Meanwhile, by early 1940 the newly-annexed
territories were proclaimed *Judenrein*, the Jews having been forced into
appallingly squalid and unsanitary ghettos in Warsaw, Cracow, Lvov, Lublin
and Radom. Life was made even more miserable when German soldiers
began what they were pleased to call 'ghetto tourism', which involved plunder, murder and taking snapshots of their hapless victims. Goebbels visited
the Lublin ghetto in September 1939 and remarked that 'Jewry must be
destroyed' since Jews 'are not humans but animals'. Hundreds of thousands
of Jews were denied even this temporary respite and were murdered by the
Einsatzgruppen. Hitler issued specific orders to exterminate the Polish intelligentsia, and 17 per cent of those listed as 'intellectuals' were murdered
in the Extra-Special Pacification Action known as Operation A. Also in early
1940 the SS built a concentration camp in the former cavalry barracks at
Auschwitz where Polish prisoners were treated as slave labour and were
executed at will.

The SS and the Wehrmacht were given *carte blanche* in Poland so that
every sadist and fanatical racist could give vent to their basest instincts without fear of reprisal. Whatever the various motives it was known that they
could do whatever they wished with the 3 million Jews in Poland and that
Hitler would raise no objections. Gradually the pressure mounted for a radical
solution to the various problems consequent upon the deportation and

ghettoization of Poland's Jews. Some argued that the ghettos were sources of deadly diseases that could all too easily spread. Others complained that their upkeep was an unacceptable burden. There were complaints that the movement of such large numbers of people placed an excessive strain on the transportation network, or that the process of 'de-Jewing' (*Entjudung*) and resettlement by Germans should be speeded up. All the while the Einsatzgruppen took perverse pride in their murderous duties.

For the time being efforts were concentrated on forcing all remaining Jews into the ghettos. Himmler in March 1940 condemned 'the Bolshevik method of physical extermination' as 'unGermanic and impossible'. Heydrich argued that three options were open: Jews should all be forced into the ghettos, a huge Jewish 'reservation' or 'Reich ghetto' could be formed in the area around Lublin, or the Jews could be forced to emigrate. For the time being ghettos seemed the least problematic solution. Hitler needed the area around Lublin as a deployment area for the invasion of the Soviet Union, and emigration was not a viable option since the Jews were likely to join the ranks of Germany's enemies or flee to Palestine where they would plot revenge. Franz Rademacher at the foreign office was particularly concerned that Palestine might become a 'second Rome', the centre of the world Jewish conspiracy. Furthermore the transport network was tied up bringing Germans from the Baltic States, the Bukovina and Dobruja under the terms of the Soviet-German treaty. Earlier attempts to force Jews across the Soviet border with generous support from the Wehrmacht had not been successful. The Soviets drove the Jews back again into the General Government where they were shot by the Einsatzgruppen. The aim of creating a Jewish Reservation beyond the Ostwall in an area between the Vistula and the Bug would obviously have to be postponed until after the defeat of the Soviet Union.

Adolf Eichmann was entrusted with the task of deporting Jews from Austria, but here too it initially proved impossible to find anywhere they could be detained. Initially, a large group was herded together around Nisko on the San, a small town roughly half way between Lublin and Przemýsl. The operation was not a success. The forced immigrants were not welcomed by the German authorities and were forced across the Soviet border, resulting in such a chaotic situation that the operation had to be stopped. Heydrich was impressed by Eichmann's dedication and promoted him to head section IVB4 in the RSHA with a broad responsibility to 'clear the eastern provinces'. On 7 October Himmler was given plenipotentiary powers in Poland and 10 days later Hitler told Keitel that Poland was to become the glacis for the deployment of the German Army against the Soviet Union.

[310] On 25 October the military government in Poland ended and Hans Frank, head of the BNSDJ, president of the Academy of German Law and minister without portfolio, was appointed governor of the General Government, while Danzig, East Prussia and the Wartheland were formally annexed. This meant that the SS and the Totenkopfverbände were no longer under military control, which admittedly had been extremely lax. The military authorities remained in command in Western Europe, but in France and Belgium the Sipo and the SD were given special powers to deal with Jews without having first to consult the military.

Himmler acted immediately, issuing an order on 30 October calling for the expulsion of 500,000 Jews and an equal number of Poles from the recently annexed provinces. This proved to be an impossible undertaking, so that by mid-December only 88,000 people, mostly Jews, had been deported. Hans Frank, who announced that the only good Jew was a dead Jew, objected vigorously to his General Government being converted into a dumping ground for Europe's Jews, and placed as many obstacles in Himmler's way as possible. Goebbels responded by saying of Frank: 'a great deal of cackling, but no eggs'[3]. The deportation of Jews from Germany began in February 1940, beginning with 1,000 people from Stettin, but it was not possible to accommodate more than a handful of these unfortunates, even in the most unspeakable of conditions. In March Jews from Schneidemühl in Pomerania were deported to Poland on the orders of the Gauleiter, but this had to be stopped for lack of room. On 12 March 1940 Hitler petulantly pointed out that the Jewish problem was a 'problem of space – and that no space was available'. In October Jews from Alsace-Lorraine, the Saarland, the Palatinate and Baden were shipped off to Poland, but the numbers were still relatively small. By the end of 1941 it had proved possible to find room in the General Government for only 20,000 of the 350,000 German Jews and 110,000 Jews from the western provinces of Poland. Some 2,800 of Germany's 30,000 Gypsies joined these victims and awaited the same uncertain fate. On 4 December 1940 Eichmann announced that 5.8 million Jews would soon be moved to an as yet undesignated area as a preliminary to the 'final solution of the Jewish problem'.

The situation in the ghettos was frightful. Between 410,000 and 590,000 inmates of the Warsaw ghetto lived on average 6 to 7 people per room; 100,000 had died by the autumn of 1941. Those who did not die as a result of such attrition were to be worked to death. From the outset the 'attritionist' and 'productionist' approach to the elimination of Europe's Jews existed side by side, and were in no sense contradictory.

Franz Rademacher as head of Section III of department D (Germany) in the foreign office was made responsible for the Jewish question. He favoured a scheme, first suggested by a couple of British anti-Semites and entertained by those on the wilder shores of racism in France, Poland and Romania, which involved shipping all Europe's Jews to the French island colony of Madagascar. The French foreign minister and leading appeaser, Georges Bonnet, had told Ribbentrop in December 1938 that France wanted to get rid of some of its Jews by sending them to Madagascar. The viciously anti-Semitic Polish government entertained similar schemes. The climate was known to be particularly unhealthy, so it was assumed that the mortality rate would be extremely high. The Madagascar plan was first drawn up in the RSHA and finalized on 15 August 1940. Hitler was kept fully in the picture. It called for the deportation of 4 million Jews at a rate of 3,000 per day. This suggestion was forwarded to Rademacher, who complained that the numbers were far too low and upped them to 6 million. He also made a sharp distinction between eastern and western Jews. In his view eastern Jews provided 'reproductively vigorous and talmudically trained young people who would form the future Jewish intelligentsia'. They were to be held as hostages so as to keep American Jews in check. Western Jews could be sent to Madagascar. A number of officials in the RSHA also favoured the Madagascar Project, in spite of the fact that it would be virtually impossible to convoy some 3 million Polish Jews, to be followed by 7 million others from elsewhere in Europe, in the face of British naval supremacy to a colony which formally belonged to Vichy France. The idea of creating a vast 'reservation' somewhere in the east, preferably behind the Urals, was also not a valid option. All depended on the fortunes of war. Meanwhile the local satraps, such as Gauleiter Greiser in Wartheland, were demanding radical methods to get rid of the Jews. Discussions began in the summer of 1941 about the possibility of building huge concentration camps into which the Polish Jews could be herded.

The fate of the Soviet Jews

In the course of planning the invasion of the Soviet Union it became clear that there would be about another 4 million Jews in the area under German control. Hitler refused to consider any moral restraints on his racial war of extermination. In July he told the Croatian Marshal Kvaternik that Europe would be rid of Jews and that he did not care where they went. Himmler instructed his Einsatzgruppen that they were to shoot all the Jews they found

[312] behind the front. On 13 March 1941 Himmler was given 'special duties under orders from the Führer'; the SS was made fully independent from the Army and given the right to decide who was a member of the 'Jewish-Bolshevik intelligentsia' and who should be liquidated. Clearly murder on such a massive scale could not be carried out without the cooperation of the Wehrmacht, as the Einsatzkommandos did not have enough men. Lengthy discussions were held between the Wehrmacht and the SS that resulted in an agreement that SS liaison officers should be attached to each army group. On 11 June Halder issued instructions that the army was to give the SS its full support in its murderous endeavours behind the front line.

Himmler ordered that all Jews between the ages of 17 and 45 should be regarded as partisans and should therefore be executed. The age restrictions were soon lifted and the large-scale murder of women and children began as early as July 1941. Two days after the invasion of the Soviet Union he ordered a General Plan East to be drawn up. The details were worked out by officials in the Reich Commissariat for the Strengthening of the German Race (RKF) and the RSHA. The report was presented to him on 19 July 1941 and called for the elimination of 31 million people, the 'de-Jewing' (*Entjudung*) of the entire area under German control and the settlement of some 10 million 'racial Germans' in Poland and the Soviet Union. On 28 July 1941 Himmler told officials in Rosenberg's Commissariat for Eastern Affairs that the Führer had 'placed the responsibility for carrying out this difficult order [to murder the Jews] on my shoulders'. There is absolutely no doubt whatsoever that Himmler, a man who was slavishly subservient to Hitler, was telling the truth. At the end of July 1941 Göring ordered Heydrich to make the necessary preparations for an 'overall solution' (*Gesamtlösung*) of the Jewish question in the parts of Europe under German influence. Heydrich dragged his feet, presumably because he was given no indication from on high as to what form it should take, and also because a fierce debate was still raging about how to define who was Jewish. Among the more bizarre instances of such confusion was whether or not the Soviet Karaman and the Krimshak peoples were Jewish, and therefore should be murdered. The matter was referred to Professor Franz Alfred Six in Section VIIB of the RSHA, who handed it on to an underling, one Dr Ballenseiffen. The resulting opinion was that the Karaman, who had practised a heterodox form of anti-rabbinical Judaism founded by Anan ben David in AD 760, were not 'racially Jewish', whereas the Krimshaks, who had no connection whatsoever with Judaism, were Jewish and therefore were to be liquidated.

The Einsatzkommandos designated for duties in the Soviet Union were given intensive ideological training at Pretzsch on the Elbe, beginning in

May 1941. They were told that their principal task, as it had been in Poland, was to liquidate the political elite. The order to kill all Jews who were Communist Party members had not yet been given. As soon as Barbarossa was launched they set about their murderous business with grim determination and with the enthusiastic cooperation of the local population. From the outset Soviet Jews were to be shot as reprisals, or used as slave labour and given minimal rations. A curfew was imposed at 6 p.m., all those over the age of 14 were to wear the Star of David badge, no Jew was permitted to work in public office and all Jewish businesses were seized. The task of identifying who was Jewish was made much simpler by the fact that Soviet Jews were considered to be a nationality and were identified as such in their papers. There is strong evidence that an order to murder all Soviet Jews, regardless of whether or not they were party members, was issued in August 1941. Mass murder on this scale was also felt to be desirable as a means of relieving the pressure on food supplies. It was argued that there was no need for skilled Jewish labour given the de-industrialization policy in the Soviet Union. Those who insisted that certain industries were essential to the war effort managed to get a stay of execution for any Jews deemed to be irreplaceable. The Germans found themselves faced with something of a dilemma. They needed Jews to work in army hospitals, as cleaners in their offices or as labourers in Organisation Todt (OT); on the other hand they faced the ideological imperative to murder those who posed such a deadly threat to the 'racial community' and who placed such an intolerable strain on the food supply. Added incentives were that the mass murder of Jews left a million empty dwellings, private individuals profited greatly from plunder, and about 3 per cent of the cost of the civil administration was subsidized by commandeering Jewish property.

By the second half of 1942 the murderers got the upper hand over the pragmatists, so that even skilled Jewish workers were killed. Slightly more than half of the Soviet Jews were killed between March 1942 and March 1943. In some cases, such as in Białystok, the local SS and police chief and the civil administration argued that the Jews were needed to work in industry, whereas Himmler insisted that ideological considerations were paramount. The result was that in some instances this grim process was somewhat slowed down. The civil and military authorities were responsible for the millions who starved to death. The SS preferred swifter and more immediate methods. Similarly it was the civil administration, aided by the military, not the SS, SD or Sipo, that was responsible for defining who was Jewish, for building ghettos, and for overall health and housing. Responsibility for all these horrors was widely distributed, an awkward

[314] fact that was long disguised by attempting to shift all the blame on to the shoulders of a small group of corybantic fanatics in the SS.

In Estonia SS-Standartenführer Martin Sandberger, formerly from RSHA Section IIIB dealing with the immigration of 'racial Germans', was ably assisted by Estonians in rounding up 60,000 suspects: 5,634 were killed, 5,623 were sent to concentration camps, and 18,893 were incarcerated in more conventional establishments. SS-Oberführer Erich Ehrlinger was a cold-blooded killer who had thoroughly enjoyed his tour of duty in Poland with Einsatzgruppe IV and was given command of Einsatzgruppe 1B in Lithuania where his bestial inclinations were no longer partially restrained by having to report to a superior officer. Eager locals joined in an orgy of slaughter of which the notorious massacre of Jews in Kowno was but one horrific example. SS-Brigadeführer Erwin Schulz, former head of Section 1B in the RSHA, responsible for training and education, as head of Einsatzkommando 5A found that he did not have the stomach for his new assignment and managed to get himself posted back to Berlin, ending the war in comparative safety and comfort as head of the Sipo and SD in Salzburg. Schulz (born in 1900), Ehrlinger (born in 1910) and Sandberger (born in 1911) were all university educated, and were typical of the intelligent, ideologically driven young men in the upper echelons of the RSHA.

Einsatzgruppe B under SS-Obergruppenführer Erich von dem Bach-Zelewski, acting behind the front of Army Group Centre, announced that they had killed 30,000 people by August, 90 per cent of whom were Jews, and in October began the systematic murder of all Jews in the area under their control, except for those still able to work. Bach-Zelewski usually left the shooting of children to Ukrainian units who took special delight in throwing babies up in the air and shooting them like clay pigeons. The army group commander, Field Marshal Fedor von Bock, sent a message to Bach-Zelewski congratulating him on his excellent work, and when General Walter von Reichenau, commander of 6th Army, was informed that Jewish children were being murdered he expressed his heartfelt approval. Bach-Zelewski, who turned state's evidence at Nuremberg, said: 'Of course the liquidation of women and children is a crime . . . but my conscience has remained clear, because I have always acted humanely, even when I was full of hatred.'

Hermann Fegelein, a sadistic brute and former stable boy who was to rise to prominence as Hitler's brother-in-law when he married Eva Braun's sister, commanded the SS Cavalry Brigade responsible for a series of mass executions of Jews in the Pripit marshes in August. Fegelein was executed on 28 April 1945 on Hitler's orders, charged with desertion for having left the bunker without permission.

To the south SS-Obergruppenführer Friedrich Jeckeln, who along with Bach-Zelewski had been among the prominent guests at the gala opening of Rosenberg's Institute for Research into the Jewish Question in Frankfurt in June 1941, proudly announced that he had killed 44,125 people by August, most of whom were Jews. In September he was responsible for the murder of 33,771 Jews at Babi Yar near Kiev, an unspeakable atrocity that he proudly reported 'met with the full approval of the Wehrmacht'. Jeckeln's men, ably assisted by Romanian units, had killed 100,000 people by the end of October. SS-Gruppenführer Otto Ohlendorf's Einsatzgruppe D began their mass executions of Jews at the end of August 1941 when Ohlendorf claimed that he had been given a 'Führer order', passed down by Himmler and Heydrich, that all Soviet Jews had to be killed. Ohlendorf began this grim task by rounding up 20,000 Jews at Kamenets Podolsky, where their murder was witnessed by army units. In September 5,000 Jews were murdered by Ohlendorf's men at Nikolaiev. Previously they had mostly been forced back across the border to Romania, where they were slaughtered by fascist thugs; now the Ukraine was systematically 'worked over' (*bearbeitet*) by Einsatzgruppe D.

Between 21 and 28 September 1941 2 Company 306 Police Battalion took part in Operation Chicken Farm and reported 6,000 'eggs laid' – in other words they had murdered that number of Soviet prisoners of war.

In October SS-Standartenführer Heinrich Seetzen, commanding Sonderkommando 10A of Einsatzkommando D, ordered the Jews in Mariupol to elect a 30-man council that was charged with rounding up all the Jews and making an inventory of their possessions. Eight thousand were murdered in front of an audience that included members of the SS Leibstandarte Adolf Hitler and Wehrmacht personnel. General Ewald von Kleist, commander of 1 Panzer Army in Ukraine, objected vigorously to this outrage and hauled Seetzen over the coals, but it was all to no avail. Sepp Dietrich, the commander of the Leibstandarte, gave Seetzen his full and enthusiastic support and Kleist had to accept the attachment of an Einsatzkommando from Einsatzgruppe C to his Panzer army. Kleist's superior officer, Field Marshal von Manstein, had no such scruples. In November 1941 he wrote: 'Jewry provides the middlemen between the enemy behind our backs and the remnants of the Red Army that is still fighting . . . The Jewish-Bolshevik system must be destroyed once and for all.' When Sonderkommando 10B in the Crimean town of Kertsch found itself short of personnel needed to murder 7,500 Jews, Manstein's army command stepped into the breach and provided transport, ammunition and riflemen from 46 Infantry Division to finish the job.

[316]   Even mixed marriages offered no asylum. The children were murdered along with the non-Jewish partner. Elsewhere, the Wehrmacht massacred Jews of their own accord, but by the end of August 1941 an order was issued that mass executions should be left to the Einsatzkommandos, and that army personnel were not permitted to witness them. This order was more honoured in the breach than in the observance. In the autumn of 1941, 707 Infantry Division murdered thousands of Jews. In January 1942 Einsatzgruppe D was ordered to murder 60,000 Jews in the area around Vinnitza, north-east of Czernowitz, where Hitler intended to build his head-quarters. At least 28,000 Jews were promptly murdered. The Wehrmacht was responsible for 10,000 of these deaths.

In Posen SS-Obersturmbannführer Rolf-Heinz Höppner, the 31-year-old SD commander, wrote to Eichmann on 16 July 1941 suggesting that a camp for 300,000 Jews should be built in the Wartheland where the women would be sterilized and the men put to work. He added his concern that by the onset of winter there might not be enough food to feed these people and therefore: 'Serious consideration should be paid to whether it might not be the most humane solution to finish off those Jews who are incapable of working by use of a method that works quickly.'

On the following day Heydrich wrote a memorandum in which he ordered that all important state functionaries, civil servants in charge of local offices, leading figures in the economy, Soviet intelligentsia, all Jews, agit-ators and 'fanatical Communists', criminals, 'socially inferior elements', and 'Asiatics' should be arrested, placed in camps, sorted out and either be killed or released. Heydrich had already issued an order to this effect to the HSSPFs in the east. From the outset exceptions were made. One official pointed out that the 'total eradication' of the Jews would have dire consequences since many of them were skilled craftsmen who were needed in 'industries essen-tial for the war effort'. 'Asiatics' were first seen as fanatical Communists who had been moved to the West to ensure ideological conformity, but many of them were Muslims whom the Germans saw as potential allies and who were therefore spared. On 12 September 1941 Heydrich issued strict instructions that 'Asiatics' were to be spared and groomed as allies.

On 2 October 1941 Hitler gave a speech in which he is reported to have said:

> There can be no compromises, an absolutely clear and unambiguous solution is essential, and that means especially here in the east the total annihilation of our enemies. These enemies are not even human beings by the standards of Euro-pean culture, but they are raised up from childhood to be criminals and are trained as criminal animals. Such animals must be destroyed.

He proclaimed that 'the law of existence demands endless killing, so that the better can live'. On the day after Pearl Harbor Hitler announced that the time had come to 'clear the table' of the Jewish question. Hans Frank gave a speech in Cracow on 16 December in which he reported on a meeting with Hitler four days previously: 'We must destroy the Jews wherever we find them and wherever it is possible, in order that the entire structure of the Reich can be preserved.' He added that it would not be possible to shoot or poison 3.5 million people. Other methods had to be found. On 18 December Himmler noted: 'Jewish question – to be exterminated as partisans.' In February 1942 Hitler said: 'Today we must carry on the same fight as Pasteur and Koch led!' Speaking before 10,000 officer cadets on 15 February, he gloated over the fact that the Jews now faced a catastrophe of their own making and that they would be annihilated. In 28 July 1942 Himmler told his loyal vassal Gottlob Berger, head of the SS Main Office: 'The occupied eastern territories will be made free from Jews. The Führer had placed the responsibility for carrying out this extremely onerous order on my shoulders. No one can take that responsibility away from me.'

Einsatzgruppe A under SS-Brigadeführer Walter Stahlecker in the Baltic relied on the assistance of local murderers, rather than units of the Waffen-SS, to murder 135,567 Jews, Communists and psychiatric patients. The murder of psychiatric patients began in October 1941 when the first batch was gassed in Mogilew in Belarus. A large number of 'Asiatics' were also killed and the mass murder of Gypsies began in 1942. These 'protection units' (*Schutzmanschaften*) were made up of sundry riff-raff from the Baltic States, Ukraine and Belarus and were notoriously sadistic. At first Stahlecker had argued in favour of creating a 'Jewish reservation' with strict segregation of the sexes, where they would be made to work until they could be deported to a country outside Europe. Gauleiter Hinrich Lohse, the Reichskommissar for Ostland, was initially in favour of ghettos where Jewish labour could be exploited. Both men overlooked the fact that thousands of Jews had already been murdered. SS-Standartenführer Karl Jäger, commanding Einsatzgruppe 3 in Lithuania as well as the SD and Security Police, bitterly complained that Lohse and the army authorities were putting obstacles in the way of killing 'working Jews' and their families. He was unable to override such objections and somewhat sourly reported on 1 December 1941 that he had murdered 137,346 Jews and that 'the object of solving the Jewish problem, apart from the working Jews and their families, has been solved by EK 3'. Clearly he felt that his mission was not yet fully accomplished. Stahlecker reported in November that 'the

[318] Jewish question can be considered as resolved in Ostland'. All Jews, except those working in the ghettos, had been murdered.

Whereas throughout Eastern Europe the Germans acted according to the slogan 'expel, exploit and expunge' ('*aussiedeln, ausbeuten umhringen*'), in the Caucasus they acted quite differently. Here they posed as saviours of the subject peoples from Muscovite tyranny and, with a close eye on Turkey as a potential ally, as champions of Islam. The Caucasus was the key to a successful strategy. Only if Operation Blue, aimed at Stalingrad and the Caucasus, was combined with a successful campaign in North Africa could there be any hope for a limited victory. As it was, the Germans were defeated at Stalingrad and in North Africa, and the Soviets destroyed the oilfields that were essential to the Wehrmacht. The situation was further complicated by a typical struggle over jurisdiction in the area between the Wehrmacht, the foreign office and Rosenberg's office with the delightful acronym RmfdbO. The army wanted to tread softly with the native peoples, but officials in Göring's Four-Year Plan demanded that the region had to be ruthlessly exploited to provide supplies for the Wehrmacht. There was much talk of ending 'the slavery of the collective farms' and of freeing the people from 'Jewish-Bolshevik tyranny', but the population was forced to bring in the harvest and feed the troops. Sauckel's men continued to hunt for labour to work for the German war machine. The German variant of St Paul's and Lenin's injunction was now: 'He who does not work shall suffer death by starvation!' Meanwhile the Einsatzkommandos as the most radical instrument for the creation of *Lebensraum* hunted down Jews with ruthless determination. As in Ukraine and the Crimea, there were no ghettos that offered temporary respite and no attempt was made to exploit Jewish labour. Jews were murdered on the spot and many Muslims were among these victims simply because they were circumcised.

Wannsee and beyond

Pressure mounted in the summer of 1941 for a drastic solution to the 'Jewish question'. Disease was rampant in the Polish ghettos and the German authorities began to worry that they had a serious health hazard on their hands. There was already a serious food shortage, which would probably become chronic if millions of 'useless eaters' were not killed. As the British began their strategic bombing campaign a housing crisis loomed, although it was not until after a raid on Hamburg in September 1942 that Gauleiter Karl Kaufmann asked Hitler to order the deportation of Hamburg's Jews to free up housing for homeless 'racial comrades'. Faced with the astronomical cost of the war, economists cast greedy eyes on Jewish property and cooked up ingenious schemes whereby it could be stolen at home and abroad without violating the letter of international law. There was also increasing pressure to extend the definition of who was Jewish beyond the criteria laid down in the Nuremberg Laws. Goebbels insisted that 'half-breeds' (*Mischlinge*) should be included. The RSHA enthusiastically supported the propaganda minister and demanded that they should all be deported. SS-Obergruppenführer Walter Stuckart, secretary of state in the ministry of the interior, felt that 'half-breeds' were especially dangerous in that they combined all that was reprehensible in Jews with the sterling leadership qualities of the Germans. He insisted that they should all be sterilized. A fierce argument ensued between Stuckart and the RSHA until it was decided to shelve the question until after the war. The RSHA ignored this agreement and murdered 'half-breeds' in the east and in the concentration camps in Germany. In August Hitler ordered that all German Jews should wear a yellow Star of David. German Jews in concentration camps were murdered by the euthanasia experts, and Jews from Bohemia and Moravia were deported to Poland. In September Hitler decided that all Jews should be deported to the east, before the end of the campaign against the Soviet Union, and Goebbels suggested that this could be presented as a response to Stalin's deportation of the Volga Germans. Others warmly welcomed the proposal on the grounds that a large amount of housing would thus be made available for those who had lost their homes in the bombing raids. All shares owned by Jews had to be handed over to the state and exchanged for non-negotiable treasury bills, the debt wiped out when the bondholder was murdered. Initially their property was sold off, but in April 1942 it was decided to put an end to this unseemly profiteering in pilfered real estate, in the hope that investors would put their money into war loans.

In September 1941 Heydrich was appointed Neurath's deputy in Bohemia and Moravia, where he immediately set about making the Protectorate 'cleansed of Jews'. Neurath, an old-fashioned conservative nationalist now serving as Reich Protector, raised no objections, since he had already come to the conclusion that the only viable solution was to expel all the Czechs and settle the area with Germans.

The evacuation of German Jews began in October under terrible conditions. A third of the deportees from Stettin died on the journey east. The problem was then to find room for them. Most of those who survived the journey became the victims of mass executions by the Einsatzgruppen who were working overtime. Twenty-seven thousand Jews were killed in the

[320] Riga ghetto to provide room for the new arrivals. Within a few weeks of the invasion of the Soviet Union they had murdered half a million Jews, and by the time they finished their gruesome duties their victims numbered about a million. The local populations were encouraged to indulge in pogroms that were described in Nazi German as 'self-cleansing efforts'. Some 3,800 Jews in Lithuania were killed, often by unimaginably savage methods, in one such operation. Elsewhere the results were less satisfactory. It was reported that the 'more difficult' inhabitants of Riga killed 'only' 400 Jews.

This was clearly far too few and far too slow for those who were overeager to carry out the Führer's murderous will. Beginning in the autumn of 1941 six major concentration camps were built, designed for industrialized mass murder: Auschwitz and Majdanek (begun in September), Belzec (October), Chelmno (December), Sobibor (March 1942) and Treblinka (July 1942). This was not the result of a master plan, but was typically the result of individual drives at the local level, as ambitious activists seized the initiative within the overall context and atmosphere of encouragement and approval from on high. On 17 and 18 July 1942 Himmler visited Auschwitz and Lublin and expressed his satisfaction at the progress that had been made. On the next day HSSPF Friedrich-Wilhelm Krüger, the SS and police chief in Cracow, who had been made state secretary for security in the General Government in May that year, ordered that all Jews in the General Government should be killed by the end of the year. Krüger had gleefully supervised the murder of 12,000 Jews on 'Bloody Sunday in Stanislau' in October 1941, a large sausage in one hand, a pistol in the other. He had almost achieved his goal by the time he was posted to the front in November 1943. Political voluntarism once again was combined with functional rationality to murderous effect. The mass executions were beginning to take their toll on the nerves of all but the more perverted of the members of the Einsatzkommandos and the Wehrmacht, and it was suggested that poison gas, which had been used to murder the victims of the euthanasia campaign, was a viable alternative. T4's movable gas chambers using carbon monoxide from the exhaust and mounted on trucks were first used in Chelmno, but they were too small and inefficient to be of much use. The Wehrmacht also used mobile gas chambers that were built by Jewish workers and were capable of killing 400 people per day per truck. They were first used in Belarus in the winter of 1941. Since mass executions by firing squads could result in 10,000 deaths per day, mobile gas chambers were not considered very efficient. Albert Widmann from the Criminal Technical Institute took part in gassing victims with carbon monoxide, which was provided for him by IG Farben (now known as BASF) in Ludwigshafen. He then went on to murder psychiatric patients in Minsk, for which crime he was obliged by a Stuttgart court in 1967 to give 4,000 DM to an institution devoted to helping the handicapped. Widmann was welcomed by Arthur Nebe who was complaining that it was unreasonable for his Einsatzgruppen to be expected to engage in mass shootings. His other preferred method was to put his victims in a bunker, wall them in and blow them up. This proved swift, but the mopping-up operations were both unpleasant and time-consuming. As early as 22 July 1941 the army group proudly announced that there were no more Jewish intellectuals left in Minsk.

In September 1941, 900 Russian prisoners of war were killed in the gas chambers of Auschwitz using Zyklon B gas, based on hydrocyanic acid, which had been developed to exterminate vermin. After this successful experiment the method was used to murder Jews in Belzec in October 1941. The population of the Lublin ghetto were murdered in Belzec in order to make rooms for Jews who had been deported from the Reich and Slovakia. They were given a brief respite before being sent to Majdanek and Sobibor. Jews from Galicia were sent directly to the death camps. By December 1941 the shortage of food was used as a justification for the indiscriminate murder of 'useless eaters'.

Heydrich finally acted on Göring's instructions in July by calling a meeting for 9 December 1941 to discuss the 'Final Solution', but it was postponed because of the attack on Pearl Harbor and Germany's declaration of war on the United States. Goebbels noted in his diary[4]: 'The world war has come and the annihilation of the Jews must be the necessary consequence.' The meeting was finally held on 20 January 1942 in a delightful villa on the Wannsee in Berlin that had been Aryanized a few years previously. Heydrich was in the chair and Eichmann took the minutes. It was attended by five representatives of the police and the SD, eight politicians and civil servants from various government agencies, two representatives of the NSDAP, one from the party chancellery and one from the SS Race and Settlement Office. The state secretary in the propaganda ministry, Leopold Gutterer, and the chief of staff of the RKF, Ulrich Greifelt, did not attend because they were involved in negotiations in Italy. None of those present raised any objections as the chairman announced that it was his intention to render all of Europe, including Britain and Sweden, as well as North Africa, 'uncontaminated by Jews'. He estimated that a total of 11 million Jews would be deported to the east. In fact the total Jewish population in Europe was between 9 and 10 million. Those capable of working would be subjected to 'natural reduction'; the rest would be killed. Those who were

[322] not worked to death would be given 'appropriate treatment', since they would otherwise represent an exceptionally tough 'germ-cell' of a Jewish revival. Exception was to be made for German Jews over the age of 65 who were to be placed in an 'old folks ghetto' in the concentration camp at Thereslenstadt. This was to serve as a model institution to counter any Allied charges that the Jews were being badly treated. There was some debate of the problem on rounding up Jews in allied countries, but this was quickly discounted. Questions whether 'grade one and grade two half-breeds' and Jews who were married to non-Jews should be treated equally as 'full-Jews', whether they should be sterilized or killed and whether mixed marriages should be dissolved were all shelved. Joseph Buhler, Hans Frank's deputy in the General Government, and seconded by Rosenberg's deputy Alfred Meyer who was also head of the German Red Cross, requested that the 'final solution' should begin as soon as possible, since most of the Jews were unable to work and posed a serious economic and health problem. This was granted and was accompanied by a frank and open discussion of the merits of different methods of mass killing.

In one sense the Wannsee Conference was a confirmation of what had already happened. The decision to murder vast numbers of Jews had already been taken, hundreds of thousands had died and the death camps were being built. But now for the first time the decision to murder every single Jew in Europe had been formally taken, the order widely dissemin-ated, and the somewhat haphazard massacres were now to be carefully coordinated into systematic genocide. There had been a number of previous 'final solutions', but this was the definitive 'Final Solution' by means of cold-blooded, pedantic, carefully planned, industrialized and centralized genocide. It was a horror unparalleled in human history.

The status of those living in racially mixed marriages was decided by Hitler in 1938. It was inexplicably determined by the religion of children resulting from such a union. If the children were raised as Christians the marriage was deemed to be 'privileged'. The parents were not required to wear the Star of David badge and the children were permitted to attend school and pursue normal careers. But their situation was desperately insecure. If a non-Jewish husband were killed in the war, or died from whatever cause, the Jewish wife ceased to be 'privileged' and faced deporta-tion and death. A Jewish man was treated similarly if his Aryan wife died or decided to sue for divorce. Hitler also ordained that half-Jews should be treated as Jews, but quarter-Jews were to be regarded, up to a certain point, as members of the German racial community. All this was somewhat vague and gave the SS ample opportunity to make arbitrary decisions over life and death. 'Aryans with Jewish relations' were dragged into the circle of the persecuted and from 1942 a number of 'half-breed camps' were set up where an increasing number of Aryan partners of mixed marriages were interned as forced labourers. Half-Jews were dismissed from the armed forces, used as slave labourers and later sent to the model concentration camp at Theresienstadt. Some of these unfortunates were sent on to Auschwitz. Thirty-seven per cent of prisoners were categorized as 'non-Mosaic Jews' when the camp was liberated in April 1945.

In February 1942 the mass murder of Jews in Auschwitz got into full swing, with up to 10,000 deaths in one day. When Goebbels heard of the use of gas as an instrument of mass murder in March 1942 he described it in his diary as 'a barbarous method that beggars further description', but added 'once again the Führer is the tireless pioneer and advocate of a radical solution'[5]. Amid all these horrors Wilm Hosenfeld wrote to his wife from Warsaw in August 1942[6]:

> You simply cannot imagine what is happening here in W. to the Jews. There has been nothing like this since human beings have populated the earth. One loses every ounce of faith and hope. How deep have we sunken! I consider that a recovery and a victory for our way of thinking are unthinkable. Even the Blacks in Africa have a right to protect themselves against us. This is a world without God and without moral responsibility.

The Einsatzkommandos, eagerly supported by Latvians, Ukrainians and Romanians, with the cooperation of the Wehrmacht, continued with their murderous work. In October 1943, for example, Romanian units murdered 25,000 Jews in Odessa. Croatians set about murdering Jews with enthusiasm and cooperated fully with the German authorities sending others to Auschwitz. The viciously anti-Semitic Slovaks paid the Reichsführer 500 RM for every Jew deported to Auschwitz. It was a deal that left both sides more than content. It was not until November 1944 that Himmler ordered the extermination camps to close, by which time 6 million Jews had been killed.

At first sight it would seem that murder on such a horrific scale was totally counter-productive and the result of ideological frenzy and blind hatred. Transport that was badly needed to supply the front and bring up reserves was diverted to ship Jews from Crete, Thessaloniki and Budapest. Millions were murdered who could have been put to useful work. Rosenberg's ministry bluntly stated in December 1941 that 'economic considerations should not be taken into account in dealing with this

[324] problem'. It was not long before this strict observance was ignored. SS-Standartenführer Karl Naumann, who was placed in charge of agriculture and nutrition in the General Government in July 1941, announced that he needed 300,000 Jews to work, adding that: 'The remaining Jews, altogether 1.2 million of them, will no longer be provided with food.' Naumann, who was regarded as a harmless bureaucrat, escaped unpunished and had a successful political career in Lower Saxony in post-war Germany. In 1942 the SS began to hire out concentration camp inmates as slave labourers to German firms. By 1944 there were 700,000 such helots and the SS was raking in the money. But these unfortunates were so badly nourished, diseased and weakened that only a few of the very strongest survived. The rest were, in the parlance of the day, 'worked out' (*abgearbeitet*). It has been estimated that the productivity of such slave labour was a mere 17 per cent of the average.

Albert Speer, who managed to lie his way into a reputation for being a 'good Nazi', was the most vicious and callous employer of slave labour from the concentration camps. Almost 500,000 such victims worked for his armaments industry, 140,000 in the horrific underground death traps where weapons of particular importance, such as the V1 and V2 rockets, were produced.

The Nazi leadership was perfectly well aware that mass murder on such an unimaginable scale was a gross violation of established moral norms and of generally acceptable civilized behaviour. They also knew that it was highly doubtful whether there would be any general public support or even sympathy for this most monstrous of crimes. For this reason it was felt prudent to preserve the highest possible degree of secrecy about the Final Solution. In his three-and-a-half-hour speech to the Gauleiter and Senior SS officials in Posen in October 1943 Himmler argued that it would be better 'to take the secret with us to our graves'. Hitler told Goebbels as early as 15 June 1941 that Germany had better win the war because otherwise the German people, with the likes of the minister of propaganda at the top of the list, would be 'rubbed out' in retribution for the crimes they had committed. Even as late as 1945 soldiers who spread rumours about the extent of the murders were summarily executed.

It was of course utterly impossible to keep an operation on such a scale secret. Thousands of SS, police and soldiers were directly involved in murder, thousands more direct witnesses. Railway officials planned the transport to the death camps; others ran the trains, rounded up the victims and acted as guards. Millions heard graphic accounts of what was happening. If Victor Klemperer, deprived of his civil rights and denied access to public places, could learn what was happening at Auschwitz, then this was indeed common knowledge. The appalling fact is that although these terrible events were widely known there was virtually no protest. The great exception to this shocking moral blindness were those who, with exceptional courage and moral fortitude, saved the lives of thousands of Jews. It is often forgotten that although outside the borders of the Reich harbouring a Jew carried an automatic death sentence, this was not the case at home, where such instances were not even reported in the press.

The acts of outright violence against Jews during peacetime, such as the pogrom on 9 November 1938, met with a mixed reception, and the systematic whittling away of the rights of German Jews was treated with ethical indifference and silent acceptance, often with malicious approval. Years of state-sponsored anti-Semitism fanned the omnipresent anti-Semitism, but this was still a long way from endorsing the mass murder of Europe's Jews.

The killing began in September 1939, often in a haphazard manner, by men sworn to secrecy. Gauleiter Greiser, for example, ordered the murder of 100,000 Jews without bothering to ask permission from either Hitler or Himmler. Both subsequently endorsed this initiative. There followed a gradual escalation with the creation of 'Jew-free' areas and the herding of Polish Jews into the ghettos, which in turn created serious hygiene problems. Heydrich issued strict instructions that Jewish doctors should be spared as they were needed to maintain basic standards of hygiene. Radical anti-Semites now demanded a 'final solution' to the problem and the extermination of the arch-enemy and deadly threat to the German race. All restraints were removed with the invasion of the Soviet Union as officials calmly discussed the murder of between 30 and 40 million people, 6.5 million of whom were Jewish, so that the army could live off the land and the desperate food shortages at home be relieved. The way would also be cleared for the vast agricultural settlements in Germany's eastern empire. By the end of 1941, 500,000 people had been killed, about 90 per cent of whom were Jewish, but this only served to whet the appetites of those searching for a radical solution.

An army of SS and police, ably assisted by the Wehrmacht and with the enthusiastic support of Latvian, Lithuanian, Ukrainian, Romanian, Hungarian and French thugs, set to work. Rudolf Höss' concentration camp at Auschwitz was greatly expanded so as to accommodate victims from Western Europe, the Balkans and the Czech protectorate. The original camp (Stammlager) was now called Auschwitz I, the extermination camp at Birkenau Auschwitz II, and the IG Farben factory at the work camp at

[326] Monowitz Auschwitz III. Forty thousand workers slaved away for four years at these Buna works under the most appalling conditions and to no avail. No synthetic rubber was ever produced at the Buna works. Meanwhile the Einsatzgruppen and police scoured the area behind the front for Jews, rounded them up in synagogues and burnt them alive or shot them in mass executions. Army units did their bit, often describing such atrocities as 107 Infantry Regiment's murder of 10,000 Jews in Belarus as 'counter-measures against partisans'. Such actions were approved by anti-Semitic desktop murderers among the generals. Some, such as the commanding general in Białystok, raised objections. He complained that the mass execution of Jews in a park near his quarter disturbed his rest. He did not register a complaint when some 500–700 men, women and children were burnt alive in a local synagogue. Army units murdered Jewish prisoners of war, with OKW and 'Gestapo' Müller reaching an agreement on the 'purification of POW camps' that formed the basis of Einsatz Order Number 8. The Wehrmacht was directly responsible for the deaths by starvation of 3.3 million of the 5.7 million Soviet prisoners of war. Some 38,000 Soviet prisoners of war who were held in camps in Germany were executed, along with 140,000 in the Soviet Union.

The 'Final Solution' in east and west

Six million people died in the Holocaust, two-thirds of Europe's Jews. Given the organized chaos of Nazi rule it is hardly surprising that the 'Final Solution' was applied with differing degrees of intensity in the various parts of Europe under German control. Some areas, such as Danzig, West Prussia, South-east Prussia and Upper Silesia, were formally annexed. Alsace-Lorraine, Luxembourg, Lower Styria, Carinthia and Carniola, as well as the area around Białystok, were incorporated into the Reich but were never formally annexed. Denmark had a civilian administration and was placed 'under the Reich's protection'. Norway and Holland were within the Greater Germanic Sphere and were earmarked for annexation. The Reich Protector, the General Governor and the Reich Commissars ruled supreme in Bohemia and Moravia, Poland, the Ukraine and Ostland, which included the Baltic States and White Ruthenia. Other areas, including France, Belgium, Serbia, Greece and the operational areas of the Soviet Union, were under military control.

Eastern Europe was thus under the ideologically frenzied and murder-ous sway of the likes of Hans Frank in the General Government, Arthur

Greiser in the Wartheland, Hinrich Lohse in Ostland, Erich Koch in East [327] Prussia and Ukraine, and Wilhelm Kube in Belarus. Alfred Rosenberg as minister for the occupied eastern territories was initially without influence. His hopes that the Ukraine might be secured as an ally were dismissed as absurdly heterodox and ideologically suspect, although it was an idea that was seconded by a number of German generals. The SS and police bands were given free rein so that the entire area became a vast laboratory for the dystopian racial new order. Zealots in the SS and the RSHA could safely claim to be acting in accordance to the Führer's will, and had no difficulty in overriding any reservations or objections from the military or civilians. The situation in the west was somewhat different. In Holland effective control was in the hands of the Reich Commissar, Arthur Seyss-Inquart, who ruled supreme without interference from the foreign office or any other ministry. Here the SS and police could get to work to deadly effect, with

Figure 9.1   Felix Nussbaum's 'Self-portrait with a star of David and Jewish identity card'. Nussbaum lived in exile in Belgium from 1935, was denounced in July 1944 and shortly after was murdered in Auschwitz

[328]   the result that 105,000 of the 140,000 Jews in Holland, of whom 112,000 were citizens and 28,000 immigrants, were murdered. At 75 per cent this is roughly the same percentage as in Eastern Europe. Belgium was under military control and was bled white, but it was free from senior SS and police officials. As a result 22,000 of the 50,000 Jews in Belgium survived. France was divided into various zones. Most of the north was under direct military control, the north-east was treated as part of Belgium, and Alsace came under Gauleiter Robert Wagner, who was also Gauleiter of Baden. Lorraine was combined with the Saarland-Palatinate under Gauleiter Josef Bürckel. Vichy France was theoretically independent and there was a small area in the south occupied by the Italians. There were frequent conflicts between the military and the SS and police, with the military commander Carl Heinrich von Stülpnagel, a confirmed anti-Semite who had previously cooperated fully with Einsatzkommando 4B, warning about the danger of creating 'Polish conditions' in France. Hitler was incensed at this spineless attitude towards such a pressing necessity. These squabbles were compounded by the problems involved in cooperating with the anti-Semitic Vichy regime, and mounting resistance from the population that resulted in three-quarters of the Jews in France being saved. Seventy-three thousand Jews were deported from France, of whom only 24,000 were French citizens; 250,000 survived. In Denmark where the SS and police remained relatively aloof and where the population showed exemplary civil courage, most of the 7,000 Jews were saved; 930 escaped to Sweden. The Reich plenipotentiary, SS-Obergruppenführer Werner Best, who had played an active part in mass murders of Jews in Poland and in the deportation of French Jews, managed to deport only 770 Jews and erroneously reported to the foreign office that the country was 'de-Jewed' (*entjudet*). Some Jewish communities were saved by merciful twists of fate. The German legation in Sofia was told in June 1942 that should the Bulgarian government express the wish to deport the Jews they should be 'given a fundamentally positive response', but that there was no immediate possibility of 'taking them on'. Bulgaria had a number of discriminatory laws against Jews, but the Germans insisted in the summer of 1942 that they should be toughened up. Bulgaria took notice, but continued to prevaricate about deportation. The Finnish government told Himmler that since there were only 2,000 Jews in the country they did not have a 'Jewish problem'. The Reichsführer-SS had enough on his plate not to worry about this for the time being. Jews in Tunisia had their property confiscated and 5,000 became slave labourers. They were saved by the Allied victory in North Africa. Where there was no restraint on the SS and police the death toll was unspeakably

horrific; elsewhere the catastrophe was still terrible and only pales by [329] comparison.

Croatia had anti-Jewish legislation on the German model and sent 4,927 Jews to Auschwitz in the summer of 1942. All of them were murdered. Romania was in an exceedingly ugly mood. On 28 June 1940, the day that peace between Germany and France was formally signed, Romania was forced to hand over Bessarabia, the northern Bukovina and part of Moldavia to the Soviet Union. In the Second Vienna Ruling of August that year Romania lost south Dobruja to Bulgaria and part of Transylvania to Hungary. Within two months the country thus lost a third of its territory. On 20 January 1941 the fascist Iron Guard, egged on by a special unit of the SS, mounted a coup against the Antonescu regime. An appalling pogrom ensued, which included the murder of a 5-year-old Jewish girl in an abattoir where she was hung up on meat hooks and advertised as 'kosher meat'. Antonescu succeeded in putting down the putsch and ordered the SS out of the country, but the anti-Semitic outrages continued. Eichmann sent SS-Sturmbannführer Gustav Richter to Bucharest as Consultant for Jewish Questions in April 1941, where he remained until August 1944 when he was taken prisoner by the Soviets. He could rely on the enthusiastic support of the local population, the Wehrmacht and the SS. The bestial brutality of the Romanians was too much even for the SS, who complained that their behaviour amounted to a '*Schweinerei*', largely because they were hopelessly disorganized and they did not bother to bury their victims. The town of Jasy was soon reported to be 'cleansed of Jews'. Some 150,000 Jews were forced into the area between the Dniester and the Bug known as Transnistria where they were shunted back and forth between the Germans and the Romanians; 65,000 died in the process. The situation became so chaotic that on 8 September 1941 OKW ordered this to stop. Thugs in the ethnic German self-defence groups (Selbstschütz) hunted down Jews and murdered them on the spot. In the summer of 1942, 320,000 Jews who had managed to survive these massacres were sent to Auschwitz, where the vast majority perished. In 1943 all the Polish ghettos, with the exception of Łódź were cleared, the inmates either murdered on the spot or sent to the death camps. This process was intensified with the uprising in the Warsaw ghetto between 19 April and 16 May.

The Germans were initially frustrated in their efforts to get their hands on Greek Jews because many were in the Italian zone of occupation. Himmler therefore decided to bide his time until February 1943 when the deportation specialists SS-Hauptsturmbannführer Alois Brunner and SS-Hauptsturmbannführer Dieter Wisliceny were sent to Thessaloniki, a city

[330] with a large and prosperous Jewish community: 45,000 Jews were sent to Auschwitz shortly thereafter. The Italian authorities refused to deport the Jews in their occupation zone, but with the fall of Mussolini, whom the Germans considered hopelessly pusillanimous on the Jewish question, the persecution of Greek Jews was intensified. In April 5,000 Jews from mainland Greece were transported and in May the Wehrmacht began to round up the Jews in Corfu, Rhodes and Crete. Some 63,000 of Greece's 70,000 Jews were murdered. This is often represented as an example of ideological madness whereby transport essential to the army was purloined for pointless murder. In fact the cost of the Wehrmacht in Greece was covered to a large extent by property stolen from the Jewish community. Between 14 May and July 1944, 437,000 Hungarian Jews were sent to Auschwitz and only 10 per cent survived this hell. Admiral Horthy tried to stop the murder of the Hungarian Jews on 7 July, whereupon the SS engineered his dismissal and placed the fascist Arrow Cross in power. They promptly murdered 9,000 Jews and a further 75,000 were force-marched to Auschwitz as there were not enough trains available. In March 1944 there were 700,000 Jews in Hungary; 293,000 survived. Murder in Auschwitz stopped in November 1944, but tens of thousands were still to die in the death marches, in labour camps and in random executions.

The staggering rate of inflation in the occupied countries, caused by the manipulation of rates of exchange and the paucity of consumer goods, was blamed on the Jews. Stolen Jewish property was then used to stabilize currencies by helping supply meet the demand, thus proving the point to the simple-minded that Jews were indeed to blame.

Reaction and inaction

Although confronted with horror on such a scale the churches remained silent, the traditionally anti-Semitic officer corps offered a helping hand, the sensitivities of the vast majority of Germans were numbed by years of war, and few could spare a thought for anyone outside the immediate circle of family and friends. Experts estimate that about 300,000 people were directly involved in the murder of men, women and children in hitherto unimaginable numbers. There were only 3,000 men in the Einsatzgruppen, but they were supported by the 4,000 men in the 1st SS Brigade, and the 7,200 men in the SS Cavalry Brigade, both of which were under Himmler's direct command. In addition there were 23 battalions of Order Police with 420 officers and 11,640 men in the east along with units of the Security

Police, the military police, units from the Wehrmacht and the SS Totenkopf
guards in the concentration camps. Precious few of these people were
either 'ordinary men' or 'willing executioners'; the officers and NCOs were
mostly professionals from the police and the army. Many were highly educated. It is impossible to give an accurate figure of the numerous foreign
units and volunteers who willingly participated in this orgy of killing. Only
500 people were called to account for their crimes in the Federal Republic,
and most lived to pursue prosperous careers and enjoy years of peaceful
retirement untroubled by pangs of conscience.

CHAPTER 10

THE WAR

National Socialism revealed its true face during the war. With its restless activism the 'movement' always saw itself as being at war: against the Weimar Republic, the Versailles settlement, Marxism in all its forms, against a liberal-democratic world order, and against the sinister machinations of world Jewry. It struggled for the restoration of German greatness, for domination over Europe, for *Lebensraum* and for the purification of the Aryan race. This could not possibly be achieved without a major war that would undo the decision of November 1918, and from the very outset the regime prepared for war, regardless of the ruinous expense.

This was a radically different kind of war. The segregation, persecution and murder of Poles and Jews were coincidental with the mass murder of the handicapped and psychiatric patients at home in the so-called euthanasia programme. This was a racist war of annihilation, exploitation and colonization in which the army, contrary to persistent myth, was complicit from the outset. For long after the war it was argued that there were in a sense two wars: one a war fought by Germany's armed forces according to time-honoured rules of engagement, and another a criminal campaign of mass murder carried out by a small group of fanatics in the SS. Unfortunately the historical record clearly shows that this is far from the truth. This fact was partly obscured because the campaign in the west in 1940 was fought according to observed laws of war, but when Hitler turned east once more in 1941 the war entered its final and horrific stages, resulting in millions being uprooted, exploited, enslaved and murdered. This was a war for 'living space' designed to render Germany free from the fear of blockade, and with the race purified by the industrialized mass murder of Jews and other undesirables. Germany could then finally make its bid for 'world power'. It was a war inspired by a perverse dystopian vision, unleashed by a megalomaniac gambler and which, as many of his generals knew full well, had precious little chance of success.

With the annexation of Austria in 1938 Hitler had completed Bismarck's work of unification and created the 'greater Germany' (*Grossdeutschland*) for which many nationalists had longed. He had no intention of resting on his laurels and as early as November 1938 Himmler told his senior SS commanders that the Führer was intent on building a vast empire, the like of which had never been seen before. Czechoslovakia was destroyed in March 1939, Bohemia and Moravia absorbed as a colony, as was Memel in the same month. Hitler's birthday on 20 April 1939 was celebrated with a gigantic display of military might, an indication that he had no intention of curbing his expansionist ambitions. Confident that neither Britain nor France was willing to send troops to die for Danzig, he attacked Poland on 1 September 1939, thus starting first a European and then a world war.

What factors prompted Hitler to take this fatal step? It has often been argued that the chronic level of government indebtedness and desperate shortage of foreign currency were such that he simply had to take a leap in the dark, in the hope that a successful war of conquest would bring relief to an overwrought economy. Quite apart from the fact that there is no evidence to suggest that this was indeed his motive, deficit spending on an astronomic scale in post-war economies shows that aggressive war is not a necessary consequence. Nor was civil discontent so widespread that there was any temptation to deflect attention from troubles at home by adventures abroad. On the contrary, following a series of successes both at home and abroad, Hitler's prestige and charismatic appeal had never been greater. The answer, as in so much else in Nazi Germany, although to some it will sound pitifully old-fashioned and woefully unscientific, lies in Hitler himself. As he so often reiterated, he was unable to make any play other than *va banque*. In the early stages of his career he was painfully hesitant and reluctant to make decisions, driving men like Goebbels to distraction by his indecisiveness. Later he took to brooding at length in his Bavarian mountain fastness while his minions waited in awestruck anticipation for his next daring move. Having pulled off a series of astonishing victories he became totally convinced that his instincts were infallible, a delusion that was strengthened by the adulation of his closest associates. His self-confidence grew into an overweening sense of self-importance, became self-seeking hubris and finally descended into megalomania. National Socialism depended on action, struggle and success and Hitler was the motive force behind this activism, ever fearful that the 'movement' would come to a standstill, degenerate into routine and ossify in normality. He was also obsessed with the idea that he would die at a young age. His health was bad and

[334] worsened by hypochondria, an unhealthy diet and an eccentric lifestyle. He was utterly convinced that he alone could carry out the great tasks he had set himself and that he had little time in which to fulfil his mission and his destiny.

Hitler was a hectic and charismatic improviser, but he also pursued certain long-term goals. Although he had no fixed plans as such, he was determined to destroy the Versailles settlement, carve out vast areas of 'living space' in the east, purify and strengthen the Germanic race, and create a true 'racial community'. In even vaguer terms he dreamt of world domination after an epic struggle with the United States. Speaking to a group of students in 1930 he said that every race (*Volk*) aspired to dominate the world, which was 'a prize to be won by the strongest power', and that 110 million Germans would win the cup. At times he told his closest associates that his aim was to undo the Treaty of Westphalia of 1648, but it was never clear what he meant by this, beyond a determination radically to redraw the map of Europe. He could see nothing that seriously stood in his way. For him the Soviet Union was run by a maniac, bent on slaughtering his closest associates, and with a worthless military. Britain and France were craven and degenerate nations whose pusillanimous leaders would abandon Poland just as they had stood silently by when he annexed the Rhineland, or when they shabbily betrayed Czechoslovakia. Thus Hitler had his long-term plans, had implicit trust in his instincts, and the foreign political constellation appeared to be highly favourable. Above all he was in a position of such absolute power that he, and he alone, could make all decisions without fear of contradiction and certain of absolute obedience.

The war began with two major disappointments. Ordinary Germans showed little initial enthusiasm for the war, in spite of months of intensive propaganda ever since Munich, designed to steel the people for war. Even more serious was Britain's decision to go to war. Hitler always saw Britain as the best of all possible allies, and he had not given up the idea that the country would eventually come round to his point of view. Goebbels did not agree, describing the English as 'plutocrats – the Jews among the Aryans' and a 'stinking race' who were sending 'their racehorses and pluto-cratic children' off to Canada. Hitler's luck held. As Jodl pointed out at Nuremberg, had France and Britain attacked in the west, Germany would have been in serious trouble, since the much-vaunted West Wall offered very little protection. Goebbels was also in constant fear of a two-front war, but although the campaign in Poland showed up many serious deficiencies in the German army, it was all over in three weeks and Goebbels' propaganda machine made it out to be a masterpiece of German military proficiency, a dire warning for Germany's remaining enemies and in marked [335] contrast to the 'phoney war', the *drôle de guerre* or *Sitzkrieg* in the west.

One week before the invasion of Poland Hitler told his generals that he intended to destroy Poland and enslave the population. He added: 'In future there will never be anyone who has more authority than I have!' Himmler's Einsatzgruppen, supported by local German self-defence groups (*Volksdeutsche Selbstschütz*), began their murderous handiwork within days of the invasion. They set about slaughtering the Polish intelligentsia and rounding up, humiliating, robbing and killing Jews. The literary critic Marcel Reich-Ranicki, a survivor of the Warsaw ghetto, gives a graphic account of these dreadful events in a chapter entitled 'Hunting down Jews is fun' in his autobiography, in which he points out that army units were enthusiastically involved in these atrocities. Sixteen thousand men were murdered in September 1939 on Heydrich's orders that Poland's leadership should be rendered 'harmless' while the rest of the population could be employed as seasonal labourers on the land. Franz Halder, the army chief of staff, using the same vocabulary as the SS, spoke of the 'ethnic consolidation' (*Flurbereinigung*) of Jews, clerics and the intelligentsia. Jews were herded into ghettos in the cities in occupied Poland, henceforth known as the General Government, and some 750,000 Jews were deported to Governor Hans Frank's satrapy. By 1944 1.3 million Poles had been sent to work in Germany.

On 7 October 1939 Himmler added another title to his already impressive list when he was made Reich Commissar for the Strengthening of the German Race (RKFDV) with the remit to 'de-Pole', 'de-Jew' and 'Germanize' Poland. Here at last was an opportunity to put National Socialist racial-biological theories into practice in a far-reaching programme of deportation, resettlement and mass murder. Himmler and the HSSPFs operated in the space between the army and the civilian authorities. They were outside the law, with each HSSPF doing whatever he wished within the area under his command. Only General Blaskowitz had the courage to complain about what he euphemistically called the 'unchivalrous behaviour' of the SS.

An area amounting to 90,000 square kilometres of Poland with 10 million inhabitants, 80 per cent of whom were Polish, was annexed by Germany. This left Hans Frank as lord over 12.5 million Poles in the truncated General Government of Poland. The annexed provinces were labelled Danzig-West Prussia under Gauleiter Albert Forster and Wartheland under Gauleiter Arthur Greiser, who had been Forster's deputy in Danzig before the war. Both men were fanatical bullyboys who cooperated enthusiastically with the SS in Germanizing the new provinces. Hitler was delighted when Geiser told him in September 1939 that he intended to 'liquidate the Polish intelligentsia'. The entire population was divided into five racial categories. There was an elite of 1.724 million 'racial Germans' (*Volksdeutsche*) and 'Poles who were capable of being Germanized'. These were granted full citizenship. Next came 1.7 million 'provisional candidates for Germanization'. They were given limited rights, but if they passed the test could become full citizens after 10 years, or if they were decorated while serving in the armed forces. The third category comprised 83,000 'provisional nationals' who had even less rights. By early 1944 most of categories two and three had been elevated to the status of 'racial Germans', even though most of them could barely speak German. Then came the 6 million Polish 'protected persons' who had virtually no rights and were subjected to every form of discrimination and exploitation. Last of all came the Jews, whether German or Polish, who were deported. Those that did not die in the overcrowded and pestilent ghettos were sent to the gas chambers in the extermination camps. Thus mass murder, ethnic cleansing and resettlement began long before the attack on the Soviet Union in June 1941. Parallel to this radical policy in Poland was the systematic murder of the handicapped, the psychologically disturbed and 'asocials' in Germany.

The campaign in the west

Hitler ordered the invasion of Denmark and Norway in April 1940 in order to stop the British from establishing bases there and to secure the transport of vital Swedish iron ore via the Norwegian port of Narvik. Meanwhile the attack on France was postponed. The weather had been unsuitable in the winter of 1939, and the generals were concerned to correct the many mistakes and deficiencies that had marked the Polish campaign. Then there were acute shortages of ammunition, fuel, raw materials and wheeled vehicles. These shortages were eventually overcome thanks to the prompt delivery of supplies from the Soviet Union. Most important of all the generals, mindful of the experience of the Great War, were extremely nervous about tackling the French Army, which was as well equipped as the Wehrmacht. The commanders of the three army groups in the west, Leeb, Bock and Rundstedt, had serious misgivings about Hitler's plans to extend the war, but Leeb's proposal that they should all resign in protest fell on deaf ears. General Thomas also argued that Germany had neither the manpower nor the material resources to conduct a lengthy war. On 5 November the Wehrmacht's commander-in-chief, Field Marshal Walther von Brauchitsch, made a final attempt to persuade Hitler not to attack in the west, but he was treated to a thunderous denunciation of the 'spirit of Zossen', the suburb of Berlin where the general staff had its headquarters, and the opposition crumbled.

Planning went ahead based on Hitler's directives of 9 October and the OKW's on the following day. Most planners felt that a revamped version of the Schlieffen Plan, a thrust through Belgium, along the Channel coast and encircling Paris, was the only viable strategic solution, even though it had been a spectacular failure in 1914. Hitler wisely did not agree. He supported an ingenious plan developed by General Erich von Lewinski, who had prudently changed his name to von Manstein, that involved an offensive through the Ardennes and on to the Channel coast, thereby encircling the bulk of the French Army in north-eastern France.

Manstein's 'cut of the sickle', which began on 10 May 1940, worked like clockwork and six weeks later France capitulated. An armistice was signed in the same railway carriage in the forest of Compiègne where the Germans had surrendered to Marshal Foch in 1918, and at the beginning of July an elaborate victory parade was held in Paris. Alsace and Lorraine once again returned to Germany, France was divided into an area under military occupation in the north while in the south the ancient Marshal Pétain, the hero of Verdun, formed an authoritarian and anti-Semitic government based in the spa town of Vichy that readily cooperated with the Germans.

Hitler was now at the very pinnacle of his power and popularity. He had undone the 'shame of Versailles' and Germany dominated Europe, from the Bug to the Atlantic coast, from Norway to the Brenner. Keitel proclaimed him to be 'the greatest commander of all times'. The charismatic Führer basked in the undivided adulation of his people, whose morale was high after the crushing defeat of the 'hereditary enemy', and who profited from the plunder and exploitation of those outside the 'racial community'. The British had ignominiously retreated at Dunkirk, their escape made possible by Hitler's blundering interference, leaving the bulk of their equipment behind. Final victory seemed to be only a matter of time. The SD and Sipo got ready for the invasion, drawing up a lengthy list of prominent figures to be liquidated shortly after the arrival of the Wehrmacht on British soil. On 31 July, confident that Britain was already beaten and entertaining the extraordinary idea that the country's hope for salvation lay in the Soviet Union, Hitler issued instructions to the Wehrmacht for planning to begin for a two-pronged attack on the Soviet Union towards Moscow and Kiev. The invasion was to begin in May 1941. The Wehrmacht, ever eager to oblige, had already begun planning such an attack.

Attention now turned to Operation Sea Lion to deliver the *coup de grâce* to Britain. For an invasion to be successful Germany had first to gain control over British airspace, but Göring's Luftwaffe made the fatal mistake of stopping the attack on airfields and radar installations in southern England and concentrating on bombing cities and towns. The Germans did not count on Churchill's dogged determination to continue the fight against all the odds and whatever the cost, nor on the gallantry and skill of the fighter pilots in 'The Few', many of whom were exiled Poles. They saved Britain and ultimately Europe from Nazi tyranny. This was indeed Britain's 'finest hour'. On 17 September Hitler cancelled Operation Sea Lion, the invasion plan, but he still clung to a vague hope that Britain would in the end come round to see that an alliance with Nazi Germany was in its best interest.

Barbarossa

There was now no viable alternative for Hitler to an attack on the Soviet Union. Churchill would not even consider making peace, and Hitler felt that it was far too risky remaining so dependent on deliveries from the Soviet Union, especially at a time when the Soviets were stepping up demands for far greater influence in the Balkans and the Straits. It was generally agreed that the Red Army was in a state of disarray and would offer no serious resistance. It had performed poorly in the campaign against Finland, and the outstanding success of General Georgi K. Zhukov in the campaign at Khalkin Gol against the Japanese in 1939 was completely overlooked. This was a textbook piece of modern armoured warfare by a man who was to prove to be the greatest general in the war. Britain was in no position to offer any support to the Soviets were Germany to attack, because it was imagined that this would be yet another swift campaign. Germany would then have the living space and the resources that would enable it to make a final bid for world domination.

On 18 December 1940 Hitler issued 'Directive 21' formally ordering the general staff to draw up plans for an attack on the Soviet Union. Much preliminary planning had been competed, but the general staff's proposal for the annexation of the Baltic States, Belarus and the Ukraine fell far short of Hitler's intent to destroy the Soviet Union and to carve out a vast area of living space in the east, thus at last making Germany into a world power. On 30 March 1941 Halder transmitted Hitler's orders that the eastern campaign was to be a 'war of annihilation' (*Vernichtungskampf*) in which the commissars and Communist intelligentsia would be destroyed. Military law was to be set aside, Soviet citizens could be summarily executed. Military personnel were not to be punished for crimes against Soviet citizens, except for rape (which was considered objectionable on racial rather than moral grounds) and in cases where 'criminal intent' was involved. The SS was far more stringent in disciplinary matters than the Wehrmacht and took an exceptionally dim view of matters of 'racial pollution'.

Hitler was unable to concentrate entirely on the forthcoming campaign in the east. Italian forces were routed in North Africa, obliging him to send one of his favourite generals, Erwin von Rommel, at the head of an excellently equipped and mechanized Afrikakorps to bale out his ally in February 1941. In March there was an anti-German coup in Yugoslavia coupled with yet another Italian setback in Greece, which Mussolini had attacked in October, and where Churchill had sent British reinforcements against the better judgement of General Sir Archibald Wavell, the one-eyed and obdurately taciturn commander-in-chief in the Middle East. This prompted Hitler to act in order to secure the southern flank of his attack on the Soviet Union, codenamed Barbarossa, on 3 February 1941. The Germans attacked Greece on 6 April 1941, about a month later than had been planned in November, and although the fighting lasted less than three weeks, valuable forces had to be withdrawn from the east and the attack on the Soviet Union had to be postponed. Since the planners were convinced that the campaign would last only a matter of weeks this delay caused no concern.

Barbarossa was intended not merely to achieve living space and sufficient raw materials to ensure Germany's self-sufficiency; it was also designed to bring about what in the ugly Nazi neologism was termed a 'racial catastrophe' (*Volkskatastrophe*). Slavs were to be slaughtered on an unimaginable scale and those that survived turned into the helots of Germanic settlers. Not only would the 'Jewish-Bolshevik' elite be destroyed, but all Jews and card-carrying Communists. Himmler issued his general orders to the Einsatzgruppen on 13 March 1941 and at the end of the month Hitler told his generals that this was a 'struggle between two world views' in which the Soviet Union would not have simply to be defeated, but the 'Jewish-Bolshevik intelligentsia' and 'asocial and criminal' Bolsheviks would have to be eliminated. Himmler repeated Hitler's orders to Halder to the effect that this would be a 'war of annihilation' in which the enemy were to be denied any of the conventional rights of warfare. In May Himmler's deputy, Reinhard Heydrich, spelt out the details, ordering that all Jews, Bolshevik functionaries and 'Asiatic subhumans' should be shot. On 14 May Hitler suspended military law, so that any German soldier could mistreat Soviet citizens with impunity, short of actions that seriously threatened military

[340] discipline. Five days later an addition was made to Barbarossa calling for 'fanatically drastic action' against 'Bolshevik agitators' and Jews. On 6 June Hitler issued the notorious 'commissar order' whereby all 'Jewish-Bolshevik functionaries' were to be shot. It was issued with the full endorsement of Brauchitsch and Halder, and the commissars were to be executed by the Wehrmacht rather than the SS. Shortly afterwards the High Command issued an order to the troops which read:

> It would be insulting to animals were one to describe these Jewish oppressors of humanity as animals. They are the embodiment of the infernal and insane hatred of everything honourable in mankind. In the form of the commissar we witness the revolt of the subhuman against noble blood.

The army raised some mild objections to the commissar order, arguing that it might strengthen Soviet determination to resist, and also objected that military discipline would be threatened by the limitation of the army's jurisdiction in the earlier decree. It made no principled stand on these issues and the army was fully complicit with Hitler in this monstrous undertaking. It cooperated fully with the SS and their Einsatzgruppen, and was guilty of countless atrocities in this most terrible of wars.

That the German officer corps, which still preserved to a large extent its conservative, aristocratic and Protestant values, should so readily abandon all considerations of morality, legality and common decency is truly astonishing. So incredible indeed that many still insist, with all the mounds of evidence to the contrary, that this never happened and that the army preserved its honour until the bitter end. There are many factors that partially explain this appalling moral collapse, but they leave a nagging doubt as to their adequacy. The army had enjoyed a series of extraordinary successes and seemed invincible. Hitler's status as a charismatic Führer was unchallenged, unquestioned and awe-inspiring. The generals were already complicit in atrocities committed in Poland, to say nothing of having planned and executed an aggressive war. They had colluded and connived with Hitler and were bound together as a criminal band who now had no alternative but to continue as his faithful minions or go down together to utter destruction. They agreed with Hitler in the absurd idea inherited from the previous generation that Germany faced a simple choice between world power and annihilation. They were in full agreement with most of Hitler's aims. They saw the need for living space and autarky. They shared his hatred of Marxism in all its forms. Their anti-Semitism might not have been quite so murderous, but it was deep-rooted and unquestioned. An instructional manual issued by the OKW in 1939 stressed the importance of the struggle against 'world Jewry', which should be exterminated like 'a dangerous parasite'. They regarded all Slavs as inferior, fit only for menial labour on behalf of their German masters. They saw the 'racial community' as a necessary requirement of total war. Very few thought that Barbarossa would be anything other than a walkover, or imagined that Britain posed any serious threat. It was only when the tide turned against the Wehrmacht that there was any serious questioning of the depths to which this great nation had sunk, and then the question was to see what could be saved from the wreckage, both moral and material.

This already deplorable situation was made even worse when dramatic changes were made in the criteria for officer selection. With the rapid expansion of the army in peacetime the personnel department was faced with the increasingly difficult problem of maintaining the quality and the homogeneity of the officer corps. There were about 3,200 officers in 1933, but the number rose to almost 90,000 by 1939 and 180,000 by October 1942. When Hitler took over the supreme command of the army (OKH) on 19 December 1941 he ordered that henceforth experience in battle should be the main criteria for commissions and promotions, rather than educational qualifications and seniority. He shared the front-line soldier's detestation of staff officers that he coupled with his social-Darwinist belief that all problems could be surmounted with fanatical will-power, heroic self-sacrifice and unwavering fortitude. At first the vast army bureaucracy managed to frustrate his intentions, but in September 1942 he decided to take the matter into his own hands. First he fired the chief of general staff, Franz Halder, a man who was the very personification of everything he detested and whom he accused of having spent the entire previous war behind the lines where he had not even earned the Iron Cross second class for a wound. Then he appointed his adjutant and lickspittle Rudolf Schmundt head of the personnel department. Schmundt, who died from injuries sustained in the attempt on Hitler's life on 20 July 1944, issued an order on 31 October 1942 which read:

> Every single officer must be thoroughly cognisant of the fact that it is primarily the influence of Jewry that stands in the way of the German people's claim to living space and for its claim to greatness, and which for the second time has forced our people to sacrifice our sons' blood in defence against a world of enemies . . . There is no difference between a so-called 'decent Jew' and others.

The result was a dramatic change in the social composition of the officer corps. Ninety per cent of officer cadets in 1941 had the school-leaving certificate (*Arbitur*), but this soon dropped to 50 per cent. Two-thirds of the field marshals were from the nobility, but only 16.6 per cent of the generals. Fourteen per cent of lieutenants in 1937 were aristocrats, but the percentage dropped to 3.9 by May 1943. An increasing number of officers had only attended elementary school, and a number of generals had been promoted from the ranks. This new breed of officer believed unquestioningly in the Führer, was fanatically committed to National Socialism and was immune to any suggestion that the war could ever be lost. After the failure of the 20 July plot Hitler wreaked a terrible revenge on the old officer corps when thousands were executed. The majority of those who remained were ideologically committed, fanatically loyal and determined to fight on whatever the cost and against all the odds. Wherever possible they faithfully executed Hitler's demented orders in the final weeks of the war and were thus directly responsible for the appalling loss of life in the final hopeless battle.

On 2 May 1941 General Georg Thomas, head of logistics in the ministry of war, called a meeting of the secretaries of state to discuss the forthcoming campaign in the east. He told his audience that the campaign would be successful only if the army could be fed from Soviet sources for the next three years and that this meant that millions would have to die. A few days before this meeting the head of the nutrition department of the Four-Year Plan, Herbert Backe, told Goebbels that Germany faced a serious food shortage that could only be overcome by the ruthless exploitation of the Soviet Union. Backe, who was born in Batum, fancied himself as an expert on Russia. He announced that: 'The Russian has put up with poverty, hunger and frugality for centuries. His stomach is ductile, therefore sympathy would be misplaced.' Germany would have to seize the agricultural areas of the Ukraine and starve the rest of the population to death. Given that the productivity of Ukrainian agriculture was half that of Germany's, that agriculture would be seriously disrupted by warfare, that there was a severe transportation problem with a shortage of east–west routes with a different railway gauge, and having analysed the experience of the First World War, it was estimated that between 30 and 40 million Soviet citizens would have to die of starvation so that the army could be fed and the home front adequately provided. Such appalling ideas were not new. As early as January there had been much talk of murder on an unimaginable scale to dispose of 'useless eaters' and the Einsatzkommandos which were to carry out this grim task began to be organized in February. At the beginning of June the meat ration was reduced from 500 to 400 grams per week, roughly the same as the allowance in Britain, and shortly thereafter potatoes were rationed. The attack on the Soviet Union was thus in part a *va banque* play to overcome Germany's food shortages. Hitler was full of confidence, telling Goebbels on 4 June that the Red Army would be smashed within a fortnight.

The offensive began on 22 June 1941 with 3 million German soldiers and 600,000 allies from Hungary, Romania, Slovakia and Finland facing a Red Army of 2.9 million. The Soviets were far better equipped with 15,000 tanks, some of which were vastly superior to the German models, against a mere 3,648, and 9,000 aircraft against 2,510, but they were caught off balance. This was partly because of Stalin's disastrous miscalculation of Germany's intents, but also because the Red Army was positioned for a forward defence, with airfields at the front and armour poised to disrupt the Wehrmacht's deployment. It was a helpless stance when called upon to stand and fight. Barbarossa went like clockwork in the initial stages, the army advancing 400 miles within three weeks in a series of brilliantly executed battles of encirclement. On 3 July Halder confided in his diary that the war would be over within a fortnight. But the Soviets still had three vital factors in their favour: time, space and resources, including 14 million men in the reserve. These were to frustrate Hitler's three intentions announced on 16 July: the Soviet Union was to be mastered, divided up and exploited. Hitler was so confident of victory that he overlooked the need for building up reserves or equipping the army for a winter campaign. Instead he ordered the armaments industry to concentrate on building ships and aircraft for an attack on Britain, and 5 million men were temporarily relieved from military duty.

It soon became uncomfortably obvious that this optimism was ill placed. By the end of August 1941 the Wehrmacht had suffered 410,000 casualties, considerably less than the Red Army, but they could find only 232,000 replacements. At the beginning of September Goebbels noted in his diary that[2] 'The military development is not such that we would have wished' and blamed the situation on Brauchitsch whom he described as both insecure and 'a vain fop'. Wilm Hosenfeld noted in his diary in September that if the war were not won within the next few weeks it would be lost[3]. At the beginning of October Hitler announced to the adulatory crowd in Berlin's Sportpalast that the Russians were defeated. Soldiers at the front greeted the broadcast with bitter laughter. Then the rains began and the roads turned into a sea of mud. Still the Germans pushed on, reaching the outskirts of Moscow by mid-November, but the temperature dropped to 40 below zero and the Red Army clung tenaciously to every inch of ground. On 5 December the Soviets at last launched their counter-attack west of Moscow. The Germans were forced back between 60 and 150 miles and

[344] Hitler was obliged to place the entire front on the defensive. Barbarossa had failed, and the Soviets had wrested the initiative from the Germans. Britain was now spared the threat of invasion, the European resistance movement was given much-needed encouragement, and with the Japanese attack on Pearl Harbor on 7 December the war took on a wholly different dimension.

The main reason for Germany's defeat in 1918 had been the chronic lack of manpower compared to the Entente's almost inexhaustible supply. Now they were facing the same problem. Between 1 November 1941 and 1 April 1942 the Wehrmacht suffered 900,000 casualties, many caused by freezing to death in their summer uniforms. Only half that number could be replaced. The loss of matériel was equally serious; 2,340 tanks, 8,000 aircraft and 74,200 wheeled vehicles had been destroyed. The minister of munitions, Fritz Todt, and the commander of the reserve army, who was also the officer in charge of armaments, General Friedrich Fromm, realized that the war could not be won and begged Hitler to make peace with the Soviet Union. Hitler would not listen to such advice and rambled on about 'iron will' and 'fanatical determination'. He denounced his generals as ana-chronistic incompetents who failed to understand the basic concepts of modern warfare, and began to interfere with the conduct of war down to the tactical level. With obscene disregard for the suffering of his troops, and in accordance with his appalling social-Darwinist ideology, he announced that if the German people were not tough enough and were not prepared to make the necessary sacrifices they deserved to be destroyed and replaced by a stronger breed. None of this disguised the fact that his prestige and charisma had suffered a severe denting and his long-suffering troops on the eastern front began to refer to him with heavy irony, shortening the appella-tion 'the greatest commander of all times' to '*Gröfaz*'.

The Soviet Union outmatched Germany not only in manpower, but also in armaments production. By halting the German advance in December the bulk of industrial plant in the west could be shipped back behind the Urals, an astonishing achievement that most experts felt was impossible, and the Germans had no long-range bombers capable of attacking this industrial base. Whatever had to remain was destroyed, so that whereas Soviet arma-ments production almost doubled, the Germans found precious little left behind. Whereas the German war machine had been adequately supplied by the Soviets before 22 June 1941, Germany was now desperately short of critical raw materials. By March 1942 Goebbels came to the sad conclu-sion that Germany could not face another winter in the Soviet Union. The army would have to go on the defensive in October and fight on for another hundred years if necessary.

The key figure in the economic exploitation of the occupied territories in the east was General Eduard Wagner, the quartermaster general in the General Staff who was responsible for supplying the army and the Einsatzkommandos, relations with the SD, civil administration, prisoners of war, and hunting down partisans. He worked in close cooperation with Backe and the Four-Year Plan, as well as Heydrich and the RSHA, and it was he who was largely responsible for the decision to let Leningrad starve, as well as for the exceptional brutality of the Stalingrad campaign. There were 19,000 civilians working in the Economic Staff East that was responsible for exploiting the resources of the Soviet Union.

The administration of the occupied eastern territories was nominally under Rosenberg and his ministry for the east, but once again there were no clear limits to Wagner's and Rosenberg's jurisdictions, or between the army, the SS and the civilians. The situation was further complicated by serious divisions within Rosenberg's ministry between those who wanted to coop-erate with the Soviet peoples and those who wanted to exploit them. The Reich Commissars were theoretically subordinate to Rosenberg, but acted independently and were frequently locked in battle with the military. Hinrich Lohse, the Reich Commissar in Ostland (the Baltic States and White Ruthenia), a man whom Goebbels described as 'an everlasting mischief-maker'[4], had a series of fist fights with a senior army officer to whom he was nominally subordinate. Most of the junior officials in Himmler's RKFDV thought that his plans for German settlements in the east were totally unrealistic. Yet in spite of all these difficulties the administration was relatively efficient. In the First World War there were 10,800 German civil servants working in Belgium, in the Second World War there were only 800. Ostland and Ukraine had 30 million inhabitants and were administered by 13,000 civilians. Most of these people were young men with university training, whereas their superiors such as Rosenberg, Backe, Sauckel and Kube were 'old warriors'. The resulting generational conflict was almost inevitable. Most of the younger generation were volunteers, and those who fell prey to what was known as 'eastern rage' (*Ostkoller*) were posted home without any questions being asked. They were assisted by tens of thousands of Soviet citizens who were under constant attack from partisans, seriously disrupting their efficiency. Army Group Centre co-opted 200,000 local policemen, in addition to whom there were 45,000 Germans in the OD, which in the view of one senior German official were little more than organized robber bands.

In spite of these auxiliary forces the German Army was far too thin on the ground to control so vast an area. Even with stringent curfews, frequent

[346]   pass controls, police raids and draconian punishments, only a semblance of order could be maintained. For all the talk of ending the 'tyranny of the collective farms' the exploitation of the peasantry was far worse than it had been under Stalin. Elaborate schemes were put in train to collect agricultural produce and ferocious punishments were meted out to those who failed to meet their quotas. Officials soon came to the bitter realization that whereas the machine-gun was quite an efficient instrument for collecting produce it was virtually useless as a means of production. It was impossible for Army Group Centre in Belarus to live off the land and vast quantities of food had to be brought in from Ukraine. The Army Group needed 1,200 head of cattle per day to provide 1.5 kilos of meat per man per week (which was more than three times the civilian ration in Germany). Cattle got thinner for lack of fodder, with the average weight falling by 52 per cent so that twice the number of animals had to be killed. Combined with partisan raids, plunder and black-market racketeering, this created an intolerable situation that was further aggravated by the increasingly drastic remedial measures. The Wehrmacht was far from being the highly disciplined force that it is often thought to have been, and the line between requisition and plunder was exceedingly thin, even with death penalties for plunder. The German-occupied Soviet cities were soon desperately short of food, causing widespread disorder and disease. By July 1941 it was clear that rationing would have to be imposed.

On 31 July General Thomas wrote: 'the intelligentsia has been killed, the commissars have gone, large areas left untended (starvation)'. He then set priorities for the allocation of food. First came the front-line soldiers, then the army of occupation, followed by food for Germany, then for Soviet citizens working in Germany, and lastly for other Soviet citizens. Soviet workers in the occupied territories were to be allowed 1,200 calories per day, non-workers got 850 calories and Jews a mere 450. That more did not die was due solely to the ingenuity of an army of black marketeers, smugglers and squirrelers. The situation would have been even worse had the Soviets not evacuated between 10 and 17 million people as the Germans advanced, but on the other hand they took large amounts of agricultural machinery with them and dismantled a number of important factories.

The Germans set about the systematic depopulation of the cities in order to provide additional labour on the land and to relieve the pressure for food in the urban areas. Thus the population of Kalinin, some 120 miles north of Moscow, was 250,000 in 1941; when the Germans arrived this had dropped to 160,000, and on liberation there were only 16,000 left. The Germans were thus able to increase the area under cultivation, but they were still hampered by the lack of agricultural machinery and a shortage [347] of fuel for what they had. This was only partially offset by importing machinery, seed grain and farm animals from the Reich. This movement away from the towns resulted in a serious shortage of labour and the process soon had to be reversed. Since 80 per cent of the craftsmen and artisans in Belarus were Jewish, most of whom were murdered, skilled labour was exceedingly hard to find.

In spite of all the talk about starving 30–40 million people and for all Göring's bluster that 'Whoever does not work for Germany, should perish', it soon became clear that such a policy was unworkable. It was possible to starve Soviet prisoners of war, Jews in the ghettos, a select group of Poles and the mentally ill, but it was not possible to murder such a vast number of people by such means. The German authorities were deeply concerned about the spread of disease that was bound to result from mass starvation, even to the point of Heydrich issuing strict instructions that Jewish doctors should be kept alive. Equally important was the obvious fact that such a course of action would turn the entire population against the German invaders and swell the ranks of the partisans, who already presented a major problem. Between 30,000 and 50,000 Soviet Jews joined the partisans in whose ranks they were not always welcomed. With the deeply ingrained Russian anti-Semitism there were frequent vicious incidents and a number of Jewish partisans were murdered by their comrades. The food problem was somewhat relieved by establishing communal kitchens in the occupied towns that provided a modest supplement to the inadequate rations. In Belarus, where the food shortage was exceptionally severe, the Wehrmacht began to put all males between the ages of 15 and 45 in civil prison camps so as to keep them under close control. In some instances the age limit was extended to 60.

Setbacks

Hitler's decision, made in the night of 10/11 December 1941, to declare war on the United States was yet another example of his *va banque* mentality. It did not come as a great surprise, for most observers had been expecting this to happen ever since June. Now at last Hitler had a chance to lash out at a power that was sending vast quantities of supplies to Britain and the Soviet Union and which was Germany's greatest rival in the ultimate bid for world power. Would he now make good his vow made on 30 January 1941 in a broadcast speech to destroy all Jews if the United States were to enter the war? Hitler hoped that the United States would concentrate its forces in the Pacific, allowing him to concentrate on a U-boat offensive in the Atlantic to sever Britain's umbilical cord. Had he perhaps begun to realize that the war was lost and was orchestrating a national suicide? Whatever the case, his reference to the United States as 'half Jewish and half Nigger', wallowing 'like a sow in a sty full of shit', shows that his sense of reality was becoming alarmingly tenuous. On the eastern front the Wehrmacht was ordered to press on to the industrial region of the Donetz basin, to the oilfields of the Caucasus and to the Volga, an important transport artery. He imagined that the army would then be well supplied and poised to press on into Persia, Afghanistan and India. In North Africa Rommel's Afrikakorps was ordered to advance to the Suez Canal, enflame anti-British sentiment in the Arab world, and eventually link up with German forces from the eastern front. Lastly, as the Wehrmacht advanced the Jews in the area under occupation would be murdered, either by the SS Einsatzgruppen, ably assisted by army units, or in the death camps.

On 8 February 1942 Fritz Todt, the efficient and clear-headed minister of munitions, was killed when his plane flew back from a visit to Hitler's headquarters in East Prussia. It was widely rumoured that he had been murdered because he had deigned to criticize Hitler and was thus regarded in the Führer's immediate entourage as a defeatist. Todt was flying in a twin-engine Heinkel 111, a notoriously unreliable machine, even though Hitler had forbidden his top officials from flying in twin-engined aircraft. He was replaced by Albert Speer, a 37-year-old ambitious, self-seeking toady, who had won Hitler's affection with his gigantomanic plans for rebuilding Berlin, to be renamed Germania as the capital of the vast new empire. He was also an organizational genius and a tough infighter, who succeeded in greatly increasing Germany's industrial output, thus prolonging a war that many believed could not possibly be won.

German armaments production was grossly inefficient and lacking in central control. The weapons were of high quality, but there were far too few of them. Speer set about centralizing production. When he took office Germany was producing 180 Me 109s per month in a series of small factories. By 1943 production had increased to 1,000 per month in three large factories. This was an impressive increase, but Germany still lagged far behind the Soviet Union in aircraft production. That Speer achieved a 555 per cent increase in aircraft production is often taken as evidence that the Allied bombing campaign was both ineffectual and immoral. This is far from being the case. Speer frequently complained about the devastation done to armaments factories, transport networks and fuel supplies. After the

Figure 10.1   Hitler and Speer admiring a model of the new Berlin

Hamburg raid in August 1943 he said that if this were to happen to six more cities the war would be lost. On 6 October 1943 he reported that air raids had disastrously cut back the rate of growth of the armaments industry. Goebbels' diaries are full of expressions of concern over the effects of the bombing campaign on morale, and Hitler was well aware of the fact that 'fortress Germany' no longer had a roof[5]. Leaving aside questions of morality, the Allied bombing campaign made a major contribution to the defeat of Nazi Germany. Allied bombing, expulsion from the east and the mass rapes committed by the Red Army are all too often either seen as adequate atonement for Nazi crimes, or used to place the victors on the same moral plane as the vanquished.

Speer did an excellent job in covering his traces and thus saving his neck at Nuremberg. He claimed to have saved those Jews in Berlin who were working in the armaments industry when in fact they were temporarily saved due to a lack of transport. He ruthlessly expelled Jews from their apartments in Berlin to make way for his Brobdingnagian buildings. He lorded over the Hasag company with its six camps in Poland that were run by Poles and where conditions were even worse than in the concentration camps, with rations of 200 grams of bread and 1.5 litres of watery soup per day. The hapless slaves in these camps produced a third of the ammunition used on the eastern front. Hundreds of thousands of others worked in

Figure 10.2   Dresden after the raid on 13–14 February 1945

intolerable conditions in underground factories, concentration camps and makeshift workshops. The mortality rate was appallingly high. Albert Speer, presented to us by Joachim Fest as the good bourgeois, a person like us, misled in his youth, blinded by power, but remaining ever upright and contrite in middle age, in short the 'good Nazi', was a mass murderer, slave driver and a go-getting sycophant[6].

Three million Germans scored some impressive successes on the eastern front in 1942 against 5 million far better equipped Soviet troops. The Germans occupied the Crimea, which was designated as Germany's future Riviera where Germans from South Tyrol would be settled, as well as reaching the Caucasus. At 4 in the morning of 3 July 1942 Hitler issued orders that all but the Tartars and the 'ethnic Germans' were to be evacuated from the Crimea, adding that detailed plans should be ready by 9.30 that morning. It was pointed out that this would involve the expulsion of 700,000 people, thus leaving the Crimea somewhat short-handed for the harvest, where-upon the scheme was dropped. In mid-September 1942 General Paulus' 6th Army reached the strategically important town of Stalingrad, but soon became bogged down in ferocious house-to-house fighting, and was gradually encircled and cut off from supplies. Although 1 million Red Army soldiers were lost in this the most ferocious battle of the war, the recently promoted Field Marshal Paulus had no alternative but to surrender on 2 February. Ninety thousand of the 250,000 men under his command were taken prisoner; only 5,000 lived to tell the terrible tale. Hitler made the right strategic decision to hang on to Stalingrad at whatever cost, because it enabled him to save his troops in the Caucasus. Stalingrad was undoubtedly a great victory for the Red Army, but its significance should not be exaggerated. The German Army had suffered a severe setback, and Hitler's prestige was further battered, but it was still an awesomely professional fighting machine as the third battle of Kharkov was soon to show.

For Goebbels Stalingrad amounted to 'a virtually irreparable loss of prestige' and he commented 'it must be absolutely devastating for us to imagine that in the end we, by far the most superior race in Europe, have become the victims of the technology of a race of semi-apes'[7]. He agreed with Göring that Hitler had aged terribly. He sat all day in his bunker brooding and worrying, finding it increasingly difficult to make up his mind. The only encouragement was that 'a people who have burnt their bridges usually fights with greater ruthlessness than one that still has the possibility of retreating'. Hitler, who was rapidly retreating into a world of fantasy, would have none of this, announcing in May that Germany would soon conquer Europe and then make a bid for world power.

The Germans also suffered a major defeat in North Africa in 1942–43. Montgomery failed to deliver the *coup de grâce* to Rommel's Afrikakorps at El Alamein in early November 1942, but in any case Rommel had to turn back to face the Americans who landed in Morocco and Algeria a few days later. Rommel flew to see Hitler at his headquarters in Rastenberg in East Prussia, where he argued that the situation was hopeless and that North Africa should be evacuated. Hitler insisted that the defence of Tunisia and Tripolitania was essential and poured in reinforcements. The result was that when the inevitable defeat came in May 1943 the bag was even bigger, with the Allies taking 250,000 prisoners. For Goebbels this was 'a second Stalingrad' and the suggestion that the entire North Africa campaign was designed simply to make time for the building of the Atlantic Wall[8] against an Allied invasion of France convinced but a few.

The U-boat offensive was initially extremely effective with the Allies losing an average of 750,000 tons of shipping every month in 1942. The American chief of staff, General George C. Marshall, predicted imminent disaster if drastic measures were not taken. Soon the tide turned. American shipyards built far more shipping than the Germans could sink. The German production of new U-boats began to falter. The Allies greatly improved convoy defence, air surveillance, submarine detection devices and depth charges. The German naval codes were cracked so that the movement of U-boats could be tracked easily. By May 1943, when of the 118 U-boats in service 38 failed to return, it was clear that the Allies were winning the Battle of the Atlantic, and American men and matériel flooded into Britain in preparation for the final showdown.

The turn of the tide

There was increasing disillusionment with Hitler's leadership among senior army commanders by the spring of 1943 and it was widely felt that the *Gröfaz* had lost his grip. A group of senior officers, including Manstein, Zeitzler, Milch and Guderian, argued in favour of appointing a Supreme Commander East so that Hitler's meddling with operational and tactical matters could at least be reduced, but Hitler would hear nothing of a proposal that challenged his supreme leadership. Others thought in more drastic terms. A group of young officers around Colonel Henning von Tresckow, a senior staff officer in Army Group Centre, who was close to General Beck, and civilians associated with Dr Carl Goerdeler, a conservative nationalist and former mayor of Leipzig, argued that Hitler had to be assassinated. With the complicity of General Hans Oster of military intelligence and General Friedrich Olbricht of the reserve army, a bomb was placed in Hitler's plane when he visited Army Group Centre in Smolensk on 13 March 1943, but unfortunately it failed to detonate.

The critical battle on the eastern front was fought in the Kursk salient in July when 2,000 German Panzer faced 4,000 Soviet tanks in the greatest tank battle in history. It was an appalling bloodbath, matching Stalingrad in ferocity, which ended in a Soviet victory. The Germans had at last been defeated at armoured warfare, the game they knew best. Their elite armoured units, equipped with the latest Panzer models and manned by fresh troops, had been smashed, and the Soviets had finally gained the strategic initiative. Kursk, not Stalingrad, was the turning point in the war on the eastern front. From now on Germany fought a desperate defensive campaign as the Red Army made its relentless advance towards Berlin.

The Allies now landed in Sicily and crossed to the Italian mainland; Mussolini was toppled and the Allies began their painfully slow advance up the boot of Italy against resolute German resistance. The Germans had occupied Vichy France in November 1942 in anticipation of an Allied landing, which did not occur until 6 June 1944. Half of the total wartime casualties occurred in these terrible last nine months as the Allies slowly closed in from the west, the Soviets from the east.

In retrospect it is easy to see why Germany was defeated, but it is still difficult to imagine how it was possible to prolong the unequal struggle and fight fanatically until the bitter end. Fear of the Russians played a major role, and was fanned by Goebbels' propaganda machine, but the real answer lies in Hitler's charismatic leadership that met with such extraordinary resonance. Here was the saviour who overcame the shame and humiliation of a lost war, who undid the ignominious Versailles settlement, who brought full employment, completed the process of national unification and restored the country's status as a great power. His prestige was further enhanced by stunning victories in Poland, Scandinavia, France and the Balkans and the shining prospect of a powerful and prosperous new Germany lay ahead. As success followed success and as Goebbels' propaganda machine churned out hyperbolic paeans to his all-encompassing genius, more and more Germans fell prey to the Führer's charisma and his entourage was reduced to a collection of apple-polishers and toadies bitterly competing with one another for his grace and favour. Hitler had an astonishing ability to convince those who initially opposed him that he was right, inspiring the doubtful and the fearful with his absolute conviction, all the evidence to the contrary, that victory would soon be theirs. All who worked closely with him were astounded by his phenomenal memory and command of the smallest details, and found his fanatical self-confidence hard to resist and his single-minded passion truly inspiring.

Now that we know of the total moral depravity, the mean-spirited narrow-mindedness, and the suicidal recklessness of this loathsome creature it is hard to believe that the overwhelming majority of Germans regarded him as their Messiah and were drugged into a state of mindless adulation. Where they saw the omnipotent and omniscient Führer we see Charlie Chaplin's Great Dictator or Bruno Ganz's megalomaniac living in a world of illusion[9]. But Hitler had had six years of breathtaking successes when he unleashed his war. War leaders, such as Hitler's opponents Churchill, Stalin and Roosevelt, can always exploit the deep-rooted hopes and desires of

[354] their people and inspire their confidence. Hitler was able to draw on the capital of the six peacetime years to further enhance his prestige, to which he added two years of successful campaigning. He enjoyed the unquestioning loyalty of the vast majority of his people, even when he led them to disaster, ruin and defeat. By March 1944 Goebbels no longer believed Hitler's confident analyses of the situation and he was deeply frustrated by his inability to take decisive action. He admired Stalin for having generals he did not trust shot, and for taking appropriate action against 'God botherers' (*Pfaffen*). But he still believed blindly in Hitler, now because he had no other choice. The appalled reaction to news of the attempt on Hitler's life on 20 July 1944 is testament to the virtually undiminished power of his charisma when it was obvious that the great gambler had lost all. Without Hitler's amazing charisma Germany would never have been able to continue fighting for three and a half years after the reverse before the gates of Moscow in December 1941. Even when his lustre began to dim after the defeats at Stalingrad and in North Africa, Hitler was seen as the only man who could save Germany from the savage revenge of the Bolshevik hordes and bring the war to an end with its territory intact. Hitler's unquestioned authority and seductive power remained virtually undiminished even during the final horrific days in the Berlin bunker. Some of the more prominent rats, such as Himmler and Göring, swam away from the rapidly sinking ship, but there was never a hint of revolt. Most generals carried out his insane orders, and hard-nosed campaigners allowed themselves to believe that his much vaunted 'miracle weapons' would turn the tide, or that what Goebbels called 'the perverse coalition between plutocracy and Bolshevism' would fall apart. These weapons had first been promised in the spring of 1943 so that most of the other ranks had long since ceased to believe in them.

By September 1944 Goebbels knew that Hitler was living in a world of fantasy. He confided in his diary[10]: 'I am afraid that the Führer is operating with divisions that either no longer exist or only partially exist.' When the Japanese ambassador Oshima told him that Germany should make peace with the Soviet Union he did not protest and simply forwarded this suggestion to Himmler and Bormann to pass on to Hitler. The war had long since been lost and it was criminal folly to continue fighting. More than half of Germany's total casualties were inflicted after 20 July 1944, 90 per cent of them by the Red Army.

In August 1944 Hitler began planning for an offensive in the Ardennes. It was his final *va banque* play, but it was one where the odds were so impossibly high that it amounted to an act of national suicide, a dress rehearsal for the 'Nero Order' of 19 March 1945. A makeshift 6th SS

Panzer Army under Sepp Dietrich was tacked together at the cost of seriously weakening the eastern front, thus effectively delivering up Germany to the Red Army. The remnants of Manteuffel's 5th Panzer Army could offer precious little support. The Germans were hopelessly outnumbered and desperately short of fuel and ammunition. The Allies had absolute command of the air and a spot of bad weather gave the Germans only temporary relief. Even a dyed-in-the-wool Nazi like Field-Marshal Model knew that the offensive was doomed, although it was likely to have brief initial success by throwing everything against a weak spot between the US 1st and 3rd armies. Hitler would not listen to reason and as a result only managed to hold up the Allied advance for a few weeks at the cost of 120,000 men and tons of irreplaceable equipment. He had no reserves to counter the Red Army's offensive on the Vistula, and the Big Three, far from falling apart, were to meet at Yalta where there was no serious dissension.

Germany fought two distinct wars. In the west and in North Africa the conventions of warfare were respected, soldiers accused of crimes against the civilian population were subject to military justice, and occupation regimes were relatively benign until resistance movements provoked savage reprisals and Jews were rounded up for deportation and death. The war in the east was quite different. SS Einsatzgruppen began their murderous handiwork behind the front from the very beginning of the campaign in Poland, and army units were guilty of numerous atrocities against civilians. This was merely a foretaste of the campaign in the Soviet Union. Some 3.3 million Soviet prisoners of war died in captivity, and often no prisoners were taken. Most were starved to death, others were less fortunate. In winter prisoners were sprayed with cold water and froze. One POW camp was set on fire and when the inmates fled in panic they were mown down. At a post-war trial in the Federal Republic this outrage was excused as a legitimate response to a revolt. The Wehrmacht killed more prisoners of war in the Soviet Union than the Einsatzkommandos killed Jews. One hundred hostages were shot for every German killed by partisans and 50 for every German wounded, resulting in hundreds of thousands of deaths. The Red Army meted out similar treatment on those that fell into its hands so that German units would fight to the last bullet rather than surrender to a terrible fate. Christian Gerlach[11] has shown that of the 345,000 'partisans' killed in Belarus the vast majority were Jews, women and children. Women who were prepared to abandon their children to be killed were spared and then sent to work, often to the Reich. There are no statistics as to how many took this option. Most of the anti-partisan operations were designed to kill Jews and other 'useless eaters', destroy unproductive villages, round up forced labour and seize livestock and crops to feed the Wehrmacht. The partisans were not very successful at killing Germans, but they did attack the collective farms, denied the Wehrmacht food and fuel, and above all disrupted the railway system, destroying more engines than could be produced in occupied Europe. The anti-partisan campaign was thus primarily designed as a convenient cover for murder and plunder on a truly appalling scale.

The Wehrmacht was fully complicit in all these atrocities. Admittedly it did not condone rape or plunder, more out of concern for military discipline, but it saw this as a radically new form of warfare in which conventional rules no longer applied. On 10 October 1941, shortly after the massacre at Babi Yar in which 33,771 Jews were murdered, General Walter von Reichenau told his men in the 6th Army that they were the 'bearers of an inexorable racial idea' who should mete out just punishment on 'Jewish humanity' and set about the 'merciless extermination of racially foreign maliciousness'. General Erich Hoepner, who was later executed for his part in the plot to kill Hitler, ordered that all means were justified in the defence of European culture against 'Asiatic barbarity' and 'Jewish Bolshevism'. General von Manstein proclaimed that all Jews deserved to be 'liquidated'. The army cooperated fully with the Einsatzgruppen in shooting hundreds of thousands of Jews and in rounding up millions of others for the death camps.

This shameful descent into barbarity was caused in part by the brutalization of warfare in which no holds were barred and in which soldiers were desensitized to the point where all consideration for the dignity of human life was lost. An equally important factor was the deep-rooted and long-standing contempt for Slavs as subhumans at the forefront of the Asiatic hordes. The same is true of an all-pervasive anti-Semitism that, within the context of a brutal war, could all too easily become infused with murderous intent. There was also a powerful economic motive behind this appalling butchery. The more people killed the more food there was to go round. Jewish property was used to subsidize the cost of the occupation and to provide housing for Soviet citizens deemed to be of use to the Germans. In addition there were tactical considerations. On 10 July 1943 Himmler ordered North Ukraine and Central Russia to be depopulated, men and women put to work, children thrown into prison camps. The partisans would then be denied all popular support, the food situation could be further regulated, and the entire region would be under firm control. The Red Army put paid to this scheme, but for millions this was too late.

According to paragraph 45 of the *Manual of Military Law* any soldier issuing an order that resulted in a breach of the law was fully responsible, and any subordinate who carried out that order in the knowledge that it was in breach of civil or military law was equally liable. Furthermore, there is no recorded instance of a member of the Einsatzgruppen or soldier who refused to take part in mass murder receiving any punishment more severe than the loss of a few days' leave. Most were simply posted to other duties. That so few had the moral fibre to refuse to participate in what according to military law was a crime is testament to the exceptional degree to which ordinary and normally decent human beings were barbarized by the experience of warfare, by propaganda, by orders from above, and by a charismatic Führer with his uncompromising genocidal mission.

Thanks to Christian Gerlach's meticulous study of German occupation policies in Belarus[12] we can get a glimpse of the horrors they perpetrated in the Soviet Union. In this region alone between 1.6 and 1.7 million people were murdered, amounting to between 18 and 19 per cent of the population. Of these victims 700,000 were prisoners of war, 500,000–550,000 Jews, 345,000 'partisans' and their supporters, with 100,000 in other groups such as 'Asiatics' and Gypsies. Not included are the hundreds of thousands of Belarussians who died in the Red Army, and these frighteningly cold statistics take no account of the terrible suffering of those who somehow managed to survive this barbarous invasion.

Such brutality was by no means confined to the Soviet Union. The army and the SS cooperated closely in their campaign against 'Jews and commissars' in the campaign in Yugoslavia and Greece. Thirty-one thousand hostages were shot in Yugoslavia in the first few weeks and the army soon announced that Serbia was 'cleansed of Jews' (*Judenrein*). Croatian fascist bands slaughtered 200,000 Serbs, prompting Tito's partisans to seek terrible revenge on the Germans who had made this massacre possible. As in the Soviet Union hostages were shot in huge numbers and whole villages destroyed. A fierce partisan war in Greece resulted in similar atrocities. The pattern was repeated in Italy after the surrender to the Allies and in France.

Resistance

'Resistance' is a word of extreme elasticity, and the precise point where discontent, grumbling and refusal to toe the line become active resistance has proved hard to define. Did refusal to give the Nazi salute, or to insist on saying 'good morning' rather than 'Heil Hitler', constitute resistance, and what about refusal to join the party, or offering help to Jews and other victims of the regime? Was expression of uncertainty about the outcome of the war, at the risk of one's life, a deliberate attempt to undermine the morale of the fighting forces, or was it a realistic assessment of a hopeless situation? The obvious forms of resistance such as handing out leaflets, sabotage, passing on information to the enemy, or attempted assassination, lack any such ambiguity. The problems were further compounded by historians in the former German Democratic Republic insisting that Communists were the only true resisters, using them to reinforce the anti-fascist legend. In the Federal Republic the emphasis was initially on the men behind the 20 July plot, and the role of the Communists, who were numerically the most important group of active resisters, was largely ignored. Then, under the dominant influence of social and cultural historians anxious to illustrate history from below, youthful pranks, an enthusiasm for Benny Goodman or even doing nothing at all, were seen as acts of resistance. The time had now come to make a clear distinction between mere non-conformity and active opposition, while admitting that the demarcation lines are vague and the scale ranges from hesitation and reluctance to dissent, from protest to active opposition, from conspiracy to an actual attempt to remove the tyrant and overthrow the regime.

No regime, however brutal, has ever been able to impose absolute conformity and consent; the human propensity to complain and to grumble is indefatigable, the 'totalitarian' model much beloved of old cold warriors in the social sciences is an ideologically motivated over-simplification. The Nazis were villains, but they were not fools, and were well aware of the need for people to let off steam at the expense of minor officials and over daily grievances. Those who were in active opposition were quite another matter. At the outset their enemy was clearly defined as the 'Marxists', with the KPD at the top of the list. They were an easy prey. Communist opposition to National Socialism had been rendered totally ineffectual by the ridiculous theory of 'social fascism', which held that social democracy was equal to or, in some versions, worse than National Socialism. Communists actively cooperated with Nazis to destroy the Weimar Republic, and some even welcomed Hitler's appointment as chancellor as a sure sign that capitalism in Germany was on its last legs. With the Reichstag fire and the subsequent violent suppression of the KPD, German Communists suddenly awoke to the fact that there was a subtle difference between the two. The KPD made no preparations for an underground organization and the Nazis had little difficulty in destroying the remnants of a demoralized party. Stalin finished off what Hitler left undone. More German Communists were dispatched by Soviet executioners than by their homologues in Germany.

The Hitler–Stalin Pact left European Communists in a state of helpless confusion that was only relieved with the attack on the Soviet Union; but the fundamental problem of the KPD's resistance was that it strove to replace one brutal dictatorship by another, a prospect that had only limited appeal.

The Comintern had managed to build up a reasonably effective commun- ications network in Germany, using party activists working for the post and telephone services, for the railways and Rhine shipping under the leadership of Willi Gall. He was arrested in 1940, his place taken by Wilhelm Knöchel, the German representative of the Red Trades Union International and a member of the KPD's central committee. He was initially based in Amsterdam where he worked with the Comintern's representative Daan Goulooze, who was in radio contact with Moscow and sent instructions to the major European centres. Knöchel moved to Berlin in 1942 when radio contact with Moscow from Amsterdam was seriously compromised. He was arrested by the Gestapo in January 1943, tortured into collaboration and executed in July 1944. This resulted in the virtual destruction of the Comintern's network.

The outstanding Communist organization in Nazi Germany was the Soviet spy network run by a Polish Jew, Leopold Trepper, first from Brussels and then from Paris. He had his agents in all Western European countries, forming a network known to the Gestapo as the Red Orchestra. The German section was led by Harro Schulze-Boysen, a Luftwaffe officer working in the air ministry, and Arvid Harnack, a civil servant in the ministry of economics. These two colourful characters, genuine anti-fascists rather than principled Communists, had a vast network of influential people and gathered a considerable amount of valuable intelligence that was forwarded to Moscow. They also spread propaganda at home, aimed principally at foreign workers. German counter-espionage uncovered the Brussels transmitter in 1942, a number of arrests were made, and by the systematic use of torture the extent of the conspiracy was revealed. The Berlin group was arrested in 1942 and the ringleaders hanged.

The SPD was far less active and was in a state of complete demoralization after Papen's coup in Prussia in 1932. Their efforts were further hampered by a deep-rooted distrust of the KPD that rendered it impossible to make a common front against a deadly enemy. The exiled leadership, based initially in Prague, collected information on developments in Nazi Germany, and maintained contacts with small resistance groups, some members of which became actively involved in the conspiracy of 20 July.

The Catholic Church

In spite of the heroic resistance of a number of Catholic priests and some Protestant clergymen, the churches' record in the Third Reich was shameful.

The democratic republic was destroyed, the rule of law rendered a mockery, the left brutally suppressed, tens of thousands were murdered in the euthanasia programme, hundreds of thousands forcibly sterilized, Jews were humiliated, excluded from society and finally murdered by the million. Yet in the face of these horrors and the flagrant violation of all the fundamental tenets of the Christian faith, the churches remained silent. The churches at least offered a space outside the coordinated Nazi world, but this was more than offset by their capitulation in the face of evil and their tacit acceptance, and not infrequently active support, of National Socialist criminality.

Eugenio Pacelli wrote an effusive letter to Hitler assuring the 'Führer' that he was 'deeply attached to the German people who were under his care' shortly before he was crowned as Pope Pius XII on 12 March 1939. This was a remarkable document coming after six years of Nazi terror and the Anschluss during which 800 priests had been arrested, to say nothing of the pogrom of 9 November 1938. The Pope removed the anti-Nazi bishop O'Rourke of Danzig and replaced him with Carl Maria Splett, whose shameful activities earned him life imprisonment after the war. He remained silent over the invasion of Poland, but condemned the Soviet attack on Finland as a 'cold, calculated crime without parallel'. He maintained his silence when the Germans murdered 4 bishops, 1,996 priests, 113 clerics and 238 nuns in Poland. After Germany's victory over France Pius XII ordered thanksgiving masses for the Führer in all German churches. Bishop Galen of Münster, the Catholic Church's favourite example of heroic resistance to National Socialism, thanks to his stand against euthanasia, rejoiced at Germany's victory over the 'English plutocrats' who only thought of their 'sacks of coffee and their cotton plantations' and not of Jesus Christ, the heavenly redeemer. Galen was delighted when Germany attacked the Soviet Union and proclaimed: 'Our thoughts will be with our brave soldiers night and day so that God will help them in their successful defence against the Bolshevik threat to our people.' One week after the invasion Pius XII said in a radio address that there was 'light amid the darkness of the storm which gives rise to sacred hopes: heroic courage in the defence of the foundations of Christian culture and a confident hope in its triumph'. For him the Nazis were fighting a holy war for the reconversion of mother Russia.

The German Catholic episcopate was seriously divided, with an influential group, led by the bishop of Berlin, Count Konrad von Preysing, arguing that National Socialism was a denial not only of the basic tenets of the Christian faith, but also of fundamental human rights. 'Brown Konrad' Gröber of Freiburg, a member of the SS who had played an important part in negotiating the Concordat, assured the Pope that National Socialism was 'at its best a copy of Christianity', and waited until Hitler was dead to [361] announce that: 'It is wrong to come under the spell of an extreme and merciless anti-Semitism in order to destroy a race which, by being forced to defend itself will be an even greater danger than the largest enemy army.' The autocratic and ultra-conservative Cardinal Faulhaber of Munich called upon the bishops to protest against the murder of the Jews, but the Pope argued that this would do nothing to help and would probably make the situation worse. After the war Faulhaber announced that the killing of 6 million Jews was no worse a crime than the Allied bombing of Germany. Subsequently Bishop von Preysing begged the Pope to speak out on behalf of the suffering Jews, but Pius XII said that he could do nothing to help 'non-Aryans' and that caution and restraint was needed '*ad maiora mala vitanda*' (to prevent a great evil). On 16 October 1943 1,259 Jews were arrested in Rome and 1,007 were sent to Auschwitz. Even then the Pope remained silent, but at least the Vatican helped a number of Jews by providing passports and asylum.

There were some notable exceptions to this mute acceptance of the most terrible of crimes. Bernhard Lichtenberg, a parish priest in Berlin, included the Jews in his prayers continually following the pogrom of 1938. He protested openly against the euthanasia programme and was arrested in October 1941. He died under highly suspicious circumstances on his way to Dachau. He was one of the very few priests and ministers who spoke out on behalf of the victims of this monstrous regime and died a martyr's death.

Assistance, protest and resistance

There were very few punishments meted out to those within the borders of the Reich who gave assistance to Jews, and incidents of this sort were not reported in the press. Outside Germany such behaviour earned an automatic death sentence. Yad Veshem memorializes 264,500 people from Germany, Austria and the Czech provinces of Bohemia and Moravia who helped their persecuted Jewish fellow citizens in one way or another. Since tens of millions of others either actively hunted down Jews or stood passively aside, precious few were saved. Of the 5,000–7,000 'submarines' in Berlin only 1,400 lived to pay tribute to those honourable people who resisted a terrible evil that appeared in the guise of ethnic virtue and who refused to accept the barriers between 'us' and 'them'.

In 1942 a tiny group of 10–15 students in Munich formed a resistance group known as the White Rose. It was a disparate bunch of brave, idealistic but hopelessly unrealistic young people, united in their disgust at the apathy of the German people when confronted with incontrovertible evidence of the regime's criminal nature. Although they had been told that the Gestapo was on their heels they distributed pamphlets in Munich University, were arrested, hauled up in front of the dreadful Roland Freisler and promptly executed. It is unfortunate that the White Rose is now only remembered by the names of Hans and Sophie Scholl, after whom countless schools and streets are named. They certainly deserve their place in history for their courage, but so do Alexander Schmorell, Willi Graf and Christoph Probst.

Once Hitler was firmly in power the military was the only group capable of overthrowing the regime, but this was unlikely to become a hotbed of resistance. From the outset Hitler had skilfully wooed the armed forces. He privileged them, giving them the weapons for which they longed, along with the manpower. He had dealt drastically with the challenge from the SA. His triumphant campaigns had silenced the faint-hearted. The officer corps was also in broad agreement with the aims and ideology of National Socialism. They might disapprove of the plebeian rowdiness of some of its aspects, but they shared its racism and anti-Semitism, its ultra-nationalism and its militant expansionism. Hitler could count on the submissive loyalty of a military bound to him by a solemn oath of allegiance. It was not until the appalling crimes committed in the Soviet Union, in which the Wehrmacht was fully implicated, and the dramatic reversal in the fortunes of war that there was any serious opposition.

The longest-standing and most effective resistance group was known as the Kreisau Circle, named after the Silesian estate of Helmuth James von Moltke, a lawyer in civilian life who became the OKW's legal expert. This was a very mixed bag of Christian socialists, anti-militarists, supporters of the League of Nations and New Dealers, much under the influence of the hazy notions of Eugen Rosenstock-Huessy, a professor of law in Breslau who emigrated to the United States in 1933, and bound together by a fervent detestation of National Socialism. For all its aristocratic elitism, the Kreisau Circle was admirably open in debate and far from socially exclusive. It was in close touch with more conservative, authoritarian, nationalist and monarchist figures such as the former mayor of Leipzig, Carl Goerderler, and the former ambassador in Rome, Ulrich von Hassel. Another group of young staff officers, such as Count Claus von Stauffenberg and Henning von Tresckow, were outraged at the barbarity of Germany's campaign in the east and, knowing that the war was lost, wanted to save what they could from the ruins. Goerdeler did not believe that Germans could be entrusted with a democracy and was in favour of a dictatorship. Stauffenberg announced that he was opposed to 'Jewry, capital and the Catholic Church' [363] and claimed that he stood for 'true National Socialism'. Nor should it be overlooked that among the conspirators and those associated with them, such as Count Peter Yorck von Wartenburg, Baron Rudolf-Christoph von Gersdorf, Henning von Tresckow, Count Fritz-Dietlof von der Schulenburg, Arthur Nebe, commander of Einsatzkommando B, General Georg Thomas, and General Eduard Wagner, were men who were implicated in appalling crimes committed in the Soviet Union in the name of National Socialism. Theirs was indeed a selective morality.

There were certain fundamental issues over which this heterogeneous group could agree. Hitler had to be removed, the war had to be brought to an end, and the rule of law restored. But there was no agreement about how Hitler should be put out of business, on what terms the war should be ended, or on the fundamental principles on which the new Germany should be based. Most serious of all was the obvious fact that the conspirators had virtually no support among the people. Hitler's charismatic appeal was enhanced by a series of spectacular victories, and although it was somewhat diminished after Stalingrad it was still astonishingly powerful as the German people became inextricably implicit in his crimes and clung to the hope that the Führer could save them from dire retribution. All too many of the conspirators imagined that it would be possible to preserve Germany's great power status; some even hoped that they could keep some of the territory that Hitler had conquered. Much of their thinking about domestic politics was also strongly flavoured with notions from the Wilhelmine empire and from the ultra-conservative and corporatist thinkers of the Weimar Republic with their anti-democratic, elitist gallimaufry of 'Prussian traditions' and 'Prussian socialism'. The more democratically inclined and less nationalistic members of the Kreisau Circle subscribed to a Christian socialism that was also vague, emotionally overcharged and distinctly removed from harsh political reality.

In the later stages of the war the only active conspirators who had a chance of getting close enough to Hitler to be able to kill him were from the military. These men were mostly young aristocrats, or came from the upper reaches of the bourgeoisie, who before the war had enthusiastically endorsed the regime. Both their social background and their earlier enthusiasm made it very difficult for members of the left-wing opposition to overcome their reservations and misgivings. They were also keenly aware that they were unlikely to win much support from ordinary Germans, and troubled by the realization that they had remained silent for so long in the face of countless crimes and injustices that they were seriously compromised.

[364] The more they planned, the more the conspirators realized that they had little chance of success. They were after all officers and gentlemen, not hired guns or SS killers. General Henning von Tresckow, chief of staff of the 2nd Army, wrote to Stauffenberg:

> The assassination attempt must go ahead, whatever the cost. Even if it does not succeed, we must act in Berlin. It is not a question of the practical end, but rather that the resistance movement has made this daring move in the eyes of the world and of history. Everything else is unimportant.

The 20 July plot thus resulted from moral fortitude rather than political resolve; it was an action of exculpation, not a future-oriented effort to reshape Germany.

Those who actively resisted Hitler were a tiny minority. They showed such exceptional courage that it seems churlish to criticize them. In struggling against an evil regime they not only risked their lives, they were despised and rejected by the vast majority of their compatriots as traitors. Theirs was a remote and somewhat snobbish elite, whose ideas seem at best old-fashioned and which met with no resonance in the post-war years. Their idealistic notions of a 'third way' between totalitarian Communism and materialistic capitalism and of an organic society ruled by an elite seemed oddly antiquated. When coupled with hopelessly unrealistic territorial ambitions for a Germany rid of National Socialism, their vision appears as alarmingly reactionary and nationalistic. Such ideas were deeply rooted in the German tradition, going back to the days of the Freiherr vom Stein and the Napoleonic wars, and they were reinforced by the precarious situation in which they found themselves. Obliged to conspire in the utmost secrecy, permanently dodging the Gestapo and the SD, they were unable to appeal for mass support, quite apart from the fact that the glaring shortcomings of parliamentary democracy in the Weimar Republic offered them little encouragement. They were thus forced by circumstances to seek refuge in utopian visions that today seem neither practical nor desirable. But this is hardly the point. By bravely confronting a brutal, corrupt and immoral regime, they upheld fundamental ideals of human decency, morality and essential human rights. Their vision of a better world than that of Nazi Germany, however blurred and distorted at times it might have been, was a positive and inspiring attempt to face a number of social and moral issues which in our present-day complacency we ignore at our peril. They had the courage to dream of a better world and, even if many of their ideas seem quaintly antiquated, hopelessly metaphysical or frankly reactionary, it should be remembered that they had the courage to act, regardless of the [365] cost, against an inhuman tyranny. The theologian Dietrich Bonhoeffer, a Protestant martyr, agreed with Henning von Tresckow in seeing the resistance in its true light. For him the struggle against this evil regime was an act of contrition from which no foreign political advantage could or should be made. Most of the Kreisau Circle eventually shared this selfless view.

The end

Hitler's triumphant campaigns against Poland and France further enhanced his charismatic authority. He had overcome the humiliation of a lost war and torn up the few remaining shreds of the Treaty of Versailles. National honour had been restored and the Führer was at the pinnacle of his power and prestige. Here was a politician who had gambled and won, proving himself to be a soldier of genius. The war transformed Hitler from demagogic politician to commander. His place was at the front, far away from the seat of government in Berlin. At first, Hitler's transformation from a 'hands-off' to a 'hands-on' dictator was scarcely noticed, for in a sense he had always been a hands-off leader, first in the party, then as the unchallenged tyrant. What to some, like Goebbels, had at first seemed to be indecisiveness was in fact a deliberate tactic. He had always allowed his underlings to battle it out while he hid his real intentions from even his closest associates, and then either acted as the honest broker, or made a sudden and surprising decision, catching his myrmidons off balance as they jockeyed for positions of power and influence. The result was a flurry of activity and a dynamic vitality that never ossified into bureaucratic routine. As the war dragged on Hitler became increasingly remote in his distant headquarters, his attention focused on the conduct of war. The affairs of state were ignored; the head of the chancellery, the indefatigable Hans Lammers, was left virtually powerless, to be shunted aside in 1944 by the brutal and ambitious Martin Bormann. Bormann replaced Rudolf Hess as head of the party chancellery after his flight to Scotland in 1941 and was promoted to the rank of minister. In April 1943 he was appointed secretary to the Führer. He gradually managed to determine who had access to Hitler, and therefore who had real power. It was he who interpreted the Führer's will that was the ultimate source of legislative and executive authority. It was Bormann who transformed the 'Führer's will' into the 'Führer's orders'. There was still much that remained beyond Bormann's power and influence. Hitler communicated directly with the armed forces via the OKW and OKH or through his adjutants. Himmler assiduously guarded his vast SS empire from any outside influence. The Gauleiter remained truculently independent, taking orders from Hitler alone.

Hitler became increasingly isolated, surrounded by a small group of worshippers, gradually removed from reality and finally living in a megalomanic dream world into which the light of day was never allowed to enter. Jodl described the atmosphere at Hitler's headquarters as being 'a mixture of monastery and concentration camp'. Goebbels and Himmler were closest to him, along with Albert Speer, for whom he showed something approaching affection. Göring was initially among the elect but with the failure of the Luftwaffe and with his indolence, drug addiction and increasingly sybaritic lifestyle his star began rapidly to wane. His military entourage changed with increasing rapidity, but the obsequious Keitel and the diligent and colourless Jodl remained within the magic circle.

The result was that the organizational chaos that characterized the Third Reich, although occasionally given some shape and direction by an order from the Führer, became ever more pronounced. That the entire system did not fall apart, but was actually remarkably effective, is at first sight amazing. In part this was due to Hitler's charismatic power, although greatly weakened, still having its magic hold over an entire people, for he now seemed to be the only hope for a solution to the host of problems that beset Germany, even though he was ultimately their prime cause. It was also due to a state of permanent emergency that vitiated administrative routine and red tape. Special agencies were encouraged, determined leaders were given their head, and innovative solutions promoted, as polycratic governance and charismatic leadership reinforced one another. The mass murder of Europe's Jews was a paradigmatic example of how this system worked as the Führer's will was carried out with ideological frenzy and deadly efficiency.

When the fortunes of war turned against Germany, with the Red Army steadily advancing and the fatherland reduced to a pile of rubble by Allied bombers, the Führer's charismatic appeal diminished still further, but it did not vanish. Hitler was now seen as the only hope for a miraculous salvation from the deadly vengeance of the Bolshevik hordes and of world Jewry. Those who had precious little faith in such an unlikely turn of the tide were silenced by mounting terror as special courts sprouted up to ensure that the 'racial community' was not threatened by violations of 'the healthy sentiments of the race'. The police and security services ran amok to an extent that was even too much for Hans Frank, the murderous General Governor of rump Poland who had proclaimed in December 1941 that 'We must kill Jews wherever we find them', and who in August 1942 had amused an audience in Lemberg (Lvov) by saying: 'I am told there used to be thousands of flat-footed Indians in this town, but now there are none to be seen. I hope you haven't done anything nasty to them.' Frank, who was also Reich Legal Leader and head of the German Academy of Law, complained in 1942 that: 'The extent of the wilful use of the plenipotentiary powers of the executive organs of the police has now reached such proportions that one can now speak of an utter disrespect for the law by certain racial comrades.' By April 1945, 40,000 people had been hauled up in front of special courts. Sixteen thousand death sentences were carried out; the remainder of those convicted were given lengthy prison sentences. Five thousand of these death sentences were handed down by Roland Freisler's People's Court after the attempt on Hitler's life on 20 July 1944. A major achievement of Allied bombing was that it killed this vile creature, who had been a prisoner of war in Russia, had learnt Russian and had fought with the Bolsheviks, returning to Germany in 1920 and joining the NSDAP in 1924. Hitler announced that he did not trust the man, whom he regarded as an unprincipled opportunist. Military justice was even more ferocious with 30,000 death sentences, at least 20,000 of which were by drumhead court martial.

Blind faith and murderous violence could not halt the rapid waning of Hitler's charismatic appeal. Henriette von Schirach, the daughter of Hitler's court photographer Heinrich Hoffmann, remarks in her memoirs that her husband, the Reich Youth Leader, once likened Hitler to Dorian Grey. Those around him refused to recognise the rapid deterioration of his health and his increasingly violent mood swings, still seeing in him the idealized Führer, thus avoiding a painful cognitive dissonance. With Allied and Soviet troops firmly placed on German soil and with virtually unchallenged Allied air supremacy all hopes were dashed. Goebbels tried desperately to persuade Hitler to address the nation, but the Führer knew in his heart of hearts that his magic had gone. On 20 February 1945 Hermann Esser, the secretary of state in Goebbels' propaganda ministry, the proud owner of party membership card number two, widely known as 'the little Hitler' because of his mimicry of Hitler's mannerisms and speech, and author of *The Worldwide Jewish Plague* (1939), was chosen to read a brief proclamation on behalf of the Führer. It met with a generally negative response. The Führer had finally lost his magic hold, except over a few fanatics in the bunker who had inextricably tied their fate to his. But still there was no revolt or mutiny, no expression of disgust or shame, as Germany headed for the fall.

Göring, Ribbentrop and Speer left Berlin on 20 April, Hitler's 56th birthday. Hitler threw Göring out of the party on 23 April and Himmler on the 28th. Goebbels remained until the bitter end and was rewarded by being appointed chancellor on Hitler's death. Grand Admiral Dönitz, another blindly loyal disciple, was to be president. Thus on 30 April, when Hitler took his wretched life, the offices of president and chancellor were once again separated. The new chancellor followed in his master's footsteps within hours. On 6 May the laconic General Eisenhower reported to the Combined Chiefs that his mission was accomplished, Jodl having signed an act of surrender at Reims. On 9 May Keitel signed a second act of surrender in the presence of Marshal Zhukov and Air Marshal Tedder in Berlin, thus bringing Hitler's war to a formal end.

It was also the end of National Socialism. The Third Reich left nothing behind it but horror. The horror of tens of millions of dead, of a continent laid waste, the horror of a great nation reduced to barbarism, moral squalor and mass murder, soon to be crippled by guilt. Six million of Germany's 23 million dwellings had been destroyed and there were 17 million refugees wandering among the rubble. It is a horror that still refuses to go away, that still baffles and bewilders, remaining as a permanent challenge to historical understanding. It is the horror of the unfathomable.

Charisma and community

That Hitler's image becomes increasingly blurred is due in part to the natural process whereby the present fades into the past to become history, but it is also because Hitler was nothing without his charisma, which began to dim in December 1941 and could only survive his death among a handful of besotted devotees. Where once the great thaumaturge would call the children to step forward so that he could place a salving hand upon their heads, a prematurely aged, trembling and defeated Führer, abandoned by his partners in crime, could only pat the cheek of an adolescent warrior in a pathetic gesture of resignation. A man who had described himself as a living god had shrivelled into a ranting megalomaniac who had lost touch with reality. Once the masses, swayed by his masterly demagogy, had absolute trust and faith in him. Now in his final years he could not appear in public or on film for fear that his rapid ageing and declining health would shatter his charismatic spell. He was still the focal point of collective hopes and fears, but as failure heaped upon failure hopes faded, fears grew and his magic dimmed. Max Weber argued that charismatic leadership is not reality oriented[13]. This is both its strength and its weakness. It can inspire, demand superhuman effort and achieve the seemingly impossible, but it can all too easily be overwhelmed by reality. Charismatic leadership is a form of psychosocial disorder in which morality and a sense of reality begin to crumble, giving rise to gigantomania and an overpowering hubris. Only so can it be explained that Hitler imagined that succeeding generations would be grateful to him for having murdered 6 million Jews. That they would regard such an unparalleled crime with utter horror would never have occurred to him.

Gustave LeBon offers some explanation as to how it was possible for the German people to contribute to Hitler's monstrous project with a clear conscience[14]. The sense of belonging to a group enhances the individual's sense of power to the point of feeling omnipotent. The everyday restraints on the individual are removed, giving rise to an alarming potential for extreme violence. Hitler at the height of his charismatic power, commanding the total allegiance of his people, could induce a form of collective megalomania, so that everything seemed possible: even the murder of every single Jew in Europe. But by December 1941 there were nagging doubts that the war could be won, doubts that are echoed in Himmler's remarkable speech in Posen in October 1943. Soon it became obvious that nothing short of a miracle or a providential stroke of luck could save the situation. Then there was the bitter realization that all was lost, the German people had let their Führer down and deserved to be destroyed, but at least he had saved Europe from the Jews. Then at last in a moment of clarity he realized that he could expect nothing but humiliation and death from his enemies and he prudently took his own life, thus leaving the German people to face the consequences of their actions. The destruction of the Jews was of far greater importance to Hitler than the survival of Germany, indeed he called for the collective suicide that he had contemplated as early as December 1941. That would have been, as Simon Wiesenthal has argued, a historical exit very much to his perverse taste. That faith in such a leader could have survived so long can only be explained in terms of individual psychopathology. The charismatic bond had long since begun to dwindle.

What was left of the 'racial community' that was at the very heart of National Socialism? How far were the National Socialists able to realize their promise that all the social barriers based on class, wealth, property or education would be removed, to be replaced by the natural inequality inherent in human beings? How far was a society in which the 'leadership principle' had replaced the democratic pluralism of liberty, fraternity and equality, the 'ideas of 1789', acceptable to ordinary Germans? Was the slogan *Gemeinnutz vor Eigennutz* (the good of the community must come before the good of the individual) generally accepted? The sense of community was heightened by the gigantic party rallies, national holidays, festivals, parades and mass meetings in which the participants were roused to a state of impassioned frenzy and blind obedience. Those deemed to be 'alien to the community' (*gemeinschaftsfremd*) had been excluded, 'racial vermin' (*Volksschädlinge*) had been exterminated, but what was left? The 'racial community' had no rational or empirical basis, but was a cultic, sacral community held together by blind faith in an increasingly remote mystagogue. Since the 'racial community' depended upon a complete and utter subordination of the individual will to the charismatic leader, it fell apart as his hold was gradually broken as failure piled upon failure. The crushing defeat of the German armed forces brought the 'destined community of the German *Volk*' to a bitter end.

The concept of a 'racial community' was not unique to National Socialism. It was a key component of the romantic ideology of the *völkisch* youth movement known as the Wandervogel; it was widespread in right-wing circles and among Christian groups. In a society as divided politically, socially and economically as Weimar Germany there was a hankering after the mythical 'spirit of 1914' and the 'community of field grey', a widespread desire to remove the barriers of class and estates, a longing for a sense of community that was skilfully exploited by the National Socialists and which was the key to their appeal right across the social spectrum. Against the background of a lost war followed by a humiliating peace settlement, of hyperinflation, depression, mass unemployment and near civil war, the vision of a heroic, disciplined, austere, virtuous Germanic race, ready for every sacrifice even unto death, a master race tied by German blood to German soil but steeled for the conquest of 'living space', had such a powerful appeal that people were prepared to submit to such catchphrases as 'You are nothing, your *Volk* is everything' or the Hitler Youth's 'The flag is more important than death'. There was a fundamental contradiction within National Socialism between the ideology of the 'racial community' and the social-Darwinist principle of each for his own in the struggle for power and privilege. As Victor Klemperer noted in his diary on 31 January 1938[15]: 'I am struck every day anew by this trivial antithesis: such incredible things are created – radio, airplanes, the talkies – and yet insane stupidity, primitiveness and bestiality cannot be rooted out. All this inventiveness will lead to murder and war.'

The first massive demonstration of the desire to create a 'racial community' was the National Labour Day on 1 May 1933, during which Hitler denounced the 'arrogance of the estates' and the 'insanity of class' and Goebbels proclaimed the end of the class struggle and the creation of a 'racial community'. All this was accompanied by folk dancing and costumed parades to underline the fact that this was a national festival that had nothing to do with international working-class solidarity, Robert Ley's DAF was designed to strengthen the 'ideology of the racial community and the community of the workplace' in which the concept of employer and employee was to be replaced by 'soldiers of labour, some who give orders, others who obey'. Consideration of the national good was to overcome economic and social conflicts and antagonisms, the militarization of labour to be offset by the attractive offerings of KdF.

None of this could possibly have worked had the regime not managed to overcome unemployment and had a series of startling foreign political successes. Life in Germany was still grim and austere, but Germany was back at work and the future looked promising. The destruction of the labour movement and the emphasis on piecework led to a rapid erosion of working-class solidarity and the gradual formation of a consumer-oriented mass society which many former Social Democrats and Communists found hard to resist. Massive propaganda to the effect that this was an equal society for 'racial comrades' with equal opportunities for all was eagerly accepted, until it was gradually shown to be a cruel illusion. Similarly, unemployment had been overcome to a large extent by colossal investments in road building and rearmament that resulted in a crushing burden of debt and rising inflation. Wages limped behind prices, leading to mounting discontent that was combated by increasingly strident propaganda and outright terror.

The German people went reluctantly to war in 1939, even though it was widely felt that Britain was to blame for refusing to accept Hitler's reasonable demands over Danzig and the Corridor, but the startling successes in the early stages of the war further enhanced Hitler's charismatic hold over his people. With their determination to strengthen the 'racial community' and boost civilian morale so as to avoid a repeat of the collapse of the home front in the First World War, the Nazis tried to fight the war on the cheap under the motto: 'as much normality as possible, as much war as necessary'. All this began to fall apart when the Wehrmacht was halted outside Moscow in December 1941 and was defeated at Stalingrad and in North Africa, and when the Soviets seized the strategic initiative after the battle of Kursk. As the Red Army relentlessly advanced and Germany was pulverized by Allied bombing, Hitler's charismatic hold was reduced to a vain hope in a miracle, as the Germans huddled together in air-raid shelters or, spurred on by lurid propaganda, made a last-ditch stand against the Bolshevik hordes.

It is truly astonishing that so few realized that National Socialism was a gigantic fraud that ruled by terror, deprivation and hunger and that left

[372]   Germany an accursed outcast among nations. One such was Wilm Hosenfeld, who wrote in his diary in January 1942[16]:

> They ally with the ruling classes of finance and industry and uphold the capit alist system, while preaching socialism. They proclaim the rights to individual and religious freedom while destroying the Christian churches and fighting an underground war against them. They talk of the 'leadership principle' and the rights of the skilled to develop freely, while everything depends on being a party member. Even the hardest working people of exceptional talent are overlooked if they decline to join. Hitler promises peace while rearming to an incredible extent. He promises the world that Germany has no intention of taking over other peoples and denying them the right to be independent states, but what did he do with the Czechs, the Poles and the Serbs? . . . Look at the way the National Socialists live according to their principle of 'the good of the community takes precedence over individual well being'. They demand this of the little fellow, but do not even think of it themselves. Who is in the front line – the people, not the party. Now even physically weak people are drafted, while one sees perfectly robust and healthy young men in party offices and in the police, who do their duty far from harm's way. Why are they excused? They steal the property of Poles and Jews, in order to help themselves to it and enjoy it, while they have nothing to eat, waste away and freeze. They see nothing wrong in taking everything from them and squandering it.

Survival and an end to the horror of war was now all that mattered. Charisma had vanished, Hitler's order for a national suicide fell on deaf ears, the 'racial community', such as it had ever existed, disintegrated, National Socialism was totally discredited. Anything that was worth saving from the ruins was there in spite of National Socialism, and those who claim that there was anything remotely positive about the Third Reich make a cruel mockery of a terrible tragedy. The new Germany, ethically and aesthetically transformed according to racial principles, a community in which the old tensions of class and station were overcome, turned out to be nothing but a pile of rubble that had cost the lives of tens of millions. That there could be no hankering after 'the good old days', no repeat of a 'stab in the back' legend, and the claim that confrontation with the total moral bankruptcy and murderously destructive force of the National Socialist project provided valuable food for thought and the chance of a new beginning, all provided exceedingly cold comfort for victims and survivors alike. It took many years before a traumatized nation was able to begin the painful process of confronting its past.

NOTES

Chapter 1 Background

1. Walter Benjamin's 'Angel of History' is a very well known comment on Paul Klee's famous painting 'Angelus Novus'. It is in the chapter 'Über den Begriff der Geschichte' in Walter Benjamin's *Illuminationen*.

2. The Heimwehr was a nationalist, right-wing, paramilitary organization. 'Comrade Mauser' was a widely used description of Bolshevik violence, the Mauser being a pistol invented by a German gunsmith, Paul Mauser.

3. 'Techne' is the application of reason to production, i.e. craftsmanship in the original Greek sense, technology in its modern meaning. Heidegger, like Socrates and Aristotle, saw it as a threat to the higher knowledge of the 'episteme'.

4. Papen dissolved the Social Democratic government of Prussia on 20 July 1932 by emergency decree.

5. J. Goebbels, *Tagebücher 1924–1945*, ed. R.G. Reuth, 5 vols., (Piper, Munich, 2003).

6. All quotes from Hosenfeld from: W. Hosenfeld, *'Ich versuche jeden zu retten' – Das Leben eines deutschen Offiziers in Briefen und Tagebüchern*, (Munich, 2004).

7. This was the pseudonym of Paul Bötticher (1827–1891).

8. H.S. Chamberlain, *The Foundations of the Nineteenth Century*, (1899).

9. Tucholsky (1890–1935) was a prominent satirist during the Weimar Republic.

10. F. von Reck-Malleczewan, *Diary of a Man in Despair*, (Duck Editions: London, 2000).

11. J.P. Stern, *Hitler, The Führer and the People*, (Fontana: London, 1975).

12. 'Cunctator' refers to someone who is notoriously hesitant. The nickname of the Roman general Fabius Maximus.

13. M. Burleigh, *The Third Reich: A New History*, (Pan Books: London, 2001).

[374] ## Chapter 2 The origins of National Socialism

1. W. Hosenfeld, *'Ich versuche jeden zu retten'* – *Das Leben eines deutschen Offiziers in Briefen und Tagebüchern*, (Munich, 2004).

2. J. Goebbels, *Tagebücher 1924–1945*, ed. R.G. Reuth, 5 vols., (Piper, Munich, 2003).

3. Gregor Johann Mendel (1822–1884), priest and scientist. The father of modern genetics.

4. A referendum held in December 1929 against the Young Plan, supported by Hugenberg and the DNVP, the veterans' organization 'Stahlhelm' (Steel Helmet) and the NSDAP.

5. Goebbels, op. cit.

6. G. Aly, *Hitlers Volksstaat*, (Fischer S. Verlag: Frankfurt, 2006).

7. As mentioned, Hitler's 'Second Book' was not published during his lifetime. It first appeared as *Hitlers Zweites Buch*, edited by Gerhard Weinberg in 1961. An official English translation appeared in 2003.

Chapter 3 Hitler as chancellor

1. 'Old Warriors' (*alte Kämpfer*) were those who had joined the party at the beginning of 'the movement'.

2. D. Rebentisch, *Führerstaat und Verwaltung im Zweiten Weltkrieg. Verfassungsentwicklung und Verwaltungspolitik 1939–1945*, (Steiner Franz Verlag: Stuttgart, 1986).

3. A burning of un-German books by radical students.

4. Victor Klemperer's diary was published as *Tagebücher* in 1995 (Aufbau: Berlin). A three-volume English translation followed, *I Will Bear Witness* (1933 to 1941), *To The Bitter End* (1942 to 1945) and *The Lesser Evil* (1945 to 1959).

5. See H. Ott, *Martin Heidegger. A Political Life*, (HarperCollins: London, 1993) and 'Nur noch ein Gott kann uns retten', *Der Spiegel*, 31 May 1976.

6. I. Kershaw, *Hitler 1889–1936: Hubris* (Penguin Books: London, 2001), p. 441.

7. The notion of a 'weak dictator' comes from Hans Mommsen.

8. J. Goebbels, *Tagebücher 1924–1945*, ed. R.G. Reuth, 5 vols., (Piper, Munich, 2003).

9. E. Fraenkel, *The Dual State*, (1941).

10. F. Neumann, *Behemoth: The Structure and Practice of National Socialism*, (London, 1942).

11. Goebbels, op. cit.

12. S. Volkov, 'Antisemitism as a Cultural Code. Reflections on the History and historiography of Antisemitism in Imperial Germany', in: *Yearbook of the Leo Baeck Institute, XXIII* (1978), 25–45.

13. A. Hitler, *Mein Kampf,* (1925).

14. Ibid.

15. Unfettered, free-trading capitalism.

16. Goebbels, op. cit.

17. Lombroso (1835–1909) was an Italian criminologist and founder of the Italian School of Positivist Criminology.

18. K. Binding and A. Hoche, 'Permission to Destroy Life That Is Unworthy of Living. Extent and Form', (1920).

19. D. Peukert, *Volksgenossen und Gemeinschaftsfremde. Anpassung, Ausmerze und Aufbegehren unter dem Nationalsozialismus,* (Bund Verlag: Cologne, 1982).

20. D. Rebentisch, *Führerstaat und Verwaltung im Zweiten Weltkrieg. Verfassungsentwicklung und Verwaltungspolitik 1939–1945,* (Steiner Franz Verlag: Stuttgart, 1986).

21. Goebbels, op. cit.

22. A. François-Poncet, *Als Botschafter in Berlin 1931–1938,* (1947).

23. W. Shirer, *Berlin Diary, 1934–1941* (1941).

Chapter 4 Reordering society and the economy

1. D. Henderson, *Innocence and Design: The Influence of Economic Ideas on Policy,* (Blackwell Publishers: Oxford, 1986).

2. R. Overy, *The Nazi Economic Recovery,* (Cambridge University Press: Cambridge, 1996).

3. Karl Ballod (1864–1931) was a Latvian economist and Zionist.

4. D. Ricardo, *On the Principles of Political Economy and Taxation,* (John Murray: London, 1817).

5. W. Sombart, *Der Moderne Kapitalismus,* (1916).

6. 'Old Reich' refers to Germany before the Anschluss.

7. Stakhanov was the hero worker who greatly exceeded his norm, setting an example that other workers were called upon to emulate.

8. Shoah – the modern Hebrew word for the mass murder of European Jews by the Nazis in World War II.

9. Böll contributed to the plunder by making extensive purchases while serving in the German Army in France.

[376]   10. G. Aly, *Hitlers Volksstaat*, (Fischer S. Verlag: Frankfurt, 2006).

11. R. Dahrendorf, *Society and Democracy in Germany*, (London, 1968)

12. D. Schoenbaum, *Hitler's Social Revolution*, (W.W. Norton & Company: New York, reissue edition, 1997).

Chapter 5 The churches and education

1. J. Goebbels, *Tagebücher 1924–1945*, ed. R.G. Reuth, 5 vols., (Piper, Munich, 2003).

2. Ibid.

3. Inner emigration refers to those who opposed the regime, but did not play any active part in the resistance.

4. See H. Ott, *Martin Heidegger. A Political Life*, (HarperCollins: London, 1993) and 'Nur noch ein Gott kann uns retten', *Der Spiegel*, 31 May 1976.

Chapter 6 The arts and propaganda

1. J. Goebbels, *Tagebücher 1924–1945*, ed. R.G. Reuth, 5 vols., (Piper, Munich, 2003).

2. Ibid.

3. Aryan paragraphs: the law excluding Jews from the professions.

4. K. Zuckmayer with G. Nickel, J. Schrön and H. Wagener, *Deutschlandbericht für das Kriegsministerium der Vereinigten Staaten von Amerika*, (Göttingen: Wallstein, 2004).

5. The famous altar from Pergamon, now in Berlin.

6. Goebbels, op. cit.

7. W. Hosenfeld, *'Ich versuche jeden zu retten' – Das Leben eines deutschen Offiziers in Briefen und Tagebüchern*, (Munich, 2004).

8. Widukind was the legendary 8th century Duke of Saxony. Henry the Lion (1129–1195), also a Duke of Saxony, was one of the most powerful men in Germany.

9. The Horst Wessel Song was the Nazi Party anthem.

10. 'Neue Sachlichkeit' was a neo-realistic and socially critical art movement.

11. Pfitzner's 'Palestrina' was composed during 1912–1915 and the première was in Munich in 1917.

12. Hartmann's 'Mourning Music' or *'Trauermusik'* was written in 1939.

13. Konrad Henlein was the Nazi leader in the Sudetenland, appointed Gauleiter
    in the Sudetenland in 1938.

14. The pseudonym for Hermann Nielebeck.

15. 'Tin Pan Alley' – the source of popular music.

Chapter 7 The SA, SS and police

1. Darré's 'Pig' article appeared in the journal *Volk und Rasse* in 1926 and '*On Blood and Soil*' appeared in 1929.

2. O. Spann, *On the Sociology and Philosophy of War*, (1913).

3. Refers to those who joined the party after March 1933, i.e. who jumped on the bandwagon. The original 'March fallen' were those who died on the barricades in Berlin in March 1848. The expression is thus bitterly ironic.

4. Hechaluz (The Pioneer) was a left-wing Zionist organization.

5. The equivalent of an 'armchair strategist', a person who organizes murder bureaucratically, without actually pulling the trigger.

6. C. Koonz, *The Nazi Conscience*, (The Belknap Press: Cambridge, MA, 2003).

7. H. Arendt, *Eichmann in Jerusalem*, (Penguin Classics: London, 2006).

Chapter 8 Foreign policy

1. J. Goebbels, *Tagebücher 1924–1945*, ed. R.G. Reuth, 5 vols., (Piper, Munich, 2003).

2. Ibid.

3. Ibid.

Chapter 9 The Shoah

1. J. Goebbels, *Tagebücher 1924–1945*, ed. R.G. Reuth, 5 vols., (Piper, Munich, 2003).

2. Poles from the Reich Protectorate of Poland.

3. Goebbels, op. cit.

4. Goebbels, op. cit.

5. Goebbels, op. cit.

6. W. Hosenfeld, *'Ich versuche jeden zu retten' – Das Leben eines deutschen Offiziers in Briefen und Tagebuuhern*, (Munich, 2004).

Chapter 10 The war

1. M. Reich-Ranicki, *The Author of Himself: The Life of Marcel Reich-Ranicki*, (Phoenix, an imprint of Orion Books Ltd; London, 2002). Originally published in Germany in 1999 under the title *Mein Leben*.

2. J. Goebbels, *Tagebücher 1924–1945*, ed. R.G. Reuth, 5 vols., (Piper, Munich, 2003).

3. W. Hosenfeld, *'Ich versuche jeden zu retten' – Das Leben eines deutschen Offiziers in Briefen und Tagebuuhern*, (Munich, 2004).

4. Goebbels, op. cit.

5. Goebbels, op. cit.

6. J.C. Fest, *Speer: The Final Verdict*, (New York, 1999).

7. Goebbels, op. cit.

8. The Atlantic Wall refers to the coastal defences in France.

9. Ganz in the film *Der Untergang* (translated as *The Downfall* in English), 2005.

10. Goebbels, op. cit.

11. C. Gerlach, *Kalkulierte Morde: Die deutsche Wirtschafts- und Vernichtungspolitik in Weissrussland 1941 bis 1944*, (Hamburg, 1999).

12. Ibid.

13. M. Weber, *Wirtschaft und Gesellschaft*, (1922).

14. G. LeBon, *La psychologie des foules*, (1895).

15. Klemperer, V., *I Shall Bear Witness: The Diaries of Victor Klemperer 1933–1945*, (Weidenfeld & Nicolson: London, 1998).

16. Hosenfeld, op. cit.

FURTHER READING

Fascism and National Socialism

Arendt, H., *The Origins of Totalitarianism*, (New York, 1958)

Bessel, R. (ed.) *Fascist Italy and Nazi Germany: Comparison and Contrasts*, (Cambridge, 1996)

Blinkhorn, M., *Fascism and the Right in Europe 1919–1945*, (London, 1990)

Brady, R.A., *The Spirit and Structure of German Fascism*, (London, 1937)

Carsten, F.L., *Fascist Movements in Austria: From Schönerer to Hitler*, (London, 1977)

Carsten, F.L., *The Rise of Fascism*, (Berkeley, CA, 1980)

Cassels, A., *Fascism*, (New York, 1975)

De Grand, A.J., *Fascist Italy and Nazi Germany: The 'Fascist' Style of Rule*, (London, 1995)

Friedrich, K. and Z. Brzezinski, *Totalitarian Dictatorship and Autocracy*, (New York, 1967)

Gentile, E., 'The sacrilisation of politics: definitions, interpretations and reflections on the question of secular religion and totalitarianism', *Totalitarian Movements and Political Religions*, **1** (2000)

Gregor, J.A., *Interpretations of Fascism*, (Morristown, NJ, 1974)

Griffin, R., *The Nature of Fascism*, (London, 1993)

Griffin, R., *International Fascism – Theories, Causes and the New Consensus*, (London, 1998)

Hamilton, A., *The Appeal of Fascism: A Study of Intellectuals and Fascism 1919–1945*, (New York, 1971)

Kitchen, M., *Fascism*, (London, 1976)

Kitchen, M., *The Coming of Austrian Fascism*, (London, 1980)

Laqueur, W., *Fascism: A Reader's Guide*, (Berkeley, CA, 1976)

Larsen, S.U., *Who Were the Fascists? Social Roots of European Fascism*, (Bergen, 1980)

Mosse, G.L., *International Fascism: New Thoughts and New Approaches*, (London, 1979)

Mosse, G.L., *Masses and Man: Nationalist and Fascist Perceptions of Reality*, (New York, 1980)

Nolte, E., *Three Faces of Fascism: Action Française, Italian Fascism, National Socialism*, (New York, 1969)

Passmore, K., *Fascism: A Very Short Introduction*, (Oxford, 2002)

Pauley, B.F., *Hitler, Stalin, and Mussolini: Totalitarianism in the Twentieth Century*, (Wheeling, IL, 1997)

[380] Payne, S.G., *A History of Fascism, 1914–1945*, (London, 1995)

Rabinbach, A.G. 'Towards a Marxist theory of Fascism and National Socialism', *New German Critique*, **1**, (1974)

Schapiro, L., *Totalitarianism*, (London, 1972)

Sohn-Rethel, A., *Economy and Class Structure of German Fascism*, (London, 1978)

Turner, H.A. (ed.), *Reappraisals of Fascism*, (New York, 1975)

Turner, S.P. and D. Käsler (eds), *Sociology Responds to Fascism*, (London, 1992)

Weber, E., *Varieties of Fascism: Doctrines of Revolution in the Twentieth Century*, (New York, 1964)

Weiss, J., *The Fascist Tradition: Radical Right-Wing Extremism in Modern Europe*, (New York, 1967)

General studies

Ayçoberry, P., *The Nazi Question: An Essay in the Interpretation of National Socialism (1922–1975)*, (New York, 1981)

Bracher, K.D., *The German Dictatorship: the Origins, Structure, and Effects of National Socialism*, (London, 1971)

Broszat, M., *The Hitler State: the Foundation and Development of the Internal Structure of the Third Reich*, (London, 1981)

Burleigh, M., *The Third Reich: A New History*, (London, 2000)

Childers, T. and J. Caplan, *Re-evaluating the Third Reich*, (New York, 1993)

Dülffer, J., *Nazi Germany 1933–1945: Faith and Annihilation*, (London, 1996)

Evans, R.J., *In Hitler's Shadow: West German Historians and the Attempt to Escape from the Nazi Past*, (New York, 1989)

Evans, R.J., *Rereading German History: From Unification to Reunification 1800–1996*, (London, 1997)

Evans, R.J., *The Third Reich in Power*, (London, 2005)

Fraenkel, E., *The Dual State: A Contribution to the Theory of Dictatorship*, (New York, 1941)

Frei, N., *National Socialist Rule in Germany: The Führer State 1933–1945*, (Oxford, 1993)

Hirschfeld, G. and L. Kettenacher (eds), *The 'Führer State': Myth and Reality: Studies in the Structure and Politics of the Third Reich*, (Stuttgart, 1981)

Kershaw, I., *The Nazi Dictatorship: Problems and Perspectives of Interpretation*, (London, 2003)

Kitchen, M., *Nazi Germany: A Critical Introduction*, (Stroud, 2004)

Koonz, C., *The Nazi Conscience*, (Cambridge, MA, 2003)

Lee, W.R. and E. Rosenhaft (eds), *The State and Social Change in Germany 1880–1980*, (Oxford, 1990)

Lehmann, H. and J.V.H. Melton, *Paths of Continuity: Central European Historiography from the 1930s to the 1950s*, (Cambridge, 1994)

Meinecke, F., *The German Catastrophe: Reflections and Recollections*, (Cambridge, MA, 1950)

Mommsen, H. (ed.), *The Third Reich Between Vision and Reality: New Perspectives on German History 1918–1945*, (Oxford, 2001)

Neumann, F., *Behemoth: The Structure and Practice of National Socialism*, (London, 1942)

Noakes, J. and G. Pridham (eds), *Nazism 1919–1945*, 4 vols, (Exeter, 1983–98)

Overy, R.J., *The Dictators: Hitler's Germany and Stalin's Russia*, (New York, 2004)

Shirer, W.L., *The Rise and Fall of the Third Reich: A History of Nazi Germany*, (New York, 1960)

Stachelberg, R., *Hitler's Germany: Origins, Interpretations, Legacies*, (London, 1999)

Stachelberg, R. and S.A. Winkle (eds), *The Nazi Germany Sourcebook: An Anthology of Texts*, (London, 2002)

Stachura, P.D., *The Shaping of the Nazi State*, (London, 1978)

Hitler

Bullock, A., *Hitler: A Study in Tyranny*, (London, 1953)

Domarus, M. (ed.), *Hitler: Speeches and Proclamations, 1932–1945: The Chronicle of a Dictatorship*, 4 vols, (London, 1990)

Fest, J.C., *Hitler*, (London, 1982)

Genoud, F. (ed.), *The Testament of Adolf Hitler: The Hitler-Bormann Documents*, (London, 1961)

Hamann, B., *Hitler's Vienna: A Dictator's Apprenticeship*, (Oxford, 2000)

Hanfstaengel, E., *Hitler: The Missing Years*, (London, 1957)

Jäckel, E., *Hitler's Weltanschauung: A Blueprint for Power*, (Middletown, CT, 1972)

Jetzinger, F., *Hitler's Youth*, (London, 1958)

Kershaw, I., *Hitler: Hubris 1889–1936*, (London, 1998)

Kershaw, I., *Hitler: Nemesis, 1936–1945*, (London, 2000)

Kershaw, I., *The 'Hitler Myth': Image and Reality in the Third Reich*, (Oxford, 1987)

Lewis, W., *The Hitler Cult*, (London, 1939)

Miskolczy, A., *Hitler's Library*, (Budapest, 2003)

Peterson, E.N., *The Limits of Hitler's Power*, (Princeton, NJ, 1969)

Roberts, S., *The House that Hitler Built*, (London, 1938)

Schwaab, E.H., *Hitler's Mind: A Plunge into Madness*, (New York, 1992)

Schwarzwäller, W.C., *The Unknown Hitler: His Private Life and Fortune*, (Bethesda, MD, 1989)

Staudinger, H., *The Inner Nazi: A Critical Analysis of Mein Kampf*, (London, 1981)

Stern, J.P., *Hitler, the Führer, and the People*, (London, 1975)

Zitelmann, R., *Hitler: The Politics of Seduction*, (London, 1999)

Autobiographies, biographies, diaries, group portraits

Abel, T., *Why Hitler Came into Power: An Answer Based on the Original Life Stories of Six Hundred of His Followers*, (New York, 1938)

[382] Below, N. von, *At Hitler's Side: The Memoirs of Hitler's Luftwaffe Adjutant 1937–1945*, (London, 2003)

Bendersky, J.W., *Carl Schmitt: Theorist for the Reich*, (Princeton, NJ, 1983)

Bloch, M., *Ribbentrop*, (London, 1992)

Breitmann, R. *The Architect of Genocide: Himmler and the Final Solution*, (Hanover, NH, 1991)

Buber-Neumann, M., *Under Two Dictators*, (London, 1949)

Burdick C. and H.-A. (eds), *The Halder Diary, 1939–1942*, (London, 1988)

Conradi, P., *Hitler's Piano Player: The Rise and Fall of Ernst Hanfstaengl, Confidant of Hitler, Ally of FDR*, (New York, 2004)

Fest, J.C., *Speer: The Final Verdict*, (New York, 1999)

Fest, J.C., *The Face of the Third Reich*, (London, 1979)

Gisevius, H.B., *To the Bitter End*, (London, 1948)

Haffner, S., *Defying Hitler: A Memoir*, (London, 2000)

Junge, T., *Until the Final Hour: Hitler's Last Secretary*, (London, 2003)

Kersten, F., *The Kersten Memoirs, 1940–1945*, (London, 1952)

Klemperer, V., *I Shall Bear Witness: The Diaries of Victor Klemperer 1933–1945*, (London, 1998)

Manchester, W., *The Arms of Krupp*, 1587–1968, (New York, 1968)

Maschmann, M., *Account Rendered: A Dossier on My Former Self*, (London, 1964)

Neville, P., *Appeasing Hitler: The Diplomacy of Sir Neville Henderson, 1937–39*, (Basingstoke, 1999)

Nevin, T., *Ernst Jünger and Germany: Into the Abyss 1914–1945*, (London, 1997)

Niemöller, M., *From U-boat to Pulpit*, (London, 1936)

Ott, H., *Martin Heidegger: A Political Life*, (London, 1993)

Overy, R.J., *Goering: The 'Iron Man'*, (London, 1984)

Overy, R.J., *Interrogations: The Nazi Elite in Allied Hands*, 1945, (London, 2001)

Padfield, P., *Himmler: Reichsführer SS*, (London, 1990)

Papen, F. von, *Memoirs*, (London, 1952)

Preston, P., *Franco: A Biography*, (London, 1993)

Reck, F., *Diary of a Man in Despair*, (London, 2000)

Reuth, R., *Goebbels*, (London, 1993)

Ribbentrop, J. von, *The Ribbentrop Memoirs*, (London, 1954)

Rolfs, R.W., *The Sorcerer's Apprentice: The Life of Franz von Papen*, (Lanham, MD, 1996)

Schacht, H.H.G., *My First Seventy-Six Years: The Autobiography of Hjalmar Schacht*, (London, 1955)

Schlotterbeck, F., *The Darker the Night, the Brighter the Stars: A German Worker Remembers (1933–1945)*, (London, 1947)

Sereny, G., *Albert Speer: His Battle with Truth*, (London, 1995)

Shirer, W.L., *Berlin Diary: The Journal of a Foreign Correspondent, 1934–1941*, (London, 1970)

Smelser, R.M., *Robert Ley: Hitler's Labor Front Leader*, (Oxford, 1988)

Smelser, R.M. and R. Zitelmann (eds), *The Nazi Elite*, (Basingstoke, 1993)

Smith, B.F., *Heinrich Himmler 1900–1926: A Nazi in the Making*, (Stanford, CA, 1971)

Speer, A., *Inside the Third Reich: Memoirs*, (London, 1970)

Stachura, P.D., *Gregor Strasser and the Rise of Nazism*, (London, 1983)

Taylor, F., *The Goebbels Diaries 1939–1941*, (London, 1982)

Thyssen, F., *I Paid Hitler*, (London, 1941)

Turner, H. A. (ed.), *Hitler: Memoirs of a Confidant (Otto Wagner)*, (New Haven, CT, 1995)

Weitz, J., *Hitler's Banker: Hjalmar Horace Greeley Schacht*, (London, 1998)

Wright, J., *Gustav Stresemann, Weimar's Greatest Statesman*, (Oxford, 2002)

The Weimar Republic

Abraham, D., *The Collapse of the Weimar Republic: Political Economy and Crisis*, (New York, 1986)

Bessel, R., *Germany after the First World War*, (Oxford, 1993)

Breitman, R., *German Socialism and Weimar Democracy*, (Chapel Hill, NC, 1981)

Crew, D.F., *Germans on Welfare: From Weimar to Hitler*, (New York, 1998)

Diehl, J.M., *Paramilitary Politics in Weimar Germany*, (Bloomington, IN, 1977)

Evans, R.J. and D. Geary (eds), *The German Unemployed: Experiences and Consequences of Mass Unemployment from the Weimar Republic to the Third Reich*, (London, 1987)

Fowkes, B., *Communism in Germany under the Weimar Republic*, (London, 1984)

Fritzsche, P., *Rehearsals for Fascism: Populism and Political Mobilization in Weimar Germany*, (New York, 1990)

Haffner, S., *Failure of a Revolution: Germany 1918–1919*, (Chicago, 1973)

Kocka, J., 'German history before Hitler: The debate about the German Sonderweg', *Journal of Contemporary History*, **23**, (1988)

Koshar, R., *Social Life, Local Politics, and Nazism: Marburg 1880–1935*, (Chapel Hill, NC, 1986)

Mommsen, H., *The Rise and Fall of Weimar Democracy*, (Chapel Hill, NC, 1996)

Nicolls, A.J., *Weimar and the Rise of Hitler*, (London, 2000)

Nicolls, A.J. and E. Matthias, *German Democracy and the Triumph of Hitler: Essays in Recent German History*, (London, 1971)

Panayi, P. (ed.), *Weimar and Nazi Germany: Continuities and Discontinuities*, (London, 2001)

Patch, W.L. Jr., *Heinrich Brüning and the Dissolution of the Weimar Republic*, (Cambridge, 1998)

Röhl, J.C.G., *From Bismarck to Hitler: The Problem of Continuity in German History*, (London, 1970)

Speier, H., *German White-Collar Workers and the Rise of Hitler*, (New Haven, CT, 1986)

Steinberg, M.S., *Sabres and Brown Shirts: The German Students' Path to National Socialism, 1918–1935*, (Chicago, 1977)

Stern, F., *Dreams and Delusions: The Drama of German History*, (New York, 1987)

Waite, R.G.L., *Vanguard of Nazism: The Free Corps Movement in Postwar Germany 1918–1923*, (Cambridge, MA, 1952)

NSDAP 1919–1933

Allen, W.S., *The Nazi Seizure of Power: The Experience of a Single German Town, 1922–1934*, (New York, 1984)

Bessel, R. 'The Potempa murder', *Central European History*, **10**, (1977)

Bessel, R. *Political Violence and the Rise of Nazism: The Storm Troopers in Eastern Germany 1925–1934*, (London, 1984)

Broszat, M., *Hitler and the Collapse of Weimar Germany*, (Leamington Spa, 1987)

Brustein, W., *The Logic of Evil: The Social Origins of the Nazi Party 1925–1933*, (New Haven, CT, 1996)

Burden, H.T., *The Nuremberg Party Rallies: 1923–39*, (London, 1967)

Childers, T., *The Nazi Voter: The Social Foundations of Fascism in Germany, 1919–1933*, (Chapel Hill, NC, 1981)

Evans, R.J., *The Coming of the Third Reich*, (London, 2003)

Fischer, C., *The Rise of the Nazis*, (Manchester, 2002)

Gordon H.J., *Hitler and the Beer Hall Putsch*, (Princeton, NJ, 1972)

Grill, J.H., *The Nazi Movement in Baden 1920–1945*, (Chapel Hill, NC, 1983)

Jablonsky, D., *The Nazi Party in Dissolution: Hitler and the Verbotzeit 1923–1925*, (London, 1989)

Kater, M., *The Nazi Party: A Social Profile of Members and Leaders, 1919–1945*, (Oxford, 1983)

Massing, P.W., *Rehearsal for Destruction*, (New York, 1949)

Merkl, P., *Political Violence Under the Swastika: 581 Early Nazis*, (Princeton, NJ, 1975)

Noakes, J., *The Nazi Party in Lower Saxony 1921–1933*, (Oxford, 1971)

Orlow, D., *The History of the Nazi Party*, 2 vols, (Newton Abbot, 1973)

Pauley, B.F., *Hitler and the Forgotten Nazis: A History of Austrian National Socialism*, (Chapel Hill, NC, 1981)

Pridham, G., *Hitler's Rise to Power: The Nazi Movement in Bavaria 1923–1933*, (London, 1973)

Rauschning, H., *Germany's Revolution of Destruction*, (London, 1938)

Rauschning, H., *The Conservative Revolution*, (New York, 1941)

Szejnmann, C.-C.W., *Nazism in Central Germany: The Brownshirts in 'Red' Saxony*, (New York, 1999)

Ideology and philosophy

Baird, J.W., *To Die for Germany: Heroes in the Nazi Pantheon*, (Bloomington, IN, 1990)

Birken, L., *Hitler as Philosopher: Remnants of the Enlightenment in National Socialism*, (Westport, CT, 1995)

Burleigh, M., 'National Socialism as political religion', *Totalitarian Movements and Political Religions*, **1**, (2000)

Burrin, P., 'Political religion. The relevance of a concept', *History and Memory*, **9**, (1997)

Burrow, J.W., *The Crisis of Reason: European Thought, 1848–1914*, (New Haven, CT, 2000)

Butler, R. d'O., *The Roots of National Socialism 1783–1933*, (London, 1941)

Cecil, R., *The Myth of the Master Race: Alfred Rosenberg and Nazi Ideology*, (London, 1972)

Cristi, R., *Carl Schmitt and Authoritarian Liberalism*, (Cardiff, 1998)

Gasman, D., *The Scientific Origins of National Socialism*, (London, 1971)

Gispen, K., 'Visions of Utopia: Social emancipation, technological progress and anti-capitalism in Nazi inventor policy 1933–1945', *Central European History*, **32**, (1999)

Gottfried, P., *Thinkers of Our Time: Carl Schmitt*, (London, 1990)

Herf, J., *Reactionary Modernism: Technology, Culture, and Politics in Weimar and the Third Reich*, (Cambridge, 1984)

Kolnai, A., *The War Against the West*, (London, 1938)

Lane, B.M. and J. Leila (eds), *Nazi Ideology Before 1933: A Documentation*, (Manchester, 1978)

Lauryssens, S., *The Man Who Invented the Third Reich*, (Stroud, 1999)

Lewis, W., *The Hitler Cult*, (London, 1939)

Mosse, G.L., *The Crisis of German Ideology: Intellectual Origins of the Third Reich*, (London, 1964)

Mosse, G.L., *The Nationalization of the Masses: Political Symbolism and Mass Movements in Germany from the Napoleonic Wars through the Third Reich*, (New York, 1975)

Pois, R.A., *National Socialism and the Religion of Nature*, (London, 1986)

Rhodes, J.M., *The Hitler Movement: A Modern Millenarian Revolution*, (Stanford, CA, 1980)

Rosenberg, A., (ed. R. Pois), *Selected Writings*, (London, 1970)

Saldern, A. von, *The Challenge of Modernity: German Social and Cultural Studies, 1890–1960*, (Ann Arbor, MI, 2002)

Sluga, H., *Heidegger's Crisis: Philosophy and Politics in Nazi Germany*, (Cambridge, MA, 1993)

Smith, W.D., *The Ideological Roots of Nazi Imperialism*, (New York, 1986)

Stern, F., *The Politics of Cultural Despair: A Study in the Rise of the German Ideology*, (New York, 1977)

Theweleit, K., *Male Fantasies. Male Bodies: Psychoanalysing the White Terror*, (Oxford, 1989)

Vieler, E.H., *The Ideological Roots of German National Socialism*, (New York, 1999)

Viereck, P., *Metapolitics: From the Romantics to Hitler*, (New York, 1941)

Voegelin, E., *The New Science of Politics: An Introduction*, (Chicago, 1952)

Wachsmann, N., 'Marching under the swastika? Ernst Jünger and National Socialism, 1918–1933', *Journal of Contemporary History*, **33**, (1998)

Anti-Semitism and the Shoah

Abella, I.M. and H. Troper, *None Is Too Many: Canada and the Jews of Europe, 1933–1948*, (New York, 1983)

[386]   Allen, M.T., 'The banality of evil reconsidered: SS mid-level managers of extermination through work', *Central European History*, **30**, (1997)

Allen, M.T., *The Business of Genocide: The SS, Slave Labor, and the Concentration Camps*, (Chapel Hill, NC, 2002)

Aly, G., *'Final Solution'. Nazi Population Policy and the Murder of the European Jews*, (London, 1999)

Bajohr, F., *'Aryanization' in Hamburg: The Economic Exclusion of the Jews and the Confiscation of Their Property in Nazi Germany*, (New York, 2002)

Bankier, D. (ed.), *Probing the Depths of German Anti-Semitism: German Society and the Persecution of the Jews, 1933–1941*, (Jerusalem, 2000)

Bankier, D., *The Germans and the Final Solution: Public Opinion under Nazism*, (Oxford, 1992)

Barkai, A., *From Boycott to Annihilation: The Economic Struggle of German Jews, 1933–1943*, (Hanover, NH, 1989)

Bauer, Y., *My Brother's Keeper: A History of the American Jewish Joint Distribution Committee, 1929–1939*, (Philadelphia, 1974)

Berenbaum, M., *A Mosaic of Victims: Non-Jews Persecuted and Murdered by the Nazis*, (New York, 1990)

Bergen, D., 'The Nazi concept of the Volksdeutsche and the exacerbation of Anti-Semitism in Eastern Europe 1939–1945', *Journal of Contemporary History*, **29**, (1994)

Beyerschen, A., 'Rational means and irrational ends. Thoughts on the technology of racism in the Third Reich', *Central European History*, **30**, (1997)

Browning, C., *Ordinary Men: Reserve Police Battalion 101 and the Final Solution*, (Cambridge, 1992)

Browning, C., *The Path to Genocide: Essays on Launching the Final Solution*, (Cambridge, 1992)

Burleigh, M., *Ethics and Extermination: Reflections of Nazi Genocide*, (Cambridge, 1997)

Burleigh, M., *Germany Turns Eastwards: A Study of Ostforschung in the Third Reich*, (Cambridge, 1988)

Burleigh, M. and W. Wippermann, *The Racial State: Germany 1933–1945*, (Cambridge, 1991)

Burrin, P., *Hitler and the Jews: The Genesis of the Holocaust*, (London, 1994)

Caron, V., *Uneasy Asylum: France and the Jewish Refugee Crisis, 1933–1942*, (Stanford, CA, 1999)

Cary, N.D., 'Anti-Semitism, everyday life, and the devastation of public morals in Nazi Germany', *Central European History*, **55**, (2002)

Cesarini, D., *Eichmann, His Life and Crimes*, (London, 2004)

Cesarini, D. (ed.), *The Final Solution: Origins and Implementation*, (London, 1994)

Cohen, A. (ed.), *The Shoah and the War*, (New York, 1992)

Cohn, N., *Warrant for Genocide: The Myth of the Jewish World-Conspiracy and the Protocols of the Elders of Zion*, (London, 1967)

Dean, M., *Collaboration in the Holocaust: Crimes of the Local Police in Belorussia and Ukraine, 1941–1944*, (London, 2000)

Dean, M., 'The development and implementation of Nazi denaturalization and [387] confiscation policy up to the Eleventh Decree of the Reich Citizenship Law', *Holocaust and Genocide Studies*, **16**, (2002)

Dwork, D. and R.J. Van Pelt, *Holocaust: A History*, (New York, 2002)

Evans, R.J., *Lying About Hitler: History, Holocaust, and the David Irving Trial*, (New York, 2001)

Fleming, G., *Hitler and the Final Solution*, (London, 1985)

Friedländer, H., *The Origins of Nazi Genocide: From Euthanasia to the Final Solution*, (Chapel Hill, NC, 1995)

Friedländer, S., *Nazi Germany and the Jews: The Years of Persecution 1933–1939*, (London, 1997)

Gerlach, C., 'The Wannsee Conference, the fate of the German Jews, and Hitler's decision in principle to exterminate all European Jews', *Journal of Modern History*, **70**, (1998)

Goldhagen, D.J., *Hitler's Willing Executioners: Ordinary Germans and the Holocaust*, (New York, 1996)

Gordon, S.A., *Hitler, Germans, and the 'Jewish Question'*, (Princeton, NJ, 1984)

Graml, H., *Anti-Semitism in the Third Reich*, (Cambridge, MA, 1992)

Gutman, Y. (ed.), *Encyclopedia of the Holocaust*, 4 vols, (New York, 1990)

Gutman, Y. and M. Berenbaum (eds), *Anatomy of the Auschwitz Death Camp*, (Bloomington, IN, 1994)

Heer, H. and K. Naumann, *War of Extermination: The German Military in World War II 1941–1945*, (Oxford, 2000)

Herbert, U., *National Socialist Extermination Policies: Contemporary German Perspectives and Controversies*, (Oxford, 2000)

Hirschfeld, G., *The Politics of Genocide: Jews and Soviet POWs in Nazi Germany*, (London, 1988)

Höss, R., *Commandant of Auschwitz*, (London, 1959)

Johnson, E.A., *Nazi Terror: The Gestapo, Jews and Ordinary Germans*, (New York, 1999)

Kaplan, M.A., *Between Dignity and Despair: Jewish Life in Nazi Germany*, (New York, 1998)

Katz, J., *The Darker Side of Genius: Richard Wagner's Anti-Semitism*, (Hanover, NH, 1986)

Kogon, E., Langbein H. and A. Ruckerl (eds), *Nazi Mass Murder: a Documentary History of the Use of Poison Gas*, (New Haven, CT, 1993)

Lewy, G., 'Gypsies and Jews under the Nazis', *Holocaust and Genocide Studies*, **13**, (1999)

Lifton, R.J., *The Nazi Doctors: Medical Killing and the Psychology of Genocide*, (London, 1986)

Lipstadt, D.E., *Beyond Belief: The American Press and the Coming of the Holocaust, 1933–1945*, (New York, 1986)

London, L., *Whitehall and the Jews, 1933–1948: British Immigration Policy, Jewish Refugees, and the Holocaust*, (Cambridge, 2000)

Longerich, P., *The Unwritten Order: Hitler's Role in the Final Solution*, (Stroud, 2001)

[388] Marcuse, H., *Legacies of Dachau: The Uses and Abuses of a Concentration Camp, 1933–2001*, (Cambridge, 2001)

Mazower, M., 'Military violence and National Socialist values: The Wehrmacht in Greece 1941–1944', *Past and Present*, **134**, (1992)

Meyer, M.A. (ed.), *German-Jewish History in Modern Times*, 4 vols, (New York, 1998)

Milton, S., 'The expulsion of Polish Jews from Germany October 1938 to July 1939: a documentation', *Leo Baeck Institute Yearbook*, **29**, (1984)

Morse, A.D., *While Six Million Died: A Chronicle of American Apathy*, (New York, 1967)

Mosse, W.E., *The German-Jewish Economic Elite, 1820–1935: A Socio-Cultural Profile*, (Oxford, 1989)

Nicosia, F.R., *The Third Reich and the Palestine Question*, (London, 1985)

Paucker, A. *et al.* (eds), *The Jews in Nazi Germany, 1933–1945*, (Tübingen, 1986)

Pauley, B.F., *From Prejudice to Persecution: A History of Austrian Anti-Semitism*, (Chapel Hill, NC, 1992)

Pehle, W.H., *November 1938: From 'Reichskristallnacht' to Genocide*, (New York, 1991)

Peukert, D., *Inside Nazi Germany: Conformity, Opposition and Racism in Everyday Life*, (London, 1987)

Pulzer, P., *The Rise of Political anti-Semitism in Germany and Austria*, (London, 1988)

Read, A., *KristallNacht: Unleashing the Holocaust*, (London, 1989)

Rigg, B.M., *Hitler's Jewish Soldiers: The Untold Story of Nazi Racial Laws and Men of Jewish Descent in the German Military*, (Lawrence, KS, 2002)

Rose, J. (ed.), *The Holocaust and the Book*, (Amherst, MA, 2001)

Roseman, M., 'Recent writing on the Holocaust', *Journal of Contemporary History*, **36**, (2001)

Roseman, M., *The Villa, the Lake, the Meeting: Wannsee and the Final Solution*, (London, 2002)

Safrian, H., 'Expediting expropriation and expulsion: The impact of the "Vienna Model" on anti-Jewish policies in Nazi Germany, 1938', *Holocaust and Genocide Studies*, **14**: 3, (2000)

Sherman, A.J., *Island Refuge: Britain and Refugees from the Third Reich, 1933–1939*, (London, 1973)

Strauss, H.A., 'Jewish emigration from Germany: Nazi policies and Jewish responses', *Leo Baeck Institute Yearbook*, **25**, (1980) and **26**, (1981)

Volkov, S., 'Antisemitism as a Cultural Code: Reflections on the history and historiography of antisemitism in Imperial Germany', *Year Book of the Leo Baeck Institute*, **23**, (1978)

Wasserstein, B., *Britain and the Jews of Europe, 1939–1945*, (Oxford, 1979)

Wiesen, S.J., 'Morality and memory: Reflections on business ethics and National Socialism', *Journal of Holocaust Education*, **10**, (2001)

Wollenberg, J. (ed.), *The German Public and the Persecution of the Jews, 1933–1945: 'No One Participated, No One Knew'*, (Atlantic Highlands, NJ, 1996)

Zimmermann, M., *Wilhelm Marr: The Patriarch of Anti-Semitism*, (New York, 1986)

Economics

Abelhauser, W. (ed.), *German Industry and Global Enterprise: BASF: The History of a Company*, (Cambridge, 2004)

Abelhauser, W., 'Germany: guns, butter, and economic miracles', in Harrison, M. (ed.), *The Economics of World War II: Six Great Powers in International Comparison*, (Cambridge, 1998)

Aldcroft, D.H., *From Versailles to Wall Street 1919–1929*, (London, 1977)

Balderston, T., *Economics and Politics in the Weimar Republic*, (London, 2002)

Balderston, T., *The Origins and Course of the German Economic Crisis, 1923–1932*, (Berlin, 1993)

Barkai, A., *Nazi Economics: Ideology, Theory, and Policy*, (Oxford, 1990)

Bellon, B.P., *Mercedes in Peace and War: German Automobile Workers, 1903–1945*, (New York, 1990)

Borchardt, K., *Perspectives on Modern German Economic History and Policy*, (Cambridge, 1991)

Borkin, J., *The Crime and Punishment of I.G. Farben*, (New York, 1978)

Carroll, B., *Design for Total War: Arms and Economics in the Third Reich*, (The Hague, 1968)

Clavin, P., *The Great Depression in Europe, 1929–1939* (Chapel Hill, NC, 2000)

Ericson, E.E., *Feeding the German Eagle: Soviet Economic Aid to Nazi Germany, 1933–1941*, (Westport, CT, 1999)

Evans, R.J., *The Great Disorder: Politics, Economics, and Society in the German Inflation, 1914–1924*, (New York, 1993)

Feinstein, C.H. *et al.*, *The European Economy Between the Wars*, (Oxford, 1997)

Feldman, G.D., *Allianz and the German Insurance Business, 1933–1945*, (Cambridge, 2001)

Gregor, N., *Daimler Benz in the Third Reich*, (London, 1998)

Guerin, D., *Fascism and Big Business*, (New York, 1973)

Guillebaud, C.W., *The Economic Recovery of Germany*, (London, 1939)

Harrison, M. (ed.), *The Economics of World War II: Six Great Powers in International Comparison*, (Cambridge, 1998)

Hayes, P., *Industry and Ideology: IG Farben in the Nazi Era*, (New York, 1987)

Hayes, P., *From Cooperation to Complicity: Degussa in the Third Reich*, (New York, 1995)

Holtfrerich, C.-L., *The German Inflation 1914–1923, Causes and Effects in International Perspective*, (New York, 1986)

James, H., *The German Slump: Politics and Economics, 1924–1936*, (Oxford, 1986)

James, H., *The Deutsche Bank and the Nazi Economic War Against the Jews*, (Cambridge, 2001)

Kindelberger, C.P., *The World in Depression 1929–1939*, (Berkeley, CA, 1987)

Klein, B.H., *Germany's Economic Preparations for War*, (Cambridge, MA, 1959)

Milward, A.S., *The Nazi Economy at War*, (London, 1965)

Nicolls, A., *Freedom and Responsibility: The Social Market Economy in Germany 1918–1963*, (Oxford, 1994)

Nissen, O., *Germany – Land of Substitutes*, (London, 1944)

[390] Overy, R.J., *War and Economy in the Third Reich*, (Oxford, 1994)

Overy, R.J., *The Nazi Economic Recovery 1932–1938*, (Cambridge, 1996)

Silverman, D.P., *Hitler's Economy: Nazi Work Creation Programs, 1933–1936*, (London, 1998)

Tooze, J.A., *Statistics and the German State, 1900–1945: The Making of Modern Economic Knowledge*, (Cambridge, 2001)

Turner, H.A., *German Big Business and the Rise of Hitler*, (New York, 1985)

Webb, S.B., *Hyperinflation and Stabilization in Weimar Germany*, (Oxford, 1989)

Youth

Pine, L., 'Creating conformity: The training of girls in the Bund Deutscher Mädel', *European History Quarterly*, **33**, (2003)

Stachura, P.D., *The German Youth Movement, 1900–1945: An Interpretative and Documentary History*, (London, 1981)

Stephens, F.J., *Hitler Youth: History, Organisation, Uniforms and Insignia*, (London, 1973)

Women

Boak, H.L., '"Our Last Hope": Women's votes for Hitler – a reappraisal', *German Studies Review*, **12**, (1989)

Bridenthal, R., A. Grossmann and M. Kaplan (eds), *When Biology Became Destiny: Woman in Weimar Germany and Nazi Germany*, (New York, 1984)

Frevert, U., *Women in German History*, (Oxford, 1989)

Heinemann, E.D., *What Difference Does a Husband Make? Women and Marital Status in Nazi and Postwar Germany*, (London, 1999)

Kirkpatrick, C., *Women in Nazi Germany*, (London, 1939)

Koonz, C., *Mothers in the Fatherland: Women, the Family, and Nazi Politics*, (London, 1988)

Owings, A., *Frauen: German Women Recall the Third Reich*, (London, 1993)

Sachse, C., *Industrial Housewives: Women's Social Work in the Factories in Nazi Germany*, (London, 1987)

Stephenson, J., *Women in Nazi Germany*, (London, 1975)

Stephenson, J., *The Nazi Organisation of Women*, (London, 1981)

Stibbe, M., *Women in the Third Reich*, (London, 2003)

SA, SS and police

Browder, G.C., *Foundations of the Nazi Police State: The Formation of the Sipo and SD*, (Lexington, KY, 1990)

Browder, G.C., *Hitler's Enforcers: The Gestapo and the SS Security Service in the Nazi*
Revolution, (New York, 1996)

Fischer, C., *Stormtroopers: A Social, Economic and Ideological Analysis 1929–1935*,
(London, 1983)

Gellately, R., *The Gestapo and German Society: Enforcing Racial Policy 1933–1945*,
(Oxford, 1990)

Hackett, D.D. (ed.), *The Buchenwald Report*, (Boulder, CO, 1995)

Höhne, H., *The Order of the Death's Head: The Story of Hitler's SS*, (New York, 1969)

Jaskot, P.B., *The Architecture of Oppression: The SS, Forced Labor and the Nazi Monumental Building Economy*, (London, 1999)

Koehl, H.W., *The Black Corps: The Structure and Power Struggles of the Nazi SS*,
(Madison, WI, 1983)

Krausnick, H. and M. Broszat, *Anatomy of the SS State*, (London, 1970)

Lozowick, Y., *Hitler's Bureaucrats: The Nazi Security Police and the Banality of Evil*,
(London, 2000)

Reilly, J. *et al.* (eds), *Belsen in History and Memory*, (London, 1997)

Sydnor, C.W., *Soldiers of Destruction: The SS Death's Head Division, 1933–1945*,
(Princeton, NJ, 1990)

Ziegler, H.F., *Nazi Germany's New Aristocracy: The SS Leadership, 1925–1939*,
(Princeton, NJ, 1989)

Outsiders

Connelly, J., 'Nazis and Slavs: from racial theory to racist practice', *Central European
History*, **32**, (1999)

Gellately, R. and M. Stolzfus (eds), *Social Outsiders in Nazi Germany*, (Princeton, NJ,
2001)

Grau, G. (ed.), *Hidden Holocaust? Gay and Lesbian Persecution in Germany 1933–1945*,
(London, 1995)

Lewy, G., *The Nazi Persecution of the Gypsies*, (Oxford, 2000)

Plant, R., *The Pink Triangle: The Nazi War against Homosexuals*, (Edinburgh, 1987)

Schoppmann, C., *Days of Masquerade: Life Stories of Lesbian Women during the Third
Reich*, (New York, 1996)

Medicine, eugenics and euthanasia

Adams, M.B. (ed.), *The Wellborn Science: Eugenics in Germany, France, Brazil, and Russia*,
(New York, 1990)

Burleigh, M., *Death and Deliverance: 'Euthanasia' in Germany 1900–1945*, (Cambridge,
1994)

Clay, C. and M. Leapmahn, *Master Race: The Lebensborn Experiment in Nazi Germany*,
(London, 1995)

[392] Kater, M., *Doctors Under Hitler*, (Chapel Hill, NC, 1989)

Kühl, S., *The Nazi Connection: Eugenics, American Racism, and German National Socialism*, (New York, 1994)

Proctor, R.N., *Racial Hygiene: Medicine under the Nazis*, (London, 1988)

Weindling, P., *Health, Race and German Politics between National Unification and Nazism 1870–1945*, (Cambridge, 1989)

Law

Jones, J.W., *The Nazi Concept of Law*, (Oxford, 1939)

McKale, D.M., *The Nazi Party Courts: Hitler's Management of Conflict in His Movement*, (Lawrence, KA, 1974)

Müller, I., *Hitler's Justice: The Courts of the Third Reich*, (London, 1991)

Stolleis, M., *The Law under the Swastika: Studies in Legal History in Nazi Germany*, (Chicago, 1998)

Wachsmann, N., *Hitler's Prisons: Legal Terror in Nazi Germany*, (New Haven, CT, 2004)

Press and propaganda

Bramsted, E.K., *Goebbels and National Socialist Propaganda, 1925–1945*, (East Lansing, MI, 1965)

Eksteins, M., *The Limits of Reason: The German Democratic Press and the Collapse of Weimar Democracy*, (Oxford, 1975)

Hale, O.J., *The Captive Press in the Third Reich*, (Princeton, NJ, 1964)

Hardy, A.G., *Hitler's Secret Weapon: The 'Managed' Press and Propaganda Machine of Nazi Germany*, (New York, 1968)

Herzstein, R.W., *The War that Hitler Won: The Most Infamous Propaganda Campaign in History*, (London, 1979)

Welch, D., *The Third Reich: Politics and Propaganda*, (London, 2002)

Welch, D. (ed.), *Nazi Propaganda: The Power and the Limitations*, (London, 1983)

Zeman, Z., *Nazi Propaganda*, (Oxford, 1973)

The churches

Baranowski, S., *The Confessing Church, Conservative Elites, and the Nazi State*, (New York, 1986)

Barnett, V., *For the Soul of the People: Protestant Protest Against Hitler*, (Oxford, 1992)

Barth, K., *The German Church Conflict*, (London, 1965)

Bentley, J., *Martin Niemöller, 1892–1984*, (Oxford, 1984)

Bergen, D., *The Twisted Cross: The German Christian Movement in the Third Reich*, (Chapel Hill, NC, 1996)

Conway, J.S., *The Nazi Persecution of the Churches 1933–1945*, (London, 1968)

Cornwell, J., *Hitler's Pope: The Secret History of Pius XII*, (London, 1999)

Douglas, P.F., *God Among the Germans*, (Philadelphia, 1935)

Ericksen, R.P., *Theologians Under Hitler: Gerhard Kittel, Paul Althaus, and Emanuel Hirsch*, (New Haven, CT, 1985)

Friedländer, S., *Pius XII and the Third Reich*, (London, 1966)

Griech-Polelle, B.A., *Bishop von Galen: German Catholicism and National Socialism*, (New Haven, CT, 2002)

Harrison, E.D.R., 'The Nazi dissolution of the monasteries: A case study', *English Historical Review*, **109**, (1994)

Heilbronner, O., *Catholicism, Political Culture and the Countryside: A Social History of the Nazi Party in South Germany*, (Ann Arbor, MI, 1998)

Helmreich, E.C., *The German Churches Under Hitler: Background, Struggle, and Epilogue*, (Detroit, MI, 1979)

Lewy, G., *The Catholic Church and Nazi Germany*, (New York, 1964)

Matheson, P., *The Third Reich and the Christian Churches*, (Edinburgh, 1981)

Scholder, K., *A Requiem for Hitler and Other New Perspectives on the German Church Struggle*, (Philadelphia, 1989)

Steigmann-Gall, R., *The Holy Reich: Nazi Conceptions of Christianity, 1919–1945*, (Cambridge, 2003)

Stoakes, G., *Hitler and the Quest for World Domination*, (Leamington Spa, 1986)

Zabel, J.A., *Nazism and the Pastors: A Study of the Ideas of Three Deutsche Christen Groups*, (Misoula, MT, 1976)

The arts

Adam, P., *Arts of the Third Reich*, (London, 1992)

Alter, R., *Gottfried Benn: The Artist and Politics (1910–1934)*, (Frankfurt am Main, 1976)

Baird, J.W., 'From Berlin to Neubabelsberg: Nazi film propaganda and Hitler Youth Quex', *Journal of Contemporary History*, **18**, (1983)

Barron, S., *'Degenerate Art': The Fate of the Avant-Garde in Nazi Germany*, (New York, 1991)

Bergmeier, H.H. and R.E. Lotz, *Hitler's Airwaves: The Inside Story of Nazi Radio Broadcasting and Propaganda*, (New Haven, CT, 1997)

Bussmann, G., *German Art of the Twentieth Century*, (Munich, 1985)

Cuomo, G.R., 'Purging an "Art-Bolshevist": The persecution of Gottfried Benn in the years 1933–1938', *German Studies Review*, **9**, (1986)

Cuomo, G.R. (ed.), *National Socialist Cultural Policy*, (New York, 1995)

Deak, I., *Weimar's Left Wing Intellectuals: A Political History of the Weltbühne and its Circle*, (Berkeley, CA, 1968)

Deischmann, H., *Objects: A Chronicle of Subversion in Nazi Germany and Fascist Italy*, (New York, 1995)

[394] Dümling, A. (ed.), *Banned by the Nazis: Entartete Musik: The Exhibition of Düsseldorf, 1938 in Texts and Documents*, (London, 1995)

Etlin, R.A., *Art, Culture, and Media under the Third Reich*, (Chicago, 2002)

Fallada, H., *Little Man – What Now*, translated by S. Bennett, (London, 1996)

Gay, P., *Weimar Culture: The Outsider as Insider*, (London, 1969)

Golomstock, I., *Totalitarian Art in the Soviet Union, Third Reich, Fascist Italy and the People's Republic of China*, (London, 1990)

Hake, S., *Popular Cinema in the Third Reich*, (Austin, TX, 2001)

Hoffmann, H. (ed.), *The Triumph of Propaganda: Film and National Socialism, 1933– 1945*, (Providence, RI, 1997)

Hull, D.S., *Film in the Third Reich: A Study of the German Cinema, 1933–1945*, (Berkeley, CA, 1969)

Infield, G.B., *Leni Riefenstahl: The Fallen Film Goddess*, (New York, 1976)

Kater, M., '"Forbidden fruit?" Jazz in the Third Reich', *American Historical Review*, **94**, (1989)

Kater, M., *Different Drummers: Jazz in the Culture of Nazi Germany*, (New York, 1992)

Kater, M., *The Twisted Muse: Musicians and the Music in the Third Reich*, (New York, 1997)

Kater, M., *Composers of the Nazi Era: Eight Portraits*, (New York, 2000)

Kater, M. and A. Riethmüller (eds), *Music and Nazism: Art under Tyranny, 1933– 1945*, (Laaber, 2003)

Kracauer, S., *From Caligari to Hitler: A Psychological History of the German Film*, (Princeton, NJ, 1974)

Kreimeier, K., *The Ufa Story: A History of Germany's Greatest Film Company 1918– 1945*, (New York, 1996)

Lane, B.M., *Architecture and Politics in Germany, 1918–1945*, (Cambridge, MA, 1968)

Levi, E., *Music in the Third Reich*, (New York, 1994)

London, J. (ed.), *Theatre Under the Nazis*, (Manchester, 2000)

Marchand, S., 'Nazi culture: banality or barbarism?' *Journal of Modern History*, **70**, (1998)

Meyer, M.L., *The Politics of Music in the Third Reich*, (New York, 1991)

Mosse, G.L., *Nazi Culture: Intellectual, Cultural and Social Life in the Third Reich*, (London, 1966)

Norton, R.E., *Secret Germany: Stefan George and his Circle*, (Ithaca, NY, 2002)

Paret, P., *Artist Against the Third Reich: Ernst Barlach, 1933–1938*, (Cambridge, 2003)

Petropolous, J., *Art as Politics in the Third Reich*, (Chapel Hill, NC, 1996)

Petropolous, J., *The Faustian Bargain: The Art World in Nazi Germany*, (London, 2000)

Phillips, M.S., 'The Nazi control of the German film industry', *Journal of European Studies*, **1**, (1971)

Potter, P.M., *Most German of Arts: Musicology and Society from the Weimar Republic to the End of Hitler's Reich*, (New Haven, CT, 1998)

Prieberg, F.K., *Trial of Strength: Wilhelm Furtwängler in the Third Reich*, (London, 1991)

Rainbird, S., *Max Beckmann*, (New York, 2003)

Ritchie, J.M., *Gottfried Benn: The Unreconstructed Expressionist*, (London, 1972)

Ritchie, J.M., *German Literature under National Socialism*, (London, 1983) [395]

Salkeld, A., *A Portrait of Leni Riefenstahl*, (London, 1997)

Schulte-Sasse, L., *Entertaining the Third Reich: Illusions of Wholeness in Nazi Cinema*, (Durham, NC, 1996)

Scobie, A., *Hitler's State Architecture: The Impact of Classical Antiquity*, (Philadelphia, 1990)

Spotts, F., *Bayreuth: A History of the Wagner Festival*, (New Haven, CT, 1994)

Spotts, F., *Hitler and the Power of Aesthetics*, (London, 2002)

Steinweis, A.E., 'Weimar culture and the rise of National Socialism: The Kampfbund für deutsche Kultur', *Central European History*, **24**, (1991)

Steinweis, A.E., *Art, Ideology and Economics in Nazi Germany: The Reich Chambers of Music, Theater and the Visual Arts*, (Chapel Hill, NC, 1993)

Taylor, B. and W. van der Will (eds), *The Nazification of Art: Art, Design, Music, Architecture and Film in the Third Reich*, (Winchester, 1990)

Taylor, R., *Literature and Society in Germany 1918–1945*, (Brighton, 1980)

Taylor, R., *Film Propaganda in Soviet Russia and Nazi Germany*, (London, 1998)

Taylor, R.R., *The Word in Stone: The Role of Architecture in the National Socialist Ideology*, (Berkeley, CA, 1974)

Turner, H.A., 'Fallada for historians', *German Studies Review*, **36**, (2003)

Walter, B., *Theme and Variations: An Autobiography*, (New York, 1966)

Welch, D., *Propaganda and the German Cinema*, (London, 2001)

West, S., *The Visual Arts in Germany 1890–1937: Utopia and Despair*, (Manchester 2000)

Whitford, F., *The Bauhaus*, (London, 1984)

Williams, J., *More Lives than One: A Biography of Hans Fallada*, (London, 1998)

Wingler, H., *The Bauhaus – Weimar, Dessau, Berlin, Chicago 1919–1944*, (Cambridge, MA, 1978)

Germany 1933–1945: Specialized studies

Caplan, J., *Government Without Administration: State and Civil Service in Weimar and Nazi Germany*, (Oxford, 1988)

Corni, G., *Hitler and the Peasants: Agrarian Policy of the Third Reich, 1930–1939*, (Princeton, NJ, 1990)

Farquharson, J.E., *The Plough and the Swastika: The NSDAP and Agriculture in Germany 1928–45*, (London, 1976)

Herbert, U., *Hitler's Foreign Workers: Enforced Foreign Labor in Germany under the Third Reich*, (Cambridge, 1997)

Jones, L.E., ' "The greatest stupidity in my life": Alfred Hugenberg and the Forma-tion of the Hitler Cabinet', *Journal of Contemporary History*, **27**, (1992)

Komjathy, A.T. and R. Stockwell, *German Minorities and the Third Reich: Ethnic Germans of East Central Europe between the Wars*, (New York, 1980)

Tobias, F., *The Reichstag Fire: Legend and Truth*, (London, 1962)

[396] Foreign policy

Carr, E.H., *Twilight of the Comintern, 1930–1935*, (London, 1982)

Cienciala, A.M., 'Poland in British and French Policy in 1939: Determination to fight – or avoid war?', *Polish Review*, **34**, (1989)

Emerson, J.T., *The Rhineland Crisis, 7 March 1936: A Critical Study in Multilateral Diplomacy*, (London, 1977)

Finney, P. (ed.), *The Origins of the Second World War*, (London, 1997)

Förster, J. and E. Mawdsley, 'Hitler and Stalin: Secret speeches on the eve of Barbarossa', *War in History*, **11**, (2004)

Fox, J.P., *Germany and the Far Eastern Crisis, 1931–1938: A Study in Diplomacy and Ideology*, (Oxford, 1982)

Frank, W.C., 'The Spanish Civil War and the coming of the Second World War', *International History Review*, **9**, (1987)

Gorodetsky, G., *Grand Delusion: Stalin and the German Invasion of Russia*, (New Haven, CT, 1999)

Herzstein, R.W., *When Nazi Dreams Come True*, (London, 1982)

Hildebrand, K., *The Foreign Policy of the Third Reich*, (London, 1970)

Kallis, A.A., 'To expand or not to expand? Territory, generic Fascism and the quest for an "Ideal Fatherland'", *Journal of Contemporary History*, **38**, (2003)

Levine, H.S., *Hitler's Free City: A History of the Nazi Party in Danzig, 1925–1939*, (Chicago, 1973)

Meehan, P., *The Unnecessary War: Whitehall and the German Resistance to Hitler*, (London, 1992)

Mommsen, W.J. and L. Kettenacher, *The Fascist Challenge and the Policy of Appeasement*, (London, 1983)

Nekrich, A.M., *Pariahs, Partners, Predators: German-Soviet Relations 1922–1941*, (New York, 1997)

Parker, R.A.C., *Chamberlain and Appeasement: British Policy and the Coming of the Second World War*, (London, 1993)

Parker, R.A.C., *Churchill and Appeasement*, (London, 2000)

Preston, P., *The Spanish Civil War, 1936–39*, (London, 1986)

Preston, P. and A.L. Mackenzie, *The Republic Besieged: Civil War in Spain 1936–1939*, (Edinburgh, 1996)

Read, A. and D. Fisher, *The Deadly Embrace: Hitler, Stalin, and the Nazi-Soviet Pact, 1939–1941*, (London, 1988)

Rich, N., *Hitler's War Aims*, 2 vols, (London, 1973–74)

Roberts, G., *The Soviet Union and the Origins of the Second World War 1933–1941*, (London, 1995)

Schweller, R.L., *Deadly Imbalances: Tripolarity and Hitler's Strategy of World Conquest*, (New York, 1998)

Sharp, A., *The Versailles Settlement: Peacekeeping in Paris, 1919*, (London, 1991)

Smelser, R.M., *The Sudeten Problem, 1933–1938*: Volkstumspolitik *and the Formulation of Nazi Foreign Policy*, (Folkestone, 1975)

Stoakes, G., *Hitler and the Quest for World Domination*, (Leamington Spa, 1986)

Strobl, G., *The Germanic Isle: Nazi Perceptions of Britain*, (Cambridge, 2000)

Taylor, A.J.P., *The Origins of the Second World War*, (Harmondsworth, 1961)

Teich, M., *Bohemia in History*, (Cambridge, 1998)

Temperley, H. (ed.), *A History of the Peace Conference of Paris*, 6 vols, (London, 1920–24)

Thomas, H., *The Spanish Civil War*, (London, 1986)

Volkov, V.K., 'Soviet-German relations during the second half of 1940, *Voprosii Istorii*, **2**, (1997)

Watt, D.C., *How War Came: The Immediate Origins of the Second World War, 1938–1939*, (London, 1989)

Wegner, B. (ed.), *From Peace to War: Germany, Soviet Russia and the World 1939–1941*, (Providence, RI, 1997)

Weinberg, G.L., *The Foreign Policy of Hitler's Germany I: Diplomatic Revolution in Europe, 1933–1936*, (London, 1970)

Weinberg, G.L., *The Foreign Policy of Hitler's Germany II: Starting World War II*, (Chicago, 1980)

Whealey, R.H., *Hitler and Spain: The Nazi Role in the Spanish Civil War, 1936–1939*, (Lexington, KY, 1989)

Wheeler-Bennett, J.W. *et al.* (eds), *Documents on German Foreign Policy 1918–1945*, 13 vols, (London, 1950–70)

Wiskemann, E., *The Rome–Berlin Axis: A History of the Relations Between Hitler and Mussolini*, (London, 1949)

The war

Addison, P. and A. Calder, *Time to Kill: The Soldier's Experience of War in the West 1939–1945*, (London, 1997)

Bartov, O., *Hitler's Army: Soldiers, Nazis and War in the Third Reich*, (Oxford, 1991)

Bartov, O., 'The missing years: German workers, German soldiers' in D. Crew (ed.) *Nazism and German Society 1933–1945*, (London, 1994)

Bartov, O., *The Eastern Front 1941–1945: German Troops and the Barbarization of Warfare*, (New York, 1985)

Bessel, R., *Nazism and War*, (London, 2004)

Carsten, F.L., *Reichswehr and Politics 1918–1933*, (Oxford, 1966)

Cooper, M., *The Phantom War: The German Struggle Against Soviet Partisans*, (London, 1979)

Craig, G., *The Politics of the Prussian Army 1640–1945*, (Oxford, 1955)

Dallin, A., *German Rule in Russia 1941–1945*, (London, 1981)

Erickson, J., *The Road to Stalingrad*, (London, 1975)

Erickson, J., *The Road to Berlin: Stalin's War with Germany*, (London, 1983)

Erickson, J. (ed.), *Barbarossa: The Axis and the Allies*, (Edinburgh, 1994)

[398]   Glantz, D.M., *Before Stalingrad: Barbarossa – Hitler's Invasion of Russia 1941*, (Stroud, 2003)

Glantz, D.M. and J. House, *When Titans Clashed: How the Red Army Stopped Hitler*, (Lawrence, KS, 1995)

Gordon, H.J., *The Reichswehr and the German Republic 1919–26*, (Princeton, NJ, 1957)

Hancock, E., *National Socialist Leadership and Total War 1941–1945*, (New York, 1991)

Heiber, H. and D. Glanz (eds), *Hitler and His Generals: Military Conferences 1942–1945*, (London, 2002)

Homze, E.L., *Arming the Luftwaffe: The Reich Air Ministry and the German Aircraft Industry, 1919–1939*, (Lincoln, NB, 1976)

Hooton, E., *Phoenix Triumphant: The Rise and Rise of the Luftwaffe*, (London, 1994)

Hooton, E.R., *Eagle in Flames: The Fall of the Luftwaffe*, (London, 1997)

Kitchen, M., *Nazi Germany at War*, (London, 1995)

Müller, K.-J., *The Army, Politics and Society in Germany 1933–1945: Studies in the Army's Relation to Nazism*, (Manchester, 1987)

Müller, R.-D. and G.R. Überschar, *Hitler's War in the East 1941–1945: A Critical Reassessment*, (Oxford, 1997)

O'Neill, R.J., *The German Army and the Nazi Party 1933–1939*, (London, 1966)

Overy, R.J., *Why the Allies Won*, (London, 1995)

Schulte, T., *The German Army and Nazi Policies in Occupied Russia*, (Oxford, 1989)

Shepherd, B., 'The continuum of brutality: Wehrmacht Security Divisions in Central Russia 1942', *German History*, **21**, (2003)

Wheeler-Bennett, J.W., *The Nemesis of Power: The German Army in Politics, 1918–1945*, (London, 1953)

Zayas, A.M. de, *The Wehrmacht War Crimes Bureau, 1939–1945*, (Lincoln, NB, 1989)

Resistance

Baigent, M. and R. Leigh, *Secret Germany: Claus von Stauffenberg and the Mystical Crusade against Hitler*, (London, 1994)

Balfour, M., *Withstanding Hitler in Germany 1933–1945*, (London, 1988)

Deutsch, H.C., *The Conspiracy Against Hitler in the Twilight War*, (Minneapolis, 1968)

Fest, J.C., *Plotting Hitler's Death: The Story of the German Resistance*, (London, 1996)

Hamerow, T.S., *On the Road to the Wolf's Lair: German Resistance to Hitler*, (Cambridge, MA, 1997)

Hoffmann, P., *The History of the German Resistance 1933–1945*, (London, 1971)

Hoffmann, P., *Hitler's Personal Security*, (Basingstoke, 1979)

Hoffmann, P., *Stauffenberg. A Family History, 1905–1944*, (Cambridge, 1995)

Klemperer, K. von, *German Resistance against Hitler: The Search for Allies Abroad, 1938–1945*, (Oxford, 1992)

Large, D.C. (ed.), *Contending with Hitler: Varieties of German Resistance in the Third Reich*, (Cambridge, 1991)

Merson, A., *Communist Resistance in Nazi Germany*, (London, 1985)

Nicosia, F.R. and L.D. Stokes (eds), *Germans Against Nazism: Nonconformity, Opposition and Resistance in the Third Reich*, (New York, 1990)

Stolzfus, M., *Resistance of the Heart: Intermarriage and the Rosenstrasse Protest in Nazi Germany*, (New York, 1996)

INDEX